AF640844

Parallel Algorithms and Architectures

Mathematical Research · Mathematische Forschung

Wissenschaftliche Beiträge
herausgegeben von der
Akademie der Wissenschaften der DDR
Karl-Weierstraß-Institut für Mathematik

Band 38

Parallel Algorithms
and Architectures

Parallel Algorithms and Architectures

Proceedings of the International Workshop on Parallel Algorithms and Architectures held in Suhl (GDR), May 25–30, 1987

edited by
Andreas Albrecht,
Hermann Jung,
and
Kurt Mehlhorn

Akademie-Verlag Berlin 1987

Herausgeber:

Dr. Andreas Albrecht
Doz. Dr. Hermann Jung
Humboldt-Universität zu Berlin
Sektion Mathematik

Prof. Dr. Kurt Mehlhorn
Universität des Saarlandes, Saarbrücken
FB Angewandte Mathematik und Informatik

Die Titel dieser Schriftenreihe werden vom Originalmanuskript der Autoren reproduziert.

ISBN 3-05-500397-7
ISSN 0138-3019

Erschienen im Akademie-Verlag Berlin, DDR-1086 Berlin, Leipziger Str. 3-4
© Akademie-Verlag Berlin 1987
Lizenznummer: 202·100/418/87
Printed in the German Democratic Republic
Gesamtherstellung: VEB Kongreß- und Werbedruck, 9273 Oberlungwitz
LSV 1095
Bestellnummer: 763 760 7 (2182/38)
02800

P R E F A C E

This volume constitutes of the proceedings of the International Workshop on Parallel Algorithms and Architectures held in Suhl, German Democratic Republic, May 25-29, 1987.

The aim of the conference is to support research activities on parallel architectures and algorithms. The program consists of invited lectures given by acknoledged scientists as well as short communications. It covers both theoretical and practical aspects of parallel computing.

The main topics of the workshop are

- Models of parallel computations;
- New algorithms for individual problems, e.g. from graph theory, logic programming, combinatorics and computational geometry;
- Hardware algorithms, parallel architectures.

We wish to thank all who submitted papers for consideration and all members of the International Program Committee which consisted of A.Albrecht (Berlin), J.von zur Gathen (Toronto), J.Herath (Yokohama), H.Jung (Berlin), R.Kannan (Pittsburgh), A.Konagaya (Tokyo), V.Kotov (Novosibirsk), T.Leighton (Cambridge), K.Mehlhorn (Saarbrücken), J.Miklosko (Bratislava), B.Monien(Paderborn), W.Paul (Saarbrücken), H.Thiele (Berlin), C.D.Thomborson (Duluth), G.Wechsung (Jena), C.K.Yap (New York).

The workshop was organized by the Department of Mathematics of Humboldt-University (Berlin) and chaired by A.Albrecht and H.Jung.

We would like to take this opportunity to express our sincere gratitude to the Organizing Secretary of the workshop T.Zeugmann for his engagement and excellent work.

We are all very grateful for the special support given by the local organizers in Suhl who contributed their generous help in arranging the workshop.

Finally we would like to thank the publishers for their assistance and cooperation in the selection of the present volume.

A. Albrecht, H. Jung, K. Mehlhorn

TABLE OF CONTENTS

Invited Papers

Communications

LATE PAPERS

Invited Papers

Communication

Deterministic Simulation of Idealized Parallel Computers on More Realistic Ones

by

H. Alt* / T. Hagerup / K. Mehlhorn** / F.P. Preparata*****

* Fachbereich Mathematik, Freie Universität Berlin, Arnimallee 2–6, D–1000 Berlin 33, FRG. Part of the research was done while the author was a member of the Mathematical Sciences Research Institute, Berkeley, U.S.A.

** Fachbereich 10, Informatik, Universität des Saarlandes, D–6600 Saarbrücken, FRG.

*** Coordinated Science Laboratory, University of Illinois, Urbana, IL 61801, U.S.A.

Abstract: We describe a non-uniform deterministic simulation of PRAMs on module parallel computers (MPCs) and on processor networks of bounded degree. The simulating machines have the same number n of processors as the simulated PRAM, and if the size of the PRAM's shared memory is polynomial in n, each PRAM step is simulated by $O(\log n)$ MPC steps or by $O((\log n)^2)$ steps of the bounded-degree network. This improves upon a previous result by Upfal and Wigderson. We also prove an $\Omega((\log n)^2/\log\log n)$ lower bound on the number of steps needed to simulate one PRAM step on a bounded-degree network under the assumption that the communication in the network is point-to-point.

As an important part of the simulation of PRAMs on MPCs, we use a new technique for dynamically averaging out a given work load among a set of processors operating in parallel.

A preliminary version of this work was presented at MFCS 86, Bratislava. The full version is available from the authors and will appear in SIAM Journal of Computing.

This work was supported by the DFG, SFB 124, TP B2, VLSI Entwurf und Parallelität, and by NSF Grant ECS-84-10902.

1. Introduction and Models of Computation

Most parallel algorithms in the literature are designed to run on a PRAM (parallel RAM). The PRAM model was introduced by Fortune and Wyllie [FW]. A PRAM consists of some finite number n of sequential processors (RAMs), all of which operate synchronously on a common memory consisting of, say, m storage cells (also called "variables"), cf. fig. 1.

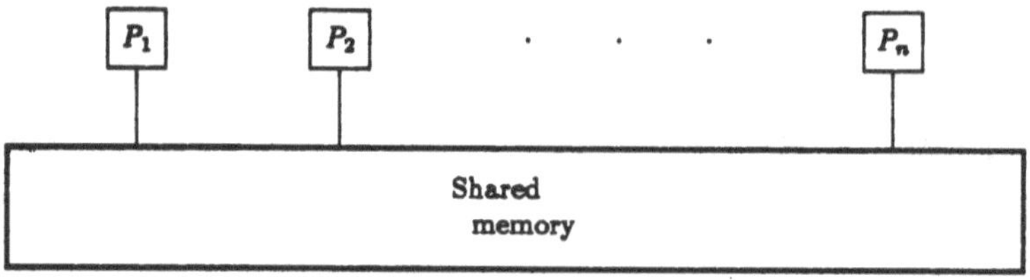

Fig. 1. The PRAM model. $P_1, \ldots, P_n$ are processors.

In every step of the PRAM, each of its processors executes a private RAM instruction. In particular, the processors may all simultaneously access (read from or write into) the common memory. Various types of PRAMs have been defined, differing in the conventions used to deal with read/write conflicts, i.e., attempts by several processors to access the same variable in the same step. In the most restrictive model, exclusive read–exclusive write or EREW PRAMs, no variable may be accessed by more than one processor in a given step. In contrast, CRCW (concurrent read–concurrent write) PRAMs allow simultaneous reading as well as simultaneous writing of each variable, with some rule defining the exact semantics of simultaneous writing.

PRAMs are very convenient for expressing parallel algorithms since one may concentrate on the problem of "parallelizing", i.e., decomposing the problem at hand into simultaneously executable tasks, without having to worry about the communication between these tasks. Indeed, any intermediate result computed by one of the processors will be available to all the others in the next step, due to the shared memory. Unfortunately, the PRAM is not a very realistic model of parallel computation. Present and foreseeable technology does not seem to make it possible for more than a constant number of processors to simultaneously access the same memory module. A model of computation that takes this problem into account is the MPC (*module parallel computer*, [MV]), cf. fig. 2.

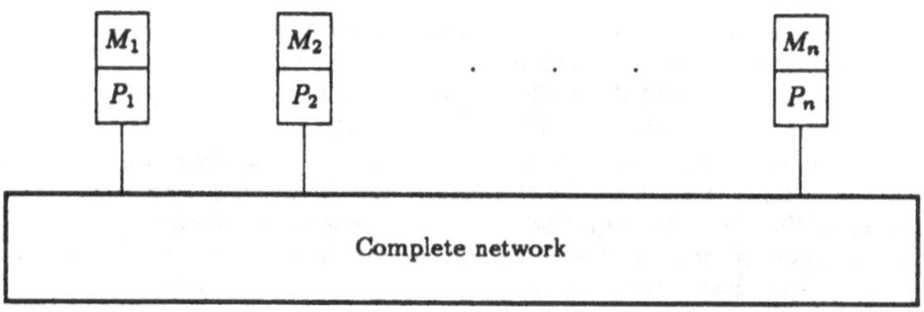

Fig. 2. The MPC model. $P_1, \ldots, P_n$ are processors, $M_1, \ldots, M_n$ memory modules.

An MPC consists of n processors (RAMs), each equipped with a memory module. Every processor may access every memory module via a complete network connecting the processors. However, the memory modules are sequential devices, i.e., able to satisfy only one request at a time. More precisely, a memory module M operates as follows: If several processors try in the same step to access a variable stored in M, exactly one of the processors is allowed to carry out its read or write instruction; the remaining access requests are discarded. All processors are informed of the success or failure of their access attempts. We make no assumptions about how the single successful processor is selected from among the processors competing to access M.

The MPC model is still not realistic for large n because of the postulated complete network connecting the processors. This leads us to consider a third model which we shall call the *network model*. Here the processors are connected via a network of bounded degree, i.e., each processor is linked directly to only a constant number of other processors, cf. fig. 3.

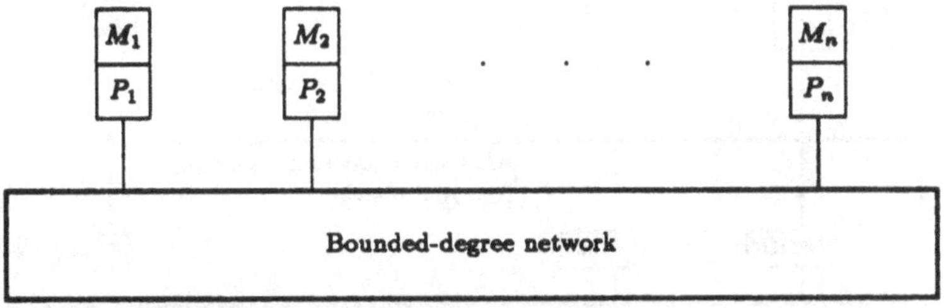

Fig. 3. The network model. $P_1, \ldots, P_n$ are processors, $M_1, \ldots, M_n$ memory modules.

Since each step of a completely interconnected processor network may be simulated by $O(\log n)$ steps of a bounded-degree network ([AKS], [L]), efficient algorithms for the MPC model translate into asymptotically efficient algorithms for the network model.

The simulation of the idealized parallel machine, the PRAM, on the more realistic one, the MPC, has been considered in several previous papers. A naive approach represents each variable x of the PRAM by one variable $\psi(x)$ of the MPC. Now if a PRAM step accesses the variables $x_1, \ldots, x_l$, collisions may occur in the simulating machine because $\psi(x_1), \ldots, \psi(x_l)$ are not necessarily located in distinct memory modules. If $m \leq n$, the m variables may be allocated to m different memory modules, and a trivial $O(1)$-time simulation is possible. However, we are concerned with the case in which m is considerably larger than n. Here a major problem is to find a memory correspondence between the PRAM and the MPC such that, for all possible access patterns of the PRAM, the maximum number of variables requested from a single MPC memory module is kept low. Note that, for specific PRAM algorithms such as matrix multiplication, there may be very efficient ways of assigning variables to modules; we refer the reader to Section 4 of the survey paper by Kuck [K]. Here we are interested in universal simulations which work efficiently no matter which algorithm is executed by the PRAM.

Some results have been obtained previously using *probabilistic* methods: Mehlhorn and Vishkin [MV] used universal hashing to define the memory correspondence. They obtained several upper bounds, for example an average of $O(\log n)$ MPC steps to simulate one PRAM step, with the total amount of memory used by the MPC larger than the PRAM memory by a factor of $O(\log n)$. Upfal [U] found a probabilistic simulation of $O((\log n)^2)$ average time for one PRAM step on a bounded-degree network; this was recently improved to $O(\log n)$ by Karlin and Upfal [KU].

This paper is concerned with *deterministic* simulations. We define the *slow-down* of a simulation as the number of steps needed by the simulating machine in the worst case to simulate one step of the simulated machine. Note that if $m \geq n^2$, the simple scheme outlined above (x is represented by $\psi(x)$) performs poorly: An adversary could make the PRAM step access n variables $x_1, \ldots, x_n$ with $\psi(x_1), \ldots, \psi(x_n)$ all in the same module. Hence the slow-down is $\Omega(n)$. This reasoning shows that each PRAM variable must be represented by several "copies" stored in different modules. Mehlhorn and Vishkin [MV] showed that read instructions can be handled very efficiently using this idea. However, they did not know how to deal with write instructions. In a beautiful paper Upfal and Wigderson [UW] resolved this problem and exhibited a simulation which uses $\Theta(\log n)$ copies of each PRAM variable. If m is polynomial in n, the slow-down is $O(\log n (\log\log n)^2)$. They also showed an $\Omega(\log n / \log\log n)$ lower bound on the slow-down for a large class of simulations.

Using similar techniques, this paper improves the upper bound to $O(\log m)$. If m is polynomial in n, this is $O(\log n)$. Consequently, a PRAM step may be simulated in $O(\log n \log m)$ time on a bounded-degree network. On the other hand, we show that $\Omega(\log n \log m / \log\log m)$ time is necessary under certain assumptions on any bounded-degree network whose communication is restricted to be point-to-point. A similar result was also obtained by Karlin and Upfal [KU]. The assumption of point-to-point communication is not satisfied by our simulation algorithm which uses more general communication patterns.

The PRAM simulations which we consider will be based on *emulations* of the PRAM's shared memory. We conceptually retain the n PRAM processors while replacing (or, equivalently, implementing) the PRAM's (physically infeasible) shared memory by a (more feasible) suitably programmed MPC or bounded-degree network with n processors, called the emulating processors. Each PRAM processor, which was formerly connected to the shared memory, is now instead connected to one of the emulating processors called its *associated* processor, each emulating processor being associated with exactly one PRAM processor, cf. fig. 4. We require the change to be completely transparent, i.e., all PRAM programs must run without change (though possibly slower) on the modified machine.

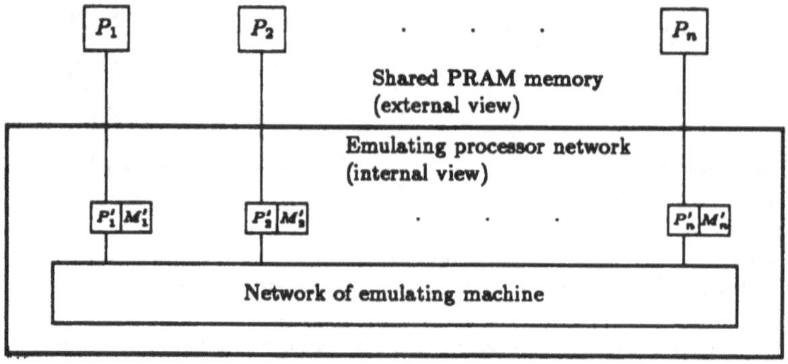

Fig. 4. Emulation of the shared memory of a PRAM.
For $i = 1, \ldots, n$, P_i is a PRAM processor and P'_i its associated emulating processor.

Note that although the most direct PRAM simulation implied by a memory emulation as above uses a total of $2n$ processors, it is a trivial matter to reduce the number of processors to n by coalescing each pair of associated processors into a single processor. For expository reasons we prefer to keep the clean separation between PRAM processors and (emulated) shared memory.

Our simulation algorithms are non-uniform. This means that they are not given explicitly. Instead we merely prove that algorithms with the desired properties exist. For fixed values of n and m, such algorithms may be found by exhaustive search in a large but finite set. We return to this question in the concluding section.

It has been known since Adleman's work [A] that probabilistic algorithms may be converted into non-uniform deterministic ones. Hence the result by Karlin and Upfal [KU] automatically translates into a non-uniform deterministic simulation of PRAMs on a bounded-degree network. However, if the translation is based on Karlin and Upfal's analysis of their algorithm and uses known techniques, it introduces an $\Omega(n)$-increase in the product of time and number of processors [R, Theorem 6]. Since it is not difficult to devise a uniform deterministic simulation which uses $O(n^2/(\log n)^2)$ processors and has a slow-down of $O(\log n)$ (the construction is similar to one presented in the remark ending Section 3), deterministic algorithms derived from Karlin and Upfal's probabilistic simulation are of little interest. The same is true of all other known probabilistic solutions.

The remaining part of the paper is structured as follows: In Section 2 we describe our simulation of PRAMs on MPCs and show that its slow-down is $O(\log m)$. As part of the development of the algorithm, we define and solve a so-called "redistribution problem". Section 3 considers the simulation of PRAMs on bounded-degree networks and establishes upper and lower bounds of $O(\log n \log m)$ and $\Omega(\log n \log m / \log \log m)$, respectively. In Section 4 we return to the redistribution problem and prove a stronger result than what was needed in Section 2. Finally, Section 5 addresses some interesting and important open issues. Sections 2 to 5 can be found in the full paper.

References

[A]: L. Adleman: "Two Theorems on Random Polynomial Time". Proc. 19'th Symp. Found. of Comp. Sci. (1978), 75–83.

[AKS]: M. Ajtai, J. Komlós, E. Szemerédi: "An $O(n \log n)$ Sorting Network". Proc. 15'th ACM Symp. Theory of Comp. (1983), 1–9.

[B]: K.E. Batcher: "Sorting networks and their applications". Proc. AFIPS Spring Joint Comp. Conf. **32** (1968), 307–314.

[BH]: A. Borodin, J.E. Hopcroft: "Routing, Merging, and Sorting on Parallel Models of Computation". Proc. 14'th ACM Symp. Theory of Comp. (1982), 338–344.

[FW]: S. Fortune, J. Wyllie: "Parallelism in Random Access Machines". Proc. 10'th ACM Symp. Theory of Comp. (1978), 114–118.

[GG]: O. Gabber, Z. Galil: "Explicit Constructions of Linear Size Concentrators and Superconcentrators". Proc. 20'th Symp. Found. of Comp. Sci. (1979), 364–370.

[K]: D.J. Kuck: "A Survey of Parallel Machine Organization and Programming". *Computing Surveys* 9:1 (1977), 29–59.

[KU]: A.R. Karlin, E. Upfal: "Parallel Hashing – An Efficient Implementation of Shared Memory". Proc. 18'th ACM Symp. Theory of Comp. (1986), 160–168.

[L]: T. Leighton: "Tight Bounds on the Complexity of Parallel Sorting". Proc. 16'th ACM Symp. Theory of Comp. (1984), 71–80.

[MV]: K. Mehlhorn, U. Vishkin: "Randomized and Deterministic Simulations of PRAMs by Parallel Machines with Restricted Granularity of Parallel Memories". *Acta Informatica* 21 (1984), 339–374.

[O]: O. Ore: "Theory of Graphs". American Mathematical Society, Providence, Rhode Island (1962).

[PV]: F.P. Preparata, J. Vuillemin: "The Cube-Connected Cycles: A Versatile Network for Parallel Computation". *Communications of the ACM* 24:5 (1981), 300–309.

[R]: J.H. Reif: "On the Power of Probabilistic Choice in Synchronous Parallel Computations". Proc. 9'th Int. Coll. Automata, Languages and Programming (1982), 442–450.

[U]: E. Upfal: "A Probabilistic Relation Between Desirable and Feasible Models of Parallel Computation". Proc. 16'th ACM Symp. Theory of Comp. (1984), 258–265.

[UW]: E. Upfal, A. Wigderson: How to Share Memory in a Distributed System". Proc. 25'th Symp. Found. of Comp. Sci. (1984), 171–180.

[VW]: U. Vishkin, A. Wigderson: "Dynamic Parallel Memories". *Information and Control* 56 (1983), 174–182.

CONVEX HULL OF RANDOMLY CHOSEN POINTS FROM A POLYTOPE
(Preliminary Version)

Rex Dwyer * and Ravi Kannan **

* Computer Science dept., Carnegie-Mellon University.
Supported by NSF Grant ECS 8418392

** Computer Science Department, Carnegie-Mellon University and Institut für Operations Research, Universität Bonn. Supported by NSF Grant ECS 8418392 and the Alexander von Humboldt Stiftung, Bonn

1. Abstract

Suppose we pick independently n random points $X_1, X_2, \ldots, X_n$ from a d dimensional polytope P. (i.e., X_i are independent identically distributed random variables each with density $= 1/volume(P)$ in P and 0 outside.) Let E_n be the convex hull of $X_1, X_2, \ldots X_n$. The following questions arise naturally :

1) What is the value of V_n the expected ratio of the volume of $P \setminus E_n$ to the volume of P ?

2) What is the expected number of extreme points of the polytope E_n ?

We show an upper bounds of $\frac{C(P)}{n}(log\, n)^{d+1}$ on V_n and $C(P)(log\, n)^{d+1}$ on M_n where $C(P)$ is a constant that depends only on P (not on n). In both cases elementary arguments will only give a bound that replaces the power of $log\, n$ by a power (less than one) of n. Previously, similar results were known only for the case of $d = 2$. (Buchta (1984) and Rényi and Solanke (1963, 1964)). There has been substantial amount of work on the problem for spheres as well as for other quantities depending on E_n in two dimensions. (see for example W.M. Schmidt (1968), G.Buchta, J.Müller and R.F.Tichy (1985), P.M.Gruber (1983) and I.Bárány and Z.Füredi (1986)) In case the polytope P has at least one vertex with exactly d adjacent vertices, we prove lower bounds of

$$d(P)(log\, n)^{d-1}\ /n \text{ on } V_n \text{ and } d(P)(log\, n)^{d-1} \text{ on } M_n.$$

Using the bounds,we are able to show that certain simple divide and conquer algorithms for finding the set of all extreme points have good sequential (linear time) and parallel (polylog time) complexitites in the expected case when the points are chosen at random independently from a polytope in a fixed number of dimensions.

The results are based on a natural notion of centrality which we introduce for convex sets.

2. The volume of the central region

Definiton : For any positive real number ϵ and a convex set P, a point p in P is ϵ-central for P, if for any hyperplane H through p, the volume of P in each of the half spaces determined by H is at least ϵ times the total volume of P.

Clearly, no point is more than $\frac{1}{2}$ central and the center of gravity is the only $\frac{1}{2}$ central point. It is also clear that if p is ϵ central then it is δ central for any $\delta \leq \epsilon$. We show below that the volume of the subset of points that are not ϵ central cannot be too high. (It is obvious that the set of non ϵ central points is Lesbeg measurable; we use volume to denote the Lesbeg measure.)

Theorem 1 *For any polytope P in R^d, there is a constant $C(P)$ depending only upon P and d such that for every positive ϵ, the volume of the set of non ϵ central points is at most*

$$C(P)\,\epsilon\,(\log \tfrac{1}{\epsilon})^d \;\cdot\; \textit{volume of } P$$

Remark It is possible to see that the volume of noncentral points is at most $C(P)(\epsilon)^{1/d}$ times the volume of P by elementary arguments - any point at distance at least $c.(\epsilon)^{1/d}$ from the boundary of P has a sphere around it of radius $c.(\epsilon)^{1/d}$, any hyperplane through the point leaves a half of this sphere (which is of sufficient volume) in either half space. Note that the bound in the theorem is stronger - there ϵ is multiplied by a power of $\log \frac{1}{\epsilon}$ whereas the elementary argument gives a bound where ϵ is multiplied by a power of $\frac{1}{\epsilon}$.

Remark The theorem is not true when P is a general convex set. For example it is easy to show that when P is a sphere, the ϵ central region is a concentric sphere of radius $(1 - c_d\epsilon^{1/d})$ times the radius of the original sphere whence the volume of the smaller sphere is $1 - O(\epsilon^{1/d})$ times that of the whole sphere.

Proof : With each unit vector c in R^d, we can associate a function $f_c : R^d \rightarrow R$ as follows : $f_c(x) =$ the volume of the set $\{y : c \cdot y \geq c \cdot x\}$, i.e., $f_c(x)$ is the volume of the half space above x determined by the hyperplane orthogonal to c through x. Further let c_o be the minimum of the linear functional $c \cdot x$ over P. It will be useful to define also $g_c : R \rightarrow R_+$ as $g_c(\lambda) =$ the volume of the set $\{x : c \cdot x \leq c_o + \lambda\}$. The following is a direct consequence of the Brunn-Minkowski theorem (Bonnesen and Fenchel (1934)).

Proposition 1 *Suppose λ, δ are real numbers such that $0 \leq \lambda \leq \delta$. Then, with the notation of the last paragraph,*

$$g_c(\lambda) \geq \left(\frac{\lambda}{\delta}\right)^d g_c(\delta)$$

Proof : Without loss of generality, we may translate P so that $c_o = 0$. For any positive real number α let $A(\alpha)$ be the $d-1$ dimensional volume of the intersection of $\{x : c \cdot x = \alpha\}$ and P. The Brunn-Minkowski theorem asserts that the $d-1$ st root of $A(\cdot)$ is a concave function. From this it follows that for any α in the interval $[\lambda \ \delta]$,

$$A(\lambda) \geq \left(\frac{\lambda}{\alpha}\right)^{d-1} A(\alpha)$$

Integrating $A(\alpha)$ from λ to δ and using the above we get that

$$g_c(\delta) - g_c(\lambda) \leq \frac{\lambda A(\lambda)}{d}\left(\left(\frac{\delta}{\lambda}\right)^d - 1\right)$$

Further, since there is some point q in P with $c \cdot q = 0$, the convex hull of q and $P \cap \{x : c \cdot x = \lambda\}$ contributes at least $A(\lambda)\lambda/d$ to $g_c(\lambda)$, so we have

$$g_c(\lambda) \geq A(\lambda)\lambda/d$$

These two inequalities together give us the proposition.

□

Let $F_i = \{x : c_i \cdot x \leq d_i\}$ $i = 1, 2, \ldots k$ be the defining inequalities of P where the c_i are unit vectors. We call a hyperplane of the form $\{x : c_i \cdot x = d_i - 2^{k/d}\epsilon\}$ where k is a natural number, a "copy" of F_i provided it intersects P. If any subset of d of the hyperplanes among the facets or their copies intersect at a point, we call the point a "grid point". It is clear that the number of grid points is at most $C(P)(log\,\frac{1}{\epsilon})^d$ for some constant $C(P)$ independent of ϵ. The facets and their copies subdivide the polytope P into what we may call "regions" - each region is a set of the form $\{x : d_i - 2^{k_i/d} \geq c_i \cdot x \geq d_i - 2^{k_i+1/d}$ for $i = 1, 2, \ldots k\}$ where the k_i are some natural numbers. It is clear that each region is the convex hull of some grid points. Finally, define for each x in P the unit vector $c(x)$ to be such that $f_{c(x)}(x) = \min\{f_c(x) : c$ a unit vector $\}$. The proof of the following proposition follows closely the lines of a proof of Lovász and Scarf (1986).

Proposition 2 *If a point x of P lies at distance at least $2^{1/d}\epsilon$ from every facet, then there is a grid point y such that*

$$f_{c(x)}(x) \geq f_{c(y)}(x)/2$$

Proof Under the hypothesis, it is clear that x is in an interior region R. Suppose R is the convex hull of grid points $y_1, y_2, \ldots y_k$. One of the y_i - call it y for short satisfies

$$f_{c(x)}(x) \geq f_{c(x)}(y)$$

Further,

$$f_{c(x)}(y) \geq f_{c(y)}(y)$$

Suppose the straight line *from x to y* intersects the boundary of P at z. By the definition of "copies", it is clear that $|x-z| \leq 2^{1/d}|y-z|$. So by proposition 1, we have

$$f_{c(y)}(y) \geq f_{c(y)}(x)/2$$

The three inequalities together establish the proposition.

Now we go back to the proof of the theorem. Let $\{f_{c(y)} : y \text{ a grid point }\}$ be $\{f^{(1)}, f^{(2)} \dots f^{(s)}\}$ where $s \leq C(P)(log\,\frac{1}{\epsilon})^d$.

$$T^{(i)} = \{x : f^{(i)}(x) \lesssim 2\epsilon\} \text{ for } i = 1, 2, \dots s$$

If $x \in P$ is at least $2^{1/d}\epsilon$ away from the boundary of P and $x \notin T^{(i)}$ for $i = 1, 2, \dots s$, we wish to assert that x is ϵ central for P. This is because, for such x, there exists some grid point y such that $f_{c(x)}(x) \geq f_{c(y)}(x)/2 \geq \epsilon$, whence of course $f_c(x) \geq \epsilon$ for every unit vector c. Obviously, $\mu(T^{(i)}) = 2\epsilon$ (here μ denotes the volume) for each i, further, the the volume of the set of points at distance at most ϵ from the boundary of P is at most $C(P)'\epsilon$ for some constant $C(P)'$. Thus the volume of the set of non ϵ-central points in P is at most $2\epsilon s + \epsilon C(P)' \leq C(P)''\epsilon(log\,\frac{1}{\epsilon})^d$. So we have proved the theorem.

3. Probablilstic results

The following simple lemma together with the theorem of the last section gives us the probabilistic results.

Lemma 1 *Suppose n points are picked at random independently from a polytope P in R^d and suppose E_n denotes their convex hull. If x is an ϵ -central point of P, then the probability that x does not belong to E_n is at most $\binom{n}{d-1}(1-\epsilon)^{n-d+1}$.*

Proof: If x is not in E_n, then it lies on a facet F of the convex hull of $E_n \cup \{x\}$. F contains at least $d-1$ of n randomly picked points. Since x is ϵ central for P, the volume of P on either side of F is at most $1-\epsilon$. Thus the lemma folows.

We use the lemma as follows : Let $t = \frac{n(d+1)}{n-d+1}$ and choose $\epsilon \approx \frac{t\,log\,n}{n}$. Then a calculation shows that if x is ϵ central for P, then the probability that $x \notin E_n$ is at most $1/n^2$.

Thus the expected volume of $P \setminus E_n$ is at most $\frac{1}{n^2}$ plus the volume of the non ϵ central region. The latter is at most $C(P)(d+1)(\log n)^{d+1}/(n-d+1)$ as a simple calculation shows. Summing, we get that the expected volume of $P \setminus E_n$ is at most $C(P)(\log n)^{d+1}/n$ for $n \geq 2d$ for a suitable $C(P)$.

To get the expected number of extreme points of E_n, note that the probability that one of the chosen n points is extreme equal to the probability that it does not belong to E_{n-1}. Thus the central region contributes at most $n/(n-1)^2 < 1$ to the expected number of extreme points , while the non central region contributes at most n times its expected volume overall at most $O((\log n)^{d+1})$. So we have proved the theorem promised in the introduction.

Theorem 2 *Suppose P is a polytope in R^d and E_n is the convex hull of n randomly and independently picked points in P . Then the expected volume of $P \setminus E_n$ is $O((\log n)^{d+1}/n)$ and the expected number of extreme points of E_n is $O((\log n)^{d+1})$ where the hidden constants depend only upon P and d.*

4. Lower bounds

We prove lower bounds on the volume of the non ϵ central region. These, we will see, also imply lower bounds on V_n and M_n.

Theorem 3 *If P is a polytope of nonzero volume in R^d, such that P has at least one vertex with precisly d neighbouring vertices, then there exists a constant $e(P)$ depending only upon P such that for any ϵ, the volume of the set of points that are not ϵ central to P is at least $e(P)\epsilon(\log \frac{1}{\epsilon})^{d-1}$ times the volume of P.*

Proof. : First, we give the argument for $P =$ the cube $\{x : 0 \leq x_i \leq 1 \text{ for } i = 1,2,\ldots d\}$. For any point $p = (p_1, p_2, \ldots, p_d)$ in the cube, consider the hyperplane $\{x : \sum x_i/p_i = d\}$. This hyperplane, call it H, passes through p. Further the region in the cube "below" H is contained in the simplex with vertices $(0,0,\ldots,0), (dp_1,0,0,\ldots,0), (0,dp_2,0,\ldots,0), \ldots, (0,0,\ldots,0,dp_d)$, whose volume is $d^d \prod p_i/d!$. Thus if the product of the p_i is less than $d!\epsilon/d^d$, then p is not ϵ central to P. The following claim finishes the proof of the lemma in the case of cubes.

Claim : The volume of the set $S_d(\delta) = \{p \in R^d : 0 \leq p_i \leq 1, \prod p_i \leq \delta\}$ is at least $\delta(\log \frac{1}{\delta})^{d-1}/(d-1)!$.

Proof. : The proof is by induction on d. For $d = 1$, it is clear. In general, let $v(d, \delta)$ be the volume of $S_d(\delta)$. Then, we have

$$v(d, \delta) = \delta + \int_{x_1 = delta}^{1} v(d-1, \delta/x_1)dx_1$$

Now the claim follows by induction.

Suppose now P is any polytope with a vertex p of degree d. By trnaslating P, assume that $p = 0$. Let $p^1, p^2, \ldots p^d$ be the vertices adjacent to 0. Then the parallelopiped $Q = \{x : x = \sum \lambda_i p^i; 0 \leq \lambda_i \leq 1/d\}$, is contained in P and furthermore, P is contained in the cone $\{x : x = \lambda_i p^i, \lambda_i \geq 0\}$. So if a point x in Q has a hyperplane passing through it so that the volume of the cone below the hyperplane is less than ϵ times the volume of P, then clearly, x is not ϵ central to P. Let τ be a linear transformation that sends Q to the unit cube. τ preserves ratios of volumes, so the theorem follows from the argument for cubes plus the fact that the ratio of the volume of Q to the volume of P is a constant that depends only upon P.

To derive lower bounds on M_n, V_n, we prove the simple converse to Lemma 1.

Proposition 3 *If x is not ϵ central to P, then the probability that x does not belong to E_n is at least $(1-\epsilon)^n$.*

Proof. : The proof is straight forward and is ommited.

Now we choose $\epsilon = t/n$ for an as yet unspecified constant t. Then the non ϵ central points comprise a set of volume at least $e(P)(\log n)^{d-1}/n)$ for some constant $e(P)$ depending only upon P (and t which is but a constant) . For each x such that x is not ϵ central to P, the probability that x is not in E_n is at least $e^{-t} = O(1)$ for t independent of n. So the expected volume of $P \setminus E_n$ is at least $O((\log n)^{d-1}/n)$. The lower bound on M_n is proved as follows. By Chernoff bounds, the probability that the number of non-ϵ central points out of the n randomly picked points is less than $s = e(P)(\log n)^{d-1}(1-e^{-1})/(2n)$ is at most 1/2 (this is a very crude estimate). Thus with probability at least a half s or more points are picked from the non central region. Each such point is an extreme point of E_n with probability a constant greater than 0. So we have shown the following :

Theorem 4 *Let E_n be the convex hull of n indpendently and randomly picked points from a d dimensional polytope P in R^d, that has at least one vertex with precisely d adjacent vertices. The expected value of the ratio of the volume of $P \setminus E_n$ to the volume of P is at least $\Omega((\log n)^{d-1}/n)$; the expected number of extreme* *points of E_n is at least $\Omega((\log n)^{d-1})$ where the hidden constants depend only upon P.*

Remark Lovász and Scarf prove the following lemma using their arguments referred to earlier - they show that if P is a polytope in R^d and we have a family of possibly infinitely many concave nonnegative functions defined on P, then for any $\epsilon > 0$, there is a subfamily of the convex functions consisting of $O((\log \frac{1}{\epsilon})^d)$ of them so that for any point x in P at distance at least ϵ from its boundary, there is a concave function g in the subfamily so that $g(x) \leq 2f(x)$ for any f in the original family. Using the arguments of this section, it is possible to show that their number of elements in the subfamily cannot be improved by more than a factor of $O(\log \frac{1}{\epsilon})$. We will do so more fully in a final paper.

5. Applications to Algorithms

Suppose we are given n randomly and independently picked points in a polytope P in R^d where d is considered fixed and n grows. One of the interesting questions is to find the set of extreme points among these n. (We will address other related problems in a final paper.)

The idea of using divide and conquer to find the extreme points is simple and well-known (see Bentley and Shamos 1978). Basically, we subdivide the set of n points randomly into two equal sets and work recursively on each of them. After we find the extreme points among each set of $n/2$ points, we again use an extreme point finding algorithm on the union of the two sets. Since the two sets are small in the expected case, the sequential time for the whole process is linear. Also, in parallel, we can work on each of the set of $n/2$ points, so for parallel expected time, we get the recurrence

$$T(n) \leq T(n/2) + T(O((\log n)^{d+1})))$$

which implies for example that $T(n) \leq O((\log n)^2)$. (More careful solution is possible .) We leave the details to the final version of the paper or the reader.

References

I.Bárány and Z.Füredi , *Approximation of the ball by polytopes having a few vertices* Technical report, Cornell University, School of Operations Research (1986)

J.L. Bentley, H.T.Kung, M.Schkolnick and C.D.Thompson On the average number maxima in a set of vectors, JACM 25:536-543, 1978.

J.L. Bentley and M.I.Shamos, Divide and conquer for linear expected time, IPL 7(2):87-91, Feb., 1978.

T.Bonnesen and W.Fenchel, *Theorie der konvexen Körper*, Springer Berlin (1934), Chelsea, New York (1948)

C.Buchta, *Zufallspolygone in konvexen Vielecken* J. reine u angew. Mathematik 347, pp 212-220

C.Buchta, J.Müller and R.F.Tichy, *Stochastical approximation of convex bodies* Math. Anna. 271 pp 225-235 (1985)

L. Devroye, A note on finding convex hulls via maximal vectors, Information Processing Letters 11(1):53-56, Aug., 1980.

L.Lovász and H.Scarf, *Neighbourhood systems in Integer Programming* , Manuscript (1986)

P.M.Gruber, *Approximation of convex bodies* in Convexity and its applications ed. P.M.Gruber, J.M.Wills, Birkhäuser Verlag (1983)

A.Rényi and R.Sulanke, *Über die konvexe Hülle von zufällig gewälten Punkten* I and II, Zeitschrift für Wahrscheinlichkeittheorie 2, pp 75-84 (1963) and 3, pp 138-147 (1964)

H. Raynaud, Sur l'envellope convexe des nuages des points ale'atoires dans R^n, I. J. Appl. Prob. 7:35-48, 1970.

W.M.Schmidt, *Some results in probabilistic Geometry* Zeitschrift für Wahrscheinlichkeittheorie 9, pp 158-162 (1968)

Dataflow Computing

Jayantha Herath*, Toshitsugu Yuba, Nobuo Saito*
* Keio University, 3-14-1 Hiyoshi, Kohoku-ku, Yokohama 223, Japan.
Electrotechnical Laboratory, Ibaraki 305, Japan.

Abstract

An abstract computing model, a base language specification for the abstract model, high-level and low-level language design, and architecture design are steps in constructing computing systems. Dataflow computing, a radical departure from von Neumann computing, supports multiple processing on a massive scale and plays a major role in next generation computing machines to achieve ultra high speeds. This paper presents an overview of dataflow computing models, languages designed for dataflow computing, and dataflow computing machines for numerical and non-numerical computations.

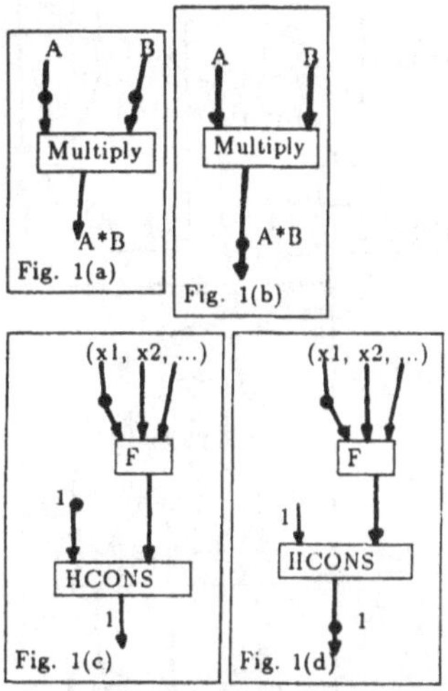

Fig. 1 Data-flow computing

1 Introduction

The dataflow approach has the potential to exploit large scale concurrency efficiently, maximum utilisation of VLSI in computer design, compatibility with distributed networks, and compatibility with functional high-level programming. In dataflow, an instruction is enabled immediately after the arrival of operands, and partial results of the execution are passed directly as data tokens. The computations are free of side effects, and independent computations proceed in parallel. In dataflow computing, there is no concept of shared data storage. Every instruction is allocated by the computing element. The dataflow concept can be easily implemented in both major computing application areas: numerical and non-numerical computations.

Several dataflow computing models have been proposed for implementing the dataflow computing concept in practical machines. These models support the building of highly parallel and asynchronous computing machines, but differ in their approach as to how the computing should proceed. Common features of these models include strict and non-strict evaluations. In strict dataflow computing, all the operands of an operation or arguments of a function must be presented to enable the execution. Figs. 1(a) and 1(b) show the strict computation, multiply. In non-strict dataflow computing, a selected number of operands of an operation or arguments of a function is sufficient to enable the execution. This avoids unnecessary computations, eliminates non-terminating computations and optimises the computations. Figs. 1(c) and 1(d) show the non-strict computation HCONS. The HCONS operator has two arguments. The result of HCONS, the first argument, is generated immediately after the arrival of first argument.

Many dataflow computing languages and machines have been developed. Section 2 of this paper discusses the static, dynamic, operator net, lazy-eager, pseudo-result and Not(operation) dataflow computing models. Section 3 overviews the dataflow computing languages used to represent dataflow computations. Section 4 discusses the representative dataflow computing machines for numerical and non-numerical computations.

2 Dataflow Computing Models

Static Computing

Static dataflow computing, [1] to [3], was proposed by Dennis for ultra high speed computing machines. This computing model consists of operators, data and control arcs, and data and control tokens. The number of tokens per arc is limited to one. In this model, switch and merge operations are introduced to support conditional computations. Fig. 2 shows the implementation of the conditional computation, IF C(x) THEN A1(x) ELSE B1(x) and the firing sequence.

Dynamic Computing

In dynamic dataflow computing, several instances of a node can be fired at a time and these nodes can be created at run time. Davis [6] proposed a dynamic computing model based on FIFO queues and recursive computations.

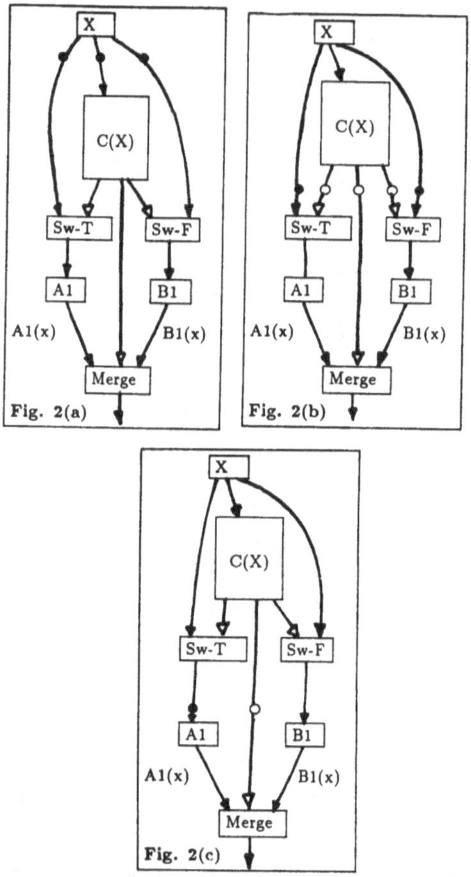

Fig. 2 Static computing

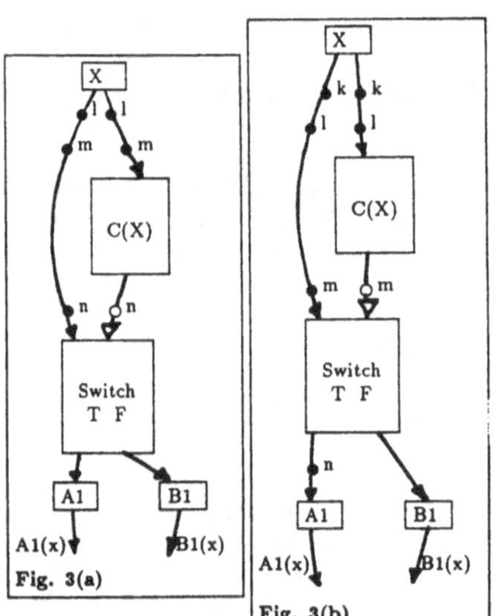

Fig. 3 Dynamic computing

The tagged token dynamic computing model, proposed separately by Arvind [4] and Gurd-Watson [5] at Manchester, is more efficient in exploiting the parallelism to a large degree. The switch operation used has two input arcs, one for boolean tokens and the other for data tokens to be switched. This operator also has two output arcs. The incoming boolean token determines the output arc along which the incoming data token is sent. The BRR operation used by Gurd's group is similar to this switch operation. Fig. 3 shows the firing sequence for tagged dynmic dataflow computing.

Operator Net Computing

Operator nets, proposed by Ashcroft [7], are a hybrid computing model of dataflow computing and demand driven computing. Fig. 4 shows the firing sequence of operator nets. The wvr node is similar to the switch-t operation. The switch operation is occasionally used. Operators such as wvr and merge need extra memory to remember the last token arrived in dynamic dataflow computing.

Eager-Lazy Computing

Eager and lazy dataflow computing models were proposed by Amamiya et al [9] for artificial intelligence applications. In eager evaluation, all possible computations are executed in parallel. It is very similar to the execution of conditional computations in parallel to the branches. This is the lenient-cons computing in AI. In lazy evaluation, selected computations are executed to optimise the computation. It is similar to the selected branch execution in conditional computations. This is the lazy-cons computing in AI. In this model eager, lazy, non-strict and demand driven computing mechanisms are selectively and efficiently implemented to get the maximum efficiency.

Pseudo-result Computing

Yamaguchi et al [26] proposed pseudo-result dataflow computing model particularly for AI applications. Pseudo-results are generated immediately after the arrival of an argument, as a result of function execution. This relaxes firing conditions. The operations in the function are executed concurrently with the evaluation of its successor. The identifiers of pseudo-results are realised by addresses on a result store and are eventually filled by actual results. A semi-result is the pseudo-result used in non-numerical computations, and the partial-result is the pseudo-result used in numerical computations. When the input to an operation or function is actual, semi or pseudo, the output is an actual or semi result. The execution of a non list operation is deferred until the inputs become actual.

Not(operation) based Computing

In this computing model, n-value logic is proposed, [29] to [31], for computing conditional computations, considering an ideal, value oriented computing environment. In n-value logic, the execution of a conditional computation does not give strictly TRUE or FALSE values or range of values between one and zero but gives any value,

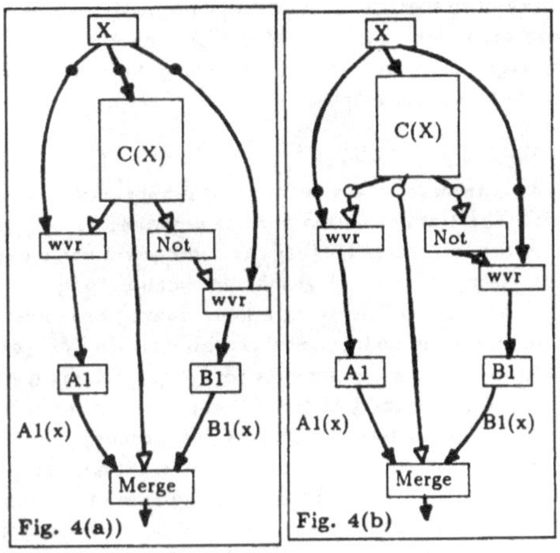

Fig. 4 Opertaor nets

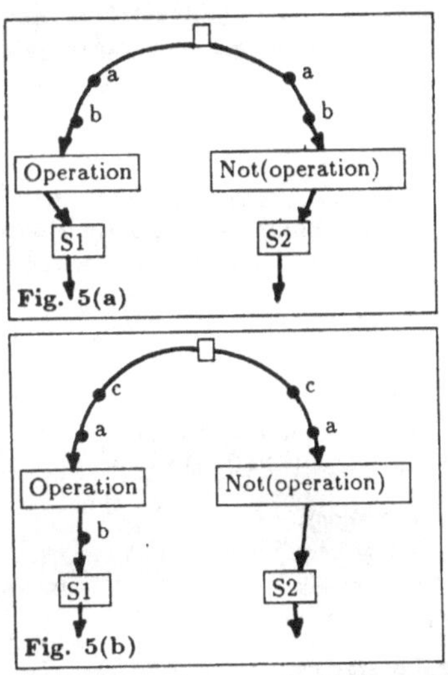

Fig. 5 Not(operation) based computing

including no value. Fig. 5 shows the conditional computation, IF (Operation) THEN S1 OR IF (Not(operation)) THEN S2. The positive state of a conditional computation is denoted by Operation and the negative state by Not(operation). Each operation receives a copy of the input token. When the operation is satisfied, input data is given as the result of execution, and the output of the other operation is frozen. This feature is extended to execute a large number of parallel conditional computations, iterative and recursive computations in parallel computing systems.

The effectiveness of the Not(operation) model over the other models in solving some general problems in dataflow computing systems such as matching bottleneck, remaining packet garbage, control of parallelism, sequential computing segments, token traffic and load balancing, parallel execution of conditional computations and optimisation of dataflow computations was discussed in [31].

3 Dataflow Computing Languages

In designing parallel computing languages, it is possible to use an existing sequential language or to use a high level language based on the hardware features of the parallel computer. The use of existing languages allows existing software to run on the new machine. The CRAY and CYBER machines use sequential languages. The compiler detects the parallelism. This approach can also be used in dataflow computing. High level languages used in ILLIAC, ICL, DAP machines reflect the machine architecture in the syntax. The use of a language which reflects the parallel machine architecture exploits the machine parallelism. Functional languages do not reflect von Neumann properties and are quite similar to single assignment languages.

3.1 High-level Languages

VAL

VAL is the high level language designed by Dennis's group at MIT [2]. VAL is value oriented, as opposed to traditional variable orientation. In a value oriented system, new values are defined and used but no values can ever be modified. Values may be bound to identifiers but identifiers are prevented from being used as variables. The design principles of VAL provide implicit concurrency and synchronization, by using completely functional language features. Expression based features inhibit all forms of side effects. Once the values of all inputs are known, execution cannot influence the results of any other operation ready to be executed. Automatic detection of parallel computations by compilers, vectorization, has been used to exploite concurrency. Side effect features, memory update and aliasing are banned. VAL helps simplify critical programming chores such as error handling, debugging and speed analysis.

Id

Id [4] was proposed by Arvind and Gostelow. Id, Irvine Dataflow, is a block structured, expression oriented, side effect free, single assignment language. A program in Id is a list of expressions. The four most basic expressions are blocks, conditionals, loops and procedure applications. Id variables are not typed. SELECT and APPEND create new and logically distinct structures. Executions of operators are dynamic compared to the static nature of Dennis's model. Id supports streams and nondeterministic programming.

LUCID

LUCID, proposed by Ashcroft and Wadge, incorporates iterations by regarding all values as histories [7]. Everything, including constants, is an infinite history. Assignment statements are equations between histories. A program in LUCID is an unordered set of equations. The result generation is stopped, when the required number of results is produced, by stopping the machine. Conventional LUCID is implemented employing demand driven computing for infinite objects.

SISAL

SISAL, the stream and iteration in a single assignment language, is a co-operative research effort of the Colorado State University, DEC, Lawrence Livermore Laboratory and Manchester University [10]. This language is a value oriented functional language for sequential, vector, multi-processor and dataflow computing machines. SISAL is implemented in the VAX, CRAY, HEP and Manchester dataflow machines. SISAL is strongly typed. Recursion has been added, error values are simplified and some Id (/MAD) features are added. Tokens are labelled to allow multiple use of arcs. Labels are used for data structures, loops and functions.

Manchester languages

Languages used in the Manchester machine [8] are conventional languages, LAPSE, MAD, SASL and SISAL.
SASL, based on LUCID, treats functions as first class objects. In particular, the function takes one argument, and currying is used to obtain the effect of multiple argument functions.
LAPSE, a single assignment language, has PASCAL-like syntax. LAPSE stores arrays during iteration or for-all loops which have used them.
MAD is based on Id but is typed using streams and has operators such as list processing operations. MAD stores arrays for longer, and garbage collection is performed using reference counts.

Valid

Valid, the value identification language, [11] designed by Amamiya et al., is a functional language with implicit and explicit parallel constructs. Lenient-cons computing is applied in function evaluation to achieve very high parallelism. Higher order function features are used in programming. List computations and higher order functions are written using an Algol and Lisp-like syntax.

EMLISP

EMLISP, is a single assignment language [26], [27]. To obtain side effect free, pure functional list processing, the features added to conventional LISP to increase efficiency in von Neumann computing, such as relatives of PROG, flow controlling operations, list modifiers, relatives of array and side effect operations such as RPLACA and RPLACD are removed. The global and free variables and loops are inhibited. Special features such as parallel COND, parallel OR, parallel AND and BLOCK are added. The low level language used in EM-3 to represent dataflow computing is EMIL.

3.2 Dataflow graph languages

Each high-level language described above has its own dataflow graph language. Two dataflow graph languages are described below.

IF1

IF1 is the intermediate language for SISAL [12]. The objective of IF1 design is to develop an intermediate form for functional languages to represent dataflow graphs. IF1 performs machine independent optimisations and machine dependent analysis. It is a well developed graph language. Two-value logic based computations are represented by these graphs.

DCBL

DCBL introduces the semantics of graphs with n-value logic. The transformation process described in [30] can be used in any other language to represent n-value logic based computations. A graph specification language is proposed using following notations. T(exp) to represent the operators of the translated expression, exp, IM.T(exp), to represent the set of imports to T(exp), EX.T(exp) to represent the exports of the T(exp) and —> to represent the links between operators. In general, two languages can be defined, using imports or exports, to represent flow graphs. Import based languages can be used to represent demand driven computations. Imports and exports show the relationship between dataflow and demand flows in computations. This implies that the optimisation of computations need both dataflow and demand flows. An extension of this graph language can specify parallel and distributed systems.

3.3 Functionality

The graph is mapped onto its semantic characteristics using the functionality. The functionality of some operators is defined below. N and e imply frozen or seized and empty exports.

- List operations:
  Fhead((x1 x2 ...)) = x1 Ffhead(( )) = E
  Ftail((x1 x2 ...)) = (x2 x3 ...) Ftail(()) = E
  Fcons(x1 (x2 ...)) = (x1 x2 ...)
- Numerical operations:
  Fplus(x y) = x+y Fdifference(x y) = x-y
  Fquotient(x y) = x/y Fremainder(x y) = rem x/y
  Ftimes(x y) = x * y
- Conditional operations:
  Fnull(()) = () Fnotnull(x1 ...) = (x1 ...)
  Fnull(x1 ...) = N Fnotnull(()) = N

  Fatom((x)) = (x) Fatom((x1 ...) = (x1 ...)
  Fatom((x1...)) = N Fnotatom(x) = N

  Fnumberp(1) = 1 Fnotnumberp(1 ...) = 1 ...
  Fnumberp(1 ...) = N Fnotnumberp(1) = N

  Fequal(x x) = x Fnotequal(x x) = N
  Fequal(x y) = N Fnotequal(x y) = x

  for integers x greaterthan y
  Fgreater(x y) = y Fnotgreater(x y) = x
  Fgreater(y x) = N Fnotgreater(x y) = N
- non-strict operators:
  Fhcons(x1 (x2 ...)) = x1
  Ftcons((x1, x2 ...) xn) = xn
  Fand(..F..) = F Fand(T,T,T... T) =T
  For(..T..) = T Fand(F,F,F... F) =F

The Fibonacci computation,
F(1) = 1;
F(2) = 1;
F(n) = F(n-1) + F(n-2); is shown in Fig. 6. Fig. 6(a) shows the code based on exports, Fig. 6(b) shows the code based on imports and Fig. 6(c) shows the dataflow graph represented by both codes. The format of the codes are similar to EMIL [28].

```
G0001 (PROCEDURE FIB 1. (G0002 MONO-0) )
G0002 (*DISTRIBUTE (G0001 MONO-0) (G0004 MONO-0) )
G0003 (*EQ (C-1 1.) (G0012 (RETURN 1.)) )
G0004 (*EQ (C-1 2.) (G0006 MONO-0)) )
G0005 (*GT (C-1 2.) (G0007 MONO-0) (G0008 MONO-0) )
G0006 (*CONSTANT (C-1 1.) (G0012(RETURN 1.)) )
G0007 (*DIFFERENCE (C-1 1.) (G0009 (ARG 1. 1.)) )
G0008 (*DIFFERENCE (C-1 2.) (G0010 (ARG 1. 1.)) )
G0009 (*CALL FIB 1.1. (G0011 0.) )
G0010 (*CALL FIB 1.1. (G0011 1.) )
G0011 (*PLUS (G0014 (RETURN 1.)) )
G0012 (*RETURN 1.)
END
```

Fig. 6(a)

```
G0001 (PROCEDURE FIB 1. )
G0002 (*DISTRIBUTE (G0001 MONO-0) )
G0003 (*EQ (C-1 1.) (G0002 2.) )
G0004 (*EQ (C-1 2.) (G0002 1.) )
G0005 (*GT (C-1 2.) (G0002 1.) )
G0006 (*CONSTANT (C-1 1.) (G0004 1.) )
G0007 (*DIFFERENCE (C-1 1.) (G0005 1.) )
G0008 (*DIFFERENCE (C-1 2.) (G0005 1.) )
G0009 (*CALL FIB 1.1. (G0007 0.) )
G0010 (*CALL FIB 1.1. (G0008 1.) )
G0011 (*PLUS (G0009 1.) (G0010 2.) )
G0012 (*RETURN (G0003 1.) ( G0004 2.) G0011 3.)
END
```

Fig. 6(b)

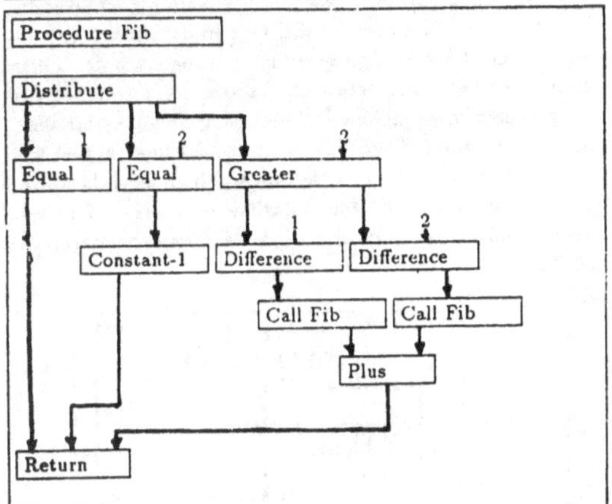

Fig. 6(c)

Fig. 6 Fibonacci - Dataflow graph

4 Dataflow Computing Machines

Several surveys on dataflow computing have been conducted by [13], [14], [15]. This section describes the representative dynamic and static dataflow computing machines for numerical computations and dynamic machines for non-numerical computations.

4.1 Dynamic Machines for Numerical Computing

4.1.1 SIGMA-1

The Electrotechnical Laboratory (ETL) started two research and development projects on dataflow computing, SIGMA-1 and EM-3, at the beginning of 1982. The SIGMA-1 project aims to develop a large-scale dynamic dataflow supercomputer, with 100 MFLOPS performance, for numerical computations in scientific and technological computations, [18] to [20]. SIGMA-1 uses a C-like high-level dataflow computing language, DFC (Dataflow C). SAS is the intermediate language used to describe the dataflow graphs. Preliminary version of the PE and SE using advanced Schottky TTL logic and MOS memories have been in operation, with 1.3 MIPS, since November 1984. Gate-array LSI chips used final version of a single group is in operation now. The full hardware configuration with the total predicted performance of 100 MFLOPS will be in operation in the end of 1987.

1. Global configuration: The SIGMA-1, Fig. 7, is constructed using 128 PEs and 128 structure elements (SEs) which are divided into 32 groups connected by a two level hierarchical network. This hierarchy corresponds to parallel execution of iterations and procedure calls which appear frequently in numerical computations. A single group consists of four PEs and four SEs, connected by a 10 x 10 crossbar switch. The remaining two ports of the switch are used for the interfaces to the global network and the maintenance architecture. The global network is a two stage omega network.

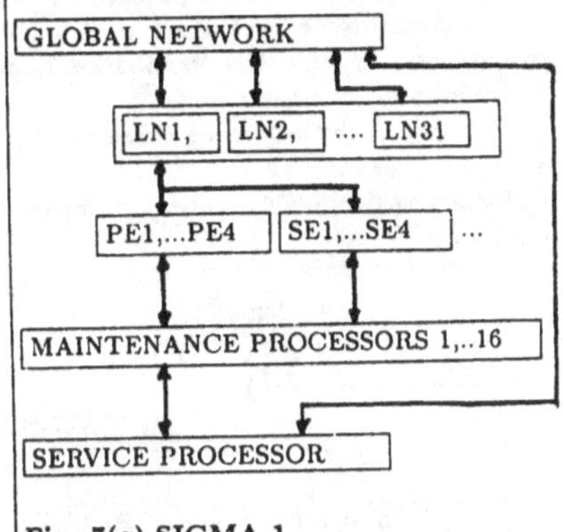

Fig. 7(a) SIGMA-1

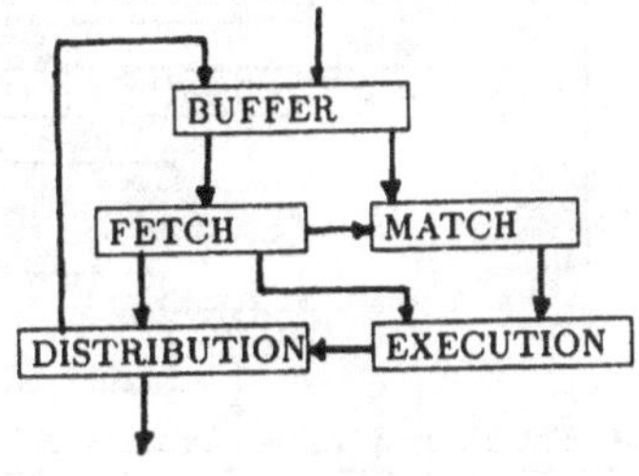

Fig. 7(b) SIGMA-1 - PE

2. Processing elements: A PE consists of several functional units, each of which works synchronously and constitutes a two stage pipeline. A chained hashing hardware with 64K cells is used as the matching memory unit. Each PE consists of about 81K logic gates, using nine types of 28 gate-array LSIs. A SE controls array structures allowing single write and multiple read operations. It is implemented by memory of 256K cells, where each cell is attached with a waiting queue for asynchronous access control.

3. Packet formats and instructions: The data transfer between PEs and SEs is in fixed length packet form. A packet consists of the PE/SE number (8 bits), the destination identifier (28 bits), the tagged data (40 bits), and miscellaneous information (12 bits). The length of the instruction is 40 bits in a primitive format. The first 20 bits indicate the operation to be performed, and the next 20 bits indicate the destination address of the result data. It is possible to allocate a maximum of three different destinations to an instruction.

4.1.2 MIT Tagged-Token Dataflow Machine

The Irvine dataflow project started in 1975 at the University of California at Irvine and is being continued at MIT by Arvind's group [4]. The major contributions include the tagged token dynamic computing model, Id language and computer architecture. The main objective is to exploit VLSI and provide highly concurrent program organisation. A 32-PE machine using Symbolic Lisp machines is being constructed.

1. Global configuration: This machine has 64 processing elements connected via a 64 x 64 communication network. The organisation minimises communication overhead by
a) Matching at the processing element holding the storage instruction;
b) Bypassing the 64 x 64 network to the processor itself.

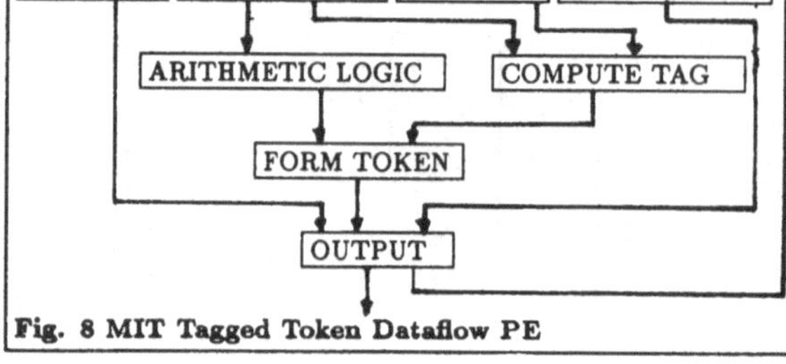

Fig. 8 MIT Tagged Token Dataflow PE

2. Processing elements: A PE, Fig. 8, consists of the input, waiting matching, instruction fetch, service and output sections. The input section accepts inputs from other processing elements, the waiting matching section forms data tokens into sets for one instruction, the instruction fetch section fetches executable instructions from the local program memory, and the output section routes data tokens containing results to the destination processing element. Enabled nodes are detected using tags carrying the information of the node. Tagged stream elements are processed in parallel using multiple instances, one for each element. Program memory stores instruction codes. The data memory, an I-structure memory, stores arrays. Waiting matching storage, an associative memory, matches or stores the incoming tokens. Recursive computations are supported by tagged tokens. Processing units asynchronously evaluate the executable instruction packets. Faults require restoring the computations at the previous checkpoint.

3. Packet formats and instructions: There is a maximum of two input tokens and several output tokens per node. 32 enabled nodes can wait for the ALU. The instruction set includes floating point, fixed point and logical instructions. The instruction and date packet lengths are 33 and 71 bits.

4.1.3 Manchester Dataflow Computer

The Manchester project was started in 1975 by the Gurd-Watson group [5], [8]. The group's main objective is to investigate the use of dynamic, tagged dataflow computing concept for very high speed computing systems. They completed the construction of 20 processor, strongly typed, tagged dataflow machine in 1980 using Schottky bit slice microprocessors. Their contributions include tagged token dynmic computing model, several high level dataflow computing languages the dataflow machine. The reported performance of the machine is approximately 6 MIPS.

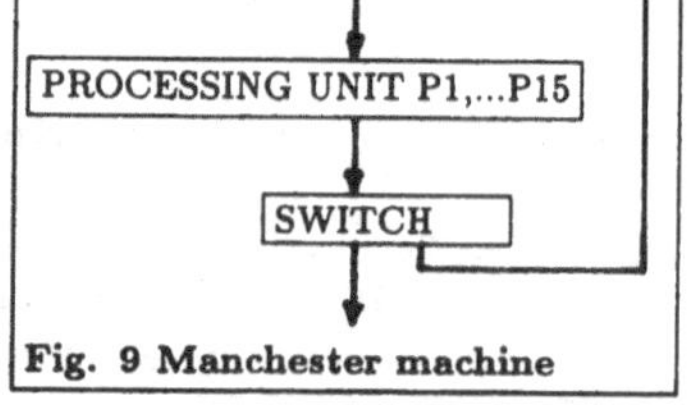

Fig. 9 Manchester machine

1. Global configuration: The machine consists of a switch, token queue, matching store, instruction store and a processing unit, Fig. 9.. A switch provides input and output for the system. The token queue is the FIFO buffer providing temporary storage for tokens. The matching store matches pairs of tokens, employing hardware hashing. The instruction store holds dataflow programs and PEs execute instructions. Access to the matching store causes a search of the store.

2. Processing elements: There are fifteen functional units in the processor. One enabled node is assigned to each functional unit. The node store supplies enabled nodes to the processing unit. Enabled nodes are assigned to the functional units using any hardware distributor. Therefore, there are no multiple assignments to a functional unit. The matching unit can hold 16K units. The PU consists of distribution and arbitration systems and a group of microprogrammed microprocessors. Streams are processed in parallel using multiple instances, one for each element. Recursion computations are supported using tags.

3. Packet formats and instructions: The instruction set supports floating point, fixed point, data branch, token label, flow control and token relabelling instructions. A maximum of two input arcs and two output arcs is allocated to operations. The lengths of instruction and data packets are 167 and 96 bits.

4.1.4 DDM1

The Data Driven Machine project [6] was started in 1975 by Davis group at Burroughs Interactive Research Center. Construction was completed in 1976, and the machine is now at the Utah University. This dynamic machine employs FIFO queues instead of tagged tokens to distinguish computations. Program execution and machine organisation are based on recursion. The DDM1 is in operation and has been used to study basic issues in dataflow. The DEC20/40 is used for software support. The graphs are generated from a high level functional language, GPL. Parenthesised strings in dataflow programs provide localised dynamic computing.

1. Global configuration: The computer is composed of an octary tree hierarchy of computing elements. This hierarchy exploits VLSI, since it is able to utilise locality of reference to reduce the critical problems of system wide communication and control.

2. Processing elements: A processing element consists of an atomic storage unit, an atomic processor, an agenda queue, an input queue, an output queue and a switch. The atomic storage unit, 4K-4bit character store, is the program memory. The atomic processor is the execution unit. The agenda queue is the message store for local atomic storage unit. The input queue acts as the buffer to the message from the superior element. The output queue is the buffer to the messages to the superior element. The switch connects to eight computer elements. The tree structure inhibits immediate rerouting of the results before the fault.

3. Packet formats and instructions: Data tokens provide all communications. Each instruction is represented as a variable length instruction packet. Each instruction has an enabling counter for input arcs. An instruction can have any number of input and output arcs. Streams are handled by pipelining the tokens. The atomic processor processes integer-oriented, logical, indexed read and write, and relational operator-oriented instructions.

4.2 Static Machines for Numerical Computing

4.2.1 VIM

The Dennis group at MIT introduced the dataflow computing concept and laid the foundation for most other dataflow projects [2]. Research and development projects on dataflow computing started in 1968, and a 1 GFLOP VAL interpretive machine, VIM, is being developed. The group's main objective is to prove the feasibility of the practical application of static dataflow computing for large scale numerical computations. In static computing, data tokens are stored in an instruction or a copy of the instruction. The nodes of a program are loaded into memory before the computation begins and at most one instance of a node is enabled for firing at a time. Enabled nodes are detected by associating a counter with each node. The group's contributions include design of dataflow graphs, dataflow computing languages and computer architecture.

1. Global configuration: The VIM machine consists of a routing network, cell blocks, functional units, and array memories, Fig. 10. Cell blocks store program graphs, operations, operands, destination addresses of nodes and recognise the instructions ready for execution. The functional unit performs operations on data values. Array memories store array structures.

2. Processing element: Functions of PEs are performed by cell blocks and functional units. Simple instructions such as duplicating values and performing tests are executed within the cell block. A PE consists of instruction enabling mechanisms and perform their execution. A PE consists of an update unit, an operation unit, a queue, a fetch unit and an activity store. The activity store holds dataflow instructions. The fetch unit picks addresses of an enabled instruction from the queue, fetches that instruction with its operands from the activity store and delivers it to an operation unit. Instruction execution gives result packets, which are sent on to the update unit. The update unit enters the address of the enabled instruction in the FIFO queue.

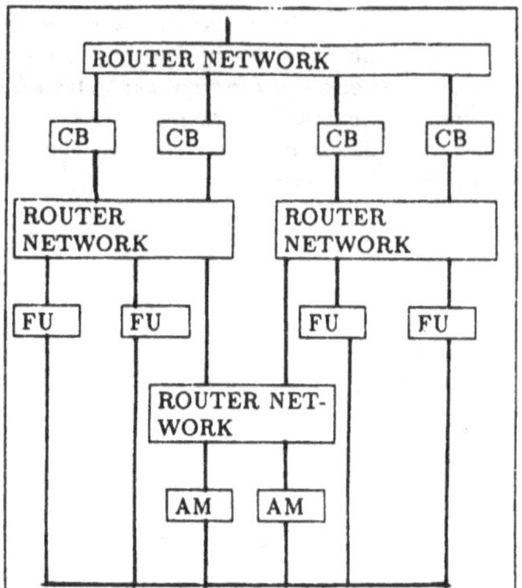

Fig. 10 VIM architecture

If the target instructions of a result packet reside in some other PE, the packet is sent off through the network. Program graph execution terminates when none of the nodes is enabled. Streams are handled by pipelining. There is no scheduler to assign nodes to a processor. Faults in the machine require restarting the computation from the beginning.

3. Packet formats and instructions: Result packets consist of a result value and a reference. Control packets contain boolean values and control values. Data packets contain integer or complex values. Floating point, fixed point, logical packet communication and shift instructions are used in the processor instruction set.

4.2.2 Texas Distributed Data Processor

The DDP was designed by Texas Instruments [21]. The project started in 1976 and the DDP has been in operation since 1978. The main objective is to investigate the feasibility of static dataflow computing for high speed computing systems. The DDP is implemented in TTL. Each dataflow computer contains 32K words of MOS memory. ADA is used in the four-processor DDP, at the computer science department of the University of Southwestern Lousiana.

1. Global configuration: The DDP system consists of four identical dataflow computers to execute programs and a TI 990/10 minicomputer acting as a front-end processor. These computing elements are connected by a DCLN ring.

2. Processing elements: Each dataflow computer consists of an arithmetic unit which processes executable instructions, a program memory holding dataflow instructions, an update controller which updates instructions with tokens and a pending executable instruction queue. Each node is associated with a counter. When an instruction completes execution, a series of token packets is released to the update controller which stores the token operand in the instruction and decrements the count by one. If this count is zero, the instruction is executable and is placed in the instruction queue. The communication bus is 28 bits wide. Two communication paths are used: one for transmitting instruction packets, and result packets and the other for maintenance and diagnostic purposes. A maintenance controller detects faulty processors. Computations can restart at the preceding checkpoint. A maintenance bus provides communication facilities to monitor the performance of each processor, load and dump contents of the memory, and diagnose the faults. The local memory of the processor has an instruction memory and a data memory. Result packets are stored in data memory. Recursive computations are not supported.

3. Packet formats and instructions: Instruction packets use up to fifteen 35-bit words. An instruction can have up to 13 input and 13 output arcs with a total of 14 input and output arcs. Result packets are two words long and contain routing information and data. Monitor call, semaphore instructions and pipelining are used in implementing streams. Floating point instructions, fixed point instructions, logical and shift instructions, loop control, memory fetch and communication with front end processor oriented instructions are used to support FORTRAN IV programs. FETCH, STORE and MC instructions are used to handle instructions and data.

4.2.3 LAU System

The LAU project started in 1976 at the CERT Laboratory, Toulouse, France [22]. The group designed the LAU high level language, programmed a large number of problems and implemented a compiler and detailed simulator. The LAU system executes programs written in a single assignment language. The LAU machine has been in operation since 1979.

1. Global configuration: The machine consists of a memory unit, control unit and 32 processing units. The memory unit is the storage for instructions and data. The control unit maintains the control memory. Six unidirectional buses are used for communication.

2. Processing elements: Each processing element is built in 16-bit microprogrammed processes using AMD 2900 bit slice microprocessors. Execution units read data from central memory. Enabled instructions are kept in a ready instruction queue until results come out of the processor. This helps to reassign instructions to a healthy processor. En-

abled nodes are detected by associating a counter with each node. The memory unit stores instructions and the data control unit maintains control memory. The von Neumann program counter is replaced by an instruction control memory which handles instructions and a data control memory which handles data.

3. Packet formats and instructions: Each node can have a maximum of two input arcs and several output arcs. The length of instruction and data packets are 64-bits. The LAU system does not handle stream data structures. The instruction set include fixed point, logical, shift, control instructions such as CASE, LOOP, CALL, RETURN and EXPAND.

4.2.4 NEDIPS

NEDIPS and IPP were the first commercially available dataflow processors [17]. They are special purpose dataflow processors with static architecture, well tuned to image processing applications developed by the Nippon Electric Co.. NEDIPS is a 32 bit machine intended for scientific computation and uses high speed logic. The IPP (Image Pipelined Processor) is a single chip processor of similar architecture. This processor is a building block for highly parallel image processing systems. Special mechanisms are used to implement multiple tokens per arc. Special hardware operations are provided for generating, splitting, and merging streams of tokens.

4.3 Dynamic Machines for non-Numerical Computing

4.3.1 EM-3

The EM-3 is the dynamic dataflow machine for symbolic manipulation of the Electrotechnical Laboratory [28] to [30]. The project started in 1982 and scheduled to continue until end of 1987. The objectives of EM-3 include evaluating the effectiveness of pseudo-result computing, to implement new parallel architectures and to evaluate the performance of a hardware simulator by executing application programs. The EM-3 prototype of the eight PE version started operation in 1984. An improved version with a 16 PE organization has been in operation since 1985, and is used to implement new parallel control mechanisms. The maximum performance of the hardware is about 10 MIPS. A highly parallel advanced version of the EM-3, which will be a more practical dataflow computer prototype, is being developed.

1. Global configuration: The EM-3 is a multi microprocessor system. 16 identical PEs are connected via a packet communication network. There is no locality in the network. The router network is adopted for communication and a special gate-array LSI chip has been developed for this purpose. The LSI chip is a four-bit slice four-by-four router and the transfer rate of a packet through the network is 150 nanoseconds.

2. Processing elements: A PE is constructed using MC68000 microprocessor with special hardware, Fig. 11. Almost all the functions, including the function evaluation mechanism, are performed sequentially within the PE. The MC68000, the packet memory control unit used as the network interface, and the I/O interface to the host computer are connected by a common bus. Each PE comprises three boards excluding the interface to the host computer PDP-11/44 and the network boards. The packet memory is accessed from the microprocessor, and each packet is represented as a pointer to the packet memory. Hence, there is no overhead in moving packets in a PE.

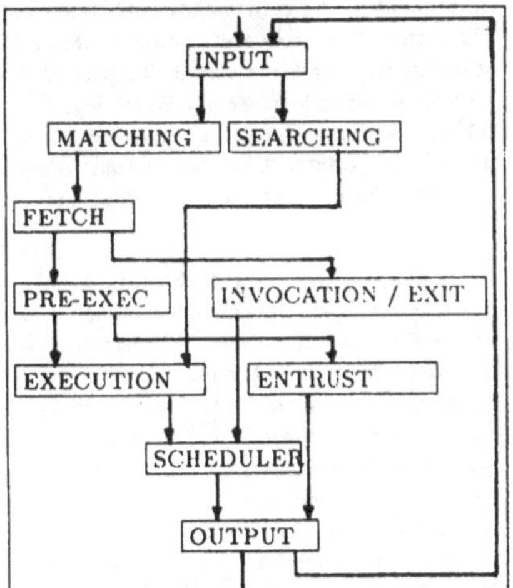

Fig. 11 EM-3 PE

3. Packet formats and instructions: The 96-bit result packet carries output data of an operation. A result packet consists of the PE number (8 bits), the type-of-packet field (4 bits), the packet length (4 bits), the destination- identifier (48 bits) and the tagged data (32 bits). The packet is divided into six 16-bit segments in the network. The length of an instruction is 48 bits, comprising the 32-bit destination field and the 16-bit operation field. The immediate data (32 bits) can be contained, and the number of destination fields within an instruction is not fixed.

4.3.2 DFM

The Nippon Telegraph and Telephone Corp. (NTT) started research and development on dataflow machines in 1980. A dataflow processor array system for scientific and technological computations, EDDY, was set up as a prototype in 1983. The main objective of DFM project is to develop a dataflow machine for symbolic manipulations [10]. using lenient and lazy cons mechanisms. The construction of the DFM-II, was started using CMOS gate-array technology in 1985. The expected maximum performance is about 15 MIPS per cluster. Parallel processing of the DFM is realized by parallel evaluation of function arguments, partial execution of a function body and pipeline processing of a delayed evaluation scheme. The two PE version of the DFM has been in operation since the beginning of 1986. The basic cycle of a PE is 180 nanoseconds and the maximum speed is about 1.4 MIPS per PE.

1. Global configuration: The DFM is constructed by connecting several clusters via a communication network. A cluster consists of eight PEs and eight structure memories which are connected by multiple buses. Structure memories are separately located from PEs for efficient list processing. Each cluster is supervised by a cluster control unit. The cluster control unit controls the load balancing among PEs within the cluster and communicates with another cluster via the network or the host computer. Two level network based on clustering; load distribution within a cluster and function distribution among the clusters. A blocked content addressable memory scheme is applied to reduce the amount of hardware.

2. Processing elements: Each PE of the DFM is composed of an instruction memory, an operand memory and an execution unit. These units work as a circular pipeline. A hardware queue is placed at the entrance of the instruction memory to ease packet traffic in the circular pipeline. Each structure memory is constructed by multiple memory banks equipped with the list operation unit. Each cell of the structure memory is composed of the cell type field (one bit), the reference count field (9 bits), the CAR field and the CDR field (23 bits each).

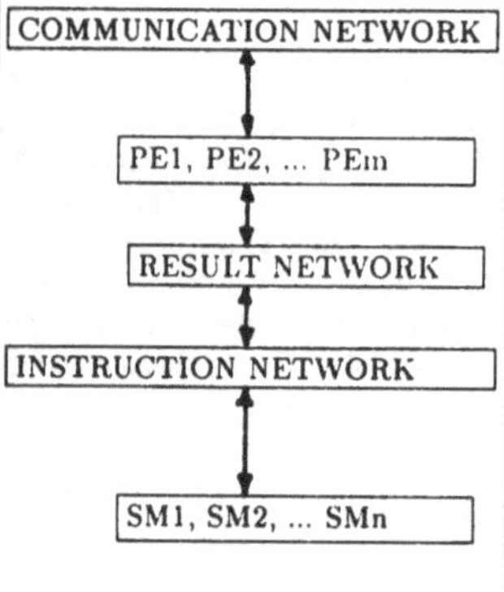

Fig. 12(a) DFM

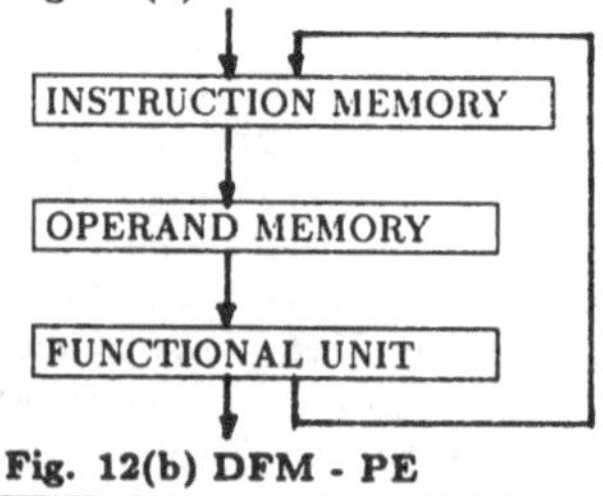

Fig. 12(b) DFM - PE

3. Packet formats and instructions: The size of a result packet is 56 bits and the contents are the destination-identifier with the function name (24 bits) and the data (32 bits). There are instructions to the cluster control unit and to the structure memory as well as to the execution unit. An instruction to the execution unit consists of the operation field (8 bits), two operand-fields (32 bits each) and the destination-identifier. An instruction to the structure memory is 90 bits and associated with the 3-bit PE number.

4.3.3 PIM-D

The research and development of a dataflow PROLOG machine started in the middle of 1982 at the ICOT. The objective is to develop the predicate logic paradigm beyond the von Neumann paradigm. This implies that all computer related technology must be looked over again from the viewpoint of predicate logic. Dataflow architecture, logic programming and natural language understanding are three research directions identified for this paradigm. The target is to achieve inference execution speed of 100M to 1,000M logical inferences per second. Three different types of architecture, PIM-D [23], a parallel reduction machine and a parallel inference machine with efficient task distribution mechanism, were studied to overcome the highly parallel processing problems in logic programs. The PIM-D employs the breadth-first search. To avoid the deadlock problem caused by the number of processes, each process is associated with execution priority. The OR-parallelism and AND-pipeline schemes are implemented using the streams. The eight PE PIM-D organisation is in operation now. LSI implementation is being developed.

1. Global configuration: The machine consists of 16 PEs, 15 structure memories (SMs) and a three level hierarchical network, implemented by a bus of 113-bit width. The PEs and SMs are divided into four clusters, each of which consists of four PEs and four SMs, except for one cluster. Each bus is connected by the network node with 128 packet buffer. The minimum transmission time is 450 nanoseconds per packet.

2. Processing elements: A PE is composed of a packet queue, an instruction control unit and two atomic processing units for execution, which are also connected via a bus. The instruction control unit serves as the matching function of dataflow control. Each hardware unit is constructed using bit-sliced microprogrammable processors and TTL ICs.

3. Data formats: A packet transferred between PEs via a bus consists of the PE/SM number (5 bits), the packet type (9 bits), the packet colour (16 bits), the destination identifier (24 bits) and the operand data (32 bits). The length of the instruction is 59 bits. A cell of a SM is composed of data (32 x 2 bits), the type flag (2 x 2 bits) and the reference count area (10 bits).

4.3.4 TOPSTAR

The TOPSTAR, a macro dataflow machine, is a highly parallel multi-microprocessor system developed from 1978 to 1982 at the University of Tokyo [24]. The TOPSTAR was originally developed to support parallel processing involved in recognising printed Chinese character patterns. The TOPSTAR-I, composed of three PMs and two CMs, is the prototype of the more advanced TOPSTAR-II. The TOPSTAR-II was easily expandable by plugging in additional modules. Both machines were in operation with the system software. The number of data buffers which causes the pipeline effect is very important to improve the performance. Using TOPSTAR-II as a testbed, some experimental studies such as the dataflow LISP compiler, logic simulation and parallel PROLOG implementation were carried out. This led to the development of the parallel PROLOG machine called PIE.

1. Global configuration: TOPSTAR consists of 16 processing modules (PM) and eight communication and control modules (CM). Each PM is connected to a maximum of four CMs, while each CM is connected to a maximum of eight PMs. Each PM or CM is separated from each other but has indirect paths through CMs or PMs. This organization is very similar to a bipartite graph. A procedure level dataflow graph is dynamically mapped into the PM-CM connection network. Each PM interrupts one of the connected CMs and requests to allocate a task by a dequeue command. Each CM contains allocated procedures of an execution program, and if executable tasks exist, their instances of procedures as well as their argument data are sent to the requested PM.

2. Processing units: Each PM or CM is constructed using a z-80 microprocessor and a direct memory access (DMA) controller. The communication between PM and CM is through the DMA system at high speed, because the data block is transferred when a new instance of a procedure is needed at an allocated PM. The CM's communication memory is shared with each PM and contains execution programs and their argument data.

3. Data formats: The data transferred from a CM to a PM has a variable length and consists of the serial number, the field indicating the stack depth, the destination addresses and the procedure instance. The serial number corresponds to a colour, and the stack depth is used for recording the history of the data passed. The data format supports the implementation of the control mechanism of iteration and recursion.

4.4 Other Projects

In addition to the projects mentioned above, there are many other ongoing dataflow research projects. These include projects at the University of Southern California; Hughes Air Craft Company; University of Adelaide, Australia; University of New South Wales, Australia; Keio University, Japan; Osaka University, Japan; Gunma University, Japan; and Indian Institute of Technology, India.

5 Conclusions

Parallel processing gives ultra-high computing speeds. The dataflow computing concept is the most effective, promising computing method to implement in machine architecture for high speed computing. This paper first discussed the static, tagged token dynamic, operator net, eager-lazy, pseudo-result and Not(operation) dataflow computing models; then the dataflow computing languages; finally, the dataflow machines for numerical and non-numerical computations. The major difficulty in realizing very high speed dataflow computing machines is the highly tuned von Neumann machines. SIGMA-1, which predicts the highest computing speeds, is a milestone in computing machines. The problems mentioned in section 2 need more attention. The construction of very high speed dataflow computing machines needs further research in the following areas.

1. Different dataflow computing models
2. High level languages suited to dataflow programming
3. Low level languages suited to dataflow architecture
4. Algorithms for specific applications and systems
5. Dataflow computing processors and system architectures
6. Operating systems with efficient resource allocation schemes
7. Optimum design of an instruction set processor
8. High-speed operand matching mechanisms
9. Efficient structure memory implementations
10. Low cost high-speed communication networks to interconnect PEs
11. Problems in dataflow computing
12. Fault tolerant computing for 1,000 to 10,000 processor dataflow computing machines
13. Impact of VLSI and device technology
14. Applications of dataflow computing concept in other fields

Acknowledgements

We wish to thank all the researchers in dataflow field for their efforts and contributions to realise dataflow machines. We thank Dr. Yamaguchi at ETL, for his valuable comments in preparing this manuscript. We would also like to thank Professor Masahiro Ishii and Professor Itoh Shuichi at University of Electrocommunications and Dr. Shimada, Dr. Hiraki, Dr. Uchibori and Mr. Toda of Electrotechnical Laboratory for their constant support and helpful discussions. We also extend our thanks to all the members of the Saito lab. Special thanks to Susantha and Rosemary for helping in many ways to produce this paper.

References

[1] J. E. Rodriguez, "A Graph Model for Parallel Computation", Tech. Rep. ESLR-398, MAC-TR-64, Lab. Computer Science, MIT September 1969

[2] J. B. Dennis, "Data flow Computation", *NATO ASI Series, Vol. F14, Control Flow and Data Flow: Concepts of Distributed Programming, Edited by M. Broy, Springer-Verlag* (1985), 346-397.

[3] J. D. Brock, "Operational Semantics of a Data flow Language", *MIT/LCS/TM-120*

[4] Arvind, David E. Culler, "Dataflow Architectures", TM-294, Lab. Comp. Sci., MIT (1986).

[5] J. Gurd and I. Watson, "Preliminary Evaluation of a Prototype Dataflow Computer", *IFIP* (1983), 545-551.

[6] A. L. Davis, "A Dataflow Evaluation System Based on the Concept of Recursive Locality", *Proc. 1979 Nat. Computer Conf. Vol 48, AFIPS,* 1979, 1079-1086

[7] E. A. Ashcroft, R. Jagannathan "Operator Nets", *Fifth Gen. Comp. Arch., IFIP* (1984).

[8] J.R. Gurd, J.R.W. Glauert, C.C. Kirkham, "Generation of Dataflow Graphical Object Code for the Lapse Programming Language" *Lecture Notes in Computer Science, vol.111, Springer-Verlag* June 1981, pp155-168

[9] M. Amamiya, M. Takesue, R. Hasegawa, M. Mikami, "Implementation and Evaluation of a List Processing-oriented Dataflow Machine", *Proc. 13th Int. Symp. on Comp. Arch.*, 10-19 (1986)

[10] J. McGraw, "SISAL: Stream, and Iteration in a Single-Assignment Language Reference Manual", *University of California, Lawrence Livermore National Laboratory, Report M-146,* (March 1985)

[11] M. Amamiya, R. Hasegawa, S. Ono, "VALID: A High Level Functional Language for Dataflow Machine", *Rev. ECL, Vol. 32, No. 5,* 793-802 NTT (1984)

[12] S. Skedzielewski, J. Glauert, "IF1 An Intermediate Form for Applicative Languages", *University of California, Lawrence Livermore National Laboratory, Report M-170,* (July 1985)

[13] T. Yuba, "Research and Development Efforts on Data-flow Computer Architecture in Japan", *Journal of Information Processing,* (vol.9, No.2 1986), 51-62

[14] P. C. Treleaven, D. Brownbridge, R. P. Hopkins, Data-Driven and Demand-Driven Computer Architecture, Joun. ACM Computing Surveys, Vol 14, No 1, March 1982, 93-142

[15] Vason P. Srini " An Architectural Comparison of Dataflow Systems", *IEEE COMPUTER,* (March 1986) 68-88.

[16] S. Ono, N. Takahashi, M. Amamiya, "Optimized Demand-driven Evaluation of Functional Programs on a Dataflow Machine" *Proc. of Int. Conf. on Parallel Processing'86* (1986) 421-428

[17] T. Temma, S. Hasegawa, S. Hanaki, "Dataflow Processor for Image Processing", *Proc. Mini and Microcomputers, Vol.5, No.3,* 52-56 (1980)

[18] K. Hiraki, K. Nishida, S. Sekiguchi, T. Shimada, "Maintenance Architecture and LSI Implementation of a Dataflow Computer with a Large Number of Processors", *Proc. of Int. Conf. on Parallel Processing' 86*

[19] K. Hiraki, T. Shimada, K. Nishida, " A Hardware Design of the SIGMA-1 - A Dataflow Computer for Scientific Computations", *Proc. 1984 Int. Conf. Parallel Processing, IEEE,* 524-531 (1984)

[20] T. Shimada, K. Hiraki, K. Nishida, S. Sekiguchi, "Evaluation of a Prototype Dataflow Processor of the SIGMA-1 for Scientific Computations", *Proc. 13th Ann. Int. Symp. on Comp. Arch.),* 226-234 (1986)

[21] M. Cornish, The TI dataflow Architectures: The Power of Concurrency for Avionics, IEEE Proc. 3rd Conf. Digital Avionics Systems, Fort Worth, Texas, November, 1979, 19-25

[22] D. Comte, N. Hifdi, J. Syre. The Data Driven LAU Multiprocessor System: Results and Perspectives, Proc. IFIP Congress 80, Tokyo, Japan, October,1980, 175-180

[23] N. Ito, M. Sato, "The Architecture and Preliminary Evaluation Results of the Experimental Parallel Inference Machine PIM-D", *Proc. 13th Int. Symp. on Comp. Arch.*, 149-156 (1986)

[24] T. Suzuki, K. Kurihara, H. Tanaka, T. Moto-oka, "Procedure Level Dataflow Processing on Dynamic Structure Multimicroprocessors", *Joun. Inf. Process., Vol.5, No.1,* 11-16 (1982)

[25] A. L. Wendelborn, "A Hybrid Data and Demand Driven Implementation of a Lucid-like Programming Language" *Proc. 9th Comp. Sci. Conf., Canberra,* (Jan. 1986)

[26] Y. Yamaguchi, K. Toda, T. Yuba, "A Performance Evaluation of a Lisp based Data-driven Machine (EM-3)", *Proc. 10th Ann. Int. Symp. Comp. Arch.,* (1983) 363-369

[27] Y. Yamaguchi, K. Toda, J. Herath, T. Yuba, "EM-3: A LISP-based Data-driven Machine", *Proc. Int. Conf. Fifth Gene. Comp. Systems, ICOT,* 524-532 (1984)

[28] K. Toda, Y. Yamaguchi, Y. Uchibori, T. Yuba, "Preliminary Measurements of the ETL LISP-based Data-driven Machine", *Proc. of the IFIP TC-10 Working Conf. on Fifth Gen. Comp. Arch.* (July, 1985)

[29] J. Herath, N. Saito, K. Toda, Y. Yamaguchi, T. Yuba, "Not(operation) for High Speed Data-flow Computing Systems", *Proc. of Int. Conf. on Super Computing Systems,* (Dec. 1985) 524-532.

[30] J. Herath, N. Saito, K. Toda, Y. Yamaguchi, T. Yuba, "Data-flow Computing Base Language with n-Value Logic", *Proc. of Fall Jont Comp. Conf.,* (Nov. 1986).

PARALLEL IN SEQUENCE - TOWARDS THE ARCHITECTURE OF AN ELEMENTARY CORTICAL PROCESSOR

E. Koerner[1),3)], I. Tsuda[1)] and H. Shimizu[2)]

Abstract

First, a short evalution of the recent progress on the question of how the brain works is given and evidence submitted for the need of large-scale computational approaches to neural computing which are as tightly as possible related to the known details of neural hardware and function. The crucial role of the firmware-level (modular) organization of neural mass for understanding the flexibility of neural computing is stressed. Based on both the anatomy of a neocortical column and an approach to the interpretation of complex scenes by the visual cortex, a functional architecture of a cortical processor is proposed with special emphasis on the dynamics of selfcontrol.

1. Hardware Does Matter

Recently, with the advent of massively parallel computers the interest in understanding the algorithms behind the brains' function resurged, since these new computing environments need a new software approach. Neurocybernetics has put from the beginning emphasis to parallel architectures. Parallelism is more than gain in speed of computing only ; it enables a qualitatively different kind of algorithms for intelligent opperations. However, there is not yet a comprehensive brain theory, but in most cases either abstract computational approaches or descriptions on the level of cellular connectivity. Currently efforts are under way for a more interactive approach. The brain was not programmed but evolved in function. Why this sensory-motor control system developed intelligent behavior is a matter of both the so called microstructure of cognition and the coordinative control in the complex system (that means not the emerged algorithms but the underlying processes and its control are the source of intelligence). With the constraints of time and resources under the selective pressure of evolution, only certain combinations of the triple <hardware, software, environment> may give enough performance [27], they are strongly interrelated, specific. Therefore, a more rapid progress in understanding this software is expected only if large-scale computational theories can be constructed in close interaction with all the details of structure and function which are offered by experimental neurobiology and

---

1) Bioholonics Research Project, Research Development Corporation of Japan, Nissho-Bldg., 5F, 14-24 Koishikawa 4-chome, Bunkyo-ku, Tokyo 112, Japan
2) Faculty of Pharmaceutical Sciences, Department of Biophysics, University of Tokyo, Hongo, Bunkyo-ku, Tokyo 113, Japan
3) Present address : The Ilmenau Institute of Technology, Dep. of Engng. and Biomedical Cybernetics, PF 327, GDR-6300 Ilmenau

which then reciprocally can guide the experimental neuroscience to selected topics of crucial importance.

2. Neural Networks and Computing

The majority of works in this field has been concentrated on associative memories. Those models of adaptive, selforganizing neural structures are based on highly formalized characteristics of the single element ("neuron") and its wiring scheme (Fig.1) : All elements arranged in a two-dimensional network receive two types of inputs, from external sources and feedback from the other elements of the same system. The weighted summation of external inputs represents a recognition process, a decoding of the input at any element. The second part of the memory weights the recurrent feedback from within the array to each element and implements either an autoassociative memory (in case of negative feedback) [8] or, in case of positive recurrent feedback, an associative memory which can retrieve a time sequence of states according to a parallel key input only [11]. The basic notion of this approach is the state vector of the elements, they compute by being appropriately connected. The programme resides in the structure of local interactions, the selection of information transmission (channeling the activity, simultaneous activity pattern in the system) is the processing result. In neural computing, decision or recall is actually the formation of an internal pattern of activity distribution. The decisive state variables are the connection strength between cells, the synaptic weights W_{ij} denoting the strength of influence from a presynaptic cell i onto a postsynaptic cell j. The W_{ij} can be positive or negative, according to excitatory or inhibitory neurons respectively. Usually, the system model is described by two sets of equations [11] [19], first for the relaxation process (dynamics of activity flow) (1) and second for the updating of the weights W_{ij} (memory dynamics), whereby the time

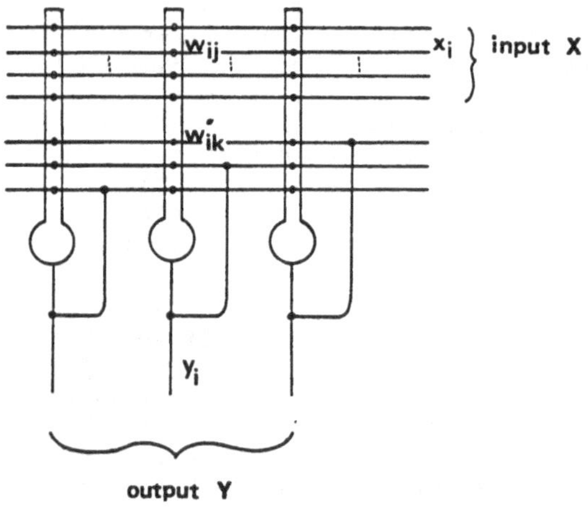

Fig.1 : General wiring scheme used in neural network models

scale of the latter is much longer than that of the relaxation in case of long term memory (which short term memory updating, e.g., in spine-structures, may well be in the same time scale [14])(2). If the connection strength between two cells changes adaptively to a value which represents the correlation in activity of both cells (Hebb-synapses), then, after rapidly approaching a steady state according to

$$Y_i = f\left(\sum_{j=1}^{n} W_{ij} X_{ij} + \sum_{k=1}^{m} W'_{ik} Y_k - \tau_i \right) \tag{1}$$

(with τ_i a threshold and $f(\cdot)$ a sigmoid function)

this stabilized pattern of "neural activity" is learned according to

$$\begin{aligned} \dot{W} &= g(x, y, w) \\ \dot{W} &= h(y, w) \end{aligned} \tag{2}$$

where $g(\cdot)$ and $h(\cdot)$ vary from simple correlation learning [6] [11], via included forgetting to sophisticated functional relation with the very local history of processing (e.g. [5]) and including more global influence [23] [25]. For a comprehensive discussion of selforganization in neural networks , see [1] [11]. A sufficient number of simulated models prove that this adaptive nets reasonably do the job of pattern mapping and recall ([6] [7] [8] [11] and others) by means of the relaxation as a parallel associative / cooperative search. However, that are still too simple systems to produce the power of flexible processing we are interested in. In recent years, a major methodological breakthrough was achieved in the theoretical treatment of complex systems in adapting the well established theory of statistical thermodynamics [9] [10]. Now the dynamics of relaxation, local and global optimal system states etc. can be quantitatively described and important fundamental problems like the crucial role of noise or irregular fluctuations for both stability and flexibility of complex systems are being investigated [18]. Within this philosophical background is the wider approach to a representation not only as a statically stable pattern of activity but also a dynamically stable reverberating activity pattern [14] [24] and to intermittent deterministic chaos as a system mode for flexible processing. Besides these recent efforts to explore the physical nature of neural computing, the connectionists try to relate this hardware to the super-software level of psychology in order to understand the microstructure of cognition [22]. And here a crucial problem in neural network modelling reappears : how to interprete the patterns of activity? In which way is the knowledge on the outer world represented inside the brain?

3. Firmware is Decisive for Flexible Computing in Neural Networks

The problem with both the abstract computational theories and formal neural network approaches is that they are not to verify experimentally and tend to interprete the neural computing in terms of known principles adapted from other fields (nevertheless, its study is the prerequisite for any more advanced approach). Substantially richer in respect of understanding the software of neural computing and its source for the power we are interested in, is the linking of those approaches to specific systems (and functions) of neural hardware. There is a very short history of approaches to a parallel theory in neural computing, rather only some successful attempts are indiscussion which may stimulate the way towards such a theory. Examples are the tensor theory of sensorimotor control [20] (in spite of the fact that a tensor-notation for the description of these processes is still under discussion [2]) and most recently the sandwich-theory of neural representation [3], which directly relate striking features of the hardware to large scale computational theories and produce exciting new hypotheses on how the brain could do its job. Here we would like to stress another important problem along this line of thinking : there is structure in the neural mass. The large entities of the brain such as the areas of neocortex are composed of "replicated local circuits, modules which vary in cell number, intrinsic connections but are basically similar within any given entity" [17,p.8]. Anatomically, the neocortex has six horizontal layers which emerge from differences both in cell types located there and its connectivity pattern. Such a basic unit, a minicolumn, is a vertically arranged group of about 110 cells heavily connected in vertical axis and more sparsely horizontally. Several hundred of the vertical cylinders of about 30μ m diameter are organized to macrocolumns with 500···1,000μ m diameter. Approximately 600,000 of such macro-columns are in the human neocortex. However, the structure of such a minicolumn is still an open problem. Neurophysiological results suggest, that solely in terms of representation and mapping processes it cannot be understood [13] [21]. Below we propose a hypothesis on a functional structure of such an unit based on a large scale computational theory on early vision processes with close fitting to anatomical details of the cortical layers. Surprisingly, the seemingly endless complexity of the hardware can be scaled down to only a few subsystems the different functional properties of which enable a specific dynamics of relaxation and pattern formation. We argue that this firmware may give rise to some of the flexibility in the neural processing we are looking for, especially by properly intermingling parallel and serial processing modes of the system. In other words, the rigid behavior of neural network models (c.f. ch.2) may be due to the use of simple formal neurons as processing nodes instead of firmware -level processors.

4. A Hypothesis on The Functional Organization of a Neocortical Columnar Unit

The input to the visual cortex is not a preselected set of objects but a very rich description of the outer worlds image in terms of very local order relations (primitives, [16]). To prevent the combinatorical explosion of the problem of interpretation, the system seemingly reduces the dimension of this parallel input (number of input channels which are accepted) by attention mechanisms, which work even between the serial scanning by eye movements [4] [7] [15]. Along this line we proposed a mechanism of random access grouping at the cortico-thalamic interface which optimally supports the cortical pattern formation (see [12] for details) and enables a rapid convergency of interpretation. In order to understand what is on in the column it is essential to understand that there is probably never a completely parallel acceptance of the sensory input, but that accepting variable sized parts of the input parallel in sequence may be the fundamental scheme in relaxation processes (formation of inner consistent patterns) under the constraints set by the input.

Modulation of the sensory input at the thalamic-cortical interface

Almost all sensory inputs enter the cortex through the thalamus, then they diverge. Hence, if there is a manipulation of the input by the

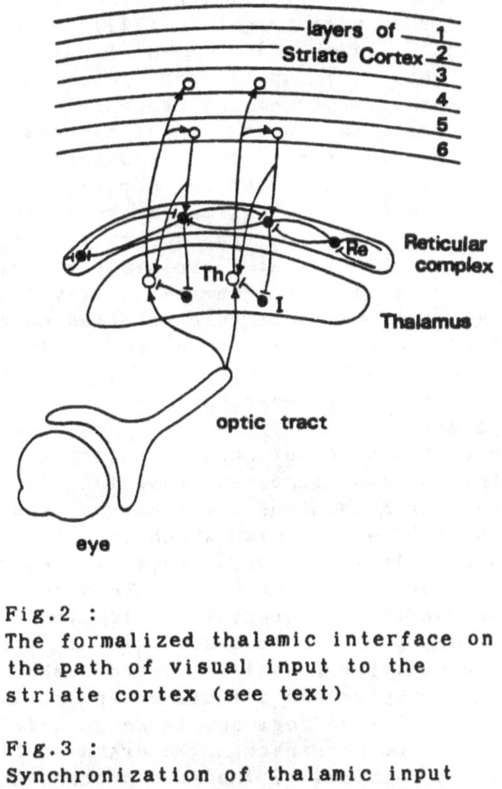

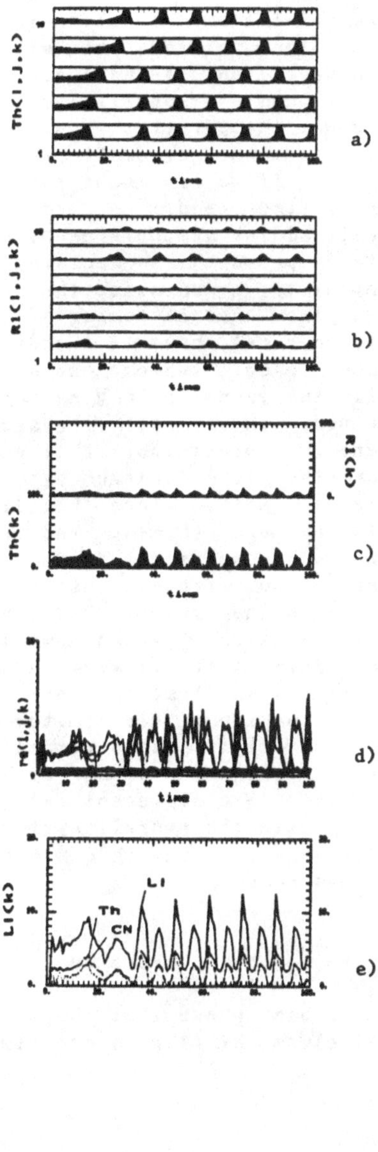

Fig.2 :
The formalized thalamic interface on the path of visual input to the striate cortex (see text)

Fig.3 :
Synchronization of thalamic input patterns (Th) of differnt syntactic complexity by cortical (R1) recall (Fig.3a,b). In c)an eeg-like summary activity, d)the related channel control by the Re-elements and e)the thalamic local inhibition LI with thalamic activity (Th) and global negative feedback (CN) is shown (see text).

cortex, it must be there for the reason of an unitary perception [4]. On its way to the cortex, the thalamic outputs pass the reticular formation the neurons of which (Re) form a mutually inhibiting network (Fig.2). The Re are activated by the passing thalamic output and more strongly by the recurrent cortical feedback to the thalamus. With its wiring scheme, any activity distribution across the Re-system is sharpened, making hot spots hotter, cool parts cooler [4]. The level of inhibition at the interface is rapidly increased with entrainment of cortical activity by the globally weighted feedback via the brainstem to the local inhibitory elements [12]. So, just after entering the interface in parallel, all channels are shut down but those which locally are disinhibited by its Re, like carving that set of channels out of the suppressed parallel input which entrained the strongest cortical recall. With strong entrainment of a cortical recall (stable pattern recall) the cortical-thalamic feedback is cancelled for some time T [12], which means the related set of input channels is purged from the input for this period and the next strongest active set of inputs can enter the cortex and so on till after a time T the first set can reappear. In this way the parallel input byte (pixel set) is turned into a ranked time sequence of smaller bytes, which enter the cortex one after each other. If we represent the 'cortex' by an associative memory like Fig.1, the recall of order relations rapidly reshuffles the sequence, freely adding and purging pixels to and from such bytes so that each byte represents a decision (recalled object) at a certain level of complexity. And since the number of bytes in this sequence is limited (not the channel number!), the system can only add more detailes onto this cortical input if the dimension of the bytes is increased. That means objects which make sense together are linked via synchronization while things not belonging together are actively desynchronized (Fig.3). However, this parallel-in-sequence algorithm is only then of use for scene interpretation, if 1) at the very beginning of such an interpretation the first ranked byte contains the most important aspects of the original image, since this first grouping determines the chances what patterns are formed, and if 2) there is a mechanism which is able to link such a sentence of parallel words to one large parallel word despite no strongly established hierarchic representation is already stored in the system. Both conditions depict the crucial problem in the interpretation of an unknown input : to separate some order out of the mass of input primitives, a highly competitive recall is needed, which determines in first instance the starting bytes and selects known parts out of the input to a limited sequence ; but to form new large parallel representations, this competition has to be decreased. We argue that these tasks are taken by different subsystems of the same processing node which are different in their dynamic characteristics and their wiring with the overall system, and, that the global state of processing defines which one is dominant at a certain time and rules the behavior of this node.

Why we may have layers in the cortex : take-grant-control

It has been shown that the seemingly endless complexity of the architecture of the neocortical column makes a lot of sense in this respect and can be strictly formalized like Fig.4 (restricted here to the dynamics of internal control only)[12]. For any subsystem, the selected internal structure is in direct relation to columnar morphology [26]. RO and R1 are autoassociative memories like Fig.1, IF2 is of the same organization like the thalamic/reticular system and R2 is a memory with characteristic differences to R1 and RO which result from differences in the characteristic connectivity of the modules : RO interacts only very locally to other RO, the autoassociative mechanism of any R1 covers a wider but still local range while additionally the R1 of a global system form a perceptron-like hierarchic coding scheme. Both RO and R1 keep strong competitive representations of parameters, objects and are reactive systems (no positive feedback within the moduls itself), hence, they form and transmit its recall in phase with the irregular frequency produced at the cortico-thalamic interface. Contrary, R2 is proposed as a kind of object file which monitores the flashing of R1 and which keeps steady but more fuzzy representations and tries with its entrainment to link the bytes out of the R1-sequence by feedforward to synchrony to form a large byte which is tolerated by the R1 systems. For being able to establish new order relations not yet coded at R1, R2 must have a short term memory mechanism like the one proposed by v.d.Malsburg [15]. Now we are in a position to discuss the evolution of selfcontrol and byte formation in a system composed of such processor element's like Fig.4. Any sensory input first starts a recall at the hardwired parameter filters RO which by its organization reduces the input byte dimension to only that channels representing the pieces of highest local syntactic complexity of the original image which belong to the largest set of smmoth relations in the image (syntactic guessing [12]). As long as only RO is active, the global inhibitory feedback $I = f(\Sigma RO)$ can be locally suppressed by the selected $Re = f(RO^*)$. Second, the triggered R1 recall reorders this set and selects the maxi

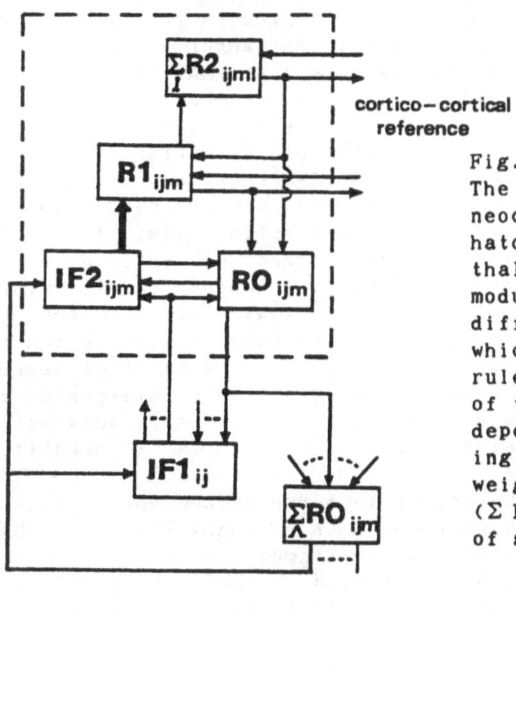

Fig.4 :
The proposed model system of a neocortical minicolumn (enclosed by hatched lines) which manipulates its thalamic interface (IF1). The R-modules of the system represent different levels of order formation which itself produce description rules of growing complexity. Which of them dominantly rules the system depends both on the state of processing and the inhibitory feedback of weighted global cortical" activity (Σ RO) which influences the balance of selfcontrol in the system.

mum number of inputs from this set which form a consistent representation. With R1 entrainment, the inhibitory feedback is increased, its local suppression is only possible with the related entrained R1 system supporting its R0, the characteristic range of R0-control is cancelled, R1 takes the control because of its more global order. In step 3, if one such consistent interpretation is established in the IF-R system interaction, these assembled channels are switched off and kept silent for a time T. This purging enables the set of next ranked pixels (parts of the original image with the next highest local syntactic complexity) which was suppressed till that moment by the stronger preceding sets (as described in step 1) to enter the system as a parallel byte which is again subject to the selection procedure of step 2. Finally, with entraining R2, more power is added to the global inhibitory feedback to the interfaces and the feedforward of R2 to R1 is a decisive advantage in the selection of channels by this winner-takes all scheme of Re-elements operation (cf. Fig.2). As a result, consensus formation at R2 guides the interpretation process as a supervisor without a strict control of R1 (see also [28]). As a conclusion, two characteristic modes of the systems' operation are to be stressed :

a) It is a semantically (by means of the recall of stored knowledge) controlled decomposition and subsequent reassembling of the image. Interpretation is pattern formation. In case of known input images, there is a high degree of parallelism in the recall, the interpretation is rapid. In case of unknown scene input, the system decomposes the image into a sequence of parallel bytes (which represent hypotheses on known parts of the image), the recognition process is more serially. With that serially flashing of hypotheses at R1 and consensus formation at R2, the system optimizes the dimension of bytes which are to be interpreted to a size which enables rapid convergency of the interpretation without the locking in of the process to a local solution only. In other words : it limits parallel computing to degree which is proper enough to have high flexibility but without the danger of exceeding a level of "speculation" on the input that is more than what can be compensated by the systems control without loosing the smooth convergency of the interpretatin process. Hence, this procedure is a fundamental scheme for managing an optimal mixing of parallel and serial processes, depending both the input and the systems knowledge ressources (time optimal use of the knowledge). This is different to the known template matching, where the image is handled as a full parallel byte. Therefore template matching is useful only for working in case of well defined, well known problems in recognition and needs a teacher for learning. Learning in this system is performed in a way, that the sequence of parallel bytes with different dimensions which is recalled most often in such relaxation processes is turned towards a new parallel representation via formation of a "sentence". The system can interprete an unknown scene by composing the unknown parts out of known ones while known order relations guide the interpretation. This is a cognitive ability.

b) That set of input channels which belong to a recognized pattern (that means which could entrain a strong recall) is switched off. By that mechanism, these channels are erased from the input and therefore the already interpreted part is out of discussion. That accelerates the process towards rapid convergency. Also, parallel solutions can develop as long as they don't access to the same set of input channels. Then the tolerance turns into competition for the share of the elementary input information (the primitives or objects - depending on the hierarchic level of the conflict). As a result the solution which can organize the largest number of the input set to a consistent solution will win and resolve the lower order competitive one. This switching off the solutions (recalled order relations) is crucial for the high flexibility of the system : this transient representations of R1 are flashing throughout the system, and at the object file R2 there is the active summary of the already understood image. Without that mechanism, if all recalled order relations would be still steadily active as strong competitive patterns, the system would lock straightforward to a certain course of the interpretation. But with this flashing at R1 and keeping at R2, the established solution at R2 can be at any time driven to a different course if a powerful alternative solution is developing as long as the interpretation is not completed (all input channels are in synchrony and switched off). The strongest consensus at R2 from R1 patterns get's the lead and organizes the smooth production of a macro-rule. Furthermore, since if we accept that the length of the 'sentence' is limited to probably about 7 such bytes [12] (different alternative decisions at the same time which are not yet linked), the cortex gets at any time an equal load : if no powerful consensus of R2 can evolve, no more details of the input can enter the interface. In case of changing the input or developing another powerful consensus out of the 7 bytes, the former one is weakened and the block of related input channels is removed, the elementary pieces of input information are free for reordering. It can be looked at as a process which enables the selfproduction of an inner language for the description of the input, whereby the selfconsistency is guaranteed by the described selfcontrol. The evolution of a macro-rule governs the interpretation but is tolerated only as long as it can unite the largest part of the input relative to other ones.

5. Conclusion

The seemingly effortless ability of the brain for perception or movement control depends on complex processes. Testing theories on such functions requires models on a more realistic scale than up to now feasible. Besides that, more complex models are neither strictly controllable nor can they get trained its knowledge in a rigid way. Simply larger pools or more layers of formal neuron nets will not do the job. We emphasize the firmware structure of a neocortical column as a possible example for an elementary processor which guarantees ultrastability [12] and high flexibility. A very suggestive aspect of that hypothesis is that in terms of the proposed dynamics of the control of pattern formation in such a heterogeneous system the columnar hardware makes a lot of sense. It is not the simple elements'mass which makes the essential difference between a reactive (peripheral) and a cognitive (cortical) system, it's the firmware organization.

References

[1] Amari, S.I. "Neural theory of association and concept formation" Biol. Cyb. 26 (1977) 175-85

[2] Arbib, M.A. & S.I. Amari "Sensorimotor transformations in the brain (with a critique of the tensor theory of cerebellum" J. Theor. Biol. 112 (1985) 123-55

[3] Churchland, P.M. "Cognitive neurobiology : a computational hypothesis for laminar cortex" Biology and Philosophy 1 (1986) 25-51

[4] Crick, F. The function of the thalamic reticular complex : the searchlight hypothesis" Proc. Natl. Acad. Sci. USA 81 (1984) 4586-90

[5] Edelman, G.M. & L.H.Finkel "Neural group selection in the cerebral cortex" In : Dynamic Aspects of Neocortical Function, G.M. Edelman, W.E. Gall, W.M. Cowan (eds.) Wiley : NewYork, Chichester, Brisbane, Toronto, Singapore (1984)

[6] Fukushima, K. "A hierarchical neural network model for associative memory" Biol. Cyb. 50 (1984) 105-13

[7] Fukushima, K. "A neural network model for selective attention in visual pattern recognition" Biol Cyb. 55 (1986) 5-15

[8] Hirai, Y. "A model of human associative processor (HASP)" IEEE Trans. Syst., Man and Cyb. SMC-13 (1983) 851-7

[9] Hogg, T. & B.A. Huberman "Understanding biological computation : reliable learning and recognition" Proc. Natl. Acad. Sci. USA 81 (1984) 6871-5

[10] Hopfield, J.J. & D.W. Tank "Neural computation of decisions in optimization problems" Biol. Cyb. 52 (1985) 141-52

[11] Kohonen, T. "Selforganization and associative memory" Springer : Berlin, Heidelberg, NewYork, Tokyo (1984)

[12] Koerner, E., I. Tsuda & H. Shimizu "Take-grant control, variable byte formation and processing parallel in sequence-characteristics of a new type of holonic processor" (subm. to publ.)

[13] Malpeli. J.G. "Activity of cells in area 17 of the cat in absence of input from layer A of lateral geniculate nucleus" J. Neurophysiol. 49 (1983) 595-606

[14] v.d.Malsburg, Ch. "Nervous structures with dynamical links" Ber. Bunsenges. Phys. Chem. 89 (1985) 703-10

[15] v.d.Malsburg, Ch. & W. Schneider "A neural cocktail-party processor" Biol. Cybern. 54 (1986) 29-40

[16] Marr, D. "Vision", Freeman : SanFrancisco (1982)

[17] Mountcastle, V.B. "An organizing principle for cerebral function : the unit module and the distributed system" Group-Selective Theory of Higher Brain Function, G.M. Edelman and V.B. Mountcastle (eds.) MIT Press : Cambridge, Mass. (1978)

[18] Nicolis, J.S. "Dynamics of hierarchical systems" Springer : Berlin, Heidelberg, NewYork, Tokyo (1986)

[19] Palm, G. "Associative Networks and Cell Assemblies" in: "Brain Theory" G. Palm & A. Aertsen (eds.), Springer : Berlin, Heidelberg, NewYork, Tokyo (1986)

[20] Pellionisz, A. & R. Llinas "Tensor network theory of the meta-organization of functional geometries in the central nervous system", Neuroscience 16 (1985) 245-73

[21] Orban, G.A. "Neuronal operations in the visual cortex" Springer : Berlin, Heidelberg, NewYork (1984)

[22] Rumelhart, D., G. Hinton & J. McClelland (eds.) "Parallel distributed processing : explorations in the microstructure of cognition", MIT Press, Cambridge, MA (1986)

[23] Singer, W. "Central control of developmental plasticity in the mammalian visual cortex", Vision Res. 25 (1985) 389-96

[24] Silverman, D.J., G.L. Shaw & J.C.Pearson "Associative recall properties of the trion model of cortical organization", Biol. Cybern. 53 (1986) 259-271

[25] Sutton, R.S. & A.G. Barto "Toward a modern theory of adaptive networks : expectation and prediction", Psychol. Rev. 88 (1981) 135-70

[26] Szentagothai, J. "The modular architectonic principle of neural centers" Rev. Physiol. Biochem. Pharmac. 98 (1983) 11-61

[27] Thagard, P. "Parallel computation and the mind-body problem" Cognitive Science 10 (1986) 301-18

[28] Tsuda, I., E. Koerner & H. Shimizu "Memory dynamics in asynchronous neural networks" (subm. to publication)

PARALLEL ALGORITHMS AND STATIC ANALYSIS OF PARALLEL PROGRAMS

N.N. Mirenkov[1)]

The present paper describes models of parallel processing, the so-called parallel algorithms, (p-algorithms), associated with the author's experience in the parallel language construction for multi-computer systems [3-4]. These models are an "asynchronous" generalization of the operator form of sequential algorithms [2], and, besides, the statement initiation conditions are specified via canonized sets of process communication schemes. Varying the sets makes it possible to proceed from one model of parallel processing to another. In this sense the concept of p-algorithm follows [5] where a metamodel of parallel processing is proposed. However, unlike [5], our model permits variations not only of semaphore functions but also message primitives and process creation/destruction primitives. To illustrate, two sets of statements describing, respectively, individual and collective schemes of process interactions are distinguished. Dead-lock freedom and uniqueness conditions are formulated for the p-algorithms. The essential conditions are that each fragment (subprocess) has information and control independence of process interactions during subprocess execution, however the next fragment may have the dependence of these interactions.

The proposed means for the description of p-algorithms and process parceling represent special extensions of conventional language structures. The extensions are made to have possibility for the static analysis of dead-lock freedom and uniqueness of parallel programs (p-programs) under the assumption that every loop terminates. As compared to [1,7] where dead-lock freedom of CSP- and ADA-programs is considered, this analysis is the detection of two above-mentioned characteristics simultaneously. Besides, the detection will be made by algorithms of the polynomial complexity.

2. CONCEPT OF PARALLEL ALGORITHM

All the actions made to solve a problem are regarded as the execution (over a shared memory $D = \{d_i, i \in I\}$) of a set of statements

$$S = \{S_k, k \in K\}, \quad S_k: \bar{D} \to \bar{D}, \quad \bar{D} = \prod_{i \in I} \bar{d}_i,$$

where K, I and $\bar{d}_i$ are finite sets of the values of k, i and d_i, respectively, $\prod$ is a sign of the Cartesian product. Each statement referred to as a c-statement in order to stress its composite structure is a triple $S_k = ([C_k^1]; T_k; C_k^2)$, where $C_k^1 \in C_1$, $C_k^2 \in C_2$, $C = (C_1 \cup C_2)$ is a finite set of special statements; the statements from C_1 allow one to define process synchronizations and data exchages. The statements from C_2 make it possible to assign c-statement-successors. The square brackets indicate that the emptiness is allowed as contents; T_k is a program fragment which

---

[1)] Computing Center, Siberian Division, USSR Ac.Sci., Novosibirsk 630090, USSR.

transforms the contents of memory locations not involving statements from C and executing the finite number of actions. In particular, the fragment can be empty. The activation (execution) of a c-statement depends on the conjunction of two conditions: its presence in <u>the successor list</u> and the validity of the individual initiation condition for $C_k^1 \in C$.

Any sequential algorithm in this interpretation, represents a succession of c-statements $S_1; S_2; \ldots; S_h$; where $S_i = (T_i, C_i^2)$, S_1 (as an example) is an "initial" statement and a set $C \equiv C_2 = \{GOTO, BC, END\}$, where BC is the branch of condition statement; END is the halt statement. At each moment only one c-statement is executed whose name (code) is in <u>the command register</u> (CR) for the given algorithm; the successor list contains only one element. The essence of the CR of an algorithm is similar to that of the CR of a processor.

In calculations which are not an execution of a sequential algorithm, several c-statements may be simultaneously executed. In our model at any moment there can exist several CR, each containing the name of one of c-statements which are executed; all together, they contain names of all the active at the moment c-statements. Each CR is connected with its own successor list. Here it should be stressed that a c-statement is a short form of the "composite statement" but not a statement of the set C.

Quadruple $\langle S, S', H, C \rangle$ is referred to as a <u>p-algorithm</u> over the shared memory D, where S is a finite set of c-statements, S' is a subset of "starting" statements ($S' \subseteq S$) initiating the execution of p-algorithm (the name of each appearing in its own CR from H); H is a set of the initially given CR, with one-to-one correspondence to the elements from S'; C is a finite set of process interaction statements, including successor selection statements $C_2 \subseteq C$ capable of 1) generating new registers or eliminating the existing ones and 2) assigning successors over any subset of existing registers[1]. The halt statement eliminates its own CR. The execution of the p-algorithm is completed when the last register has been eliminated.

In general case, if several c-statements whose individual initiation conditions are valid come to the same successor list then the most priority c-statement is assigned as the "first" successor else successor assigning is delayed. For simplicity, we will use a more partial rule, giving priority to the first statement whose individual initiation conditions may be invalid to arrive and eliminating the other statements. A successor list of a separate CR can consist of only one element, the attempt to register the second element is a "skip" statement. Thus, the execution of a p-algorithm, the general number of successors at some moment does not exceed the number of CR existing at this moment. After executing of a

[1] Examples of particular statements from C_2 are given in Section 3.

c-statement, its name in the respective CR is substituted by the name of the successor. It is considered that since this moment a new c-statement begins execution. The totality of c-statements executed on the CR is termed a "p-algorithm branch" (PA-branch).

Since a c-statement is composite, it is assumed that each CR at any moment (except for the name of the c-statement) contains the name of its composite part executed at this moment, i.e. the name of the statement from C or from T_k. A set of all the names belonging to the composite parts (in different CR) being executed at the moment under consideration, is called the current state vector of a p-algorithm.

p-Algorithm is referred to as deadlock-free if trigger condition (initiation condition) of any statement from C which appeared in CR is satisfied after execution of a finite number of statements in the other PA-branches; the current state vector never contains only statements from C with unsatisfactory trigger conditions. The memory state $\bar{D}^f \in \bar{D}$, after all the PA-branches have been finished, is the p-algorithm result. The PA-branches set, the c-statement succession occurred in every PA-branch and the execution results at each c-statement is the p-algorithm realization (the p-algorithm history). p-Algorithm is considered unique, if any realization over the same data gives one and the same result.

Architecture of a computing system is one of the main factors influencing the selection of C. Below, two examples are presented, whose elements are oriented to module multi-processor systems, each module having a processor and a memory.

3. PA-BRANCHES INTERACTION STATEMENTS

Below it is assumed that the shared memory of the p-algorithm is divided into a finite number of non-intersecting subsets: $D = \bigcup_i D_i$. Over the subset D_i, only the PA-branch with the name i is executed, except for the cases, when other PA-branches interact with the PA-branch i making use of the statements from C. The number of the PA-branch will be considered to play a role of its name.

C(I) is a set of individual interaction statements. The statements described below enable to define the individual access of the PA-branch j to the memory subset $D_i (i \neq j)$ and to control the order of execution of statements in other PA-branches; these statements define interaction of not more than two PA-branches. Some features of statements are original, the others are borrowed.

We consider that at each moment of execution of a p-algorithm there exists a finite set of vectors, generally, of different dimension, whose components are semaphores. Let X be one of such vectors whose belongness to the subsets from D will not be discussed here. Let j be the name of the PA-branch using the statements from C(I) discussed below.

The statement CHANGE (X,B) adds values of components of the integer vector B ($B \in D_j$) (the components may be positive or negative) to the values of the corresponding components of X; the vectors X and B are of the same dimension; the operation of changing X is indivisible.

The statement READ (a,i,a_1,b,B,X) inputs the value of the variable $a \in D_i$ in the place of $a_1 \in D_j$, B and X are described above. The operation of reading is realized if the condition specified by the vector b ($b \in D_j$), is valid (the dimension of b is the same as that of X). The components the vector b indicate the components of X to be used and the logic functions to be performed over these semaphores. For example, the vectors b = (1,0,1,0) and b = (0,-1,0,-1) can define conjunction and disjunction, respectively, over the odd and even components of the vector X.

The statement WRITE (a,i,a_1,b,B,X) outputs the value of the variable $a \in D_j$ in the place of $a_1 \in D_i$, b,B,X are the same as in the previous case.

Each of the above presented statements is $C_k^1 \in C_1$.

The statement DO (S_h,i,b,B,X) assigns a c-statement S_h as a successor in the PA-branch i and preliminarily defines a new CR if S_h is the first c-statement being executed in the PA-branch i. It is assumed that in the generation of a new PA-branch, the name i uniquely defines the subset D_i not intersecting with the subsets of the existing PA-branches. For S_h= END the branch i is eliminated. This statement is $C_k^2 \in C_2$.

<u>C(G) is a set of collective interaction statements</u>. These statements define the collective access of PA-branches to any memory subset or assign several successors simultaneously. The collective interaction is activated if each PA-branch passes to its copy of the statement defining this interaction.

The statement BE (l,A,L_j) defines (BE is Broadcast Exchange) the collective access of all PA-branches to the value of the variable A, l is the name of the PA-branch which reads $A \in D_j$ not using the statements from C and broadcasts the value A for all the PA-branches; L_j ($L_j \in D_j$) is a variable to which the value A is copied and to which the PA-branch j has the access not using the statements from C. The statement defining the same interaction in the PA-branch i, is of the form: BE (l,A,L_i). The statement BE enables to define a rendervous between the PA-branch-transmitter and the PA-branches-receivers. As means of the parallel programming language it was first realized in [3].

The statement SE (T,L_j,M_j) defines (SE is Shift Exchange) the shift of the values $L_j \in D_j$ in the place of $M_{j\pm 1} \in D_{j\pm 1}$, T determines direction of the shift, for example, in increasing or decreasing the numbers of PA-branches, etc.

Each of the statements is $C_k^1 \in C_1$.

The statement GB (b,F_j,S_j^1,S_j^2) defines (GB is General Branch) the generalized conditional transfer in all PA-branches, b is a logical function,

$F = \{F_j, j \in J\}$ is its argument, where $F_j \in D_j$, J is a finite set of PA-branches; c-statement S_j^1 is a successor in the PA-branch j, if b(f) = true, otherwise S_j^2 is considered a successor. This statement can belong both to C_1 and C_2.

The statement GGT (List) defines (GGT is General GO TO) the generalized unconditional transfer in all the PA-branches to the c-statements from List, L_i ($L_i \in$ List) defines a successor for the PA-branch i. To execute the generalized transfer it is necessary and sufficient that GGT appears only in one PA-branch, i.e. the copy of this statement is not **needed** in other PA-branches. If necessary GGT is assumed to define new CR of a p-algorithm and the respective new PA-branches. GGT is $C_k^2 \in C_2$.

Further we will consider that the statements DO from C(I) and GGT from C(G) are used for the assignment of successors only in the other PA-branches, in their own PA-branch conventional GOTO, Branch on condition and END statements are used. The execution of the statements described is delayed if the defined interaction assumes participation in it of the PA-branches whose processes have not started yet; the exceptions **are** DO **and** GGT statements defining the generation or elimination of these PA-branches.

4. CORRECTNESS CONDITIONS OF p-PROGRAMS

In this section, a number of theorems are formulated. Carrying out their conditions guarantees the dead-lock freedom and the uniqueness of a p-program. Based on these conditions in the next Section, the p-algorithms languages are proposed.

Let us first consider p-algorithms, using the statements from C(I). Without losing generality, we assume that each c-statement contains at least one statement from C, and any use of a statement from C has its label, identifying a c-statement to which it belongs. Let C^m denote an arbitrary element from C. A triplet $\hat{c} = \langle t, C^m, M \rangle$, where t is the moment of completion of C^m labelled with M is called <u>an event</u> of the p-algorithm execution (t is the moment of the event coming). Let in some realization of a p-algorithm with the initial data $\bar{D}°$ there take place a succession of events[1)] $\hat{c}_x(\bar{D}°) = \hat{c}_1, \hat{c}_2, \dots, \hat{c}_l$, ordered with respect to time; and in realization of the PA-branch i, the succession $\hat{c}_x^i(D°) = \hat{c}_{i_1}, \hat{c}_{i_2}, \dots, \hat{c}_{i_{l(i)}}$. If several events took place simultaneously, they were ordered with the increase of numbers of PA-branches. Two successions of events $\hat{c}_x(D°)$ and $\hat{c}_y(\bar{D}°)$ related respectively to the realizations x and y are called coincident: $\hat{c}_x(\bar{D}°) = \hat{c}_y(\bar{D}°)$ if they are of the same length and elements with the same numbers are coincident statements and labels corresponding to the statements and, also, the names of the PA-branches in which the statements were executed.

A succession of the statements was executed between the events $\hat{c}_{i_{j-1}}$ and

1) The concept of the initial data covers their partition to a totality of subsets D_i, mentioned in Section 3.

$\hat{c}_{i_j}$ (or between the PA-branch activation moment and $\hat{c}_{i_1}$ or between $\hat{c}_{i_{l(i)}}^{\,j}$ and the PA-branch halting moment), it is called the fragment j of the PA-branch realization (denoted by φ_{i_j}). Here we will consider finite p-algorithms in which every φ_{i_j} contains a finite number of actions and, besides, the number of generated processes is finite. Note that a p-algorithm will be finite if the statements GGT and DO are used only for the generation of the finite number of processes.

The fragment φ_{i_j} is <u>information</u> <u>independent</u> of the events in the other PA-branches, if the statement READ and WRITE executed between $\hat{c}_{i_{j-1}}$ and $\hat{c}_{i_j}$ are not information dependent on the statements of the fragment. The fragment φ_{i_j} is <u>control</u> <u>independent</u> of the events in other PA-branches, if between $\hat{c}_{i_{j-1}}$ and $\hat{c}_{i_j}$ there was no either realization of the statements DO or there was only one event which initiated the execution of the first statement after $\hat{c}_{i_{j-1}}$

<u>Theorem 1</u>. Let a p-algorithm with the statements from C(I) have no deadlocks. For the uniqueness of its results it is sufficient that for any $\bar{D}°$ and realizations x and y $\hat{c}_x(\bar{D}°) = \hat{c}_y(\bar{D}°)$ and any fragment φ_{i_j} has information and control independence of other PA-branches events[1].

Now we pass to consideration of p-algorithms with statements from C(G). We suppose that in any use, the statement $C^m \in C(G)$ besides the label identifying the belongness to c-statement has a label identifying collective interaction. This label is the same in the respective statements from different PA-branches. A triple $\langle t, C^m, M\text{-}N \rangle$ where t is a moment of appearance C^m labelled M-N in the successor list is called <u>an</u> <u>intermediate</u> <u>event</u>. This notion will be used for $C^m \neq$ GGT. The triple $\langle t, C^m, M\text{-}N \rangle$ where t is a moment of completion C^m labelled M-N is called <u>the</u> <u>event</u> of the PA-branch.

Let in some realization x in the PA-branch i there had place a succession of events (intermediate ones) $\hat{c}_x^i = \hat{c}_1^i, \hat{c}_2^i, \dots, \hat{c}_{l(i)}^i$ and in the PA-branch j $\hat{c}_x^j = \hat{c}_1^j, \hat{c}_2^j, \dots, \hat{c}_{l(j)}^j$. The successions $\hat{c}_x^i$ and $\hat{c}_x^j$ are called coincident if $l(i) = l(j)$ and elements with equal numbers have the same statements and corresponding to them the second labels. Let in some realizations x and y in the PA-branch i there had place successions $\hat{c}_x^i$ and $\hat{c}_y^i$. They are called coincident if $l^x(i) = l^y(i)$ and elements with equal numbers have the same statements and corresponding to them the first and the second labels.

<u>Theorem 2</u>. For the deadlock freedom of a p-algorithm with statements from C(G) it is necessary and sufficient that in any realization succession of intermediate events in all the PA-branches are equal and among PA-branches executing the statement BE $(1, A, L_j)$ there is a PA-branch with the name 1.

Let in the p-algorithm at least one PA-branch use the statement GGT. Then the following result holds.

---

1) The proof of Theorems 1-3 is presented in [6].

Theorem 3. Let PA with statements from C(G) have no deadlocks. For the uniqueness of its results it is sufficient that in any realizations the succession of events of at least one PA-branch is kept.

Although, these are essentially wide classes of problems (for example, in linear algebra and systems of differential equations) for which variation in the input data does not influence the order of interactions between PA-branches, nevertheless, a number of questions arises: how to follow the formulated conditions if we want to have the order of interactions in a p-algorithm varied by the data; how to select a more efficient succession of events if computational processes rate is unknown; how to increase flexibility of statements of collective interactions and so on.

To answer these questions it is proposed:

1) To use the statements BC and GB to change the order of appearance and the assembly of events depending on $\bar{D}^o$ and computational results.

2) In every subset D_i to distinguish a binary variable δ_i whose value determines participation of ($\delta_i=1$) or non-participation ($\delta_i=0$) of the PA-branch i in collective interactions; in this connection, the initiation condition for BE, SE and GB is that each PA-branch with $\delta_i=1$ passes to its own statement defining the same interaction. If $\delta_i=0$, the statements BE, SE and GB are taken as empty by the PA-branch i. To change the values δ_i one should use the statements $\delta_i:=1$ and $\delta_i:=0$ which can be executed only in the PA-branch i; these statements should be included due to their special importance in C(G).

3) To introduce a generalized concept of a PA-branch fragment as a succession of statements which were executed between two statements from C and which in this succession can have the other $C^m \in C$.

4) To use not a linear but a partial order in the appearance of events of a p-algorithm; to accompany each $C^m \in C$ with: a) additional initiation conditions which are a conjunctive and/or a disjunctive enumeration of the events which must or can occur before execution of C^m and b) the finish condition which is an enumeration of events before the appearance of which the execution of C^m should be completed.

5) To reject from using semaphores in $C^m \in C(I)$ since their role is to a large extent duplicated by additional initiation conditions.

Assume that a p-algorithm is presented loop-free, i.e. the statements selecting successors generate only acyclic graphs whose nodes are c-statements. Then by the additional initiation condition $C^m \in C(I)$ one of the following logical expressions is taken:

$$P_1 = A_{i_1} \wedge A_{i_2} \wedge \ldots \wedge A_{i_m}\,; \quad P_2 = (A_{j_1} \vee A_{j_2} \vee \ldots \vee A_{j_n}) \wedge P_1, \tag{1}$$

where the indices at A are the names of PA-branches, in any expression there are no two equal indices; $m \geq 1$, $n \geq 2$, $n + m$ do not exceed the maximal number of PA-branches which can be generated in the execution of a p-algorithm;

$$A_{\alpha_\beta} ::= P(R_1,\alpha_\beta) \mid P(R_1,\alpha_\beta) \vee P(R_2,\alpha_\beta) \vee \ldots \vee P(R_l,\alpha_\beta),$$

here $P(R_h,\alpha_\beta)$ = true($h=\overline{1,l}$) if the statement C^m labelled with R_h in the PA-branch α_β was executed, otherwise $P(R_h,\alpha_\beta)$= false, l is any integer.

Under the finish condition the same expressions P_1 and P_2 are taken, only $P(R_h,\alpha_\beta)$ = true, if C^m labelled with R_h in the PA-branch α_β is not executed, otherwise $P(R_h,\alpha_\beta)$ = false.

To each initiation condition the finish condition should be put in correspondence. Both in the initiation conditions and in the finish conditions there must be labels of statements from the PA-branch with which C^m defines interaction (except for the cases when interaction is fictitious). The succession of statements executed in this PA-branch between the statement from the initiation condition and the statement from the finish condition, is called a generalized fragment (GF) connected with C^m. Since GF's can intersect, the statements connected with different GF can interact with any of them. GF is called information independent of interacting with it $C^m \in C(I) \setminus DO$, if the statements of the fragment are information independent of any of the C^m-statements which are connected between by the order of succession (with the help of the trigger conditions) or information independent. The definition of control independence for GF will be considered coincident with the definition for a fragment.

For $C^m \in C(G)$, under the additional initiation condition we take one of the expressions:

$$P_1 = P(R_1) \vee P(R_2) \vee \ldots \vee P(R_l); \quad P_2 = P_1 \wedge \delta(i_1,j_1) \wedge \ldots \wedge \delta(i_n,j_n),$$

where $l \geqslant 1$, $n \geqslant 1$, $P(R_h)$=true, if the interaction defined by the statements $C^m \in C(G)$ having the second label R_h, is executed, otherwise $P(R_h)$= =false; $\delta(i_\beta,j_\beta)$=true, if in the PA-branch i_β, the statement $\delta_{i_\beta}:=0$ (or $\delta_{i_\beta}:=1$) having the label j_β was executed, otherwise $\delta(i_\beta,j_\beta)$ = =false; $\{i_\beta, \beta=\overline{1,n}\}$ is a set of names of PA-branches which must redefine its state in participation in collective interactions before execution of $C^m \in C(G)$. Under the finish condition we take one of the expressions of P_1 or P_2, only $P(R_h)$=true, if the respective actions did not take place. Note that the described initiation and finish conditions must accompany not only the statements from C(G) described in Section 3, but also the statements $\delta_i:=1$ and $\delta_j:=0$.

Let there be the texts of all possible PA-branches. A text is a list of all possible c-statements which can be executed in the respective PA-branch. Let the p-algorithm be loop-free (its loops are spreaded). Then the PA-branch interaction graph may easily be constructed. Its nodes correspond to the statements from C and the arcs - to dependences described in the additional conditions of activation, here the node corresponding to C^m includes the arcs from all the nodes corresponding to the statements which are present in these conditions. We assume that in the interaction graph there is either a curve (trace) to the node whose statement uses the name of some PA-branch from the node, whose statement defines the generation of this PA-branch, or the PA-branch is related to a "starting" subset. We also assume that there is always a curve (trace) from the node, whose statement uses the name of the PA-branch to the node, whose statement eliminates this PA-branch.

Theorem 4. For the deadlock freedom of p-algorithm with the statement from C(I) it is sufficient that the interaction graph has no loops and circuits.

Theorem 5. Let p-algorithm with the statements from C(I) have no deadlocks. For the uniqueness of its results it is sufficient that in any realization each generalized fragment has information and control independence of C^m connected with it.

Similarly, the new theorems for p-algorithms with $C^m \in C(G)$ may be formulated.

5. p-ALGORITHM LANGUAGES

Language constructions PA(I) and PA(G) are described for the presentation of p-algorithms using, respectively, the statements from C(I) and C(G). These means propose that p-algorithm is a finite set of the PA-branches; for each PA-branch, a sequential program must be written. PA(I) and PA(G) include the sequential language structures: linear, if-then-else and while-do, assignment and declaration statements, input-output statements, the set of statements C(I) or C(G), coordinated or generalized while-do structures as well.

PA(I) language. PA(I) consists of the statement READ, WRITE, DO. Their difference from those described in Section 3 is that the arguments defining the use of semaphores are excluded, but after each statement additional conditions of its initiation and finish (CIF) must be presented in the form of logical expressions, described in Section 4. CIF will be located at the place of comments; first, the initiation condition, then after a semicolon - the finish condition. We write (R_1,α_β) instead of $P(R_1,\alpha_\beta)$; the events reflecting initiation and finish of the PA-branch will be indicated by letters i and f; for example, $(i,\alpha_\beta);(f,\alpha_\beta)$ means CIF covering all the time of existence of the process α_β.

In if-structures, the statements from C(I) may only be used in the following cases. Let a fragment $\hat{s}_1$ of the program define one succession of events in the PA-branch and $\hat{s}_2$ - another one. Then the construction if p then $\hat{s}_1$ else $\hat{s}_2$ is admissible which depending on data changes the succession of events in the PA-branch. As this takes place, CIF of any C^m from $\hat{s}_1$ should not refer to the statements from $\hat{s}_2$ and vice versa. Statements of the other PA-branches dependent on the events of such a construction, must use a disjunctive form for A_{α_β} from (1). The same construction is admissible for the change of the succession of events from two PA-branches.

In the while-do structure the statements from C(I) may only be used in two cases. The first is the case when it is assumed that CIF of statements present in a loop body remain unchanged during the execution of all iterations, and statements themselves are not present in CIF of C^m from other PA-branches. In the second case the statements from C(I) may be used in the body of <u>the coordinated loop</u>, that is a loop belonging to a set of loops (all the loops from different PA-branches) which in CIF may have the dependence on the C^m execution from various loops of the set and from different iterations. To indicate the dependence on such a statement, we must write the PA-branch name, the loop label, the statement label and iteration number in the form of $j \pm k$, where k is the constant, j is the number of the iteration at which the dependent statement is executed. The dependence disappears if (i) j+k becomes greater than the number of iterations executed in the corresponding finished loop, or (ii) $j-k \leq 0$. The following example demonstrates the use of the coordinated loops for the description of asynchronous pipeline consisting of n-base processes and n-buffer processes (having fractional numbers):

PA-branch V_i $(1 < i < n)$

L_i: while P_i do	
M_i: READ$(A_{i-\frac{1}{2}}, V_{i-\frac{1}{2}}, B_i)$	$(N_{i-1}, V_{i-1}, L_{i-1}, j) \wedge (i, V_{i-\frac{1}{2}})$;
...	$(N_{i-1}, V_{i-1}, L_{i-1}, j+1) \wedge (f, V_{i-\frac{1}{2}})$;
....	...
N_i: WRITE$(Z_i, V_{i+\frac{1}{2}}, A_{i+\frac{1}{2}})$	$(M_{i+1}, V_{i+1}, L_{i+1}, j-1) \wedge (i, V_{i+\frac{1}{2}})$;
...	$(M_{i+1}, V_{i+1}, L_{i+1}, j) \wedge (f, V_{i+\frac{1}{2}})$
END L_i	

Here the PA-branch V_i at any iteration of the loop L_i executes the statement READ at first, i.e. assigns the value $A_{i-\frac{1}{2}}$ from the PA-branch $V_{i-\frac{1}{2}}$ to the variable B_i; then the statement WRITE, i.e. assigns the value Z_i (calculated in V_i) to the variable $A_{i+\frac{1}{2}}$ in the PA-branch $V_{i+\frac{1}{2}}$. The initiation condition of the statement READ is a conjunction of two partial conditions: 1) execution of the statement WRITE of j-iteration of the loop L_{i-1} by the PA-branch V_{i-1}; 2) the initiation of the PA-branch $V_{i-\frac{1}{2}}$. The finish condition of the statement READ is also the conjunction of two conditions; the statement must be executed before the statement WRITE from the PA-branch V_{i-1} is executed at (j+1)-iteration of the loop L_{i-1} and, also, before the PA-branch $V_{i-\frac{1}{2}}$ is finished.

To complete the short description of PA(I) the statement DO(S_j, i) must be mentioned. It is intended only for generating or eliminating the process in the PA-branch, that is, when S_j is from S' or END.

<u>PA(G) language</u>. C(G) includes the statements BE $(1, A, L_j)$, SE (T, L_j, M_j), GB (b, F_j, S_j^1, S_j^2) and GGT (List) described in Section 3 and, also, the statements $\delta_j := 0$ and $\delta_j := 1$.

Let the fragment $\hat{s}_1$ of the program define one succession of events in the PA-branch, and $\hat{s}_2$ - the other one. Then the expression <u>if</u> <u>p</u> <u>then</u> $\hat{s}_1$ <u>else</u> $\hat{s}_2$ is admissible if the successions may be partitioned into the equal number of fragments such that the successions in the fragments with equal numbers either coincide or at least one of two noncoincident sub-successions is passive, i.e. begins with the statement $\delta_j:=0$ and finishes with $\delta_j:=1$. To change successions of events of p-algorithm one may use also the statement GB.

In the loop structure $C^m \in C(G)$ may be used only in <u>a generalized while-do loop</u>, that is a loop belonging to a set of loops (all the loops from different PA-branches with $\delta_j=1$) which have the repetition condition in the form of GB $(b,F,\hat{s}_j^1,\hat{s}_j^2)$ where $\hat{s}_j^1$ is the first statement in the loop body, $\hat{s}_j^2$ is the first statement after the loop itself. The following example illustrates the use of the generalized loop in solving the system of linear equations $X=f(X)-Z$ by the successive approximation technique:

$$F_1=(X_1^{(k)},X_1^{(k+1)}),\ F_2=(X_2^{(k)},X_2^{(k+1)}),\ X^{(k)}=(X_1^{(k)},X_2^{(k)}),$$

$$X^{(k+1)}=(X_1^{(k+1)},X_2^{(k+1)}),\ Z=(Z_1,Z_2),\ f=(f_1,f_2),\ b=(|X_1^{(k+1)}-X_1^{(k)}|<\varepsilon)\wedge(|X_2^{(k+1)}-X_2^{(k)}|<\varepsilon);$$

CIF as well as the first label for C^m are dropped due to obviousness:

PA-branch V_1	PA-branch V_2
...	...
M_0: while GB (b,F_1,M_1,M_n)	M_0: while GB (b,F_2,M_1,M_n)
$X_1^{(k)}:=X_1^{(k+1)}$	$X_2^{(k)}:=X_2^{(k+1)}$
M_1: $X_1^{(k+1)}:=f_1(X^{(k)})-Z_1$	M_1: $X_2^{(k+1)}:=f_2(X^{(k)})-Z_2$
M_2: $BE(V_1,X_1^{(k+1)},X_1^{(k)})$	M_2: $BE(V_1,X_1^{(k+1)},X_1^{(k)})$
M_3: $BE(V_2,X_2^{(k+1)},X_2^{(k)})$	M_3: $BE(V_2,X_2^{(k+1)},X_2^{(k)})$
END M_0	END M_0
M_n: ...	M_n: ...

The statement GGT is intended for activation or elimination of processes. The process being eliminated must be suspended and wait till it is eliminated. A similar rule is also valid for the statement DO from C(I). For more details of PA(I) and PA(G) see [6]. Now we may formulate the concluding result.

<u>Theorem 6</u>. Let PA written on PA(I) or PA(G) have loops being completed. Then its deadlock freedom and the uniqueness are detected in the p-program text.

Instead of the proof we only note two aspects which are related to it. To detect deadlock freedom of the p-algorithm we must construct a graph of interactions of PA-branches. The main obstacle here are loop structures, however, it is sufficient to analyze the body of a separate while-do loop in PA(I), the bodies of the generalized loops in PA(G) and those of the coordinated loops in PA(I). This analysis avoids a complete scan of all iterations of the loops. The dimension of the scan is defined by the constants k_i used in CIF. The analysis complexity does not exceed $O(N^3)$, where N is the number of statements from C(I).

To detect uniqueness of the p-algorithm one has to elucidate the information independence of fragments, since independence of control is explicitly defined. Of great help here is the "marking" of the PA-branches defined by CIF. The analysis complexity does not exceed $O(n \cdot L)$ where L is the maximal number of statements in PA-branches texts of the p-algorithm, n is the total number of statements in PA-program text. For the p-algorithms in PA(G), the complexity of detecting uniqueness and deadlock freedom is linear.

6. CONCLUSION

Within the framework of the metamodel of parallel data processing two sub-classes of models are distinguished supported by original language means. These means allow special marking of processing into subprocesses and to define various interactions between the PA-branches of p-algorithms. The use of the proposed languages generally requires a special construction of p-algorithms, in which information dependent subprocesses must be ordered. It makes it possible to detect the uniqueness and deadlock freedom of p-programs by means of polynomial complexity static analysis of texts. It is important to note that uniqueness is ensured in the conditions of real calculation on a computer.

LITERATURE

[1] Apt, K.R.: A static analysis of CSP programs. Lecture Notes in Comp. Sci. (1984), 164, 1-17.

[2] Ershov, A.P.: Operator algorithms.I. Problemy kibernetiki (1960), 3, 5-48.

[3] Golovyashkina, L.V., Kolosova, Yu.I., Kosarev, Yu.G., Mirenkov, N.N.: Automation of parallel programming based on existing translators. Vychislitelnye sistemy.(1968), 30, 63-69.

[4] Kerbel, V.G., Kolosova, Yu.I., Korneev, V.D., Krylov, E.G., Mirenkov, N.N.:Preprint, Institut Matematiki SOAN SSSR, Novosibirsk 1979.

[5] Lipton, R., Snyder,L., Zalcstein, Y.: Comparative study of Models of Parallel Computation. 15th Ann.Symp.on Switching and Automata Theory (1974), 145-155.

[6] Mirenkov, N.N.: Construction of unique and deadlock freedom parallel programs. Vychislitelnye sistemy (1985), 109, 3-27.

[7] Taylor, R.N.: A General-Purpose Algorithm for Analyzing Concurrent Programs. Comm.ACM, 26 (1983) 5, 362-376.

Parallel Processing
of
Combinatorial Search Trees

B. Monien
O. Vornberger

Dept. of Mathematics and Computer Science
University of Paderborn

Abstract

This paper describes the implementations of parallel algorithms on distributed systems in the department of mathematics and computer science at the University of Paderborn. We report on the design and analysis of multiprocessor systems used to solve combinatorial optimization problems from the area of operations research and artificial intelligence.

1. Introduction

Many problems from the area of operations research and artificial intelligence can be formulated as combinatorial optimization problems where we are required to find a solution vector x that minimizes some criterion function f(x) subject to a set of constraints. Since the range for x is known we have a defined problem space, i.e. the number of feasible solutions is finite. In order to solve a given problem, we have to organize a systematic pass through the solution space (unless no further information about the problem is available).

We can associate with the problem a search tree where an edge represents the assignment of a value to a still undetermined solution parameter and a node represents a subproblem where some of the solution parameters are already set. In order to solve the problem, i.e. to detemine the value of the root, we grow the tree by expanding leaves and adding new nodes to the initially empty tree.

Let us classify our search problems into three main categories: the decision problems, the minimizing problems, the minimaxing problems.

For a decision problem we have to find out whether there exists a feasible solution that respects the constraints. Transfered to the search tree this means that we heve to check - while growing the tree - whether we finally create a node that represents a solution. Since no costs are involved the first such node will do. Note, that if there is no solution at all we will end up in passing the total search space.

The situation in a minimizing (resp. maximizing) problem is similar to the decision problem, however all nodes in the search tree that represent feasible solutions are now weighted and it is our goal to find among all these the cheapest one (resp. the most expensive one). We may compute heuristic values for nodes that represent subsolutions and use these values to guide the search, i.e. to determine which node is a good candidate to be expanded next.

A minimaxing problem typically occurs in the management of a negotiation where party A has certain alternatives to propose to which party B can answer with different responses.

For each of B's responses party A has again a finite number of moves and so on. This sequence is stopped after a given number of iterations (say k) and the possible "final situations" reached then, are weighted with a static evaluation function. It is the goal of party A to find an initial move that (taking into account the possible responses from B) finally leads to a situation with maximum static value.

This minimaxing concept is also used in game theory, where e.g. a best move on a chess board is determined by generating the search tree (consisting of legal chess moves) up to a given depth and bringing upwards from the leaves the values from a static board evaluation, switching between minimizing and maximizing from level to level.

Common to all three problem types is the exponential growth of the search tree. Although it is not yet proven that no efficient algorithms exist (see e.g. [8] for an introduction to complexity theory) we know up to now only of some heuristics that try to avoid to visit unnecessary parts of the tree. However, for many practical problems in the average an exponential number of nodes will be explored.

One approach to enhance the efficiency of tree search algorithms is to exploit parallelism. The design and analysis of algorithms for parallel computer architectures have become a central research area, mainly for the following two reasons:

1) The performance of sequential computers can not be improved by up-to-date technologies due to laws of physics.
2) Processing and memory units can be produced in a standardized manner and the cost per hardware unit has, due to mass production, gone down substantially.

As a result computer architectures evolve that consist of a system of identical processing units which are connected by a communication network.

In this paper we consider asynchronous multiprocessor systems that can be used to process search trees in parallel. We present implementations of our research group at Paderborn and explain the relations to work done elsewhere. Due to lack of space we can only give some introductory remarks to these projects, the interested reader is refered to the listed reports.

The experiments in Paderborn started 3 years ago with a set of personal computers, SIRIUS I, from Victor Technologies. This computer has an Intel 8088 microprocessor, 256 KB local memory, 2 serial RS-232 ports, and can be programmed in Pascal. By a few assembler routines it is possible to access the two ports and so by linking 16 Sirius to a ring our first, very simple, multiprocessor system was born. Due to the restricted topology the work load balancing became rather difficult especially for larger rings. But the system was powerful enough to produce superlinear speedups for certain problem classes (see section 2). In a next project we made accessible to a Pascal program the communication routines of a local area network (Omninet by Corvus Inc.) that is normally used to provide all PC's in the pool with system software. Now all nodes in our network can talk to each other directly, i.e. they form logically a clique (although physically the network is organized by a carrier sense multiple access bus). With this technique we were able to implement branch-and-bound algorithms that are normally designed to run on mainframes. To our knowledge is this the first time that the computing powers of several stan-

dard PC's are combined to solve problems that are too time - and space - consuming to be solved on a single PC.
The evaluation of the network performance shows 'heavy traffic' on the bus during certain periods of the computation and for our communication strategies this communication medium seems to have its limit. Half a year ago we installed in our department a multiprocessor system consisting of eight transputers. The transputer (by INMOS) is a chip with a 32-Bit processor and 4 full duplex high speed communication links that allow the configuration of any network topology only restricted by the degree 4. The transputer is programmed in OCCAM, a high level language based on Hoares concept of communicating sequential processes. Our current research projects show that the transputer is a universal tool for the construction of multiprocessor networks and supports the implementation of parallel algorithms that are based on asynchronous message oriented processes.

According to the three problem types (decision, minimizing, minimaxing) the paper is organized into three sections, that deal with the typical solution techniques for these classes, namely backtracking (section 2), branch-and-bound (section 3), and alpha-beta-search (section 4). Section 5 closes with concluding remarks.

2. Backtracking

A standard solution technique to solve a combinatorial decision problem is backtracking. Here we decompose the input problem into smaller subproblems (by restricting the solution parameters) and store these subproblems for further investigations on a stack:

```
push input problem on the stack;
repeat
   pop top problem P from the stack;
   if P has free parameters then
     begin
        split P into P1, P2,...,PK according to the k possible
        values of a free parameter
        push P1, P2,..., PK on the stack
   end
   else check if P represents a solution
until stack is empty or a solution is found.
```

Since the stack is accessed according to the last-in-first-out rule this technique corresponds to a depth-first search through the search tree for P. Note that at any time during the computation the stack stores independent and disjoint subproblems that are ready to be sent to one or more coprocessors.

This idea was used by Finkel and Manber [7] for their general purpose package DIB and the main difficulty in this approach is to determine which neighbor ih the network is asked for how much work if a processors stack gets empty. If there is no solution than an efficient implementation can reach at most linear speedup as long as all processors can be kept busy. If there is a solution then the network can stop processing as soon as the first solution is found. Clearly, additional processors may find a solution earlier than in a single-processor-operation but they may also spend their resources in vain since they work in those parts of the search tree that finally turn out to have only 'dead ends'. A very interesting fact was observed by our research group, when we implemented a parallel backtracking procedure to solve the satisfiability problem, i.e. to test whether a boolean formula in conjuntive normal form can be satisfied. It turns out that in the average a superlinear speedup can be reached. An explanation for this effect was given by a mathematical model that takes into account the solution density of a formula from a given class. This value of the solution density is not carried over to the subformulas F_x and $F_{\bar{x}}$ when formula F is splitted and so the probabilities to detect a solution in a subproblem vary very much. For details see [18,19].

3. Branch-and-Bound

A minimizing problem is a decision problem where all solutions are weighted by some integer valued function and we have to determine among all feasible solutions a cheapest one. Clearly, this problem can be approached by backtracking that visits all nodes in the search tree in depth first order and keeps a record of the cheapest 'so far'. This rather lengthy procedure (a complete pass through the search space is necessary) can be accelerated by the so called branch-and-bound technique, if at each tree node x additional information is available about the possible costs of the leave nodes originating from x. More precisely: A lower bound g(P) can be computed for a subproblem P such that any solution for P will cost at least g(P). Now all subproblems are stored according to their bounds in a priority queue and always the cheapest is explored and used for the branching step. Call a subproblem 'dead' if its bound b is at least as expensive as the cost of a tempory solution. Then the algorithm reads:

```
Find a temporary solution L (e.g. by a greedy algorithm).
Put the input problem with bound 0 in the priority queue
repeat
    remove cheapest Problem P from priority queue;
    if P has free parameters then
    begin
       take a free variable x and split P into subproblems P1, P2, ..., PK;
       compute the corresponding lower bounds g(P1), g(P2) ,..., g(PK);
       insert problems and bounds into the priority queue
    end
    else check if P can update the current solution L
until all problems in priority queue are dead.
The minimum solution is L.
```

Note that similar to the backtracking procedure the priority queue contains at any time during the computation independent, disjoint problems that are ready to be sent to idle coprocessors in the network. The main difficulty lies in the bound balancing task. Clearly, it is a waste of time for a processor to work on problems with rather high lower bounds when somewhere else in the network problems with smaller lower bounds exists. Since the bound for problem P is a measure for the probability that the optimum solution will arise from P it makes sense to work on the cheapest problem first. So, any efficient implementation for a parallel branch-and-bound strategy with distributed memories must ensure that the local priority queues are kept balanced with respect to their cheapest (i.e. top most) subproblem.

Several authors have investigated parallel versions of branch-and-bound. Wah, Li and Yu [27] give an excellent overview about multiprocessing of combinatorial problems. Besides branch-and-bound they also investigate the search in AND/OR trees, used for minimaxing. Lai, Sahni and Sprague [12, 13, 14] present conditions under which anomalies with regard to the speedup may occur: M processors need more time than N processors to solve a problem though M > N. An upper bound for the speedup obtainable by any parallel branch-and-bound algorithm was derived by Quinn and Deo [2o]. Wah and Ma [28] introduce MANIP, a multicomputer architecture for solving combinatorial extremum-search problems. Their design includes a combination of sorting and merging to be carried out between distributed memories. A unidirectional ring network is shown to be the most cost-effective interprocessor communication network. The performance is evaluated by simulations using the vertex cover problem.

A parallel branch-and-bound algorithm for the Traveling Salesman Problem was implemented by Mohan on the CM*, a multiprocessor system built at Carnegie Mellon University, consisting of a hierarchial network of LSI-11 computers [17].The memory is organized in several cluskers that are accessible to all processors as a uniform address space, local and remote access costs varying by a factor of 12. Using 16 processors, Mohan got a speedup of 8 for 3o-city-instances. A speedup of 6o was reached by 64 processors arranged in a hypercube in a Travelling-Salesman esperiment by Felten et al. [4]. However, instead of branch-and-bound they used simulated annealing that took advantage of the triangle inequality of the distance matrix and can in general not be guaranteed to come up with the optimal solution.

Our research group has also concentrated on the Travelling Salesman Problem as a classical example for a computational hard problem with important applications. (To recall the problem: We have to find a minimum cost roundtrip tour that visits each of N cities once, given the costs of travelling from one city to another.) Our approach is a simplified version of a branch-and-bound approach of Held and Karp [9]. A subproblem P = (W,b) consists of a subtour W starting at city 1 and a lower bound b with the meaning, that any solution tour starting with subtour W will cost at least b. The bound b can be determined by the cost of W plus the cost of a minimum spanning tree T calculated in the complement of W (i.e. within the still unvisited cities) plus the cheapest connections between W and T. Since a spanning tree can be computed fast and gives a rather sharp bound in sparse graphs (cities with few connections) we have an ideal candidate for a heuristic that guides us through the search space.

As heuristic that controls the balancing of the entries in the priority queue (realized by a heap) we use a procedure that monitors the increase of the cheapest lower bound. More precisely: If a processor detects that during the last iterations its own lower bound (the top most heap element) has increased by a certain constant then neighboring processors are consulted whether they have cheaper subproblems in their heaps and if so are asked to send some.

The first experiments were made on a 16-processor ring connected by RS-232 lines [23, 24]. It turned out that due to the large diameter of the network and the slow transfer rate of 96oo Band it was very difficult to transfer subproblems from one 'side' of the ring to the 'opposite side'. So long idle times for several processors reduced the average speedup for 16 processors to lo resp. 12, depending on the type of intercity distances.

When we had integrated the routines of the Omninet into our Pascal programs (see section 2) every single processor had the power of exchanging messages directly with every other processor in the network. However, since physically the communication runs via a central bus, there may be, invisible to the user, many collisions of message packages. The probability for these collisions (which reduce the throughput) depends on how often and with how many logical neighbors a processor has to talk.

So with the same graph classes and with the same balancing heuristic used in the RS-232 ring we run experiments with five different communication strategies:

S1: use the network as ring; i.e. assign to each processor one logical request neighbor

S2: use the network as ring plus one shortcut; i.e. assign to each processor two logical request neighbors

S 3: use the network as ring plus two shortcuts; i.e. assign to each processor three logical request neighbors

S 4: use the network as clique; i.e. alow each processor to request subproblems from all other processors

S 5: use the network as clique; but allow each processor to request subproblems from only one neighbor (each time randomly chosen among all network processors)

The additional logical links in strategies S2 and S3 were determined such that the resulting (logical) communication graphs had minimal diameter with regard to its degree.

These five strategies reflect a tradeoff between message density and processor availability. As the number of logical neighbors increases so does the number of messages sent across the bus, but at the same time a better "global overview" is supported. This overview allows a fast flow of subproblems between processors to balance the local heaps. It turns out that the five strategies can be ordered with regard to their performance as S1, S4, S3, S2, S5 with average speedups ranging from 11 to 14 resp. from 13 to 15, depending on the intercity distances. Clearly, S1, the ring, is the looser. That S2 outperforms S3 and even S4 (the clique) stems from the fact that two logical request neighbors per processor only cause few communication collisions but can be chosen such that the network of 16 processor has diameter 4. This distance is short enough to keep the heaps balanced with moderate forwarding. An ideal combination of good global overview and low communication density is strategy S5. Here economically reduced requests but sent within the complete network guarantee very well balanced local heaps.

In the report on our experiments with the local area network [25] we also address the issue of fault tolerance. A careful design of the data structure used for the implementation of the heap guarentees that our multiprocessor system is fault tolerant in the sense that it detects and compensates the failure of any of the network nodes except the master node (responsible for input/output). The idea is to mark subproblems in the heap, when they are sent to a processor, with the label of that processor. Later, if it is found out that one or more nodes became faulty, the 'lost' subproblems are reconstructed and recomputed.

4. Alpha-beta-search

Given a search tree with static values assigned to the leaves we have to compute the minimax value of the root. Let us classify the tree nodes, alternating from level to level, beginning with the root, as max-nodes and min-nodes. The root is a max-node, the sons of a max node are min-nodes and the sons of a min-node are max-nodes. Now the value of a max-node is the maximum of the value of its sons, the value of a min-node is the minimum of the value of its sons.

A straight forward procedure to evaluate the search tree would start with the root and recursively explore the sons. However, the subtrees emanating from the brothers of a node X may be skiped due to the information that is available about the value of X and the value of its 'uncle', a brother of its father: If the uncle is a max-node and has larger value than X, then, since X is a min-node, no further improvement for X's father is possible, An analogous consideration holds if the uncle is a min-node.

So, the alpha-beta procedure evaluates the search tree in a depth first order carrying from a node to its sons a window as possible solution range. The initial window for the root is $[-\infty,\infty]$. In the paper of Knuth and Moore [1o] it is shown that under optimal conditions (each node has the sons in a best first order) alpha-beta visits only $2 \cdot b^{d/2}$ terminal nodes (instead of b^d). Here b denotes the number of sons per node and d denotes the number of levels in the tree (not counting the root level).

Several researches have tried to parallelize alpha-beta. Baudet [2] proposes to have several processors search the tree with disjeint starting windows. It can be shown that if the correct minimax value of a tree lies within the initial window, the correct value will be found. Smaller windows accelerate the search, since they allow to cut of certain parts of the tree. Baudet observed that independent of the number of processors used a speedup of more than 6 could not be reached.

Finkel and Fushburn [5] proposed a tree of processors with a fixed fanout per processor onto which the game tree is mapped. A theoretical model predicted a speedup of order k for k processors, provided the game tree fulfills certain conditions. Akl et al. [1] implemented in a simulation language a mandatory-work-first approach. Here unevaluated nodes are given to processors according to a priority that expresses the 'nessessity' of that nodes value to be available now. Finkel and Fishburn [6] showed by a theoretical model that this approach may yield under best first ordering a speedup of order $k^{o.8}$ for k processors. Marsland, Champbell and Popowich [15,16] discuss several enhancements to alpha-beta (like transposition tables, killer heuristic, iterative deepening) and report on the implementation of a parallel chess program running on four sun workstations. The average speedup is about 3. An average speedup of 8 has been produced by a parallel chess program that our group implemented on the 16-PC-local-area-network. Since the encoding of a board position together with useful informations related to that position takes about 2ooo Bytes the communication overhead is now more dominant compared to the sending of a few bytes long subtour for the Travelling Salesman.

But the main difficulty in the approaches to parallelize alpha-beta lies in the fact that due to the sequential left-to-right nature of a depth-first search through a game tree informations about the window for a node X are not yet available when this node could be sent for evaluation to an idle processor. So, we have to fight with the following tradeoff: keep processors busy but avoid unneccessary work.

Help may be under way by the new technique SSS* proposed by Stockmann [22] , a breadth-first search through the game tree. Roizen and Pearl [21] have shown that SSS* is asymptotically equivalent to alpha-beta. Champbell and Marsland [3] report an empirical performance studies for several search techniques, applied to several tree types. Especially when the trees have a best first or nearly best-first ordering (which is a realistic assumption since in practice the sons of a node can be ordered according to some heuristic function) SSS* can compete with alpha-beta. But what is more important is the fact that SSS* seems to be more adequate for a parallel implementation. Kumar and Kanal [11] embed the search of a game tree into a general branch-and-bound sceme and propose two parallel versions of SSS*: One along the lines of Baudet [2], processing disjoint windows independently; the other by processing the k sons of the root in k processors and combining their results.

We are thoroughly convinced that SSS* can even be more adapted to a parallel branch-and-bound strategy as it is used for minimizing problems. Our group has started to implement SSS* on 16 PC's connected by a local area network. The main idea is to keep the live subproblems in local lists, sorted according to their bounds (as proposed by Stockman) and keep the costs of the lists balanced. So, instead of having k processors inserting and removing from one global list we distribute the 'main' list among the processors and exchange list items from time to time to guarantee that all list heads have about the same costs. We will report on these implementations in a forthcoming paper.

5. Conclusion

We have discussed approaches to process combinatorial search trees in parallel. It has been shown that the basic principle, namely to send messages between asynchronous processors with local memory is well suited to handle many problems from the area of operations research and artifical intelligence. For an efficient implementation of these algorithms we need besides intelligent software, i.e. problem dependent heuristics, a suitable hardware, i.e. an environment that supports program development and fulfills communication demands. The insights we have gained with our experiments with a local area network of PC's will help us to turn a system of transputers into a powerful parallel architecture. Our first project on such a universal multiprocessor network implements parallel backtracking [26], branch-and-bound and SSS* will follow.

6. Acknowledgements

Ewald Speckenmeyer, a member of our research group, introduced and developed the mathematical model for the superlinear speedup. Several students, among them Rainer Feldmann, Klaus Matuschke, Peter Mysliwietz and Walter Unger were engaged in the installation of our multiprocessor systems and programmed many variants of parallel algorithms. The transputer network used for our ongoing projects was partly financed by the Deutsche Forschungsgemeinschaft.

7. References

[1] S.G. Akl, D.T. Barnard, R. Doran: "Design, Analysis and Implementation of a Parallel Tree Search Algorithm", IEEE Transactions on Pattern Analysis and Machine Intelligence, Vol. PAMI-4, No. 2 (1982) pp.192-2o3

[2] G.M. Baudet: "The Design and Analysis of Algorithms for asynchronous Multiprocessors", Carnegie Mellon University, Technical Report #CMU-CS-78-116, 1978

[3] M.S. Campbell, T.A. Marsland: " A Comparison of Minimax Tree Search Algorithms", Artificial Intelligence 2o (1983), pp. 347-367

[4] E. Felten, S. Karlin S.W. Otto: The Travelling Salesman Problem on a Hypercube, MIMD Computer", Proceedings of the Intern. Conf. on Parallel Processing, 1985, pp. 6-1o

[5] R.A. Finkel, J.P. Fishburn: "Parallelism in Alpha-Beta Search", Artificial Intelligence 19 (1982), pp. 89-1o6

[6] R.A. Finkel, J.P. Fishburn: "Improved Speedup Bounds for Parallel Alpha-Beta Search", IEEE Transactions on Pattern Analysis and Machine Intelligence, Vol. PAMI-5, No. 1, Jan. 1983, pp. 89-92

[7] R. Finkel, U. Manber: "DIB - A Distributed Implementation of Backtracking", Technical Report #588, March 1985 Dept. of Computer Science, University of Wisconsin-Madison

[8] M.R. Garey, D.S. Johnson: "Computers and Intractability: A guide to the theory of NP-completeness (1979), Freeman, San Francisco, Calif.

[9] M. Held, R. Karp: "The Travelling Salemann Problem and Minimum Spanning Trees: Part II" Math. Prog. 1(1971), pp.6-25

[1o] D.E. Knuth, R.W. Moore: "An Analysis of Alpha-Beta Pruning", Artificial Intelligence 6 (1975), pp. 293-326

[11] V. Kumar, L.N. Kanal: "Parallel Branch-and-Bound Formulations for AND/OR Tree Search", IEEE Transactions on Pattern Analysis and Machine Intelligence, Vol. PAMI-6, No. 6, Nov. 1984, pp. 768-778

[12] T.-H. Lai, S. Sahni: "Anomalies in Parallel Branch-and-Bound Algorithms", Communications of the ACM, Vol. 27, No. 6, June 1984, pp. 594-6o2

[13] T.-H. Lai, A. Sprague: "Performance of Parallel Branch-and-Bound Algorithms", Proc. of the 1985 Intern. Conf. on Parallel Processing

[14] T.H. Lai, A. Sprague: "A Note on Anomalies in Parallel Branch-and-Bound Algorithms with one-to-one bounding functions", Information Processing Letters 23 (1986), pp. 119-122

[15] T.A. Marsland, M. Campbell: "Parallel Search of Strongly Ordered Game Trees", Computing Surveys, Vol. 14, No. 4, Dec. 1982, pp. 533-553

[16] T.A. Marsland, F. Popowich: "Parallel Game-Trees Search", IEEE Transactions on Pattern Analysis and Machine Intelligence, Vol. PAMI-7, No. 4, July 1985, pp. 442-452

[17] J. Mohan: "A Study in Parallel Computation: the Travelling Salesman Problem", Technical Report CMU-CS-82-136(R), (1983), Dept. of Computer Science, Carnegie-Mellon University, Pittsburgh

[18] B. Monien, O. Vornberger: "The Ring Machine", Technical Report No. 27, Dec. 1985, Dept. of Computer Science, University of Paderborn, West-Germany, submitted to Computers & Artificial Intelligence

[19] B. Monien, E. Speckenmeyer, O. Vornberger: "Superlinear Speedup for Parallel Backtracking", Technical Report Nr. 3o, July 1986, Dept. of Computer Science, University of Paderborn, West-Germany, submitted for publication

[2o] M. Quinn, N. Deo: "An upper Bound for the Speedup of Parallel Branch-and-Bound Algorithms", Technical Report CS-83-112, May 1983, Computer Science Dept. Washington State University

[21] I. Roizen, J. Pearl: "A Minimax Algorithm Better than Alpha-Beta? Yes and No", Artificial Intelligence 21 (1983), pp. 199-22o

[22] G.C. Stockman: " A Minimax Algorithm better than Alpha-Beta?", Artificial Intelligence 12 (1979), pp. 179-196

[23] O. Vornberger: "Implementing Branch-&-Bound in a Ring of Processors", Technical Report No. 29, Feb. 1986, Dept. of Mathematics & Computer Science, University of Paderborn, short version in: Proceedings of CONPAR 86, Conference on Algorithms and Hardware for Parallel Processing, Aachen 1986

[24] O. Vornberger: "Parallel Computing on Personal Computers", Proceedings of the 1986 ACM SIGSMALL/PC Symposium on small systems, San Francisco, pp. 115-123

[25] O. Vornberger, R. Feldmann, P. Mysliwietz: "A Local Area Network used as a Parallel Architecture", Technical Report No. 31, Sept. 86, Dept. of Mathematics & Computer Science, University of Paderborn

[26] O. Vornberger: "The Personal Supercomputer: A Network of Transputers", Proceedings of the 2nd International Conference on Supercomputing, Santa Clara, USA, May 1987

[27] B.W. Wah, G. Li, Ch.F. Yu: "Multiprocessing of Combinatorial Search Problems", Computer, June 1985, pp 93-1o8

[28] B.W. Wah, Y.W.E. Ma: "MANIP - A Multicomputer Architecture for Solving Combinatorial Extremum-Search Problems", IEEE Transactions on Computers, Vol. C-33, No. 5, May 1984, pp. 377-39o

AN O(nlogn) COST PARALLEL ALGORITHM FOR THE SINGLE FUNCTION COARSEST PARTITION PROBLEM (Extended Abstract)

A. Apostolico[1] C.S. Iliopoulos[1] R. Paige[2,3]

ABSTRACT

A CRCW PRAM algorithm is presented for computing the coarsest refinement of a partition of a finite set S of n elements with respect to a function f on S. The algorithm requires $O(n)$ processors, $O(\log n)$ time, and and $O(n \log n)$ space in the worst case.

1. Introduction

We study the complexity (on a parallel computational model) of the "single-function coarsest partition" problem [1]: given a finite set S of n elements, a partition $\pi = \{B_1, B_2, \cdots, B_k\}$ of S, and a function $f: S \rightarrow S$, compute the unique partition $\pi' = \{Q_1, Q_2, \cdots, Q_m\}$ of S that satisfies the following conditions:

(i) π' is a refinement of π; i.e.,

$$\forall Q \in \pi', \exists B \in \pi \mid Q \subseteq B$$

(ii) π' respects the function f; that is,

$$\forall Q_1 \in \pi', \exists Q_2 \in \pi' \mid f[Q_1] \subseteq Q_2$$

(iii) π' is the coarsest partition satisfying conditions (i) and (ii); i.e., it has the fewest number of sets.

We use the computational model known as CRCW PRAM (Concurrent Read-Concurrent Write Parallel RAM). Processors are unit-cost RAM's that can access a common memory. More than one processor can concurrently read-from or write into the same memory location. Writing conflicts are resolved in general in a non-deterministic fashion, i.e., one processor at random succeeds. In one case, however, we will resort to a known technique to emulate a specific deterministic resolution of write conflicts, with no substantial penalty.

We measure the complexity of parallel algorithms by the pair (t, p), where t denotes the time and p the number of processors used by the algorithm; both parameters depend on the size of the input. The product $t \times p$ is said to be the *cost* of the algorithm; the cost of an algorithm is thus the running time of that algorithm on one processor only.

In the literature, several sequential algorithms for the single-function and related partition problems are described. In [9], Paige and Tarjan give an $O(n)$ optimal algorithm for the single-function partition problem improving the worst-case complexity bounds for the same problem given by Aho, Hopcroft and Ullman in [1]. Earlier, Hopcroft in [5] gives an $O(n \log n)$ algorithm for the many functions coarsest partition problem; i.e., the partition is required to respect a set of functions $f_1, \cdots, f_k$; Paige and Tarjan in [10] give an $O(m \log n)$ algorithm for the relational partitioning problem; i.e., the refinement should respect a binary relation with m pairs. In this paper we will only consider the single function coarsest partition problem.

In [6] an algorithm on a CRCW PRAM for computing the coarsest refinement of a partition of a set S with respect to a function f is presented; it requires $O(\log n)$ time and $O(n^2)$ processors. A modified version of this algorithm reduces the cost to $O(n^2)$, where the time is $O(n^x)$ for some $0 < x < 1$. Ja'Ja' and Kosaraju [8] recently claimed a PRAM solution that runs in $O(\log^2 n)$ time with $O(n)$ processors. In this paper we present an algorithm that requires $O(\log n)$ time, $O(n \log n)$ space, and $O(n)$ processors, which improves the bound given in [6].

2. Outline of the Algorithm

We refer to the sets belonging to a partition as *blocks*. The *B-label* of an element x in S is said to be the index of the block containing x in the initial partition π. The *Q-label* of an element x in S is said to be the index of the block containing x in the final partition π'. Our algorithm makes use of the following lists (stored in the common memory of the CRCW PRAM):

(i) L_B : $L_B(x)$ is the B-label of element x in S.

(ii) L_Q : $L_Q(x)$ is the Q-label of element x in S.

[1] Purdue University, Dept. of Computer Science, West Lafayette, IN 47907, U.S.A.
[2] New York University, Dept. of Computer Science, New York City, NY 10012, U.S.A.
[3] Part of this work was supported by the Office of Naval Research under Contract No. N00014-84-K-0444.

Our algorithm exploits certain properties of the input function f. In particular, it exploits the following, easy-to-check, features of the *graph of f* (the graph of f is defined in the standard way; see Th. 2.1 below):

(i) Each connected component contains only one cycle with zero or more trees leading into and rooted in the cycle.

(ii) Each tree can be partitioned into two parts - an "initial segment" and a "final segment". A tree node x other than the root is said to be in the *initial segment* if and only if the following two conditions hold: (1) $f(x)$ is the root r or belongs to the initial segment, and (2) x has the same B-label as $f^{-l}(r) \cap C$, where l is the length (i.e., number of edges) of the path from x to r. If x does not belong to the initial segment, then it belongs to the *final segment.*

The criteria used by our algorithm in order to compute Q-labels of the coarsest partition of S are expressed in the following theorem.

Theorem 2.1 (Paige and Tarjan [9])

Let $f: S \rightarrow S$ be a finite function represented by its graph $G = (S,E)$ with nodes S and edges $E = \{ (s, f(s)) : s \in S \}$. Let π be the initial partition of S (represented by B-labels). The Q-labels (representing the coarsest partition π') of the elements of S satisfy the following:

(i) Let C be a cycle of k elements, let x be an arbitrary element of C and let P be the *smallest repeating prefix* (s.r.p.) of the string $[L_B(x), L_B(f(x)), L_B(f^2(x)), \cdots, L_B(f^{k-1}(x))]$. (The s.r.p. of a string α is the shortest string β such that $\alpha = \beta^k$ with $k \geq 1$.) Then the elements of C satisfy

$$L_Q(f^j(x)) = L_Q(f^{i|P|+j}(x)), \quad 0 \leq j < |P|, \quad 1 \leq i \leq (k / |P|) - 1$$

where $|P|$ is the length of P.

(ii) Two elements x and y of S that belong to two different cycles C_1 and C_2 satisfy

$$L_Q(f^j(x)) = L_Q(f^j(y)), \quad j=0,1,...$$

if and only if the two strings

$$[L_B(x), L_B(f(x)), \cdots, L_B(f^{k_1-1}(x))] \text{ and } [L_B(y), L_B(f(y)), \cdots, L_B(f^{k_2-1}(x))],$$

where k_1, k_2 are the lengths of C_1 and C_2, respectively, have identical s.r.p.'s.

(iii) Each element u belonging to the initial segment of a tree leading to a cycle C satisfies

$$L_Q(u) = L_Q(f^{-l}(r) \cap C)$$

where r is the root of that tree and l is the length of the path from u to the root.

(iv) If x and y are elements of the "final segment" then

$$L_Q(x) = L_Q(y) \text{ iff } L_B(x) = L_B(y) \text{ and } L_Q(f(x)) = L_Q(f(y))$$

□

Based on the above criteria, our parallel algorithm (like the sequential algorithm in [9]) proceeds in the following way.

1) Find the set of cycles.
2) Determine the Q-labels for the cycle elements by first finding the s.r.p.'s of the least lexicographic representations (l.l.r. in the following) of the B-labels of each cycle, and then sorting lexicographically such s.r.p.'s.
3) Determine the Q-labels for the tree elements of the initial segments.
4) Determine the Q-labels for the tree elements of the final segments.

3. Finding the Set of Cycles and Labeling the Cycle Elements

All the cycles can be found in $O(\log n)$ time with $O(n)$ processors and $O(n)$ space on a CRCW PRAM using Tarjan and Vishkin's biconnected component algorithm [12]. The stages for labeling the elements of the cycles are as follows:

2.1) Compute the l.l.r. of the circular string $(L_B(x), L_B(f(x)), \cdots, L_B(f^{|C|-1}(x)))$ for each cycle C. (We recall, incidentally, that there are $O(n)$ sequential algorithms for this problem; see, in particular, [11].)

2.2) **Compute the s.r.p. of every l.l.r. obtained in stage 2.1, using, for instance, Galil's parallel string matching algorithm [4].**

2.3) Assign Q-labels to every element of the cycles, according to the properties (i) and (ii) of Theorem 2.1

Lemma 3.1

There is a CRCW PRAM algorithm that finds the l.l.r. of a circular string $\alpha = a_1 a_2 ... a_{|\alpha|}$ over the alphabet $\{1,...,m\}$ in $O(\log|\alpha|)$ time using $|\alpha|$ processors and $O(|\alpha|)$ space.

Proof outline.

Below we describe the algorithm using a stronger version of the CRCW PRAM: when more than one processor attempt to write in the same memory location the one with the smallest index (i.e., serial number) succeeds. In this specific application, it can be show that the CRCW PRAM with nondeterministic resolution of concurrent write conflicts can emulate the stronger version in constant time. Such an equivalence is shown in [3] (see also [4]). In general, the equivalence of the two models is an open problem.

W.l.o.g. we assume that $|\alpha|$ is a power of 2. Through $\log|\alpha|$ stages, our algorithm maintains a partition of α into consecutive blocks of uniform size, with the property that, for each block, all but one of the positions of α in that block have been ruled out as possible starting positions of the l.l.r. of α. The size of the blocks doubles at each stage. More formally, the operation of the algorithm is as follows.

2.2) Let $\beta = b_1 b_2 ... b_{2|\alpha|} = \alpha\alpha$. Assign processor p_i to character b_i ($=a_i$) for $1 \le i \le |\alpha|$. We make use of an $1 \times |\alpha|$ array AUX (initialized to 1). At the outset, i is the starting position of a l.l.r. of α iff still $AUX(i) = 1$.

2.3) For $k = 1, \ldots, \log|\alpha|$ all alternate pairs of consecutive blocks of size 2^{k-1} are considered in parallel. Within the generic such pair, let i and $j>i$ be the positions of β such that currently $AUX(i) = AUX(j) = 1$. (There are precisely two such positions in the pair, one per block.) The 2^k processors assigned to the pair compare now (lexicographically) the substrings of β: $\gamma = (b_i ... b_{i+2^k-1})$ and $\delta = (b_j ... b_{j+2^k-1})$. This is done in two substeps: first, each processor performs one character comparison, and then all processors which detected mismatches attempt to write their outcome in a preassigned common memory location. The processor with smallest index succeeds. The outcome obtained by this processor is also the outcome of the lexicographic comparison of γ and δ. If now $\gamma > \delta$, then set $AUX(j) = 0$; otherwise set $AUX(i) = 0$.

The action of the algorithm is clearly correct in all cases where $\gamma > \delta$ or $\gamma < \delta$. More interestingly, it can be shown that when $\gamma = \delta$ then j can be safely discarded as a candidate starting position of the l.l.r. of α. To see this, observe first that, if $\gamma = \delta$, then γ and δ are overlapping occurrences of the same string. Let θ be the longest substring of β having starting positions both at i and j. If $|\theta| \ge |\alpha|$, then $\alpha = (\tau)^l$, with $|\tau| = j-i$ and $l \ge 2$. In this case each starting position of τ in the circular string α is also the starting position of a l.l.r. of α, and the algorithm would not fail in choosing i. Otherwise ($|\theta| < |\alpha|$) there are two strings σ and τ, with τ nonempty, such that $\theta = (\sigma\tau)^l \sigma$, with $|\sigma\tau| = j-i$ and $l \ge 1$. Let then θb and $\theta b'$ be the substrings of β of length $|\theta|+1$ starting at i and j, respectively. Hence b is also the first character of τ. Assume for a contradiction that j is the starting position of a l.l.r. of α. Then $b' < b$. But then there are substrings of β that start at $i + |\theta|$ and have prefix $\sigma b'$. Each such substring is lexicographically smaller than θ.

The comparison of each pair of strings, inclusive of the emulation in [3], takes constant time. The overall time complexity follows then immediately. □

Theorem 3.1

Let f represent a permutation of the n elements of set S. There is a CRCW PRAM algorithm for computing the coarsest refinement of a partition π with respect to the function f in $O(\log n)$ time, $O(n)$ space, and with n processors.

Proof.

We append the following to the construction of Lemma 3.1.

2.2) Let α be a l.l.r. of a cycle and let $\beta = \alpha\alpha$. Using, say, Galil's algorithm in [4] we find the second occurrence of α in β; let γ be the shortest nonempty string such that $\beta = \gamma\alpha\delta$. It is not difficult to see (refer, for example, to [9]) that γ is the smallest repeating prefix of α. This step can be done ([4]) in $O(\log|\alpha|)$ time using $|\alpha|$ processors. Therefore the computation of all s.r.p.'s can be done in $O(\log n)$ time using n processors.

2.3) In order to assign the Q-labels to the cycle elements, it suffices to compute all the different equivalence classes represented by the s.r.p.'s. This computation can be done in $O(\log n)$ time using n processors, as follows. The comparison of two strings can be done in constant time as in Lemma 3.1 with a number of processors equal to the sum of the lengths of the two strings. Therefore one can use the sorting algorithm in [2] to sort the list of the strings: each key comparison of the algorithm in [1] is simulated through a suitable set of concurrent character comparisons. (The outcome of each string comparison is assessed through the emulation of deterministic resolution of concurrent writes already mentioned in connection with Lemma 3.1.) Alternatively, one could partition the set of input strings into subsets of strings of equal length, and then use the lexicographic sorting in [7]. □

4. Labeling the Tree Elements

We address now the computation of the Q-labels for the tree elements. We begin by presenting the procedure LABEL, a parallel paradigm which can be adapted in particular to compute the length of the path from each tree element to the root. In conjunction with a second adaptation of LABEL, this will enable us to compute the Q-labels of the initial segments. The problem of computing the Q-labels on the final segments will be addressed last.

4.1. Computing Path Labels

Let the label $L(x) \in \{0, 1\}$ be given for each node x of a tree and let $\oplus$ be an associative and commutative, but otherwise unspecified operation over $\{0, 1\}$. The *label* of a path $(x_1 = x, x_2, \cdots, x_k = y)$ from x to y is said to be

$$L(x_1) \oplus L(x_2) \oplus \cdots \oplus L(x_k)$$

If $\oplus$ is interpreted as ordinary addition, and we assume $L(x) = 1$ for every x in the tree T, then the label of a path is the standard length of that path plus one. Later, we will also need a procedure that splits a path $(x_1, \cdots, x_t)$ into two subpaths $(x_1, \cdots, x_k)$ and $(x_{k+1}, \cdots, x_t)$, where x_{k+1} is the first node in the path that has a certain property. This can be done by first labeling with 0 (resp., 1) the nodes having (resp., not having) the given property, and then by assigning $\oplus$-labels to the paths with $\oplus$ the logical *and* (hereafter denoted &).

Given a tree with a set of nodes T (excluding the root r) together with a set of labels L, and an operation $\oplus$, the following procedure computes the labels of all paths from every node to the root.

```
Procedure LABEL (T, BB, L, r)
begin
  for each node x in T pardo
      next (x) ← f (x);
      L⊕(x) ← L(x);
  odpar
end
  repeat
    for each node x in T pardo
       if next (x) ≠ r then
            L⊕(x) ← L⊕(x) ⊕ L⊕(next (x));
            next (x) ← next (next (x));
    odpar
  until next (x) = r for all x
end
```

The procedure LABEL clearly requires $O(\log |T|)$ time, $O(|T|)$ space, and $O(|T|)$ processors in terms of the number $|T|$ of nodes of the input tree T.

4.2. Separating and Labeling the Initial Segments.

The separation and labeling of the initial segments requires the following.

3.1) For every tree and for every node of the tree compute in parallel the length l of the path from that node to the root of the tree. This is achieved simply by invoking the procedure LABEL with $\oplus$ specified as ordinary addition.

3.2) For each tree element x such that the B-label of x is different from the B-label of the l-th cycle-predecessor of the root, disconnect node x from its parent node $f(x)$. Tree elements that remain connected to a cycle belong to initial segments, while the other tree elements belong to final segments.

3.3) The Q-label of an element x in an initial tree segment and on a path of length l to the root r of that tree can now be set equal to the Q-label of the l-th cycle-predecessor of the root of the tree.

The procedure SPLIT given below splits a tree T into its initial segment and its final segment. SPLIT invokes the procedure LABEL once to compute path lengths and once to detect the elements of the initial segment. In this second case the $\oplus$-operation is logical & and the initial node labels are assigned in the following way:

$$L(x) = \begin{cases} 1 & \text{if } L_B(x) = L_B(f^{-l}(r) \cap C) \\ 0 & \text{otherwise} \end{cases}$$

Thus if the path label of a path from x to r is zero, then x belongs to the final segment; if the label is 1, then x belongs to initial segment. It is assumed that $f^{-l}(r) \cap C$ can be accessed in constant time for any value of l. A suitable precomputed table (only one such table per cycle can serve all roots on that cycle) enables to retrieve the desired f-values through trivial constant time manipulations. The details of such a preprocessing are tedious but straightforward, and they do not affect the bounds of our construction.

Procedure SPLIT

INPUT: A tree T with root r, and a cycle C ($f^i(r)$, $1 \le i \le k$, are the elements of the cycle) together with the list L_B and the values of L_Q on C.

OUTPUT: The elements of the initial segment with their Q-labels

begin

$L_+ \leftarrow$ LABEL(T, +, L, r)

for each element x in T **pardo**

$l \leftarrow L_+(x) \bmod k$;

if $L_B(x) = L_B(f^{-l}(r) \cap C)$ **then** $L(x) \leftarrow 1$;

else $L(x) \leftarrow 0$;

odpar

$L_\& \leftarrow$ LABEL(T, &, L, r)

for each element x in T **pardo**

if $L_\&(x) = 1$ **then** $L_Q(x) \leftarrow L_Q(f^{-l}(r) \cap C)$;

odpar

The procedure SPLIT separates the initial segment of the tree T and computes the Q-labels of its nodes in $O(\log |T|)$ time, $O(|T|)$ space, and with $O(|T|)$ processors. Thus we can list the following

Theorem 4.1

There is a CRCW PRAM algorithm that separates the elements in the initial segments and assigns Q-labels to them in $O(\log n)$ time using linear space and number of processors. □

4.3. Computing the Labels of the Final Segment.

We compute the labeling of the final segments as follows:

4.1) Let R denote the subset of S that already has known Q-labels and assume that the final segment F is connected to R. We begin by partitioning the set F into blocks in such a way that two elements of F belong to the same block if and only if the lengths of the paths from each element to the closest element of the initial segment are the same.

4.2) Next we refine the above partition with respect to the B-labels, i.e., we split each block into sets with the same B-label.

4.3) Finally, we refine each partition π_i, by grouping in the same subpartition all elements whose parents have the same Q-label. We make use of a "partial-sum tree" to carry out this task.

A more detailed description of the steps that lead to labeling the final segment is as follows.

a) Compute the sets

$$P_l := \{x: \text{there is a path of length } l \text{ from } x \text{ to } R\} \quad 1 \le l \le t.$$

where t is the largest value attained by the path lengths.

b) Partition each set P_l into blocks $B_1^{(l)}, \cdots, B_{l_l}^{(l)}$, where $B_j^{(l)}$ contains all elements of P_l with the same B-label.

c) Compute a refinement $\pi_1 = \{A_1, \cdots, A_k\}$ of $\{B_1^{(l)}, \cdots, B_{l_l}^{(l)}\}$ such that

$$L_Q(f(x)) = L_Q(f(y)), \; x, y \in A_i \quad 1 \le i \le k.$$

i.e., all elements of A_i, $1 \le i \le k$, have parents with the same Q-label (note that such parents are in R and their Q-labels are assumed to be known). Moreover let

$$\pi_l = \{B_1^{(l)}, \ldots, B_{l_l}^{(l)}\}, \quad 2 \le l \le t.$$

d) Each partition π_l is associated with a set

$$M_l = \{a \in \pi_l : f^{-1}(a) = \emptyset\}$$

i.e., the set of leaves in π_l.

e) **Recursively construct a balanced binary tree with leaves $\pi_1, \pi_2, \cdots, \pi_t$ as follows:**

The parent of two partitions of π_l and π_{l+1} is defined to be the coarsest refinement $\pi_{l,l+1} = \{G_1, \cdots, G_m\}$ of π_{l+1} such that

$$f^y(G_i) \subseteq B_{j_i}^{(l)}, \quad \text{for some } j_i, 1 \le i \le m$$

where y denotes the length from $\pi_{l,l+1}$ to the leaves. i.e., *the f-image of G_i, $1 \le i \le m$, is a subset of a block of π_l. Also we associate the partition $\pi_{l,l+1}$ with the set $M_{l,l+1} = M_{l+1}$.*

f) Update the nodes of the tree, starting from the root, going towards the leaves as follows:

Replace the partition π_l (child of $\pi_{l,l+1}$) by the coarsest refinement $\pi_l' = \{E_1, E_2, \cdots, E_r\}$ of π_l such that E_i is a subset of a block of the partition π_l whose preimage lies in a block of $\pi_{l,l+1}$ i.e.,

$$E_i - (E_i \cap M_l) \subseteq f^y(G_{j_i}), \text{ for some } j_i \quad 1 \le i \le r$$

Also replace π_{l+1} by its parent $\pi_{l,l+1}$.

g) Let $S' = \bigcup_{l=1}^{t} M_l = S - f(S)$ .Then compute the coarsest refinement of π_l, for $1 \le l \le t$, in the following way :

Partition $E_i \cap M_l$ for $1 \le l \le t$ and every block of each π_l into $\{X_1, X_2, \cdots, X_m, Y\}$ where

$$L_Q(f^l(z)) = L_Q(f^l(w)), \ \forall\, z, w \in X_i, \ 1 \le i \le m+1$$

and $X_{m+1} = D_i \cup Y$ (note that Y could be empty or $m = 0$).

Theorem 4.4

Suppose that $\pi' = \bigcup_{l=1}^{t} \pi_l$ is the partition of the final segment computed above. Then

$$L_Q(f^l(a)) = L_Q(f^l(b)) \tag{4.1}$$

for any pair (a,b) of members of a block of π_l, $1 \le l \le t$.

Proof outline.

The proof is by induction of l. For $l = 1$, partition π_1 satisfies condition (4.1). Now assert that (4.1) holds for $l \le r+1$. We shall show that π_{l+2} satisfies (4.1).

Let us consider the following portion of the binary tree constructed above.

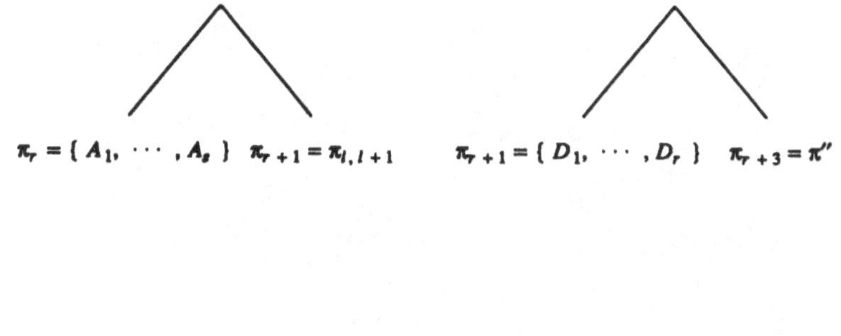

Rule (e) above guarantees that

$$f^2(H_i) \subseteq G_{j_i}, \text{ for some } j_i, 1 \le i \le q. \tag{4.2}$$

Also, Rule (f) implies that

$$D_i - (D_i \cap M_{r+2}) \subseteq f(H_{v_i}), \text{ for some } v_i, 1 \le i \le v. \tag{4.3}$$

From (4.2) and (4.3) it follows that

$$f^{r+2}(D_i - (D_i \cap M_{r+2}) \subseteq f^{r+3}(H_{v_i}) \subseteq f^{r+1}(G_{j_{v_i}})$$

which implies that (4.1) holds for $D_i - (D_i \cap M_l)$. Moreover, Rule (g) implies that $D_i \cap M_l$ satisfies (4.1). □

Theorem 4.5

There exists an algorithm for computing the Q-labels of the final segment in $O(\log n)$ time using $O(n)$ processors and $O(n \log n)$ space.□

5. REFERENCES

[1] Aho, A.V., J.E. Hopcroft and J.D. Ullman, *The Design and Analysis of Computer Algorithms*, Addison-Wesley, Reading, MA, 1974.

[2] Cole, R., *Parallel merge sort*, Proceedings of the 27-th IEEE Symp. on Foundations of Computer Science, Toronto, Canada, pp. 511-516 (1986).

[3] Fitch, F.E., R. L. Radge and A. Wigderson, *Relation between concurrent-write models of parallel computation, typescript*, Div of Comp. Science, Univ. of California at Berkeley, 1983.

[4] Galil, Z., *Optimal parallel algorithms for string matching*, Proc. 16-th ACM Symp. on Theory of Computing, pp. 240-248, 1984.

[5] Hopcroft, J.E., *An nlogn algorithm for minimizing states in a finite automaton*, in: Kohavi and Paz, ed., Theory of Machines and Computations, Academic Press, NY, pp. 189–196, 1971.

[6] Iliopoulos, C.S., *A logarithmic time parallel algorithm for partitioning*, Purdue University, CSD-TR-603, 1986.

[7] Iliopoulos,C.S., *A log-time parallel algorithm for lexicographical ordering* Purdue University, CSD-TR-602, 1986.

[8] Kosaraju, S.R., *personal communication*, 1987.

[9] Paige, R., R. Tarjan and R. Bonic, *A linear time solution to the single function coarsest partition problem*, Theoretical Computer Science 40, pp. 67–84, 1985.

[10] Paige, R. and R. Tarjan, *Three efficient algorithms based on partition refinement*, to appear in SIAM J. Computing.

[11] Shiloach, Y., *Fast canonization of circular strings* J. Algorithms 2, pp. 107-121, 1981.

[12] Tarjan, R. and U. Vishkin, *An efficient parallel biconnectivity algorithm*, SIAM J. Comput. 14, pp. 862-874, 1985.

SYSTOLIC ALGORITHMS FOR COMPUTING THE VISIBILITY POLYGON AND TRIANGULATION OF A POLYGONAL REGION

Tetsuo Asano(†) and Hiroshi Umeo(†)

Abstract

This paper first presents a naive systolic algorithm for finding a closest point for each of n given points in linear time. Then, based on the algorithm, we propose linear time systolic algorithms for computing the visibility polygon and for trapezoidal partition or triangulation of a polygonal region which may contain holes. The visibility problem among n vertical line segments in the plane is also solved.

1. Introduction

Computational geometry [4, 18, 21] is a growing field in computer science in which a number of results are being produced every year. Many geometric problems have been shown to require at least O(n log n) time in the worst case where n is the input size (for example, the number of points) if we use a sequential machine. On the other hand, a rich variety of parallel computational models have been proposed to speed up the running time on conventional machines. Very recently much attention has been paid to the study and development of parallel computational geometry algorithms. For instance, parallel geometry algorithms were presented in [1] on the concurrent-read/exclusive-write(CREW) model of computation. Chazelle[10] used one-dimensional systolic arrays to obtain linear-time algorithms for solving several geometric problems including dynamic versions of convex hulls and triangulation of the plane with n given points. A similar model was adopted by Kane and Sahni[13-14] who designed systolic arrays for design rule check of LSIs. Umeo and Asano[24] gave a survey of recent studies on systolic computational algorithms.

In this paper we also use one-dimensional systolic arrays to solve several geometric problems listed in ABSTRACT in linear-time. In our approach we make a supplementary use of the systolic arrays. In other words, we don't try to solve the whole problem by systolic arrays but try to use them in reducing the time complexity in difficult parts as one of the hardware equipments in conventional machines[9].

2. General principle

In this section we describe a general principle for systolic algorithms presented in this paper by solving a closest point pair problem as an example. The problem is to find a closest point for each of n given points in d-space. We assume the following systolic array model, shown in Fig.1, consisting of a host computer and a linear array

---

(†) Osaka Electro-Communication University, Neyagawa-shi, Hatsu-cho 18-8, Osaka, 572, Japan. The second author, H. Umeo, stays as an Alexander-von-Humboldt researcher('87, 3/1 to '88, 3/31) at Institut fur Theoret. Informatik, Techn. Universitat Braunschweig, Gaussstrasse 11, D-3300, Braunschweig, West Germany.

of systolic cells. The machine works as a controller of the array.

The systolic array must include at least O(n) processing elements(PE's) to solve geometric problems of size n. Each PE can communicate with its neighbouring PE's. The communication links with the outside are located at the left end of the array. This is the specification of the system common to all the algorithms presented in this paper. For details of the systolic array, consult [2, 15, 16, 19].

The algorithm for computing a closest point for each point using a systolic array is very simple. At the first stage, the host transmits point data consisting of point number and coordinates one by one to the systolic array through the left most PE. Each PE, folding a stream of data over the array, sends the data to its right neighbouring PE.

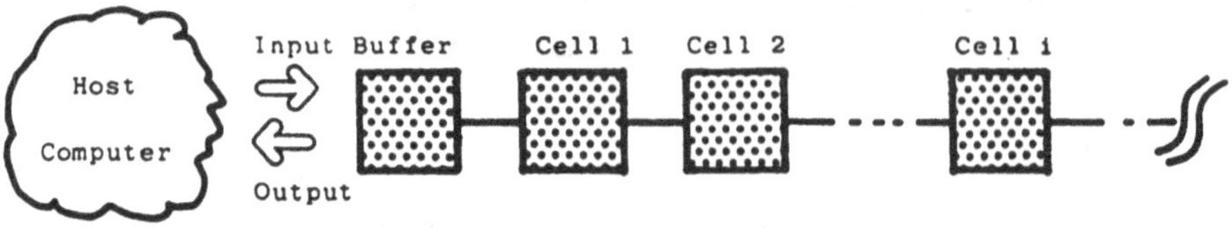

Fig.1 The overall structure of our systolic array.

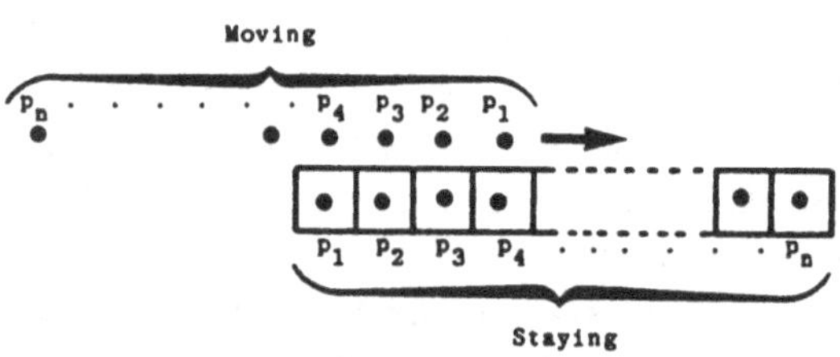

Fig.2(a)

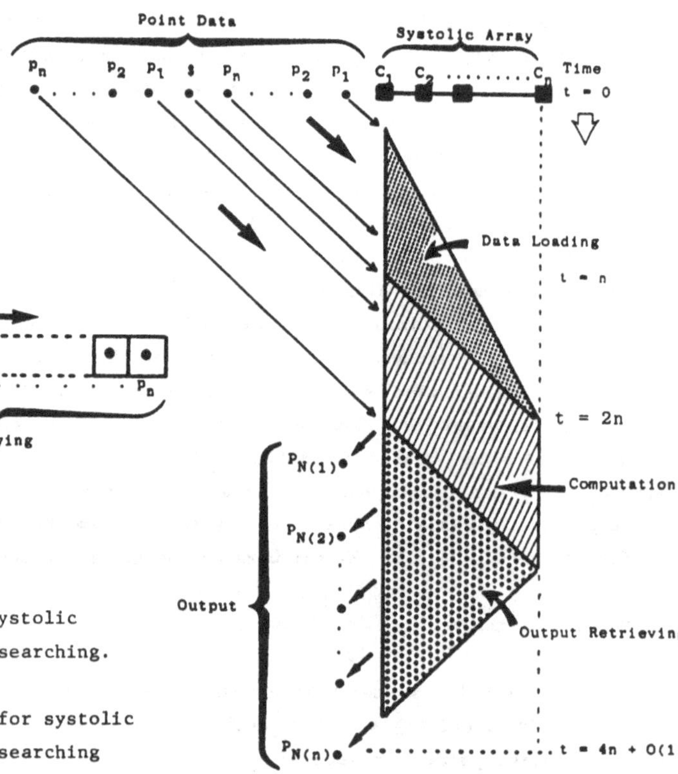

Fig.2(b)

Fig.2(a) Data movement for systolic closest-point-pair searching.

Fig.2(b) Time-space diagram for systolic closest-point-pair searching algorithm.

At the second stage, the host starts transmitting the point data through the left most PE to the array again. Note that every PE has already contained a different point data. This time each PE receives a point data from its left PEat each step, and compute the distance between the point contained in itself and that just transmitted. If the distance is less than the shortest distance computed thus far at this PE, then it is updated by the new one and the point number is stored as the closest point of the point contained in that PE. Of course, we have to skip all the computation when a PE accepts the same point as the one contained in itself. After the computation the transmitted point data is sent to the right neighbouring PE. The second stage terminates when the last point reaches the right most PE. Fig.2(a) shows the data movement on the array.

The last stage begins just after the last point is transmitted. For each PE the last stage starts when it accepts the last point data from its left PE. At that time each PE knows its closest point. Then each PE sends the point number of its closest point together with its own point number to its left PE not to its right. In practice these three stages, that is, initial data loading, computation, and output retrieving stages are pipelined and overlapped in time shown in Fig.2(b). Thus, the host can know all the closest point pairs within $4n + O(1)$ steps.

Summarizing the above systolic algorithm, the first stage is to set a point data at each PE. Then, at the second stage, each PE computes the distance to every other point by transmitting point data again. The third stage is for output. In this paper we present two more systolic algorithms both based on the above three-stage strategy. So all we have to do is to specify what kind of information should be set at each PE at the first stage and what operation should be done at each PE at the second stage.

3. Visibility-polygon search

The visibility-polygon search problem is stated as follows: (Problem): Given a polygonal region with holes in the plane and a point q in its interior, find the portion of the boundary that is visible from q.

This problem is important not only in computer graphics but also in other related problems since it is often used as a subproblem in other geometric problems such as the shortest-path problem in the plane with polygonal obstructions[7]. For this problem two linear time sequential algorithms[11,17] are known for the case of a single simple polygon. In the case of a polygonal region with h disjoint holes, Asano[3] gave an $O(n \log h)$ time sequential algorithm.

The systolic algorithm presented in this paper is based on the following classification of vertices. The types of a vertex are determined by signed area $\nabla P_0P_1P_2 = 1/2 \sum_{i=0}^{2} x(P_i)*(y(P_{i+1(\mathrm{mod}3)}) - y(P_{i+2(\mathrm{mod}3)}))$, where $x(p_i)$ and $y(p_i)$ denote the x- and y-coordinate of P_i, respectively. Note that the signed area is positive if $P_0P_1P_2$ is left turn(or counter-clockwise turn) and negative if right(or clockwise) turn. Especially it is zero if the three points are collinear. We assume that each polygon edge is directed so that its interior lies to the left of the edge. In other words, the boundary of the external polygon is directed in a counter-clockwise way, while that of each hole in a clockwise way.

To determine the type of a vertex v, we compute signed area $\nabla v_{in}vq$, $\nabla vv_{out}q$, and $\nabla v_{in}vv_{out}$, where v_{in} and v_{out} are preceding and succeeding vertices of v, respectively. Then using these quantities, the type of v is classified as in Table 1. Fig. 3 is useful for our understanding of the classification.

Then we have the following lemmas.

[Lemma 1] A vertex v of type 1 or 2 is visible from q if and only if the line segment joining v and q does not intersect any polygon edge except at endpoints that is not collinear with qv.

Type 1:	$\Delta v_{in}vq = 0$, $\Delta vv_{out}q > 0$, and $\Delta v_{in}vv_{out} < 0$,	.....(a)
	$\Delta v_{in}vq < 0$, $\Delta vv_{out}q > 0$, and $\Delta v_{in}vv_{out} < 0$,	.....(b)
	$\Delta v_{in}vq < 0$, $\Delta vv_{out}q = 0$, and $\Delta v_{in}vv_{out} < 0$,	.....(c)
Type 2:	$\Delta v_{in}vq = 0$, $\Delta vv_{out}q < 0$, and $\Delta v_{in}vv_{out} < 0$,	.....(e)
	$\Delta v_{in}vq > 0$, $\Delta vv_{out}q < 0$, and $\Delta v_{in}vv_{out} < 0$,	.....(f)
	$\Delta v_{in}vq > 0$, $\Delta vv_{out}q = 0$, and $\Delta v_{in}vv_{out} < 0$,	.....(g)
Type 3:	$\Delta v_{in}vq > 0$, $\Delta vv_{out}q > 0$, and $\Delta v_{in}vv_{out} < 0$,	.....(h)
	$\Delta v_{in}vq = 0$, $\Delta vv_{out}q > 0$, and $\Delta v_{in}vv_{out} > 0$,	.....(k)
	$\Delta v_{in}vq > 0$, $\Delta vv_{out}q > 0$, and $\Delta v_{in}vv_{out} > 0$,	.....(ℓ)
	$\Delta v_{in}vq > 0$, $\Delta vv_{out}q = 0$, and $\Delta v_{in}vv_{out} > 0$,	.....(m)
Type 4:	$\Delta v_{in}vq < 0$, $\Delta vv_{out}q < 0$, and $\Delta v_{in}vv_{out} < 0$,	.....(d)
	$\Delta v_{in}vq < 0$, $\Delta vv_{out}q = 0$, and $\Delta v_{in}vv_{out} > 0$,	.....(i)
	$\Delta v_{in}vq < 0$, $\Delta vv_{out}q > 0$, and $\Delta v_{in}vv_{out} > 0$,	.....(j)
	$\Delta v_{in}vq > 0$, $\Delta vv_{out}q < 0$, and $\Delta v_{in}vv_{out} > 0$,	.....(n)
	$\Delta v_{in}vq = 0$, $\Delta vv_{out}q < 0$, and $\Delta v_{in}vv_{out} > 0$,	.....(o)
	$\Delta v_{in}vq < 0$, $\Delta vv_{out}q < 0$, and $\Delta v_{in}vv_{out} > 0$,	.....(p)

Table 1 Classification of vertices for visibility-polygon search.

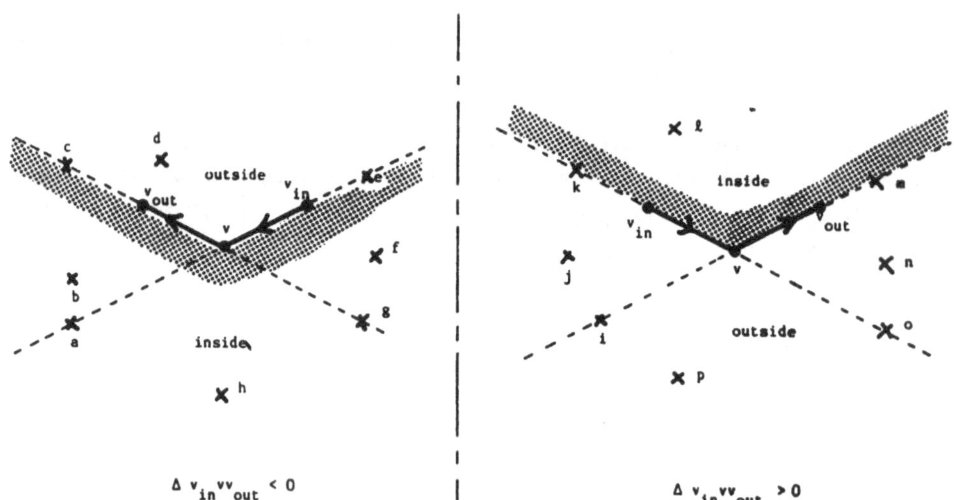

Fig.3 Classification of vertices for visibility-polygon search.

[Lemma 2] If a vertex v of type 1 or 2 is visible from q, the resulting visibility polygon contains the portion of the ray emanating from q toward v, from v to the first intersection with polygon edges including their endpoints.

[Lemma 3] A vertex u of type 3 is visible from q if and only if the line segment between u and q does not intersect any polygon edge.

[Lemma 4] Any vertex of type 4 is not visible from q.

An algorithm follows from the above considerations.

Systolic visibility-polygon search algorithm

[Stage 1] The host transmits vertex data consisting of the type of a vertex and coordinates one by one to the systolic array and sets a vertex data at each PE in the same way as before. The classification of vertices is easily done by a finite state automaton or by O(1) systolic cells within O(1) steps.
[Stage 2] The host transmits polygon edge data to the systolic array. At each PE which contains a vertex v of type 1 or 2, it checks whether the edge intersects the line segment qv and whether it intersects the ray r(v) emanating from v in the direction of qv. If it intersects r(v), it is further examined whether the intersection is near to v than is the intersection found thus far. Each PE containing a vertex v of type 3 checks whether the edge intersects line segment qv. Anyway if the transmitted edge intersects the line segment qv, the type of the vertex is altered as type 4. PE's containing vertices of type 4 only pass the edge data to the right.
[Stage 3] After the second stage terminates, all the visible vertices of types 1, 2, or 3 are sent back to the host. Especially for each vertex v of type 1 or 2, the first intersection of the ray r(v) with the polygon edges is also transmitted.

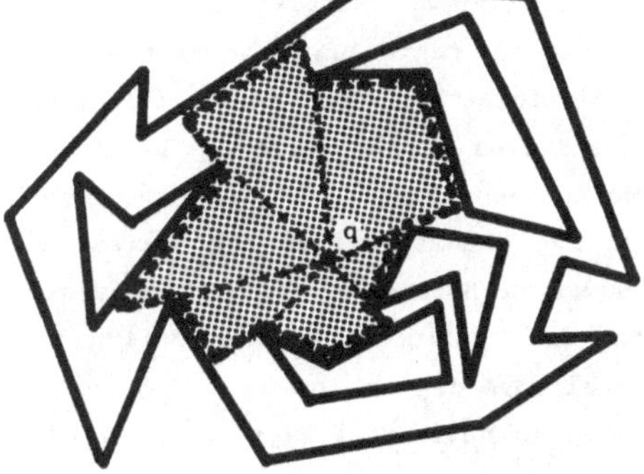

Fig.4 Visibility polygon from a point.

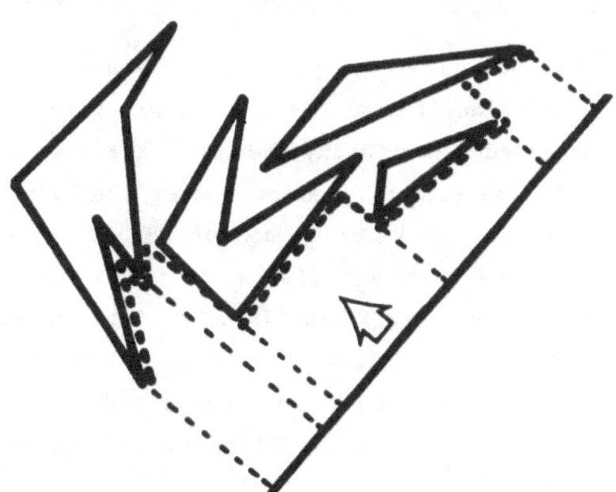

Fig.5 Parallel view.

The above systolic algorithm obtains the set of vertices on the boundary of the visibility polygon from q. Thereafter, by using a systolic priority queue as described in [19], we sort them in the angular order in the polar coordinate system with the origin at q. This is done in linear time. Note that for each vertex v of type 1 or 2 there exists another vertex v' of the same angle, which is the intersection of the above-described ray emanating from the vertex with the nearest polygon edge. We force the order (v', v) if v is of type 1 and (v, v') if type 2. See Fig.4. If there are many vertices collinear with a ray qv for a visible vertex v of type 1 or 2, it may happen that the visibility polygon contains as many duplicated edges, but we can reform it in linear time after the output is completed.

As an application of the systolic algorithm just described, we can devise a similar algorithm for computing a parallel view, which consists of the portion of the objects that are visible from a given direction(See Fig.5). In addition a dynamic maintenance of visibility segments(vertical) can also be implemented on our systolic array, where vertical visibility segment problem was studied by Lodi and Pagli[20] on mesh-of tree-connected machines.

4. Trapezoidal partition of a polygonal region

The next problem we consider is to partition the internal region of a polygonal region with holes into trapezoids with two sides parallel to the axis[5, 6, 22]. The problem arises in applications such as manipulation of VLSI artwork data, image processing, and architectural database. This problem is easily solved if we do not care about minimization of the number of trapezoids. However, it requires O(n log n) time in the worst case since it is reduced to a sorting problem. It is still open whether there exists a linear time sequential algorithm for the case of a single simple polygon. We will show a linear-time systolic trapezoidal partitioning algorithm for a polygonal region with holes.

Systolic trapezoidal partition algorithm

The systolic algorithm to be presented is very simple. What we have to do is to extend a horizontal ray from each vertex to the internal region until a polygon edge is encounted. Concretely speaking, first we set the information about a vertex at each PE, which consists of vertex number, coordinates, and type of the vertex. The type of a vertex is specified by one of LR, L, R, and Null. See. Fig.6. A vertex of type L(R, resp.) is such a vertex v that the horizontal ray emanating from the vertex to the left(right, resp.) goes into the internal region and no horizontal edge is incident to v to the left(right, resp.) of v. If both of the two horizontal rays emanating from a vertex v goes inside the region and no horizontal edge is incident to v, the vertex is classified as type LR. Vertices of type Null have no horizontal rays going inside the region.

At the second stage the host transmits edge data one after another. Each PE computes intersection of the transmitted edge with the horizontal ray(s) determined by the type of the vertex contained in the PE and stores the nearest intersection for each ray. Then, the host retrieves the set of point data which constitute the trpezoidal partition.

Similarly, a rectangular partition of any rectilinear region with some holes can also be done in linear time.

5. Triangulation of a polygonal region

Triangulation of a simple polygon or a polygonal region into triangles by diagonals between vertices has been a central issue in computational geometry problem. Especially it has been open for many years whether a simple polygon can be triangulated in linear time. Very recently Van Wyk and Tarjan[23] got an O(n loglog n) time algorithm. However, it is evident that their algorithm cannot be applied to a polygonal region with holes since it is reduced to the sorting problem[8]. The systolic algorithm to be presented in this paper which triangulates a polygonal region with holes is based on the fact that a monotone polygon can be triangulated in linear time. Recently a similar sequential algorithm was presented by Fournier and Montuno[12]. Thus, what we have to do is to partition a polygonal region into monotone polygons.

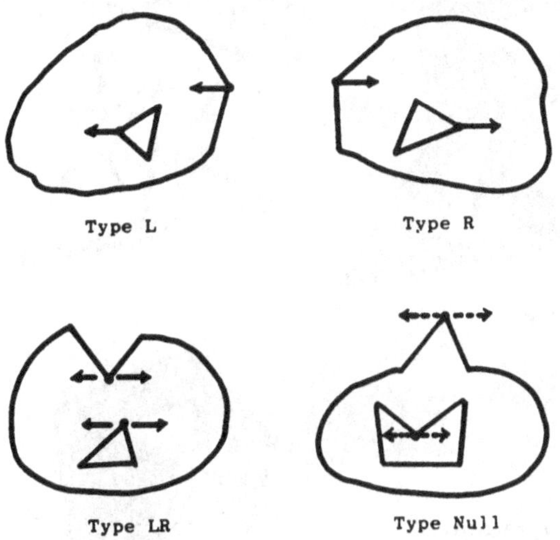

Fig.6 Classification of vertices based on rays toward the interior.

Systolic triangulation algorithm

Our triangulation algorithm is based on the previous trapezoidal partition of a given polygonal region. First of all, we classify vertices into the four types defined in the previous section. Then, using trapezoidal partition algorithm, for each vertex we find the first polygon edge encountered by the ray determined by the type of the vertex. Concretely speaking, for each vertex v of type L or LR(R or LR, resp.), by $e_L(v)$ ($e_R(v)$, resp.) we denote the first polygon edge encountered by the ray emanating from v to the left(to the right, resp.). This definition includes some ambiguity when such a ray encounters an edge just at its endpoint. Suppose that a ray emanating from a vertex u to the left encountered another vertex v. Note that the ray from v to the right encounters u. In this case $e_R(v)$ is not defined while $e_L(u)$ is defined to be the edge among the two ones incident to v that is closer to u when the distance between u and each of them is measured between u and a point on the edge which is some small distance apart. In the next stage each PE in the systolic array outputs tuples $(e_L(v), y(v), v)$ and $(e_R(v), y(v), v)$ if they are defined, where $y(v)$ denotes the y-coordinate of v.

In the last stage we sort these tuples obtained with the edge number as the first key and the y-coordinate as the second key, using again a systolic priority queue proposed by Leiserson[19]. Then, we partition the ordered sequence of those tuples by the first element(edge number). Let $(e_i, y(v_1), v_1), \ldots\ldots, (e_i, y(v_k), v_k)$ be such a subsequence associated with the edge e_i. For this subsequence we define a polygon consisting of the edge e_i and a path determined by a vertex sequence (v_0=the top vertex of the edge e_i, $v_1, v_2, \ldots, v_k, v_{k+1}$ =the bottom vertex of e_i). It is easily seen this polygon is monotone with respect to the edge e_i and that every polygon edge is contained in some monotone polygon. An example is shown in Fig.7.

Fig.7(a)

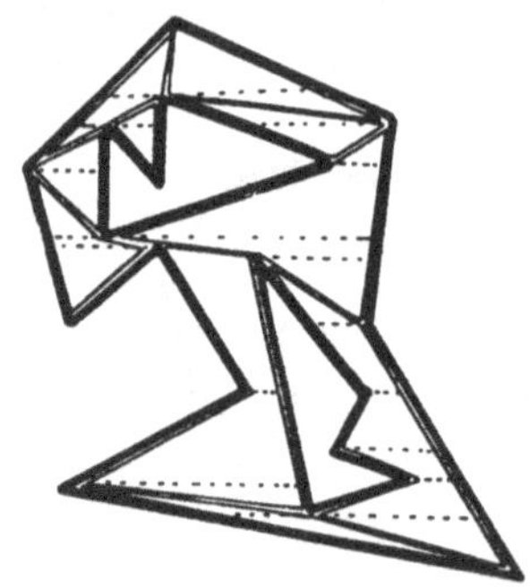

Fig.7(b)

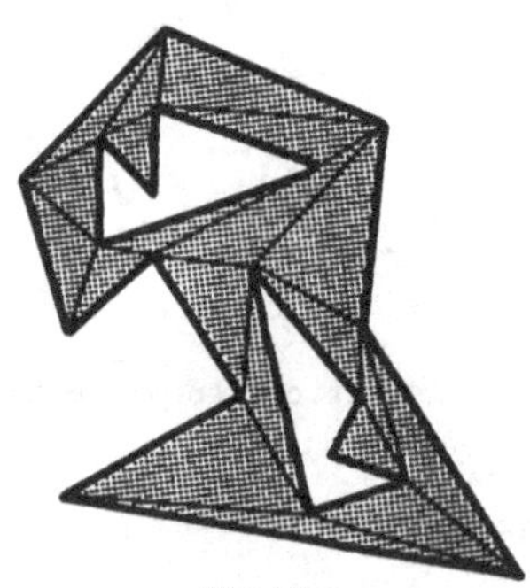

Fig.7(c)

Fig.7(a) A given polygonal region.

Fig.7(b) Decomposition into monotone polygons.

Fig.7(c) Triangulation.

Fig.7 Triangualtion of a polygonal region based on trapezoidal partition.

6. Conclusion

In this paper we have presented systolic algorithms for two fundamental problems in computer graphics: one is to find the visibility polygon from a point in the presence of polygonal obstructions and the other is to triangulate a polygonal region with holes. These two problems are known to require non-linear time complexity on conventional sequential machines. We showed that our systolic algorithms ran in linear time. Since the systolic arrays have reasonably simple architectures[2], implementation of our algorithms in integrated circuits will be easily done.

Acknowledgement

The first author is supported by the Grant-in-Aid(No.61750347) for Scientific Research of the Ministry of Education, Culture and Science of Japan. The second author is pleased to acknowledge the considerable assistance of Prof. Dr. R. Vollmar(Braunschweig Tech. Universitat). He is also supported by the Grant-in-Aid(No.61750346) and by an Alexander-von-Humboldt Fellowship.

References

[1] A. Aggarwal, B. Chazelle, L. Guibas, C. O'Dunlaing, and C. Yap;"Parallel computational geometry", Proc. of the IEEE Conf. on FOCS'85, pp.468-477, (1985).
[2] E. Arnold, H.T. Kung, O. Menzilcioglu and K. Sarocky;"A systolic array computer", Proc. of the IEEE Int. Conf. on Acoustics, Speech, and Signal Processing, pp.232-235, (1985).
[3] Te. Asano;"An efficient algorithm for finding the visibility polygon for a polygonal region with holes", Trans. of IECE of Japan, Vol. E-68, No. 9, pp.557-559, (1985)
[4] Ta. Asano;"Computational geometry and its applications", Joho-Shori, Vol. 25, No. 3, pp.208-221, (in Japanese), (1984).
[5] Te. Asano, Ta. Asano;"Minimum partition of polygonal region into trapezoids", Proc. of IEEE Symp. on FOCS, pp.233-241, (1983).
[6] Ta. Asano, Te. Asano, H. Imai;"Partitioning a polygonal region into trapezoids", to appear in J. of ACM, (1986).
[7] T. Asano, T. Asano, L. Guibas, J. Hersberger, and H. Imai;"Visibility-polygon search and Euclidian shortest paths", Proc. of IEEE Symp. on FOCS, pp.154-164, (1985).
[8] T. Asano, T. Asano, R.Y. Pinter;"Polygon triangulation:Efficiency and minimality", to appear in J. of Algorithms, (1986).
[9] Te. Asano and H. Umeo;"Systolic algorithms for computing the visibility polygon and triangulation of a polygonal region", Tech. Rep. of IECE of Japan, pp.53-60, (1986).
[10] B. Chazelle;"Computational Geometry on a systolic chip", IEEE Trans. on Computers, Vol. C-33, No. 9, pp.774-785, (1984).
[11] H. El Gyndy and D. Avis;"A linear algorithm for computing the visibility polygon from a point", J. of Algorithms, Vol. 2, pp.186-197, (1981).
[12] A. Fournier and D.Y. Montuno;"Triangulating simple polygons and equivalent problems", ACM Trans. on Graphics, Vol. 3, No. 2, pp.153-174, (1984).
[13] R. Kane and S. Sahni;"A systolic design rule checker", Proc. of the IEEE 21st Design Automation Conf., pp.243-250, (1984).
[14] R. Kane and S. Sahni;"Systolic algorithms for functions on rectilinear polygons", Proc. of Int. Symp. on Circuits and Systems, pp.1203-1206, (1985).
[15] H.T. Kung;"Let's dsign algorithms for VLSI systems ", Proc. of the Caltech Conf. on VLSI(C.E. Deitz ed.), pp.55-90, (1979).
[16] H.T. Kung and C.E. Leiserson;"Algorithms for VLSI processor arrays", in Chapter 8 of C.A. Mead and L.A. Conway "Introduction to VLSI Systems", Addison-Wesley, Reading, Massachusetts, (1980).
[17] D. T. Lee;"Visibility of a simple polygon", Computer Vision, Graphics, and Image Processing, Vol. 22, pp.207-221, (1983).
[18] D.T. Lee and F.P. Preparata;"Computational geometry-A survey", IEEE Trans. on Computers, Vol. C-33, No. 12, pp.1072-1101, (1984).
[19] C.E. Leiserson;"Systolic priority queues", Proc. of the Caltech Conf. on VLSI(C.E. Deitz ed.), pp.199-214, (1979).
[20] E. Lodi and L. Pagli;"A VLSI solution to the vertical segment visibility problem", IEEE Trans. on Computers, Vol. C-35, No.10, pp.923-928, (1986).
[21] F.P. Preparata and M.I. Shamos;"Computational geometry, an introduction", Springer-Verlag, New York, p.390, (1985).
[22] M. Sato and T. Ohtsuki;"An algorithm for partitioning polygonal regions in VLSI pattern design", Trans. of Information Processing Society of Japan, Vol. 27, No. 2, pp.269-272, (1986).
[23] R.E. Tarjan and C.J. Van Wyk;"An O(n loglog n)-time algorithm for triangulating simple polygons", Manuscript, (July, 1986).
[24] H. Umeo and Te. Asano;"A survey of recent studies on systolic computational geometry", Tech. Rep. of IECE of Japan, COMP 86-27, pp.83-94, (in Japanese), (1986).

R E L A C S - A RECURSIVE LAYOUT COMPUTING SYSTEM

L. Budach[1], E.G. Giessmann[2], H.Grassmann[2],
B. Graw[1], C. Meinel[1]

In the present the layout design for integrated circuits is in search of new ways of describing and constructing. Many systems of automatic design are in use or under development, since the manual design seems to be slow and ineffective for the requested large scale integration in the future.

The RELACS-System developed at the Humboldt University of Berlin has an other approach. It is not an automatic layout system at all, but it allows an adequate symbolic describtion of regular, hierarchical designs. Such a RELACS-description reflects the structural (Kolmogorov-) complexity of a layout design and is independent of the recursion depth and the description of the atomic elements. Nevertheless the description is short, our system can generate quickly the whole pattern or even arbitrary windows on it. On the other hand it is impossible to refine a placement by RELACS. This job remains to the designer.

While other automatic layout systems like CADIC [1] are based on logical-topological design level, RELACS is more geometrical oriented. The data base for RELACS are patterns of fixed size, i.e. rectangular blocks, length and widths of which are multiples of an elementary length λ. It can be assumed that each pattern is filled with squares of size $\lambda * \lambda$, which come from an external library and have some functional description or a description as a stick-diagram or something else. If the pattern is regular then the number of elementary squares of the pattern should be small.

Beyond this RELACS is dealing with configurations of patterns. Such a configuration represents the topological connections between the patterns composed together like in a picture of Piet Mondrian.

---

[1] Akademie der Wissenschaften der DDR, Institut für Mathematik
DDR - 1086 Berlin, Postfach 1304

[2] Humboldt-Universität zu Berlin, Sektion Mathematik
DDR - 1086 Berlin, Postfach 1297

Definition. A configuration is a spherical graph (V,E), i.e. embedded in $\mathbb{R}^2 \sqcup \{\infty\}$ without crossings, together with a compass c. A compass c assigns to each edge an an incident vertex a direction from $D=\{e,s,w,n\}$, such that for all edges $k=\{v_1,v_2\} \in E$ the set $\{c(k,v_1),c(k,v_2)\}$ is either $\{e,w\}$ or $\{n,s\}$.
In addition to this it is expected that the clockwise ordering of the edges around a vertex induced by the embedding is the usual one, i.e. if D is ordered by $e>s>w>n$ and $k_1, k_2,\ldots,k_r$ is the clockwise ordering of all edges incident with v starting with "east" then $c(k_1,v) \leq c(k_2,v) \leq \ldots \leq c(k_r,v)$.

Of course a single pattern is a 2-vertex configuration with 4 edges.
Configurations can be composed by cutting off the edges around ∞ and glueing them with respect to their directions. Compositions of configurations can be described by sequences of some elementary operations. Operations like the dihedral ones or appending and breaking.
For example appending

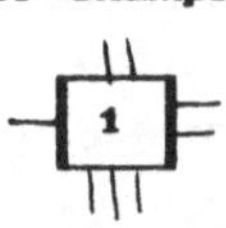

and

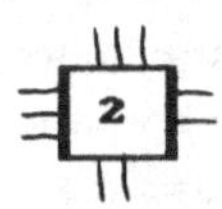

gives

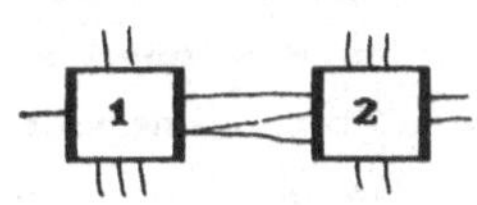

Note that there are many possibilities for glueing the east edges of 1 with the west edges of 2. They arise from the different realisations of the configuration as patterns. For example

corresponds to

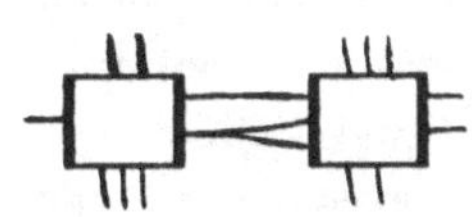

while

corresponds to

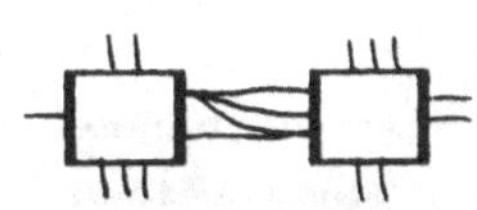

The description of the append operation keeps the indefiniteness.
Another example for an operation is the breaking off. This operation you need for describing a configuration like

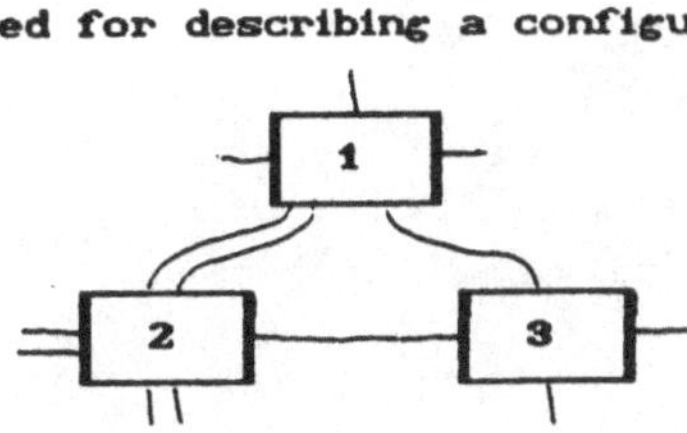

The breaking off gives

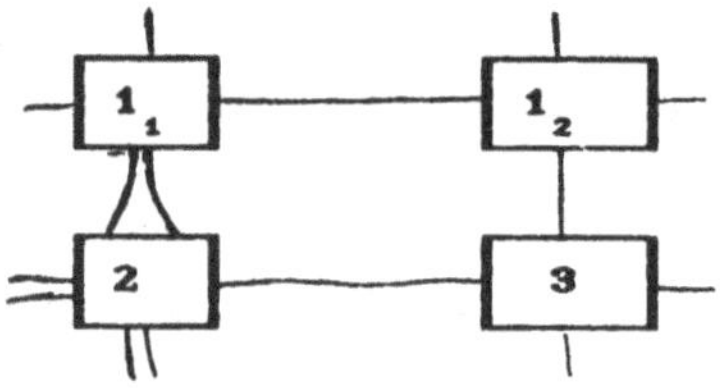

where 3 is an one pattern configuration. Now a breaked configuration can easily be decribed by a sequence of appendings. Further possible operations are the interpretation and the recribing of nodes.

RELACS generates sequences for configurations which are called the polynomial of the configuration.

As soon as polynomials are given, and the 2-vertex configurations are defined one can generate the pattern representing the whole configuration. Obviously such a pattern exists if and only if the lengths and widths of all patterns taking place in the configuration well match. This can be tested by RELACS and if it is good with each appending and breaking is joined the size of the components. Now one can by traversing down from the resulting configuration generate the representing pattern knowing the initial ones annd also arbitrary windows of it.

In different implementations of RELACS in PASCAL and MODULA 2 the procedures reported here are complemented by some modules to help the designer, as an editor and display utilities.

Experiments with standard hierarchical designs as tree-like memory, conditional sum adder or cube-connected cycles show the effectivity of the RELACS-description. The speed of the generation of windows is sufficent, the generation of the whole pattern is of course more time comsuming.

[1] G. Hotz, B. Becker, R. Kolla, P. Molitor "Ein logisch-topologischer Kalkül zur Konstruktion von integrierten Schaltkreisen" Informatik, Forschung und Entwicklung Heft 1, Springer-Verlag Berlin 1986

Parallel linear conflict-free subtree access

Reiner Creutzburg
Academy of Sciences
Central Institute of Cybernetics
and Information Processes
P.O.Box 1298
DDR - 1086 Berlin

1. Introduction

A lot of research work has been done in designing parallel memories to access arrays /1-7/. Trees are another important data structure in computer science /8,9,11/. It is an interesting problem to design parallel memories to access trees /8-10/. We use the terminology given in /11/ to describe a tree. Consider a labelled q-ary tree such that the immediate successors of the node x are qx+1, qx+2,...,qx+q, and the label of the root is 0. The level of a node is defined by initially letting the root be at level 1. The level of every node is one more than the level of its immediate predecessor. The height t of a tree is defined as the maximum level of any node in the tree.

Parallel access to trees means the conflict-free access to all the $(q^t-1)/(q-1)$ nodes of a complete q-ary subtree of height t with an arbitrary node x as root, as shown in figure 1.

In this note the parallel access to subtrees of trees is investigated. Thereby the memory module assignment function is supposed to be linear /9/ in order to simplify the hardware structure of the parallel memory. The results of SHIRAKAWA /8/ till now valid for binary trees are generalized to q-ary trees ($q \geq 1$). Furthermore the node deleting operation is introduced in order to further reduce the number of needed memory modules although nonlinear module assignment functions occur.

2. Special recursively linear module assignment functions

A module assignment function S is a mapping from the set of the labels of a complete q-ary tree to the N memory modules. We denote the set of indices of memory modules by $N = \{0, 1, \ldots, N-1\}$.

A special recursively linear module assignment function S for binary trees was introduced in /8/ by the following recurrence equations

$$\left.\begin{aligned} S(0) &\equiv 0 \\ S(2x+1) &\equiv a\, S(x) + 1 \\ S(2x+2) &\equiv a\, S(x) + 2 \end{aligned}\right\} \bmod N, \qquad (1)$$

where a is an integer with $0 < a < N$.

The following example is illustrative.

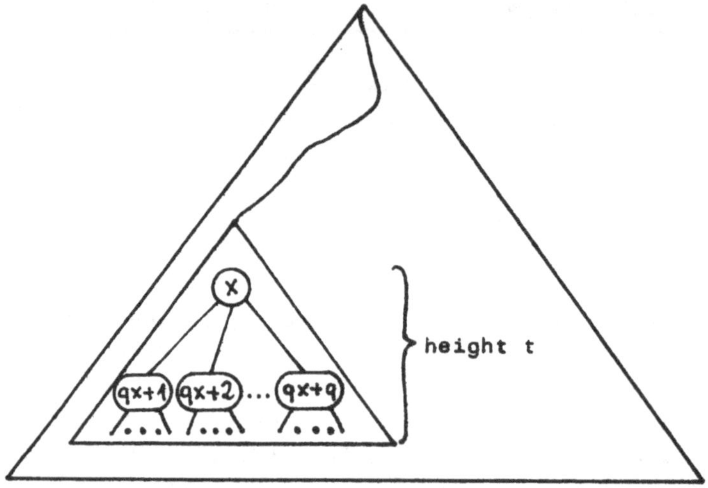

Fig.1 Labelled complete q-ary subtree of height t in a q-ary tree

Example 1. Consider the parallel access to the 7 nodes of an arbitrary complete binary subtree of height 3 in a complete binary tree.
The special recursively linear module assignment function S with

$$\left.\begin{aligned} S(0) &\equiv 0 \\ S(2x+1) &\equiv 2\,S(x)+1 \\ S(2x+2) &\equiv 2\,S(x)+2 \end{aligned}\right\} \bmod 10$$

can be written in the following table form

S(x)	0	1	2	3	4	5	6	7	8	9
S(2x+1)	1	3	5	7	9	1	3	5	7	9
S(2x+2)	2	4	6	8	0	2	4	6	8	0 .

If this function is chosen, then we obtain conflicts (marked with asterix) in the subtree access:

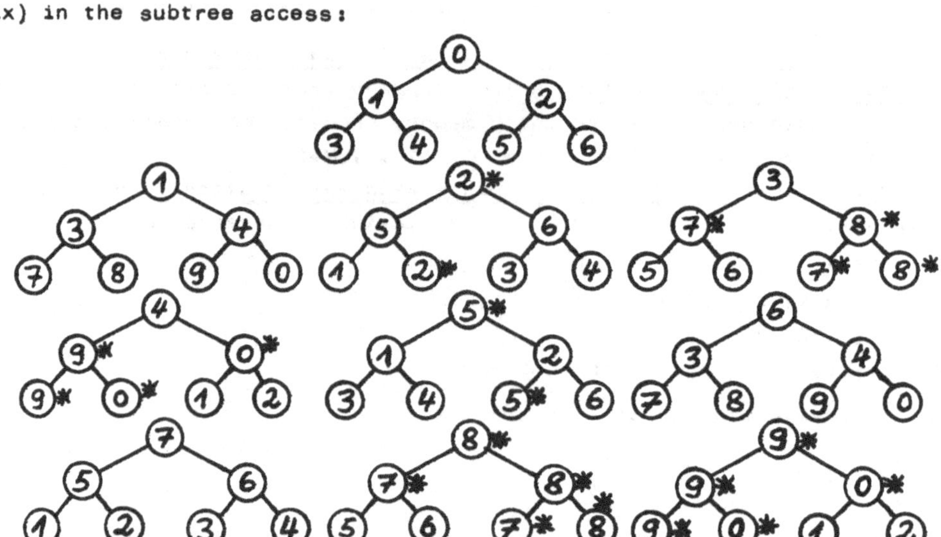

Hence a conflict-free access is impossible for subtrees with roots 2,3,4,5,8 and 9, respectively. If the special recursively linear module assignment function S with

$$\left.\begin{array}{l} S(0) \equiv 0 \\ S(2x+1) \equiv 6\ S(x) + 1 \\ S(2x+2) \equiv 6\ S(x) + 2 \end{array}\right\} \bmod 10 \qquad (2)$$

and in table form

S(x)	0	1	2	3	4	5	6	7	8	9
S(2x+1)	1	7	3	9	5	1	7	3	9	5
S(2x+2)	2	8	4	0	6	2	8	4	0	6

is chosen, then a conflict-free access to all the 7 nodes of an arbitrary complete subtree of height 3 is possible. The relating 10 subtrees are the following:

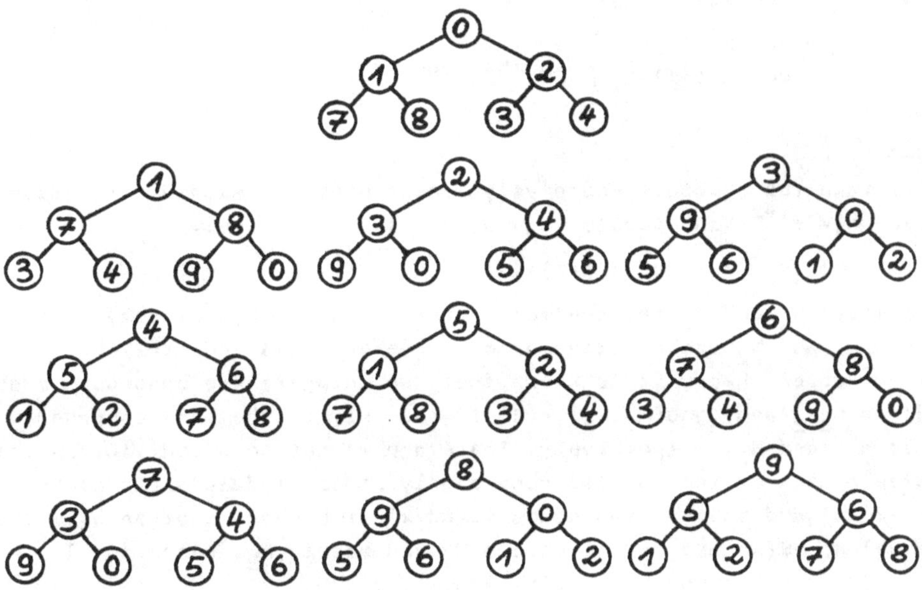

The function (2) was given by SHIRAKAWA /8/.

In order to generalize the results of /8/ to the case of q-ary trees ($q \geq 1$) we investigate in this chapter the special recursively linear module assignment function S with

$$\left.\begin{array}{l} S(0) \equiv 0 \\ S(qx+1) \equiv a\ S(x) + 1 \\ S(qx+2) \equiv a\ S(x) + 2 \\ \quad\vdots \qquad\qquad\quad \vdots \\ S(qx+q) \equiv a\ S(x) + q \end{array}\right\} \bmod N, \qquad (3)$$

where a is an integer with $0 < a < N$.

For the detailed definition of the terms given in this chapter the reader is referred to /9/.

3. Main Theorem

A number-theoretic consideration of the parameters a and N of (1) for the case of complete binary subtree access leads to the following generalization of the results given in /8,10/.

Theorem: A parallel conflictfree access to all the $(q^t-1)/(q-1)$ nodes of an arbitrary complete q-ary subtrees of height t of a q-ary tree with a special recursively linear module assignment function S according to (3) is possible, if the number of memory modules N in (3) is equal to

$$N = q^{t-2}(q(t-1)+1) \qquad (4)$$

and if the parameter a in (2) satisfies the condition

$$a \equiv \begin{cases} 1 \bmod q+1 & \text{in the case } t=2, \\ \left.\begin{matrix} 0 \bmod q \\ 1 \bmod 2q+1 \end{matrix}\right\} & \text{in the case } t=3, \\ \left.\begin{matrix} q \bmod q^{t-2} \\ 1 \bmod q(t-1)+1 \end{matrix}\right\} & \text{in the case } t>3. \end{cases} \qquad (5)$$

Proof.

Let us take the special recursively linear module assignment function S modulo $N_1 = q^{t-2}$ and modulo $N_2 = q(t-1)+1$, respectively

$$S \bmod q^{t-2}; \; S \bmod q(t-1)+1.$$

The numbers N_1 and N_2 are the two factors of N in (3). Clearly, these factors N_1 and N_2 are relative prime for every $q \geq 1$ and $t \geq 2$. From elementary number theory it is known that two integers are congruent modulo N ($N = N_1 N_2$ and $\gcd(N_1, N_2) = 1$) if and only if they are congruent modulo N_1 and N_2, respectively. Therefore we obtain a conflict in the subtree access of the special recursively linear module assignment function (2) if and only if two nodes x and x' of a q-ary subtree have the same values S(x) and S(x') modulo N_1 and modulo N_2, respectively

$$S(x) \equiv S(x') \bmod N_1 \; ; \quad S(x) \equiv S(x') \bmod N_2.$$

The next figure 2 shows that this is impossible under condition (4) for subtrees of height t=3. We consider for example the circled nodes that have the value 1 mod q in the upper part of figure 2. They are located in the lower left corner of every subtree of height 2. Note that also the root can have the value 1 mod q. The relating nodes in the lower part of figure 2 are also circled and have the values S(x), S(x)+1, S(x)+2, S(x)+3,..., S(x)+q+1, respectively. Therefore no conflicts can occur. For the other nodes the same consideration gives similar results.

The proof of our theorem for t=2 is trivial and the proof for $t>3$ is similar to the case t=3 and was given in /12/.

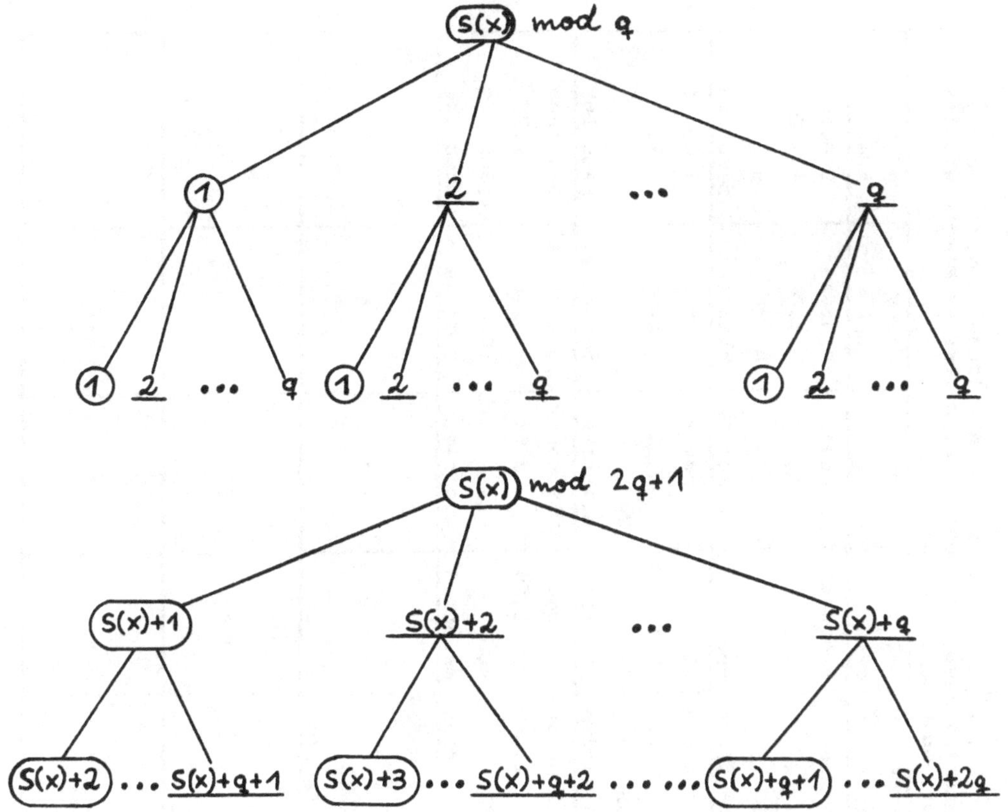

Fig.2 Complete q-ary subtree of height t=3 in the special recursively linear module assignment function taken modulo N_1=q and modulo N_2= 2q+1, respectively.

The table 1 lists a lot of special cases concerning parallel subtree access that can be derived from our theorem. Note that also the ratios of needed numbers of memory modules and accessed nodes are given. The results of SHIRAKAWA are underlined in table 1.

Example 2. From the theorem follows that the parallel conflictfree access to the 21 nodes of an arbitrary complete subquadtree of height 3 is possible with N=36 memory modules. The special recursively linear module assignment function S is

$$\left.\begin{array}{ll} S(0) & \equiv 0 \\ S(4x+1) & \equiv 28\,S(x) + 1 \\ S(4x+2) & \equiv 28\,S(x) + 2 \\ S(4x+3) & \equiv 28\,S(x) + 3 \\ S(4x+4) & \equiv 28\,S(x) + 4 \end{array}\right\} \mod 36.$$

Table 1. List of necessary memory module numbers for parallel, recursively linear complete q-ary subtree access of height t (listed are the number of nodes, the number of memory modules and the ratio of the numbers of memory modules and nodes)

height t	1-ary tree	binary tree	ternary tree	quad-tree	5-ary tree	6-ary tree	7-ary tree	oct-tree
2	2 nodes 1,0 2 memories	3 nodes 1,0 3 memories	4 nodes 1,0 4 memories	5 nodes 1,0 5 memories	6 nodes 1,0 6 memories	7 nodes 1,0 7 memories	8 nodes 1,0 8 memories	9 nodes 1,0 9 memories
3	3 nodes 1,0 3 memories	7 nodes 1,42 10 memories	13 nodes 1,61 21 memories	21 nodes 1,71 36 memories	31 nodes 1,77 55 memories	43 nodes 1,81 78 memories	57 nodes 1,84 105 memories	73 nodes 1,86 136 memories
4	4 nodes 1,0 4 memories	15 nodes 1,87 28 memories	40 nodes 2,25 90 memories	85 nodes 2,44 208 memories	156 nodes 2,56 400 memories	259 nodes 2,64 684 memories	400 nodes 2,69 1078 memories	594 nodes 2,70 1600 memories
5	5 nodes 1,0 5 memories	31 nodes 2,32 72 memories	121 nodes 2,90 351 memories	341 nodes 3,19 1088 memories	...	...	...	...
6	6 nodes 1,0 6 memories	63 nodes 2,79 176 memories	364 nodes 3,56 1296 memories	...	...	...	...	...
7	7 nodes 1,0 7 memories	127 nodes 3,27 416 memories	...	...	...	...	...	...

From (5) we obtain the following periodic table form of S:

S(x)	0	1	2	3	4	5	6	7	8	9	10	11	12	13	14	15	16	17
S(4x+1)	1	29	21	13	5	33	25	17	9	1	29	21	13	5	33	25	17	9
S(4x+2)	2	30	22	14	6	34	26	18	10	2	30	22	14	6	34	26	18	10
S(4x+3)	3	31	23	15	7	35	27	19	11	3	31	23	15	7	35	27	19	11
S(4x+4)	4	32	24	16	8	0	28	20	12	4	32	24	16	8	0	28	20	12

S(x)	18	19	20	21	22	23	24	25	26	27	28	29	30	31	32	33	34	35
S(4x+1)	1	29	21	13	5	33	25	17	9	1	29	21	13	5	33	25	17	9
S(4x+2)	2	30	22	14	6	34	26	18	10	2	30	22	14	6	34	26	18	10
S(4x+3)	3	31	23	15	7	35	27	19	11	3	31	23	15	7	35	27	19	11
S(4x+4)	4	32	24	16	8	0	28	20	12	4	32	24	16	8	0	28	20	12

It is interesting to note that the 31 nodes of an arbitrary binary subtree of height $t=5$ can be accessed with $N=72$ memory modules, but the 31 nodes of an arbitrary 5-ary subtree of height $t=3$ can be accessed with only $N=55$ memory modules (see table 1). This means that a storage in "breadth" is more efficient than a storage in "depth" in general.

4. Node deleting operation

In the previous chapters we have always considered the case of /9/ isotropic complete subtree access. This is a strong assumption and means that every node in (3) has exactly its same successor nodes in the whole infinite tree that can be built up by (3). In order to further reduce the number N of needed memory modules for isotropic complete subtree access, we consider now the method of node deleting. In chapter 2 it was shown that a parallel isotropic subtree access to the 7 nodes of a complete binary subtree of height 3 is possible with a special recursively linear module assignment function (2) and $N=10$ memory modules. In /9/ an isotropic solution with only 9 memory modules was given and it was proved that $N = 9$ is the minimum number of needed memory modules for isotropic access to the 7 nodes of complete binary subtrees of height 3. The relations between these two isotropic solutions can be well described using the node deleting operation. The following example is illustrative.

Example 3. Consider the recursively linear module assignment function (2) in its table form:

S(x)	0	1	2	3	4	5	6	7	8	9
S(2x+1)	1	7	3	9	5	1	7	3	9	5
S(2x+2)	2	8	4	0	6	2	8	4	0	6

.

The nodes which are contained in the memory module 0 are "deleted"

S(x)	~~0~~	1	2	3	4	5	6	7	8	9
S(2x+1)	1	7	3	9	5	1	7	3	9	5
S(2x+2)	2	8	4	~~0~~	6	2	8	4	~~0~~	6

(6)

and the two successor nodes (1 and 2) of 0 are put into the two "holes" (marked by squares). Then the following new conflictfree module assignment function for N = 9 occurs from (6):

S(x)	X	1	2	3	4	5	6	7	8	9
S(2x+1)	•	7	3	9	5	1	7	3	9	5
S(2x+2)	•	8	4	[1]	6	2	8	4	[2]	6 .

(7)

A simple renumbering of (7) gives:

S(x)	0	1	2	3	4	5	6	7	8
S(2x+1)	6	2	8	4	0	6	2	8	4
S(2x+2)	7	3	0	5	1	7	3	1	5 .

Clearly one can try to execute the node deleting operation on the new function again and again in order to further reduce the number of needed memory modules. We found that the number N of memory modules given in (4) can be reduced by 1 in the case t=3 for all q using one times node deleting operation for the node 0. In the case q=2 and t=4 we found isotropic solutions using two times node deleting. In the case q=2 and t=5 we used three times node deleting and obtained isotropic solutions.

Further research and extensive computations are necessary to solve the problem of optimal isotropic subtree access in general. Hopefully this will be done in the future!

References.

/1/ Budnik,P., and D.J. Kuck: The organization and use of parallel memories. IEEE Trans. Comput. C-20 (1971), pp.1566-1569

/2/ Shapiro,H.D.: Theoretical limitations on the use of parallel memories. Univ. Illinois, Dept. Comp. Sci., Rep. No. 75-776 Dec. 1975

/3/ Lawrie,D.H.: Access and alignment in an array processor. IEEE Trans. Comput. C-24 (1975), pp.1145-1155

/4/ Lawrie,D.H., and Ch.R.Vora: The prime memory system for array access. IEEE Trans. Comput. C-31 (1982), pp.435-442

/5/ Rebel,B., and M.Gössel: Ein paralleler Speicher. Report ZKI der AdW, Berlin, Nov. 1982

/6/ Gössel,M., and B.Rebel: Parallel memory with recursive address computation. Proc. Conf. Parallel Computing '83 Berlin (Ed.: M.Feilmeier, Elsevier Sci. Publ. 1984), pp.515-520

/7/ Wijshoff,H.A.G., and J.van Leeuwen: The structure of periodic storage schemes for parallel memories. IEEE Trans. Comput.C-34 (1985), pp.501-505

/8/ Shirakawa,H.: On a parallel memory to access trees. Unpublished manuscript. 1984

/9/ Gössel,M., and B.Rebel: Data structures and parallel memories. Procees. PARCELLA'86 Berlin,Akademie-Verlag Berlin 1986, (Eds.:T.Legendi, D.Parkinson, R.Vollmar, G.Wolf), pp.49-60

/10/ Creutzburg,R.: Parallel optimal subtree access with recursively linear memory function. (ibid.) pp.203-209

/11/ Horowitz,E., and S.Sahni: Fundamentals of Data Structures. Computer Science Press. Woodland Hills (Ca.) 1976

/12/ Creutzburg, R.: Parallel access to tree-like data structures. (in preparation)

A FORMAL DEFINITION FOR SYSTOLIC SYSTEMS

D. De Baer[1] and J.Paredaens[2]

1 Introduction

In recent VLSI-literature much attention has been paid to systolic systems as a way to design and implement systems in a VLSI environment ([3], [4], [6]). In this paper we give an exact definition of a systolic system. We also pay attention to some important properties of these systems, which we define rigorously. As such it becomes clear how the formalism can be used as a formal tool to reason about systolic systems.

A systolic system is a network of processing elements. This network is connected to the outside world, in most cases to a host computer. Within the system data flows in a rhythmic fashion, driven forward by the processing elements (called *processors*). Therefore the function of the processors resembles that of the heart pushing the blood through the arteries. This explains the use of 'systolic', a medical term for the contraction of heart.

Each processor executes some specific calculation on the data passing through. This is similar to an assembly line where the final product is the result of a series of parallel actions along the line. However, a systolic system might have a more complicated structure than a line.

To clarify the concept we give an example. Further examples can be found in for instance [3]. Consider the problem of ordering a row of n integers $x_1, \ldots, x_n$. A trivial way to do this is to put the maximum of this row in front, and proceed recursively in the same way with the rest of the row. It is well known however that this is not the most efficient sequential method. When turning this method into a systolic system it is quite a surprise to see that it yields an elegant and fast system.

For ordering a row of integers systolically, we start from n processors configured as drawn in figure 1. At every clock tick the first $n-1$ processors of this system take their x-input and y-input (see figure 2), push the larger of both to the left, via the y-output, and the smaller to the right, via the x-output. In case one of the inputs is empty, then the other input is sent to the corresponding output. The last processor is simply a roundabout way, that returns everything it receives. In figure 3 the third to the nineth step are illustrated. Because of the 'empty' time space between two adjacent elements all elements meet each other. It can be proven that the elements are indeed sorted when they leave the system, after $4n-3$ steps. We refer to this system as the *roundabout sort*.

The example above is representative for many systolic systems: it is composed of several processors working in parallel and the processors alternatively:

- communicate with their neighbours in a synchronized way
- process without any external communication

Typically each of the two phases only takes a constant amount of time, independent of the data or particular position of the processor in the system.

In the next section we define a systolic system formally. Actually, a simple sequential system also fulfils the requirements of a systolic system, although it works with only one processor. Thus it seems that some systems are

[1] Research assistant of the N.F.W.O.
[2] Department of Mathematics
University of Antwerp, U.I.A.
Universiteitsplein 1, 2610 Antwerp
Belgium

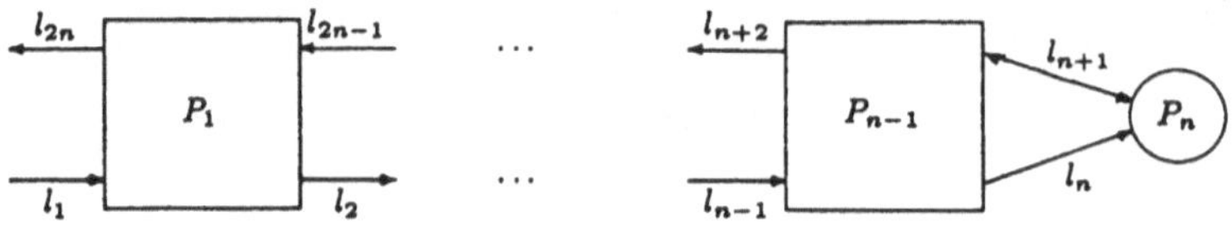

Figure 1: Example System: communication network

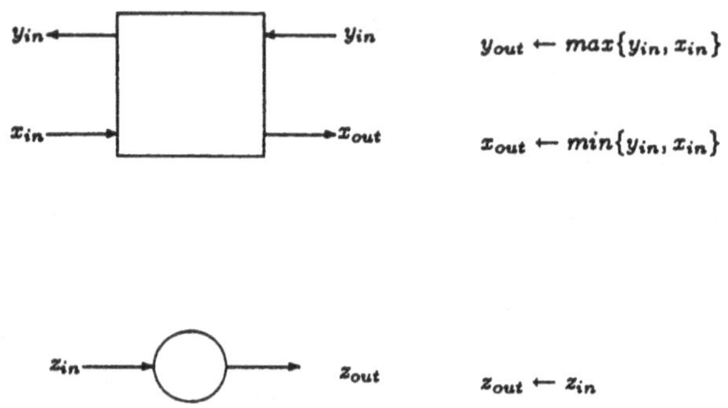

Figure 2: Example System: the nodes

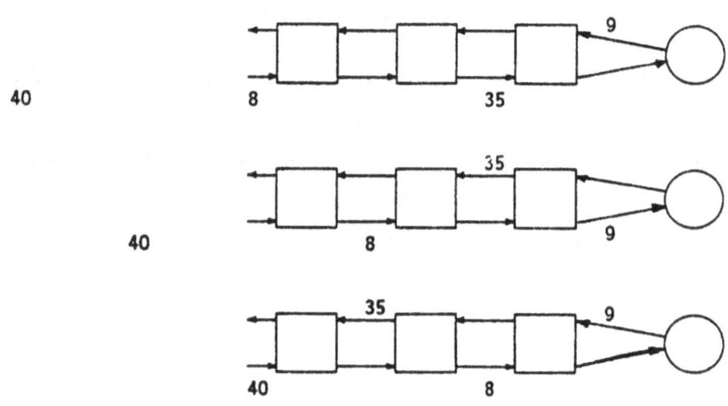

Figure 3: a few steps

more systolic than others. In section 3 we shall study different properties of systolic systems in order to measure a degree of 'systoleness' and to classify the systolic systems in different categories with comparable theoretical and practical behaviour. We shall define the dimension of a systolic system, its communication diversity and its degree of parallelism.

2 Formal Definition of a Systolic System

In this section we describe a formal model for systolic systems, which provides a notation for making statements and proving theorems about systolic systems.

2.1 Memory

Values in a systolic system reside in specific places. These posistions are called *lines*. The finite non-empty set of abstract lines is called the *lineset*. In figure 1 we have labeled the line segments with the name of the line this represent.

Lines constitute the global memory. In principle the information they contain is available to all processors connected with them. The memory cells local to a processor are called *registers*, whereas the finite set of abstract registers is referred to as the *registerset*.

All data that can circulate in the system are elements of a recursively enumerable set, called the *dataset*. The dataset of the roundabout sort contains all integers, and the element *EMP* to represent the empty time-space. The operations and predicates defined on the dataset are assumed to be very elementary, such that they are computable in a sequentially constant amount of time.

Each line and register contains an element of the dataset, which is specified by the content-mapping.

Definition 2.1 *The* **content-mapping** *of the set A with respect to the dataset D is a mapping from A to D. The set of all possible content-mappings of A with respect to D is denoted by $C(A, D)$.*

2.2 Processor

A processor is a small sequential computing device. It always has some registers containing its inputs (its *inputregisters*, and registers in which the results are stored (*outputregisters*). The task performed by a processor is described by a function called the *process* of the processor. If R_I and R_O are the set of inputregisters and the set of outputregisters respectively, then a process is a function from $C(R_I, D) \times R_O$ to D. This function must be recursive and the sequential time-complexity must be constant. Hence the computation of the function is finished after a bounded time-period. If a process does not yield a new value for a certain output register, i.e. if the function is not defined for a particular output register, then no new value will be assigned to this register.

Definition 2.2 *A* **process** *p with inputregisterset R_I, outputregisterset R_O and dataset D is a recursive function*

$$p : C(R_I, D) \times R_O \to D$$

which is computable in a constant time.

For example with registersets $R_I = R_O = \{r_1, r_2\}$ the process of one of the first $n-1$ processors in figure 1 is:

$$
\begin{aligned}
p_{rs}: C(R_I, D) \times R_O: \quad (c, r_1) &\mapsto \begin{cases} max\{c(r_1), c(r_2)\}, EMP \notin \{c(r_1), c(r_2)\} \\ c(r_1), EMP \in \{c(r_1), c(r_2)\} \end{cases} \\
(c, r_2) &\mapsto \begin{cases} min\{c(r_1), c(r_2)\}, EMP \notin \{c(r_1), c(r_2)\} \\ c(r_2), EMP \in \{c(r_1), c(r_2)\} \end{cases}
\end{aligned}
$$

Before a processor starts working it loads its inputregisters with values it takes from specified lines (its *inputlines*). Analogously, having finished, it copies the contents of its outputregisters to its *outputlines*. The lines constitute the means by which processors communicate with each other. The correspondence between inputlines and inputregisters is called the *inputconnection*. Formally it is a mapping

$$i: R_I \rightarrow L$$

The correspondence between outputregisters and outputline is called the *outputconnection*. Formally it is a surjective function

$$o: L \rightarrow R_O$$

Remark the dual analogy between input- and outputconnection.

Definition 2.3 *A* **processor** *on a lineset L and with dataset D is a triple (p, i, o) with*

- *p a process with inputregisterset R_I, outputregisterset R_O and dataset D*
- *i an inputconnection $i: R_I \rightarrow L$*
- *o an outputconnection $o: L \rightarrow R_O$*

The execution of a processor consists of three stages. The processor first copies information from inputlines to its inputregisters. Subsequently it performs some specific calculation, as described by its process. In the final stage the values from its outputregisters are copied to its outputlines. The *activity* of a processor is the composition of these stages.

Definition 2.4 *Let $P = (p, i, o)$ be a processor on a lineset L with dataset D. The function $[P]$ from $C(L, D) \times L$ to D which returns the value $p(m.i, o(l))$ for the couple (m, l), is called the* **activity** *of the processor.*

If $[P](m, l)$ is defined, the processor will write the value $[P](m, l)$ in the line l when the initial content of the lines is m. In case it is undefined, P will not overwrite the content of the line l.

2.3 Multiprocessor

Most of the time a great number of processors is active in a systolic system. An important assumption is that these processors are completely synchronized. This implies that all the processors start their first stage at the same time, copying information in their registers. When they have all finished the initial phase the processors start simultanuousl their second stage, independently performing some specific calculation. Finally, when they have all completed their second stage they start, simultanuously turn to, the final stage, copying their results into the outputlines.

The collection of processors active at the same time is called a *multiprocessor*. Remark that all processors of a multiprocessor are different, though they can execute the same proces. In that case we consider these processes as different instances of an identical process. Since these instances differ, we can distinguish their registers, which would otherwise be impossible.

Two processors may want to put a value on the same line. We do not exclude this possibility, but we require that these processors write identical values to the shared lines.

Definition 2.5 *Two processors P and Q, with lineset L and dataset D, which never write different values to a shared line when starting with the same content of L, are said to be in* **unison**. *Formally:*

$$\forall m \in C(L,D), \forall l \in L : (m,l) \in dom([P]) \cap dom([P]) \Longrightarrow [P](m,l) = [Q](m,l)$$

All processors in the roundabout sort are in unison.

Definition 2.6 *A finite set of processors which are mutually in unison, and which have the same lineset L and dataset D is called a* **multiprocessor** *with lineset L and dataset D.*

The roundabout sort contains only one multiprocessor, which consists of all processors in this systolic system.

Definition 2.7 *Given a multiprocessor M wiht lineset L and dataset D. The* **activity** *of M is defined to be the mapping [M] on C(L, D) with:*

$[M](m)(l) = [P](m,l)$ *with P a processor of M for which $[P](m,l)$ is defined.*

$[M](m)(l) = m(l)$ *if for no processor P of M, $[P](m,l)$ is defined.*

2.4 Clock

Actually the activity of a systolic system consists of the concatenation of activities of several multiprocessors. In some systolic systems the same multiprocessor is repeatedly executed (as in the roundabout sort). In general a sequence of more multiprocessors is executed. There is however, always some periodicity, such that the same sequence of multiprocessors is executed repeatedly. This periodicity is expressed by the clock.

Definition 2.8 *Given a finite set of multiprocessors $\mathcal{M}$, each with lineset L and dataset D. A* **clock** *with lineset L and dataset D is a mapping from the finite interval $[0 \ldots N-1]$ to $\mathcal{M}$. N refers to the period of the clock.*

First the processors of the multiprocessor *clock*(0) work simultaneously. When these have finished, the processors of *clock*(1) do their job, then those of *clock*(2) and so on. When *clock*($N-1$) terminates, *clock*(0) is executed again. Note that the clock is independent of the data and processors of the multiprocssors.

2.5 Systolic System

We are now able to give a formal definition of a systolic system.

Definition 2.9 *A* **systolic system** *with lineset L and dataset D is a four-tuple $S = (m, k, I, O)$ where*

- *m is a content-mapping of the lineset L with respect to the dataset D .*
- *k is a clock with lineset L and dataset D.*
- *I and O are two subsets of L.*

m is called the *initial content-mapping* of the systolic system. Generally the initial content-mapping assigns to every line the empty value *EMP*, as is the case for the roundabout sort. The lines in *I*, called *inputlines*, are the lines through which data from the outside (a host computer for example) come into the system. The lines in *O*, referred to *outputlines*, are the connections to the outside world to convey the results of the system. Line l_1 is the only inputline of the roundabout sort, and l_{2n} the only outputline.

The outside world delivers data for the systolic system, which data are stored in the input lines. Then the clock selects the multiprocessor $clock(0)$. When the selected multiprocessor has finished its task, the system delivers the first bunch of results via the outputlines. Then again new input data are stored in the inputlines, the next multiprocessor is selected and the results are delivered, and so on.

Definition 2.10 *Let $S = (m, k, I, O)$ be a systolic system with lineset L and dataset D. A function from I to D is called an* **input** *to S. We denote the collection of all possible inputs to S by $In(S)$. A mapping form O to D is called an* **output** *from S. The set of all possible outputs from S is denoted $Out(S)$.*

The write function w, which is defined next, expresses how the content-function of the lineset is altered by reading the input. Actually only the content of the lines for which the input is defined is change by reading the input.

Definition 2.11 *The* **write-function** *is defined to be a function from $In(S)$ to the set of functions on $C(L, D)$ and has the property*

$$\begin{aligned} \forall i \in In(S),\ \ \forall m \in C(L, D) &: \\ \forall l \in dom(i) &: w(i)(m)(l) = i(l) \\ \forall l \in L \setminus dom(i) &: w(i)(m)(l) = m(l) \end{aligned}$$

Definition 2.12 *The row of content-mappings $m_0, \ldots, m_j$, where j is any positive integer or even infinite, is* **the result of** *the row inputs $i_0, \ldots, i_j$ if*

- *m_0 is the initial content-mapping of S.*
- $\forall t \in \{1, \ldots, j\} : m_t = [k(t-1)].w(i_{t-1}(m_{t-1})$

Let o_t be the restriction of m_t to O. Then the row $o_0, \ldots, o_j$ is said to be the output row corresponding to $i_0, \ldots, i_m$. We denote this by $(o_0, \ldots, o_m) = [S](i_0, \ldots, i_m)$.

The essential properties of a systolic system, on which this formal definition is based, are

- A systolic system is a special purpose computing device. Except by giving input, it cannot be controlled from the outside.
- The processors are fully synchronized: they simultaneously start and end during a single clock cycle.
- The clock and the processors work independent of each other. No processor acts as a manager, controlling the other processors or clock.

Not every system obeying these rules is to be considered a "good" systolic system. In the next section we discuss some additional requirements.

3 Important properties

Other demands, beside those mentioned above, also play a part when evaluating a systolic system. In this section we concentrate on the following properties:

- The "inter-process" structure needs to be simple.

- The communication structure should be simple.
- The parallelism must be exploited as far as possible.
- The amount of time during which an input influences the output (it can be infinite) is important as to the overall behaviour of the system. The shorter it is, the easier to understand this behaviour.

We shall define, in short, some formal properties to evaluate these requirements. For a more elaborate treatment of these properties we refer to the extended version of this paper (see [1]).

3.1 Dimension

The communication scheme of a systolic system is a graphical representation of the data exchange in this system.

Definition 3.1 *Let $S = (c, k, I, O)$ be a systolic system. The directed graph G_S whose vertices are labeled by the processors of S and whose arcs represents the information flow between processors is called the* **communication graph**. *Formally, it is the graph $G_S = (V_S, E_S)$ with*

$$V_S = \cup_t k(t)$$

and

$$E_S = \{(j,l); \quad \text{there is a time } t \text{ with a processor } P_j = (p_j, i_j, o_j) \text{in } k(t), \text{ a } P_l = (p_l, i_l, o_l) \text{ in } k((t+1) mod N), \text{ and the codomain of } o_j \text{ and the domain of } i_l \text{ share a common line } \}$$

The communication graph determines to a great extend the complexity of the systolic system. We define the complexity or the dimension of the communication graph as the dimension of the grid on which this graph can be implemented. This is motivated by the way a system is implemented in hardware. The implementation of a graph on a grid is briefly defined as:

1. put each node on a crossing of the grid.
2. each edge in the graph is represented by traversals along the grid, from the starting node to the end node such that these travelsals do not cross one another.

Definition 3.2 *The* **dimension** *of a systolic system is the minimum dimension of the grid on which the communication graph can be implemented.*

The dimension of the roundabout sort is 1, i.e linear. The dimension of the hexagonal matrix product algorithm presented in [5] is 3, whereas the odd-even sort algorithm given in [2] also has a dimension of 1.

3.2 Communication diversity

The communication diversity indicates how many structurally different edges there are in the communication graph. Formally, we say that two edges are equivalent if they connect the same registers. The number of different equivalence classes gives us the communication diversity. It expresses the number of different ways processors are interconnected.

Clearly, the smaller the communication diversity is, the higher the degree of systoleness. Together with the dimension, the communication diversity provides information about the comexity of the structure of the systolic system.

The remaining measures concern the work systems perform.

3.3 Degree of parallelism

In the odd-even sort example, given in [2], not all processors are working every clock time interval. Hence this system does not use the parallellism as efficient as the roundabout system does. It might be remarked that not all processors in the roundabout sort perform real work every clock time interval; they are sometimes only busy shuffling data. However this shuffling is necessary to push the row through the system and thus forms a significant part of the solution.

As a fair estimate of the division of work amongst the procesors we shall take the average number of active processors, divided by the number of available processors. Which will be called the *degree of parallelism*. It is always a number between 0 and 1.

4 Concluding remarks

The next table gives an overview of the values for different measures we introduced for some systolic systems.

	Dimension	Communication Diversity	Degree of Parallelism
roundabout	1	4	1
odd-even	1	1	0.5
matrix product	3	3	1

All systems shown have low dimension, communication diversity and degree of parallelism, so it should not be difficult to describe these systems. It interesting to know the relation between these numbers and the description of these systems, but this is an objective for future studies.

References

[1] De Baer, D. and Paredaens, J. A Formal Definition for Systolic Systems, UIA technical report 84-14, June 1984.

[2] Kramer M.R. and Van Leeuwen J., Systolic Computation and VLSI, 4th Advanced Course on the Foundations of Computer Science, June 1982.

[3] Kung H.T. and Leiserson C.E., Systolic Arrays for (VLSI), CMU Comp. Sci. Dep. techn. rep., April 1978

[4] Kung, H.-T., Let's design Algorithms for VLSI Systems, CMU Comp. Sci. Dep. techn. rep., January 1978

[5] Mead, C.A. and L.A. Conway, Introduction to VLSI Systems, Addison-Wesley, Reading Mass, 1980.

[6] Ullman, Jeffrey D. Computational Aspects of VLSI, Computer Science Press, 1984

PARALLEL RECOGNITION OF OUTERPLANAR GRAPHS

Krzysztof Diks[1,2]

Introduction: Definitions and basic facts.

We present a parallel algorithm for the recognition of outerplanar graphs. The algorithm runs on a Concurrent-Read Concurrent-Write Parallel Random Access Machine in $O(\log_2 n)$ time and using $O(n)$ processors. In this model all processors run synchronously and have access to a common memory. Simultaneous reading by several processors from the same memory location is allowed as well as simultaneous writing. In the latter case one processor succeds but we don't know which in advance. For more details about the model and algorithms on it see [V1].

Consider an n-vertex simple graph $G=(V,E)$. In this paper we will assume that $V=\{1,2, \dots ,n\}$.

G is said to be an outerplanar graph if it can be embedded in the plane without edge crossing in such a way that each vertex touches an unbounded face.

The following basic facts hold for outerplanar graphs:

Fact 1

Each n-vertex outerplanar graph G has at most 2n−3 edges. ■

Using this Fact we can assume that the number of edges of a recognized graph is at most 2n−3.

Fact 2

The graph G is outerplanar iff its every biconnected component is outerplanar. ■

Using $O(n)$ processors biconnected components of G can be found in $O(\log_2 n)$ parallel time [TV]. Therefore, in the remaining part of the presented paper we will deal only with biconnected graphs.

Recognition of outerplanar graphs using $O(n^2)$ processors.

Outerplanar biconnected graphs have very nice structure. They can be embedded in the plane in such a way that vertices are vertices of polygons and edges their sides or noncrossing diagonals. Moreover, each edge is either a side or a diagonal and sides of an outerplanar block create the only Hamiltonian cycle in it. Hence to find an outerplanar

1) Institute of Infomatics, Warsaw University, PKiN VIIIp, 00-901 Warsaw, Poland. 2) This research was partially done during my visit at Institute of Technical Cybernetics Slovak Academy of Sciences, Bratislava.

embedding of G in the plane it is sufficient to find its Hamiltonian cycle. In other words it is sufficient to find a permutation $I=I_1,I_2,\ldots,I_n$ of its vertices which determines the Hamiltonian cycle.

An edge e of a biconnected graph G is said to be a side if G will not be biconnected after removing e.

An edge e will be called a diagonal of a biconnected graph G if G will remain biconnected after removing e.

Fact 3

Each n-vertex, biconnected, outerplanar graph G, with $n\geq 3$, possesses exactly n sides which create in it the only Hamiltonian cycle. ■

Assume that the number of vertices in a recognized graph is greater than 3, otherwise the problem is trivial.

The algorithm for a recognition, whether a given biconnected, n-vertex graph G is outerplanar is the following:

step 1 Mark sides and diagonals in G. If the number of marked sides is not equal to n then **STOP** - the graph is **NOT** outerplanar.

step 2 Create the Hamiltonian cycle from the sides. If it is impossible then **STOP** - the graph G is **NOT** outerplanar.

step 3 Test if diagonals don't cross in the outerplanar embedding of G marked by the Hamiltonian cycle. If at least two diagonals cross then **STOP** - G is **NOT** outerplanar, otherwise the Hamiltonian cycle determines the outerplanar embedding of G in the plane.

Assign processors to edges and vertices of G. Assume that the first step has been done and n sides are marked. Step 2 can be done in $O(\log_2 n)$ time using n processors assigned to sides. Apply doubling technique to create the Hamiltonian cycle if it is possible. Otherwise some vertex in the subgraph induced by sides must have a degree nonequal to 2 or that subgraph is not connected. Both condition can be easy tested in $O(\log_2 n)$ time and using n processors. The details are left to the readers.

If the sides create the Hamiltonian cycle we can assume w.l.o.g. that successive vertices on it are $1,2,\ldots,n$. It means that $\langle 1,2\rangle$, $\langle 2,3\rangle,\ldots,\langle n-1,n\rangle$, $\langle n,1\rangle$ are the sides of the graph.

We say that two diagonals $\langle i,j\rangle$, $\langle k,l\rangle$ cross if $i<k<j<l$. In step 3 it is sufficient to test if there exists a pair of crossing diagonals. If such a pair exists then G is not an outerplanar graph.

Let $\langle i,j\rangle$, $i<j$, be an edge of the graph G different from $\langle 1,n\rangle$. If there exists an edge $\langle l,j\rangle$ with $l<i$ then **next**(i,j) will denote an edge $\langle k,j\rangle$ such that $k=\max(l \mid \langle l,j\rangle\in E \ \&\ l<i)$, otherwise **next**$(i,j)=\langle j,k\rangle$, where $k=\max(l \mid \langle j,l\rangle\in E \ \&\ l>j)$. In the first case we say that **next**(i,j) is the backward edge and the forward edge in the second one. As in G there exists the Hamiltonian cycle 1,2,...,n then **next**(i,j) is determined for each edge $\langle i,j\rangle$ different from $\langle 1,n\rangle$.

Let **next*** be a closure of **next** defined as follows:

$$(*)\quad \mathbf{next*}(i,j) = \begin{cases} \mathbf{next}(i,j) & \text{if } \mathbf{next}(i,j) \text{ is the backward edge} \\ \mathbf{next*}(\mathbf{next}(i,j)) & \text{if } \mathbf{next}(i,j) \text{ is the forward edge} \end{cases}$$

If $\langle i,j\rangle$, $i<j$, is a diagonal then we will denote by **first_down**(i,j) an edge $\langle i,k\rangle$ such that $k=\max\{l \mid \langle i,l\rangle \in E \ \&\ i<l<j\}$.

The following Lemma holds:

Lemma 1

G is an outerplanar graph iff for each diagonal $\langle i,j\rangle$, $i<j$, $\mathbf{next*}(\mathbf{first\_down}(i,j))=\langle i,j\rangle$.

Proof

⇒ Suppose that G is an outerplanar graph. Let $\langle i,j\rangle$, $i<j$, be a diagonal and $\mathbf{next*}(\mathbf{first\_down}(i,j))=\langle k,l\rangle$, $k<l$. We show that $\langle k,l\rangle$ must be equal to $\langle i,j\rangle$.

Assume that

$$\mathbf{next*}(\mathbf{first\_down}(i,j)) = \underbrace{\mathbf{next}(\mathbf{next}(\ldots(\mathbf{next}}_{p\text{ times}}(\mathbf{first\_down}(i,j))\ldots))$$

for some $p\geq 1$ and for each $0\leq r\leq p$

$$\underbrace{\mathbf{next}(\mathbf{next}(\ldots(\mathbf{next}}_{r\text{ times}}(\mathbf{first\_down}(i,j))\ldots))=\langle i_r,j_r\rangle,\quad i_r<j_r.$$

It follows from the definitions of **first_down**, **next** and **next*** that:

$$(**)\quad i=i_0<j_0=i_1<\ldots<j_{p-2}=i_{p-1}<j_{p-1}=i_p=l>j_p=k.$$

Consider three cases:

(1) $i<l<j$

If $k<i$ then diagonals $\langle i,j\rangle$, $\langle k,l\rangle$ cross. Hence G is not outerplanar – a contradiction. Let $k=i$. In this case $\mathbf{first\_down}(i,j)=\langle i,s\rangle$ with $s\geq l$ and $\mathbf{next*}(i,s)$ can not be equal to $\langle l,k\rangle$ – a contradiction. At last let $k>i$. But now there is $0\leq r<p$ such that $i_r<k<j_r<l$ and G even could not be outerplanar.

(2) $l>j$

In this case there is $1<r<p$ such that $i<i_r<j<j_r$. Hence G is not an outerplanar graph – a contradiction.

(3) $l=j$

If $i<k$ then proceeding as in the case (1) we again obtain a contradiction with the assumption.

At last suppose $k<i$. But now it follows from the definition of **next** that $\mathbf{next}(i_{p-1},j_{p-1})\neq\langle k,l\rangle$. Hence k must be equal to i.

⇐ Suppose now that $\mathbf{next*}(\mathbf{first\_down}(i,j))=\langle i,j\rangle$ holds for each diagonal $\langle i,j\rangle$, $i<j$, and G is not an outerplanar graph.

If G is not outerplanar then there are two crossing diagonals $\langle i,j\rangle$,

$\langle k,l \rangle$, with $i<k<j<l$, such that there are no diagonals $\langle k,l' \rangle$ with $j<l'<l$ and $\langle k',l'' \rangle$ with $k<k'<j<l''$. It follows from the definitions of **next**, **next*** and (**) that **next*(first_down**$(k,l))=\langle x,y \rangle$ for some $x<y\leq j$. It is a contradiction with the assumption. Hence G is an outerplanar graph. ■

Let D(G) be a directed graph obtained from G by the exchange each edge $\langle i,j \rangle$ for two directed ones (i,j) and (j,i).

We define a linear order $\lhd$ on edges of D(G) as follows:

$$(i,j) \lhd (k,l) \text{ iff } i<k \vee (i=k \;\&\; (l<j<i \vee j<i<l \vee i<l<j)).$$

Suppose that edges of the Hamiltonian cycle are sides of a convex n-gon and the remining ones its diagonals. Observe, if the numbering of vertices on the Hamiltonian cycle is in the accordance with a clockwise order then the relation $\lhd$ arranges edges outgoing from each vertex on the contrary. Denote by **next**$\lhd(i,j)$ and **prev**$\lhd(i,j)$ edges, respectively next and previous for (i,j) in the order $\lhd$. Naturally, **next**$\lhd$ is not determined for the last edge in the order $\lhd$, the same as **prev**$\lhd$ for the first one. At last we obtain:

(***) **next**$(i,j)=$**next**$\lhd(j,i)$ and **first_down**$(k,l)=$**next**$\lhd(k,l)$.

(Remark: here, **next**$\lhd(j,i)$ and **next**$\lhd(k,l)$ are treated as undirected edges.)

We use the algorithm of [C] to sort edges of D(G) in the order $\lhd$. It takes $O(\log_2 n)$ time and $O(n)$ processors. Then, using (***), **next** and **first_down** can be computed in a constant time. At last we apply the doubling technique for computing **next*** using the reccurence (*). Hence the whole step 3 takes $O(\log_2 n)$ time and $O(n)$ processors.

It remains to describe the step 1. Notice, that this step can be easy done using $O(n^2)$ processors by Fact 1 and definitions of sides and diagonals. We test for each edge e if its removing from the graph leaves it still biconnected or not. We can do step 1 in $O(\log_2 n)$ time using $O(n^2)$ processors applying independently for each edge the Tarjan, Vishkin's algorithm [TV] for biconnectivity testing . In the next section we show how to decrease the number of processors to $O(n)$.

Detection of sides and diagonals with O(n) processors.

It is fascinating that to detect sides and diagonals of an outerplanar graph we use the same method as Tarjan and Vishkin for finding biconnected components.

Let $G=(V,E)$ be an n-vertex, outerplanar, biconnected graph and let T be its spanning, rooted tree with an arbitrary vertex as the root. Let $p(x)$ denote the father of a vertex x in T. We define an auxiliary graph G' with each edge of T as a vertex and with edges of the following forms:

(a) {{p(p(x)),p(x)},{p(x),x}} - iff some edge of G joins a decendant of x with a nondescendant of p(x),

(b) {{p(x),x},{p(y),y}} - iff {x,y} is an edge of G such that x and y are unrelated in T,

(c) {{u,x},{u,y}} - iff p(x)=u, p(y)=u and some edge of G joins a descendant of x with a descendant of y,

(d) {{p(x),x},{p(y),y}} - iff x is an ancestor of y and {p(x),y} belongs to G.

The following Lemma holds:

Lemma 2

An edge e of the tree T is a diagonal in G iff e is an articulation point in G'.

Proof

We apply the induction on the number of vertices in G.

(1) n=3. In this case G is simply the Hamiltonian cycle of three edges. There are two nonisomorphic, spanning rooted trees of G, one with the root of the degree 1 and the other with the root of the degree 2. Graphs G' corresponding to these trees contain only one edge. Obviously the Lemma holds. There are no articulation points in graphs G', but also their vertices correspond to sides of G (see Fig. 1).

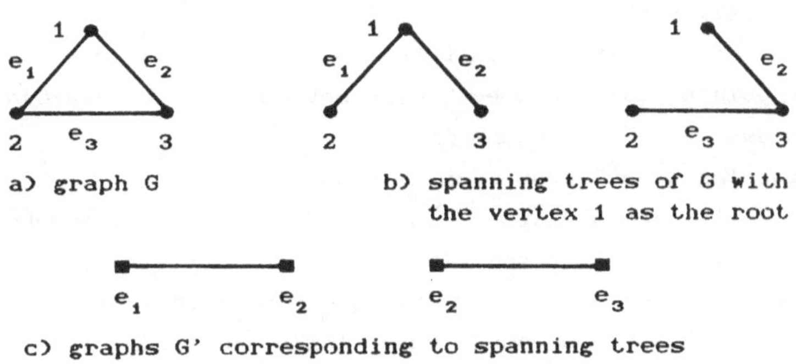

Fig. 1

(2) Suppose now n>3 and the Lemma holds for each biconnected outerplanar graph with the number of vertices smaller than n. W.l.o.g. we can assume that successive vertices on the Hamiltonian cycle of G are 1,2,...,n and the vertex 1 is the root of the spanning tree T.

Consider two cases:

(2.1) The spanning tree T contains no diagonal.

The spanning trees of such form can be partitioned into two classes: trees with roots of degree 1 (See Fig. 2a) and trees of roots of degree 2 (See Fig. 2b).

The following edges are created in the graph G' in the case of the Fig. 2a:

$\langle\langle 1,2\rangle,\langle 2,3\rangle\rangle;\langle\langle 2,3\rangle,\langle 3,4\rangle\rangle;\langle\langle 3,4\rangle,\langle 4,5\rangle\rangle;\ldots,\langle\langle n-3,n-2\rangle,\langle n-2,n-1\rangle\rangle;$ $\langle\langle n-2,n-1\rangle,\langle n-1,n\rangle\rangle$ - on the ground of the rule (a),

$\langle\langle n-1,n\rangle,\langle 1,2\rangle\rangle$ - the rule (d).

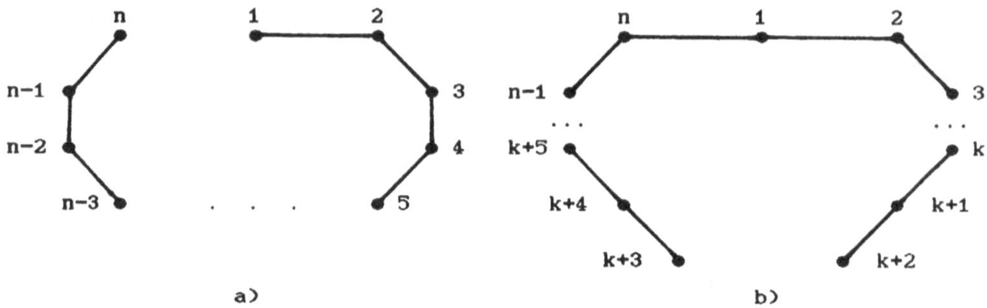

Fig. 2

The following edges are created in the case of the Fig. 2b:

$\langle\langle 1,2\rangle,\langle 2,3\rangle\rangle;\ldots;\langle\langle k,k+1\rangle,\langle k+1,k+2\rangle\rangle;\langle\langle 1,n\rangle,\langle n,n-1\rangle\rangle,$ $\ldots,\langle\langle k+5,k+4\rangle,\langle k+4,k+3\rangle\rangle$ - the rule (a),

$\langle\langle k+4,k+3\rangle,\langle k+1,k+2\rangle\rangle$ - the rule (b),

$\langle\langle 1,n\rangle,\langle 1,2\rangle\rangle$ - the rule (c).

Graphs G' are Hamiltonian in both cases. Hence they can not contain articulation points. But the tree T does not contain any diagonal. Hence the Lemma holds.

(2.2) The spanning tree T possesses diagonals.

Let $\langle i,j\rangle$, $i<j$, be a diagonal in T. Consider two graphs G_l, G_r spanned on vertices, respectively $1,2,\ldots,i-1,i,j,j+1,\ldots,n$ and $i,i+1,\ldots,j-1,j$. G_l and G_r have exactly one common edge $\langle i,j\rangle$. Naturally, both these graphs are biconnected, outerplanar and $\langle i,j\rangle$ is a side in each of them. Let T_l, T_r be spanning trees of G_l and G_r, subtrees of T. Observe that no edge of T_l different from $\langle i,j\rangle$ is connected in G' with an edge of T_r also different from $\langle i,j\rangle$ (see rules a, b, c, d.). $G'=G_l'\cup G_r'$ what denotes that sets of vertices and edges of G' are sums, respectively vertex sets and edge sets of graphs G_l' and G_r'. From the induction hypothesis an edge e of T_l (similarly for T_r) is a diagonal in G_l' iff e is an articulation point in G_l' (G_r'). If e is different from $\langle i,j\rangle$ then it does not change its status in G'. At last observe that each path in G' between vertices from G_l' and G_r' must contain $\langle i,j\rangle$. Hence $\langle i,j\rangle$ is an articulation point in G'. ■

The above Lemma allows to classify edges of T as sides or diagonals. Next three Lemmas will be used for the classification of remaining edges in G. Their proofs are similar to the proof of Lemma 2 and they are omitted.

Lemma 3

If B is a biconnected component of G' then vertices of B (edges of G) create a simple path in G. ■

Such path will be denoted by P(B).

Lemma 4

Let $\langle x,y\rangle$ be an edge from G such that x, y are unrelated in T.

Then, edges $\langle p(x),x\rangle$, $\langle p(y),y\rangle$ belong to the same biconnected component B of G' and if degrees of x and y are in P(B) equal to 1 then $\langle x,y\rangle$ is a side, otherwise a diagonal. ■

Lemma 5

Let x, y be vertices of G such that x is an ancestor of y in T and $\langle p(x),y\rangle$ belongs to G.

Then, $\langle p(x),x\rangle$, $\langle p(y),y\rangle$ belong to the same biconnected component B of G' and if degrees of y and p(x) are in P(B) equal to 1 then $\langle p(x),y\rangle$ is a side, otherwise a diagonal. ■

Observe also that the degree of each vertex in G' is at most 4 and articulation points belong to exactly two biconnected components.

We can describe step 1 as follows:

step 1.1 - Find any spanning, rooted tree of G.
step 1.2 - Build an auxiliary graph G'.
step 1.3 - Find biconnected components of G'.
step 1.4 - Mark articulation points of G' as diagonals and remaining vertices as sides.
step 1.5 - For each biconnected component B of G' build the path P(B). If it is impossible then **STOP** - G is **NOT** outerplanar.
step 1.6 - Using Lemmas 4, 5 classify nontree edges of G.

The implementation of the first three substeps of step 1 is based on the ideas from the Tarjan, Vishkin's paper about finding biconnected components [TV]. They have shown how to find a spanning tree of a given graph in logarithmic time using linear number of processors. Suppose therefore that edges of T are marked. Moreover, following further the paper of Tarjan and Vishkin we can assume that T is transformed into a rooted tree, for each vertex v ,different from the root, p(v) is computed and vertices are numbered in preorder. Identify each vertex with its preorder number.

It is possible to compute in logarithmic time the following functions on the tree T [TV].

Function 1

The number of descendants **nd**(v) for each vertex v. ■

Function 2

low(v) for every vertex v in G. Where **low**(v) is defined as the **minimum** preorder number over: v, descendants of v and vartices adjacent to a descendant of v by an edge from G\T. In other words:

low(v)=min({v}∪{**low**(w)|w is a son of v in T}∪{w|{v,w} in G\T}). ■

Function 3

high(v) for every vertex v in G. Where **high**(v) is defined as the maximum preorder number over: v, descendants of v and vertices adjacent to a descendant of v by an edge from G\T. In other words:

high(v)=max({v}∪{**high**(w)|w is a son of v in T}∪{w|{v,w} in G\T}). ■

It is also possible to form a data_structure which enables retrieval of the lowest common ancestor (**LCA**) of any pair of vertices in $O(\log_2 n)$ time by a single processor. See [V2].

We need once more function for us considerations.

Function 4

Let v be an ancestor of w in T different from **p**(w). By **FOP**(v,w) we will denote the First vertex **O**n the **P**ath in T between v and w. That is, **FOP**(v,w) is an ancestor of w such that **p**(**FOP**(v,w))=v. **FOP**(v,w) can be computed in $O(\log_2 n)$ time by a single processor. Suppose that edges outgoing from v to its sons are ordered with regard to vertices to which they direct (Remember that vertices are identified with their preorder numbers.). Such representation is easy to obtain by sorting edges in the above order. It costs $O(\log_2 n)$ time with n-1 processors. Now we can apply binary search on edges outgoing from v to find the edge {v,u} such that u<w<nd(u). **FOP**(v,w)=u. ■

Using functions defined above step 1.2 is implemented as follows:

step 1.2.1 – for every nontree edge {x,y}, x<y, such that x, y are unrelated in T (it means y≥x+**nd**(x)) add to G' edges: {{**p**(x),x},{**p**(y),y}} – according to the rule (b), {{**LCA**(x,y),**FOP**(**LCA**(x,y),x)},{**LCA**(x,y),**FOP**(**LCA**(x,y),y)}} – according to the rule (c).

step 1.2.2 – for every nontree edge {x,y} such that x is an ancestor of y (x<y<x+**nd**(x)) add to G' the edge: {{x,**FOP**(x,y)},{**p**(y),y}} – according to the rule (d).

step 1.2.3 – for every tree edge {**p**(x),x} such that **p**(x) is not the root add to G' the edge: {{**p**(**p**(x)),**p**(x)},{**p**(x),x} if **low**(x)<**p**(x) or **high**(x)≥**p**(x)+**nd**(x) – according to the rule (a).

Step 1.2 takes $O(\log_2 n)$ time on processors assigned to edges of G. To do step 1.3 apply once more the algorithm of [TV]. This algorithm produces each biconnected component as the set of its edges. The articulation points can be found in the following way. Sort edges of D(G') lexicographically. It costs $O(\log_2 n)$ time. Now it is easy to compute the degree of each vertex v in G' because all edges outgoing from v in D(G') are successive ones in the lexicographical order. If the degree of some vertex is greater than 4 then G is not outerplanar, otherwise test for each vertex v in G' whether its outgoing edges belong to different biconnected comonents. If so, then v is an articulation point. Moreover, in the same way we can compute the degree of each vertex v in every biconnected component to which it belongs (at most 2). Hence, as processors are assigned to edges and vertices of G it is possible to do steps 1.4, 1.5, 1.6 in time $O(\log_2 n)$. Details are left to the reader.

At last we summarize this section with the following Lemma:

Lemma 6

Sides and diagonals of an n-vertex, outerplanar, biconnected graph G can be detected in $O(\log_2 n)$ time on O(n) processors. ■

Concluding remarks.

In the previous two sections we have shown that each of the three steps of the outerplanarity recognition algorithm costs $O(\log_2 n)$ time and O(n) processors. Hence we obtain: •

Main Theorem

Each n-vertex outerplanar graph G can be recognized on CRCW P-RAM in $O(\log_2 n)$ time using O(n) processors. ■

Using the above algorithm some problems for outerplanar graphs can be solved in the same time and using the same number of processors, namely: finding contours [D1], optimal vertex colouring [D1], maximum flow [CD], finding DFS tree [D2].

References

[C] - R. Cole, Parallel Merge Sort, proccedings of FOCS'86, Toronto, pp 511-516.

[CD] - M. Chrobak, K. Diks, Maximum flow in outerplanar networks, submitted for publication.

[D1] - K. Diks, A fast parallel algorithm for six-colouring of planar graphs, MFCS'86, LNCS 233, Springer Verlag (1986), pp 273-282.

[D2] - K. Diks, unpublished result.

[TV] - R.E. Tarjan, U. Vishkin, Finding biconnected componenets and computing tree functions in logarithmic parallel time, proceedings FOCS'84, pp 14-20.

[V1] - U. Vishkin, Synchronous parallel computations - a surwey, Technical Report #71, Computer Science Department, New York University, New York, New York, 1984.

[V2] - U. Vishkin, An efficient parallel strong orientation, Technical Report #109, Computer Science Department, New York University, New York, New York, 1984.

SOLUTIONS FOR THE DISTRIBUTED TERMINATION PROBLEM.

Didier FERMENT (*)
Brigitte ROZOY (**)

ABSTRACT. :

Considering a network of communicating finite state machines which exchange messages over Channels, we discuss the distributed termination problem in the more general context of asynchronous environment. We first whow that this problem is undecidable. Then we discuss the possibility of superimposing algorithms that detect termination. At least we examine the case of faulty processors.

INTRODUCTION. :

In an asynchronous system of communicating machines, processors exclusively communicate by exchanging messages via connecting channels ; we first precise a simple mathematical model to describe such systems.

It is already known that the detection of deadlocks for such systems is an undecidable problem : we establish the same result for the termination one.

Therefore a weak solution for the distributed termination problem consists superimposing an algorithm on the distributed task ; it will have to conclude that termination has occured, if and only if this one has been reached.

The difficulty of the problem arises from the fact that machines have to detect global properties using local considerations only. Meanwhile, this problem has got various solutions, even in an asynchronous environment.

All of them set the assumptions that the communications are immediate and that the processors are able to test the emptiness of their buffers. Clearly, such hypothesises do not fit well with non local network ; are they other similar solutions ?

Unfortunately not : we identify three critical parameters, which, in that case, are all unfavorable for the existence of such algorithms. In order to detect termination in such environments, we definitively need clocks, real or virtual ones !

The last purpose of the paper is to deal with faulty processors. If those ones are correct with respect to the detection algorithm, this latter works. If not, the answer is again : no ; there exists no finite termination algorithm.

To sum up, the only results of this paper are negative ! Its main interest is then the formalization and the delimitation of problems in the asynchronous case !

(*) Université de Picardie - U.F.R. Maths & Informatique - 33, rue St Leu - 80039 AMIENS
(**) Labo. Informatique - Université - Esplanade de la Paix - 14032 CAEN.

The 2 authors are also affilied to L.I.T.P., 2 place Jussieu, 75221 PARIS cedex 05 France.

A MODEL OF DISTRIBUTED SYSTEM. :

We consider a network of machines which communicate by messages passing along predefined channels. Each of them follows a program, involving reception and sending of messages. The mathematical model speaking of the way of working of such systems is elaborated in [RO]. We give here an informal version of it.

Each machine is a state one, provided with one, or several, unbounded buffers which hold the messages that have been sent but not yet treated.

The messages are picked-up and delivered according to priority rules, and eventually fifo-ones.

The running of each machine is given by a transition function and a sending one,

change p : Z x MES $\rightarrow$ Z x MES'.

send p : Z x MES $\rightarrow$ $\{1, ..., n\}$ x MES'

where Z and MES are the set of states and messages, n is the total number of processors, and MES' is MES $\cup \{e\}$, e being an extra-element (whenever M is regarded as an alphabet, e will be the neutral element for concatenation).

We interpret change p(z, m) = (z', m') and send p(z, m) = (q, m'') as : being in state z and treacting message m that was in it buffer, processor p changes this buffer by deleting m, adding m', changes its state to z', and sends message m'' to processor q.

We assume that m'' is immediately deposited in the receiving buffer, and that the whole action of sending and changing is atomic. The possibility that m' = e or m'' = e has to be interpreted as the non-sending of a message, or as the loss of it.

A **distributed system** is a system of n such machines. To speak of it, at a given moment, we want to know, the state of each machine and the content of its buffer ; it is what we call a **description**.

d = (z1, buff1, z2, buff2, ..., zn, buffn).

The evolution of the system will be described in a sequential way, each description being followed by another, which results from the previous one by the **action** of a single processor :

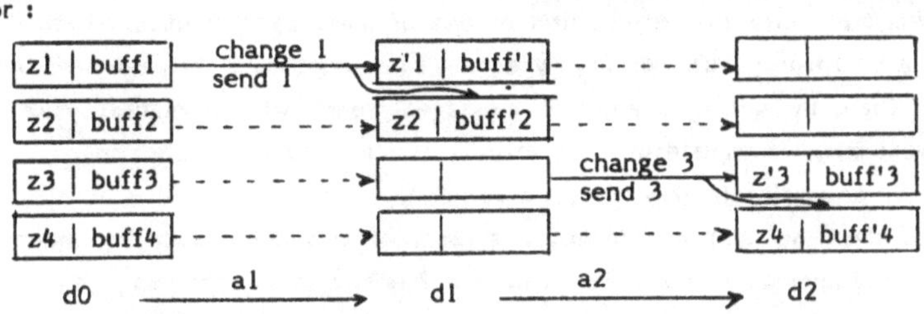

there the evolution is described by the history (d0, a1a2), leading to description d2 = d0 * a1a2.

The set of possible actions derives from the mapping functions "change" and "send" in a straight forward way. Associated with an initial description, this set of actions formally forms what we call a **distributed task** : DT = (d0, ACT).

Histories are then defined as strings of actions, together with an initial description (subject to this succession of actions being possible !).

An history is said to be **terminated** if it is finite and leads to a description such that all buffers are empty. In that case, we say that the termination has occured. Studying the evolution of the distributed system is then reducted to the study of the set of possible histories, and any classical properties have to be translated into properties of the set of actions, or of the initial description, or therefore of the histories.

For example, a task is said to be **non-spontaneous** if a machine may become active only by transmission of a message. It formally means that an action does not work on the extra element e (absence of message).

Some other properties no longer result from local considerations, as, for exemple, fairness, termination, asynchronicity of a processor, they are translated into properties of the set of histories and the problem of compelling the system to obtain them is either complex or impossible.
In that way, one can interpret the **termination problem** as the study of the set of terminated histories. We will see now that it is not decidable.

INDECIDABILITY. :

The informal idea is very simple : as soon as the number of different messages is big enough and the channels unbounded, any turing machines can be simulated by a distributed system, and the halting problem for Turing machines can be carried back to the termination one.

Similar results have already been obtained in the same way for deadlocks.

Theorem 1. : Suppose that a distributed system of communating machines exchanges at least four different messages over unbounded channels.
Then the termination problem is undecidable.

Proof. : One proof may consist in simulating any Turing machine by a system. But one may also make use of previous results ([G.R], [G.G.L.R.]) and transform the deadlock of a classical system into the termination of one of ours. Each deadlocked story is first transformed in a potentially infinite one, by adding some repetitive message sent by the processor to it-self. Then, by adding again two messages, "end" with a highest priority, and "post" with a lowest one, we transform these infinite stories into terminate ones.

In an analogous way we get also :

Theorem 2. :Suppose that a distributed system of two communicating machines exchanges messages of size at most two, and that one of the channel is bounded.
Then the termination problem is decidable.

OBSERVATION ALGORITHMS. :

As we have to forsake the wish of knowing, before the computation starts, whether and when it will terminate, our only hope is to wait for it, and to make us secure of our ability of detecting it when, or after, it occurs.

The solution we are looking for has to be a distributed one : it will be an algorithm by which a process is enabled to detect that termination has occured ; it may furthemore be required that this detection algorithm can cope with any activity of the machines without delaying the main computation, in such a way that the modification of each process is independent of the process's definition. Such an algorithm necessitates to add to machines the ability of exchanging some special messages, called signals, that propagate informations concerning the traffic.

Solutions to this problem have already been presented in numerous papers ([DFG], [FrRo], [Go], [Ma], [RO], [Fr], ...), most often in an informal way.

Formally, we add to each processor a **memory**, drawned from a set MEM. At each step of the underlying task, processors will be asked to give some informations on their actions, that they will write in this memory. This is performed by functions :

$$\text{obsp} : \text{MEM} \times \text{ACT} \rightarrow \text{MEM}$$

Then signals are exchanged by machines ; they are special messages, drawned from a set TOK. This set is eventually provided with a priority relation, connected to the priority on messages. Again a function,

$$\text{exchp} : \text{MEM} \times \text{TOK} \rightarrow \text{MEM} \times \{1, .., n\} \times \text{TOK}'$$

which expresses the way in which these messages are communicated between machines, using indications founded in the local memories and without modifying the states.

If the functions exchp are equal, the modification does not depend on the processor ; if elements in TOK are provided with a priority less than element in MES, the main computation is not delayed.

In an obvious way, the observed histories for distributed tasks are built by mixing actions with those resulting of observations. Thus the composition of a distributed task DT and an observation algorithm definies a new distributed task, DT', called **the observated one.**

We will speak of termination algorithm whenever the termination may be claimed when or after it occurs. This will be done by a special signal **claim**, belonging to TOK, such that :

(T.A.1.) when the termination occurs, some processor will end by knowing it and will send **claim.**

(T.A.2.) this special signal is sent only if termination has been reached.

The fact, for an observation algorithm, to be a termination one looks like a global property, and alway requires a delicate proof.

FINITE TERMINATION ALGORITHMS. :

If the machines are able to count, classical algorithms making use of acknowledgments will be able to detect the termination. But here we are interested in the existence of **finite algorithms** : but that we mean that the set **MEM and TOK have to be finite.** Solutions to that problem are already known ; they always suppose that the communications are immediate and that the machines are able to test the emptiness of their buffer.

But, if the network is not a local one, messages may take a rather long time to reach their destinator ; this one has to wait before being able to claim that it is idle: either communications cannot be supposed to be immediate or the test of the emptiness cannot be done in a single step.

We actually focuss on this last test, and identify three parameters that are connected with it ; let us describe them below (the letter F is refering to favorable situations for the detection).

Transmission order : F. It is favorable if messages sent over the same communication channel and if the same priority obey the fifo rule.

Priority of detection messages : F. The priority of detection messages is said to be favorable if it can be choosen such that any element in TOK has got a priority less than those of messages.

Communication synchronicity : F. The communication are said to be synchronous if their is an uniform bound for messages to be treated. Formally it means that, if a message is sent by action a for any history h, then it is treated by action b, and the size of the string a ... b is bounded by some given number.

The first parameter depends only on local considerations in the management of channels and buffers ; the second is a formal one ; within a model of immediate communication, it has to do with the transmission delay. The third parameter is a strong global one, which heavily destroyes the idea of asynchronous environment.

We will see now that, if one of this parameter is favorable, then the ability of testing the emptiness of the channels can be simulated, and thus finite termination algorithms exist. It will not be the case if the converse holds.

Theorem 3. : If as least one the threee previous parameters is favorable, then there exists a finite termination algorithm, that fits well for the whole family of distributed tasks.

Sketch of the proof. :

(1) The first point is to establish that any parameter in favorable situation allows to simulate the test of the emptiness, namely the fact that the detection signals have got a priority less that messages : when a machine treats a signal, it can affirm that there are no longer messages in its buffer.

* If the communication are synchronous with sound k, the test is simulated, for any machines possessing a signal, by sending at to itself at most k times.

* If the transmission order is fifo, the test is simulated in the following way: if processor p is applicant to idleness, it sends an "allo" to each others and wait for all receipts ; if it has got all the receipts and no other messages, it can claim that its buffer was then empty.

(2) Then we have to exhibate algorithms that detect termination. They are based on the following classical pattern.

A token is moving around in the network. Processors and token are colored either in black or white. Initially all are white, and the initiator's buffer contains a black token. A white processor sending a message becomes black ; a processor that is black, or treets a black token, transmits a black token and becomes white ; a white processor which treates a white token and has an empty buffer, transmits a white token. If the initiator, having an empty buffer, being white, receives a white token, it can claim that termination has occured.

Exemple and correctness proofs of such algorithm can be found in the literature. Clearly, the only key point here is the ability of testing the emptiness of the buffers.

Theorem 4. : Let F be the family of all non-spontaneaous tasks, and let OA be a termination algorithm for F . If the three previous parameters are both unfavorable, then OA is not finite.

We suppose that the three parameters are unfavorable. The intuitive idea used here is that, at any point, a special signal way be treated by the machines even if there were already messages in the channels.

Sketch of the proof. : We suppose that OA is finite, with the size of MEM and TOK bounded by some b . We exibit then a sequence of distributed tasks DT(k) and histories h which contradict the termination properties.

For any k , if $i \leq k - 1$ action $a_{i,k}$ is the sending by processor 1, of message m_2 to processor 2, of message m_1 to itself, when treating message m_1 ; action f_k is the destruction of message m_1 by processor 1 ; Action b is the destruction of messsage m_2 by processor 2.

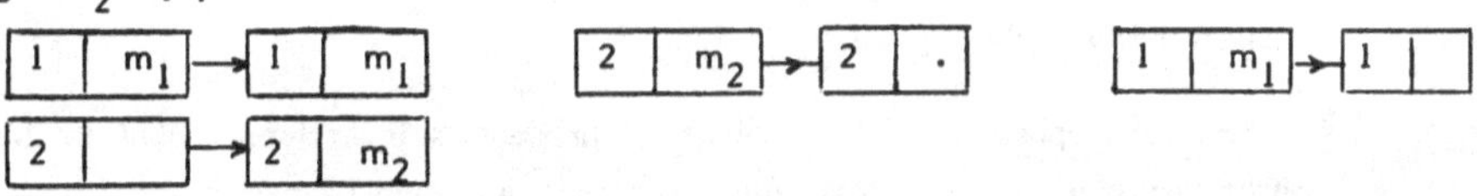

actions $a_{i,k}$ action b action f_k

For any k , set $h(k) = a_{1,k} \cdot\cdot a_{k-1,k}\, f_k(b)^k$.

As h(k) is terminated, there exists an observed history h'(k) that concluded at the termination, and whose projection on the main computation is h(k).

Let us suppose now that ℓ is big enough and let us examine the histories $h(k, \ell) = a_{1,\ell} \cdots a_{\ell-1,\ell}\, f_\ell(b)^k$, which are prefixes of $h(\ell)$. We can find ℓ and k such that the "observations" are done after $h(k, \ell)$ and h(k), and are equal (description of the memories and of the signals) because MEM and TOK are supposed to be finite ; as the communications are asynchronous and the message order not fifo, the termination message "claim" that is occuring in h(k) may occur in $h(\ell)$ at position $h(k, \ell)$, i.e. as termination is not done. Absurd.

CASE OF FAULTY PROCESSORS. :

We have to modelize the notion of faulty processor.

A processor is usually said to be faulty if it executes actions that are not in its initial task : formally, it will mean that the set of possible actions is broken into two parts, one of them being the faulty one. An history will be said to be faulty if at least one action is a faulty one.

Suppose now that AO is an observation algorithm. We will say that the processors respects the algorithm, if the function "obs" and "exch" are satisfied, even by faulty processors. If the processors respect the algorithm, classical termination algorithms, and in particular those of [Ro], works.

So it is natural to consider the case where faulty processors may destroy or falsify special signals : the termination algorithm will be said to be k-fault tolerant if it works, even in presence of (at most) k faulty processor that does not respect the algorithm. Unfortunately, there exists no such algorithm !

The most destructive type of a failure is the byzantine-one : no restriction on the possible errors ! processors may send erroneous messages, stop at any time, and act in a malicious way.

Theorem 5. : Let us, suppose that the number of processors is at least equal to 2. Let AO be any termination algorithm. Then AO is not 1-byzantine tolerant, even if all parameters are favorable.

The derives from the impossibility of consensus in the completly asynchronous case ([D.D.S.]).

Consequently the natural idea is to limit us to some classes of faults ; a dead-process is any one that destroys all messages, and no longer sends any others more. An algorithm is then said to be k-dead tolerant if it works, even in presence of k dead-processors that no longer respect the signals.

Theorem 6. : Let us suppose that the number of processors is at least equal to 2. If the three parameters are in favorable situations, any algorithm is not 1-dead tolerant.

The idea of the proof is that, if the signals have got a priority less than the messages, other processors are not able to distinguish between a dead and a very busy processor !

BIBLIOGRAPHIE. :

[A] K.R. APT. - Correctness proofs of distributed termination algorithms. - Tech. Report. 84-51 ; L.I.T.P. - Université Paris VI, 1984.

[AR] K. APT, J.L. RICHIER. - Real time clocks versus virtual clocks. - T.R. 84-34, L.I.T.P. Université Paris VI.

[B] L. BOUGE. - Symetric election in CSP. - T.R. 84-31. - L.I.T.P., Université Paris VI.

[CM] K.M. CHANDY, J. MISRA. - A paradigm for detecting quiescent properties in distributed computations. - In : Apt K.R. (ed.) Logics and Models of concurrent systems. Springer Verlag Berlin, 11 : 325-341, 1985.

[DDS] D. DOLEV, C. DWORK, L. STOCKMEYER. - On the minimal synchronism needed for distributed consensus. - Proc. 24th. IEEE 1983. - Symp. on found of Comput. Sc. : 393-402.

[DFG] E.W. DIJKSTRA, W.H.FEIJEN, A.J.M. Van GASTEREN. - Derivation of a termination detection algorithm for distributed computations. - Inf. Proc. Letters 16,5 (1983) : 217-219.

[DS] E.W. DIJKSTRA, C.S. SCHOLTEN. - Termination detection for diffusing computations. - Inf. Proc. Letters 11, 1 (1980), 1-4.

[Fe] D. FERMENT. - Finite and not finite solutions for the distributed termination problem. - T.R. 86.11 - LITP, Université Paris, 1986.

[Fr] N. FRANCEZ. - Distributed termination. - ACM, Toplas, 2, 1, pp. 42-45, 1980.

[FeRo] D. FERMENT, B. ROZOY. - Possibility and impossibility of solutions for the distributed termination problem. - TR 86-8. - LITP, University Paris, 1986.

[FrRo] N FRANCEZ, M. RODEH. - Achieving distributed termination without freezing. - IEEE - Trans. on software Engeniring, SE - 8, 3, pp. 287-292, 1982.

[Ga] P. GASTIN. - Synchronisation d'un système asynchrone d'automates. - 1985. - T.R. LITP, Université Paris VII.

[Go] M. GOUDA. - Distributed state exploration for protocol validation. - T.R. 185. - Dpt. of Comput. Sc. Univ. of Texas at Austin. - 1981.

[Gr] M.G. GOUDA, L.E. ROSIER. - Priority networks of communicating finite state machines. - T.R. 83-10 - University of Texas at Austin OR SIAM Journal Computer, 14.3, 1985, pp. 569-584.

[GGLR] M.G. GOUDA, E.M. GURARI, T.H. LAI, L.E. ROSIER. - Deadlock detection in systems of communicating finite state machines.

[LS] C.W. LERMEN, F.B. SCHNEIDER. - Dectecting distributed termination when processors can fail. - T.R. 80-449 - Cornell. University - NY.

[Ma] F. MATTERN. - New algorithms for distributed termination detection in asynchronous message passing systems. - T.R. 42/85, SFB 124, University of Kaiserslautern, 1985.

[Mi] J. MISRA. - Detecting termination of distributed computations using markers. - Proc. 2 annual Symp. on Princ. of dist. Comp. QUEBEC, p. 290-294, 1983.

[Ra] S.P. RANA. - A distributed solution of the distributed termination problem. - Inf. Process letters, 17.1, 1983, pp. 43-46.

[Ri] J.L. RICHIER. - Distributed termination in CSP. - Symetric solutions with minimal storage. - TR 84-49, LITP, Université Paris VII.

[Ro] B. ROZOY. - (1) Model and complexity of termination detection for distributed computations. - Lect. Notes in Comput. Sc. 233, 1986, p. 564-572.

(2) Termination for distributed systems : model and cost. - To be published in : Computer and Artificial Intelligence, Slovak academy of Science, 1987.

[T] R. TOPOR. - Detecting termination for distributed computation. - Inf. Proc. Lett. 18 (1984), 33-36.

Memories for Parallel Subtree-Access

M. Gössel and B. Rebel

The relatively large cycle time of large memories with respect to the cycle time of corresponding processors have led to the demand for parallel memories for different data structures such as scanning fields, matrices and trees.
Today the possiblities of parallel access to data stored in n-dimensional scanning fields, n 2, are well understood by use of elemetary number theory and the possIbilities to tesselate a scanning field by rigid templates (access formats), and a lot of papers is concerned with corresponding parallel memories. (s. e.g. /1 - 7/).

For a general data structure as defined in /8/ parallel memories are introduced in /9/.
For the interesting data structure regular n-ary tree, n 2, till now only some results concerning parallel subtree access are known.
In the first known to us paper on this subject Shirakawa /10/ has investigated for binary trees special recursively linear module assignment functions and corresponding realizations of the addressing circuitry.
These results are generalized to n-ary trees and to more general recursively linear module assignment functions in /11/.

In /12/ the notion regular (and semiregular) module assignment function (skewing scheme) is defined and some upper bounds for the number of necessary memory modules for regular module assignment functions with conflictfree access to a complete binary tree with depth d, d 1, are given.
In /9/ the notion isotropic module assignment function is defined for an arbitrary data structure and as a special case for regular trees. In this paper we show:

- To the contrary to the case of scanning fields conflictfree subtree access can not be understood by tesselating the regular tree by rigid templates.
- To the contrary to the case of a scanning field the classes of isotropic and regular module assignment functions are different.
- Isotropic module assignment functions allows a decentralized address computation and are suited for VLSI-implementation.
- A special non isotropic module assignment function which allows conflictfree parallel subtree access with an optimal number of memory modules is presented.
  Even for this function a decentralized easily implementable address computation is possible.

1. Definitions and notations

A data structure $D = (K, F)$ is here defined as a set of nodes K and a set of unary functions $F = \{f_0, f_1, \ldots, f_s\}$, $f_i: K \rightarrow K, i = 0, \ldots, s$.

For $f_i(k) = k'$ the nodes k and k' are connected by an edge, directed from k to k', which can be labeled by f_i.

To every node $k \in K$ an n_k-tupel of values $v_1(k), v_2(k), \ldots, v_{n_k}(k)$ is assigned.
In general the set F of functions can be replaced by a set of relations /8/.
For complete binary trees different representations as a data structure are known.
Three of them, D_t^1, D_t^2, D_t^3 are used within this paper.

1. $D_t^1 = \{K^1, F^1\}$ with $K^1 = \{0,1,2,\ldots\}$, $F^1 = \{L, R\}$ and $L(k) = 2k+1$,

   $R(k) = 2k+2$ for $k \in K$.

   L(k) and R(k) are the left son and the right son of k resp.

ZKI der AdW, DDR 1086 Berlin, Kurstr. 33

2. $D_t^2 = \{K^2, F^2\}$ with $K^2 = \{(l(x),x),\ x = 0,1,2,\ldots\}$

$F^2 = \{\tilde{L}, \tilde{R}\}$, and $l(0) = 0$.

$\tilde{L}((l(x),x) = ((l(x)+1, x+2^{l(x)}),\ \tilde{R}((l(x),x) = ((l(x)+1, x+2\ 2^{l(x)}),$

$l(x)$ is the level of x and $\tilde{L}(l(x),x)$, $\tilde{R}(l(x),x)$ are the left son and the right son of $(l(x),x)$ resp.

3. $D_t^3 = \{K^3, F^3\}$ with $K = \{L, R\}^*$, $F^3 = \{L, R\}$, where $\{L, R\}^*$ is the set of finite words over the alphabet $\langle L, R\rangle$ with the empty word and $L(k) = kL$, $R(k) = kR$ for k K.
The generalizations for n-ary trees are obvious. The first nodes of the data structures D_t^1, D_t^2 and D_t^3 are represented in Fig. 1.

Basic components of a parallel memory are shown in Fig. 2.
A parallel memory consists of N memory modules $S_0,\ldots,S_{N-1}$ and an address generator A, computing in dependence on the access format or window w and the emphasized node of the access format the addresses for the memory modules.
Thereby a window $w = (w_0, w_1,\ldots,w_{M-1})$, $M \leq N$, is a set of unary functions w_i: $K \dashrightarrow K$, which are superpositions of some unary functions $f_i \in F$ of the considered data structure $D = \{K, F\}$,

$w_i = f_1^i\, f_2^i \ldots f_{n_i}^i$, $f_j^i \in F$ and $w_0(k) = k$ for $k \in K$.

A window at the node $k \in K$ is the ordered set

$w(k) = (w_0(k) = k,\ w_1(k),\ldots,w_{M-1}(k))$.

The node $k \in K$ is called the emphasized node of the window $w(k)$. As an important example of a window for the data structure D_t^1 and D_t^3 the complete binary regular subtree w_{dt} of depth d consisting of 2^d-1 nodes is defined by $w_{dt} = \{\epsilon, L, R, LL, LR, RL, RR,\ldots,L^{d-1},\ldots,R^{d-1}\}$.

For D_t^2 L and R are to be replaced by $\tilde{L}$ and $\tilde{R}$ resp.

If a data structure $D = (K, F)$ is stored in a parallel memory for every node $k \in K$ the memory module $S(k)$ where the values $v_1(k), v_2(k),\ldots,v_{n_k}(k)$ are stored are to be determined.

Formally two functions, the module assignment function $S: K \dashrightarrow \{0,\ldots,N-1\}$ and the address function $a: K \dashrightarrow \{0,\ldots,a_{max}\}$ are to be defined.
In this paper we concentrate on S only. To access the data of a window w in parallel without conflict, all the data of the accessed window had to be stored in different memory modules.
A module assignment function is called w-conflictfree, if we have for $k \in K$, $k', k'' \in w(k)$

$k' \neq k''$ implies $S(k') \neq S(k')$.

For scanning fields the tesselation of the scanning field by a window w and the existence of a w-conflictfree module assignment function S are closely related /2, 13/. In general a window w tesselates the data structure $D = \{K, F\}$, if there exists a subset $\tilde{K}$ of nodes, $\tilde{K} \subset K$ such that

1. $K \subset \bigcup_{k \in \tilde{K}} w(k)$

2. $k, k' \in \tilde{K}$, $k \neq k'$ implies $w(k) \cap w(k') = \emptyset$.

In this paper we are interested in isotropic and regular module assignment functions which allow a reasonable implementation of the corresponding parallel memory.

A module assignment function in called isotropic with respect to a given data structure $D = (K, F)$ if for all $k, k' \in K$ and for all $f \in F$ $S(k) = S(k')$ implies $S(f(k)) = S(f(k'))$ /9/.

For the data structures D_t^1 and D_t^3 we have for an isotropic module assignment function S

$S(k) = S(k')$ implies $S(L(k)) = S(L(k')$ and $S(R(k)) = S(R(k'))$.

For the data structure D_t^2 L and R are to be replaced by $\tilde{L}$, $\tilde{R}$.

A module assignment function is called regular with respect to a given data structure $D = (K, F)$ if for all, $k, k', k_0 \in K$

$S(k) = S(k')$ and $k = f_{m_k}^k \dots f_1^k(k_0)$, $k' = f_{m_{k'}}^{k'} \dots f_1^{k'}(k_0)$

with $f_j^i \in F$ implies

$S(\tilde{k}) = S(\tilde{k}')$ for

$\tilde{k} = f_{m_k}^k \dots f_1^k f_l \dots f_1(k_0)$ and

$\tilde{k}' = f_{m'_k}^{k'} \dots f_1^{k'} \; f_l \dots f_1(k_0)$

with $f_l, \dots, f_1 \in F$, $l > 0$.

For the data structure D_t^3 we have for a regular module assignment function S_r:

For $k, k', \varphi \in K^3 = \{L, R\}^*$, $k_0 = \varepsilon$,

$S_r(k) = S_r(k')$ implies $S_r(\varphi k) = S_r(\varphi k')$.

For trees regular module assignment functions are defined in /12/. For the simplicity of presentation only binary trees are considered here. The generalization to n-ary trees, $n > 2$ is without difficulties.

2. Results

At first we show by simple examples that the results concerning conflictfree memory access for trees are very different from the results for scanning fields.
For a scanning field R the following theorem is valid.
Let $w = (w_0, \dots, w_{N-1})$ be a window. Then there exists a w-conflictfree module assignment function $S: R \to \{0, \dots, N-1\}$ if and only if w tesselates the plane /2, 5/.

The following example shows that there is no corresponding theorem for regular trees.
Example of a w-conflictfree module assignment function where w does not tesselate D_t^3.

Fig. 3 shows a module assignment function
$S: K^3 \to \{0,1,2,3\}$ for a regular binary tree D_t^3. S is w-conflictfree for $w = \{\varepsilon, L, LR, RL\}$, but w does not tesselate K. (Obviously we have $RL \in w(\varepsilon) \cap w(R) \neq \emptyset$). This example can be easily extended to regular n-ary trees.

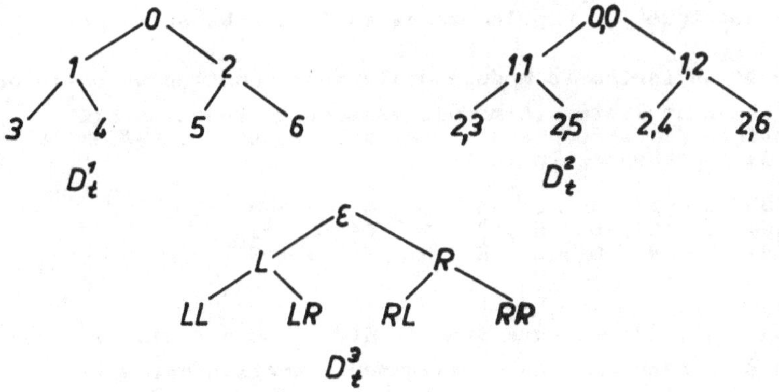

Fig. 1

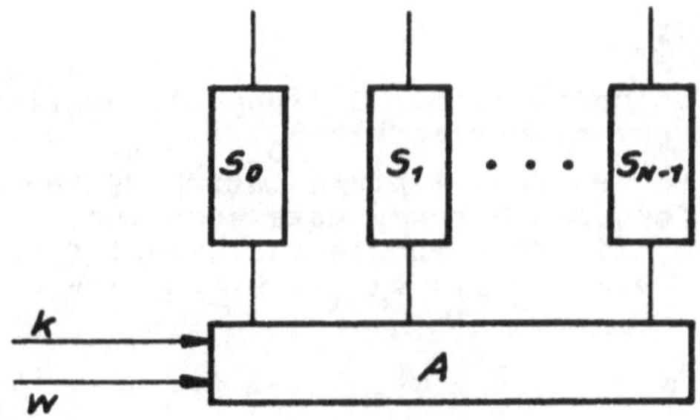

Fig. 2

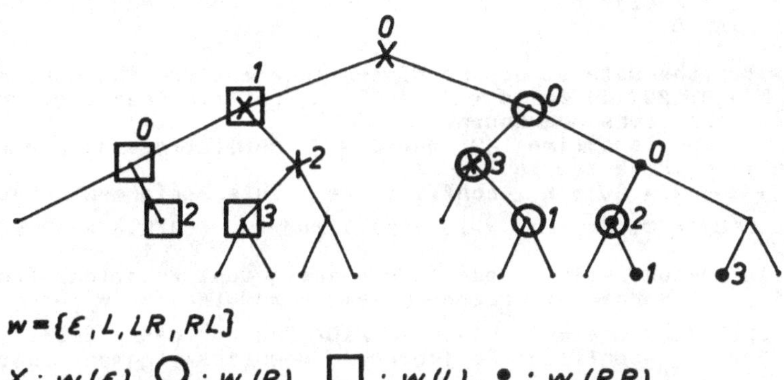

Fig. 3

In the case of a scanning field it is easy to prove that every isotropic function is regular and vice verca.

This is not true for regular trees as it can be seen from the following examples.

Example of an isotropic module assignment function which is not regular.

Fig. 4 shows an isotropic module assignment function $S:K^3 \dashrightarrow \{0,1,...,9\}$ conflictfree for a complete binary subtree of depth 3 which is not regular. S is represented in Table 1.

S	0	1	2	3	4	5	6	7	8
L(S)	1	3	5	5	7	7	0	0	1
R(S)	2	4	6	6	8	8	4	3	2

Table 1

For $\alpha = \varepsilon$, β = RRL we have $S(\alpha) = S(\beta) = 0$ and $S(R\alpha) = 2 \neq 7 = S(R\beta)$.

Example of a regular module assignment function which is not isotropic.

In Fig. 5 a regular module assignment function $S:K^3 \dashrightarrow \{0,1,2,3\}$ which is not isotropic is represented.
A basis for this module assignment function is $\{\varepsilon, LLLL\}$, $\{\varepsilon, RR\}$, $\{\varepsilon, RLR\}$, $\{L, RL\}$, $\{LL, R\}$. The set $F_{S'}$, is $\{\varepsilon, L, LL, LR\}$ (for the notions compare /12/). As it is seen from Fig. 5 we have $S(\varepsilon) =$ $= S(RLL)$ and $\{S(L(\varepsilon)), S(R(\varepsilon))\} = \{1,2\}$ and $\{S(L(RLL)) = S(RLLL),$ $S(R(RLL)) = S(RLLR)\} = \{0,1\}$ and S is not isotropic.

Now we show that for an isotropic module assignment function S the address computation for every memory module $S_0,...,S_{N-1}$ can be decentralized. (This is essential for a VLSI implementation of the addressing circuitry.) We show this for an arbitrary data structure.
Let S be an isotropic w-conflictfree module assignment function for the data structure D = (K, F), $w = (w_0,...,w_{M-1})$, $M \leq N$, where N is the number of memory modules.

Then we define a mapping $\gamma: \{0,1,...,N-1\}^2 \dashrightarrow \{w_0, w, ..., w_{M-1}\}$ by

$$\gamma(\tilde{S}, P) = w_{i_{\tilde{S},P}}$$

if and only if for $k \in K$ $S(k) = \tilde{S}$ implies $S(w_{i_{\tilde{S},P}}(k)) = P$.

For $M < N$ γ is partially defined. Since S is isotropic, γ does not depend on k.
The address computation circuitry A for the memory module P $0 \leq P < N$ is shown in Fig. 6.

Till now for the data structure binary tree and for the numbers of memory modules N = 9, 20, 69 for d = 3, 4, 5 w_{dt}-conflictfree isotropic module assignment functions are known.
For d = 3 N = 9 is optimal /9/ and a w_{3t}-conflictfree module assignment function is represented in Tab. 1.
For d = 4 and N = 20 a w_{4t}-conflictfree module assignment function S for $k \in K^1$ is $S(0) = 0$, $S(L(k)) = 13\,S(k)+1 \bmod 20$, $S(R(k)) = 17\,S(k)+7 \bmod 20$ (s. /11/).
For special recursively linear module assignment functions (which are isotropic) the number of necessary memory modules for w_{dt}-conflictfree access for binary trees is given in /10/ and for n-ary trees in /11/.
For d = 3,4 w_{dt}-conflictfree isotropic module assignment functions are very favourable for the implementation of parallel memories. But for $d > 5$ the ratio of necessary memory modules and 2^d-1 will be to large.

To overcome this difficulty we use for the data structure D_t^2 the module assignment function

$$S(l(x),\ x) = x \bmod 2^d - 1.$$

We proof that S is w_{dt}-conflictfree.

For $(l(x),x) \in K^2$ the set of nodes of $w_{dt}(l(x),x)$ is

$\{ (l(x_i),x_i)/x_i = x+i2^{l(x)}\ ,\ i=0,\dots,2^d-2 \}$.

Supposing

$$x_i \bmod 2^d-1 = x_j \bmod 2^d-1 \quad \text{for} \quad 0 \leq i,\ j < 2^d-1$$

we have with $q = l(x) \bmod d$

$$(x_i - x_j) \bmod 2^d-1 = ((i-j)\cdot 2^q) \bmod 2^d-1 = 0.$$

Since 2^q and 2^d-1 are relatively prime we conclude $i = j$,

$$x_i \bmod 2^d-1 \neq x_j \bmod 2^d-1 \text{ for } i \neq j,\ 0 \leq i,\ j < 2^d-1$$

and S is w_{dt}-conflictfree.

Now we show how to implement a decentralized address modification circuitry A_P.

Let $(l(x_{i_P}),\ x_{i_P})$ the node of $w_{dt}(l(x),x))$ stored in memory module

$P,\ 0 \leq P < 2^d-1$. From $x_{i_P} = x+i_P \cdot 2^{l(x)}$ we conclude

$P = S(x_{i_P}) = \{ S(x) + i_P 2^{l(x) \bmod d} \} \bmod 2^d-1,$

$i_P = ((P - S(x))\delta\ ) \bmod 2^d-1$ with $(\delta \cdot 2^{l(x) \bmod d}) \bmod 2^d-1 = 1,$

$x_{i_P} = x + [((P - S(x)\delta\ ) \bmod 2^d-1] \, 2^{l(x)}$

and finally

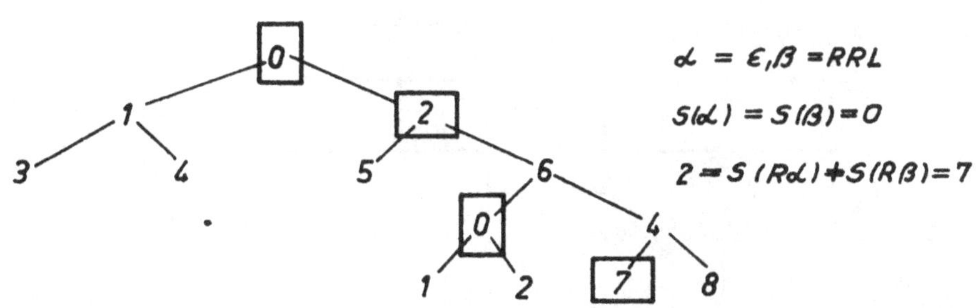

Fig. 4

$$a(x_{i_P}) = a(x) + a\left[(((P - S(x))\,\delta) \bmod 2^d-1)\; 2^{l(x)}\right] \qquad (x)$$

if the address function in linear in some field GF(p).

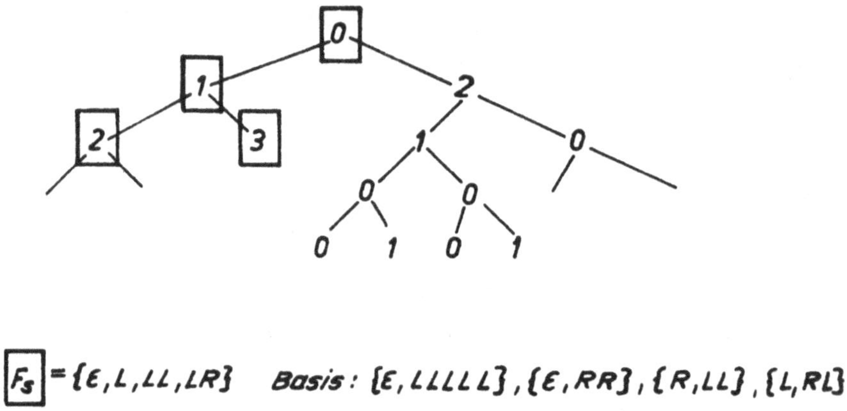

Fig. 5

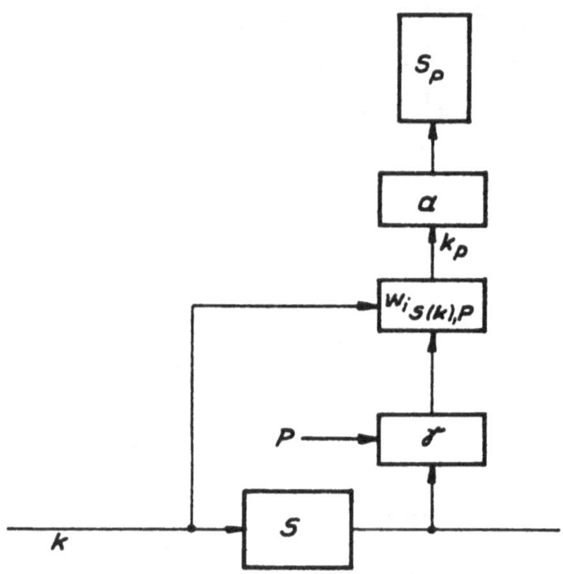

Fig. 6

Remark. Since $2^{l(x) \bmod d}$ and 2^d-1 are relatively prime, δ exists and δ is of the form $\delta = 2^{\eta}$.

The address modification circuitry A_p is a direct implementation of (x) and represented in Fig. 7. The technical realization is simple but without of the scope of this paper.

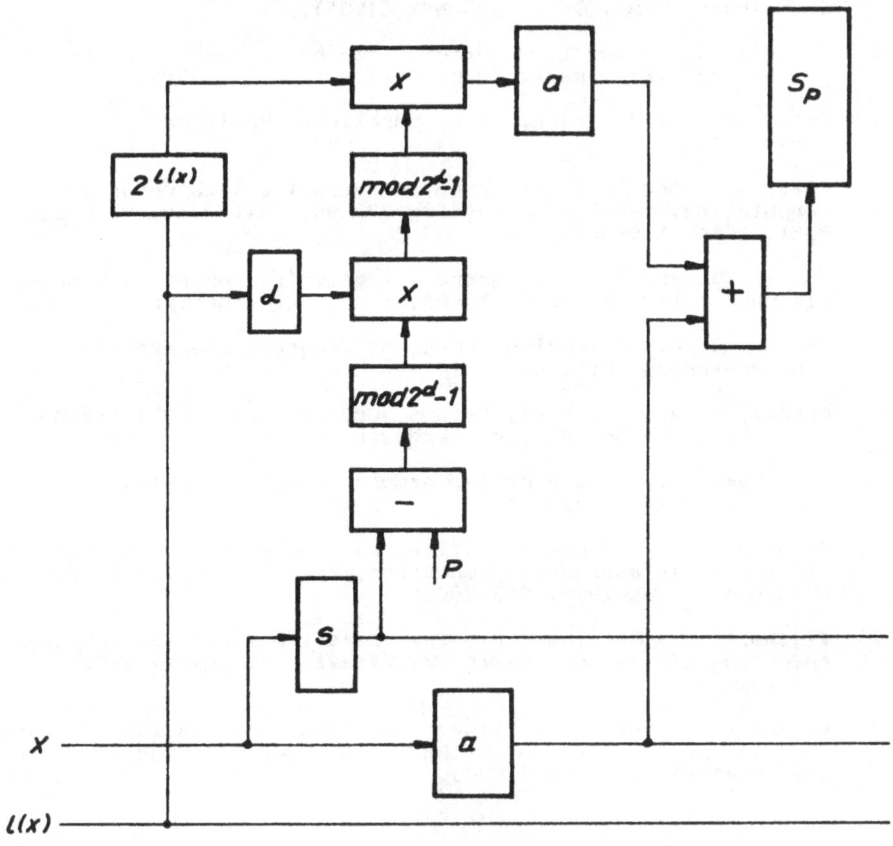

Fig. 7

References

1. Budnik, P. and D. K. Kuck. The organization and use of parallel memories. IEEE Trans. Comp. C-20, 1566-1569 (1971).

2. Shapiro, D. H.. Theoretical limitations on the use of parallel memories. Ph. D. Thesis, Dep. Comp. Sc. Univ. Illinois, UIUCDS-R-75-776 (1975).

3. Lawrie, D. H. and R. Vora. The prime memory system for array access. IEEE Trans. Comp. C-31, 435-442 (1982).

4. Voorhis, D. C. and T. H. Morrin, Memory system for image processing. IEEE Trans. Comp. C-27, 113-125 (1978).

5. Rebel, B. und M. Gössel, Ein paralleler Speicher. ZKI der AdW, Berlin, 1982.

6. Gössel, M. and B. Rebel. Parallel memories with recursive address computation, Parallel Computing 83, ed. Feilmeier, M. Elsevier Sc. Publ. 1984. 515-520.

7. Gössel, M. and B. Rebel. Parallel memories for picture processing (in russ.) Isv. AN SSSR, Techniceskaja kibernetika, in press.

8. Maurer, H. A., Datenstrukturen und Programmierverfahren, Teubner-Verlag, Stuttgart, 1974.

9. Gössel, M. and B. Rebel, Data structures and parallel memories, Proc. Parcella 86, Berlin, Akademie-Verlag 1986, 49-60.

10. Shirakawa, H., On a parallel memory to access trees. unpublished manuscript 1984.

11. Creutzburg, R., Parallel optimal subtree access with recursively linear module assignment functions, Proc. Parcella 86, Berlin, Akademie-Verlag 1986, 203-209.

12. Wijshoff, H., Storing trees into parallel memories. Parallel computing 85, ed. Feilmeier, M. Elsevier Sc. Publ. 1986, 253-261.

13. Wijshoff, H. and J. v. Leeuwen. Arbitrary versus periodic storage schemes and tesselation of the plane using one type of polyomino. Inf. Control 62, 1-25 (1984).

SYNAPSE: A MULTI-MICROPROCESSOR LISP MACHINE WITH PARALLEL GARBAGE COLLECTOR

Shogo MATSUI[1], Yoshinobu KATO[1], Shinsuke TERAMURA[2], Tomoyuki TANAKA[1], Nobuyuki MOHRI[1], Atsushi MAEDA[1], and Masakazu NAKANISHI[1]

Abstract

SYNAPSE is a multi-microprocessor Lisp Machine under development at Keio University. It is intended to be a multi-user Lisp machine that gives to each user a *List Processing Unit*, while list cell memory is shared by all the users. Several *Garbage Collection Units* constantly perform parallel garbage collection. This paper first gives an overview (hardware and software) of SYNAPSE, then describes the parallel garbage collector in detail.

Contents

1 Introduction

Artificial intelligence is drawing interest in a wide range of industries, and Lisp has been the language of choice for AI applications. When the size of the required memory grows large, while demand for a good interactive system persists, garbage collection becomes a problem. Other problems with existing Lisp machines have been their cost and their single-user limitation.

In view of the circumstances, we set out to design a new, low-cost Lisp machine toward these goals:

- **Large memory**
  —large enough to run practical AI programs and formula manipulation systems
- **Multi-user Lisp machine**
  Personal computer use should also be available.
- **High performance**
  The problem of garbage collection must be solved.

And the result was SYNAPSE, a multi-microprocessor Lisp machine with multiprocessor parallel garbage collector, now under development at Keio University.

Figure 1 (a) shows the configuration of SYNAPSE as a multi-user Lisp machine. SYNAPSE gives to each user a *List Processing Unit* (LPU), while *Com-*

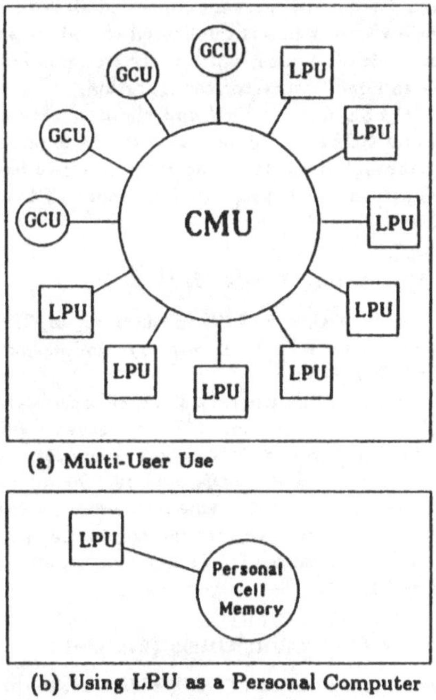

(a) Multi-User Use

(b) Using LPU as a Personal Computer

Figure 1: Configuration of SYNAPSE

[1]Department of Mathematics,
Faculty of Science and Technology, Keio University
14-1, Hiyoshi, 3 Chome, Kohoku, Yokohama 223, Japan

[2]R&D Laboratory, RICOH Ltd.
4686 Nippacho, Kohoku, Yokohama 223, Japan

mon Memory Unit (CMU), a large list cell memory, is shared by all the users. Several *Garbage Collection Units* (GCUs) constantly perform parallel garbage collection. When there aren't many users, a single user can use large cell space to execute large scale programs, while more LPUs can be attached to provide service to more users. Prototype SYNAPSE, nearing completion, comes with eight LPUs and four GCUs, and has cell memory of 8 Mbytes.

One LPU can be used as a personal computer by disconnecting it from CMU and connecting it to a personal cell memory (Figure 1 (b)).

The microprocessor used for LPUs and GCUs is Motorola's MC68000. The hardware and the software of SYNAPSE is designed with the enhanced microprocessors such as MC68020 in mind.

In Section 2 we give an overview of the hardware of SYNAPSE. In Section 3, we briefly describe SYNAPSE Lisp V 1.0, which is a subset of Common Lisp [7]. In Section 4, the parallel garbage collector, the most important feature of SYNAPSE, is described. Section 5 presents the results of the benchmark tests and our analysis. This paper closes with conclusions and future prospects in Section 6.

2 Architecture of SYNAPSE

The architecture of SYNAPSE is designed to achieve efficient parallel garbage collection. Hardware stack and tag memory are provided to meet the requirements of the parallel garbage collection algorithm. Common memory bus is duplicated to reduce access conflicts of the bus, which is the common bottleneck in a multiprocessor configuration.

SYNAPSE bus in CMU and those in each of LPUs and GCUs are connected with the external busses through bus arbiter and arbiter buffers (see Figure 2). In the figure, "PU" is either LPU or GCU.

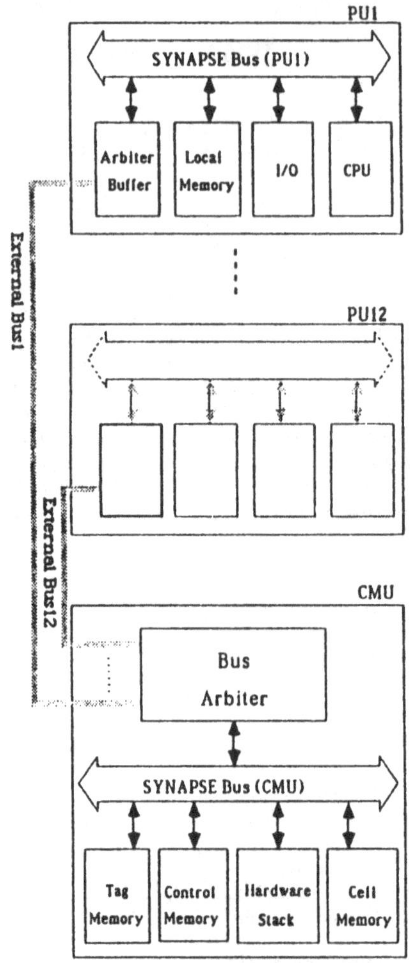

Figure 2: Connection of SYNAPSE Busses

List Processing Units (LPUs)

As shown in Figure 2, LPU is made up of CPU module, I/O module, local memory module, and arbiter buffer module.

LPUs and GCUs use MC68000 microprocessor (8 MHz clock), and support I/O interfaces for RS-232C, printer, floppy disk, and host computer.

Arbiter buffer is an interface module for the external bus, which is used to access the shared memory of CMU. It also accepts interrupts and generates interrupt vectors for communication among LPUs and GCUs.

Garbage Collection Units (GCUs)

Hardware configuration of GCU is identical to that of LPU. They are classified only by their use (GCU uses little I/O).

Common Memory Unit (CMU)

As shown in Figure 2, CMU is controlled by bus arbiter, which distributes bus cycles of CMU to LPUs and GCUs. Bus arbiter is designed so that there is never an absolute priority among LPUs and GCUs, nor is there a possibility of individual blocking.

CMU is divided into four blocks, each with its own SYNAPSE bus (see Figure 3). Bus locking for indivisible operations is restricted only to control block.

Bus arbiter consists of arbiter modules each of which is assigned to an external bus. One bus arbiter is required for each block, and thus within CMU there are four SYNAPSE busses and 12 external busses placed in a matrix form, at each element of which is an arbiter module.

Tag block is connected only to GCUs. It is used for mark bits of garbage collection. The addresses of tag block correspond exactly to those of cell block, and two blocks are distinguished by the bus cycle; for a word operation cell block is accessed, and for a byte operation tag block is accessed.

Control block is used to place the global data shared by LPUs and GCUs. It is configured just like cell block, except its bus arbiter is modified for bus locking.

Hardware stack block is used for communication among LPUs and GCUs.

Cell block is the memory module for list cells.

3 SYNAPSE Lisp V 1.0

Two main goals in the design of SYNAPSE Lisp V 1.0 were:

1. to implement the central features of Common Lisp [7], in order to give the user the ease and the power of programming in Lisp; and
2. to be as little a burden to the parallel garbage collector as possible

SYNAPSE Lisp V 1.0 is a subset of Common Lisp. While it has only a small number of data types (symbol, fixnum, cons, null, string, character, and compiled function),[1] it includes the central features of Common Lisp, such as Common Lisp control structures, lexical scoping, and multiple values. This allows the user to write clean programs in the same style as Common Lisp.

The Lisp interpreter is written using a cross assembler that we developed on the host system, UNIX 4.2bsd on the VAX-11/750.

The size of the source program for the interpreter is approximately 20,300 lines (416 Kbytes) in assembly language. The compiler is written mostly in Lisp itself (5400 lines). The Lisp structure editor is also written in Lisp (3000 lines). Other utilities written in Lisp total to 1700 lines.

SYNAPSE Lisp V 1.0 uses two stacks. The data stack is used for arguments to functions and local variables. The control stack is for return addresses and frame pointers. There is no Lisp data on the control stack, and removing the control stack from the root for garbage collection speeds up the marking phase of the parallel garbage collector.

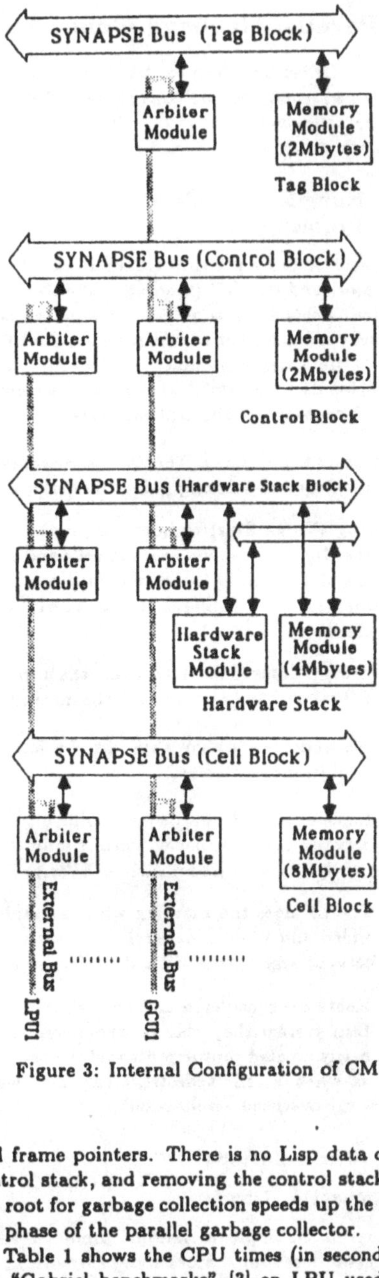

Figure 3: Internal Configuration of CMU

Benchmark	Interpreted	Slow Call	Fast Call
Tak	130.98	7.10	4.26
Takl	962.87	70.84	38.83
Destructive	887.89	34.90	28.16
Derivative	210.80	32.67	25.52
Iterative Div2	757.86	20.48	20.41
Recursive Div2	224.74	19.49	12.21
Terminal Print	9.39	9.40	9.40

Table 1: CPU Times for the Gabriel Benchmarks

Table 1 shows the CPU times (in seconds) for the "Gabriel benchmarks" [3] on LPU used as a personal computer. For the measurements, one LPU was disconnected from CMU and connected to smaller list cell memory of 2 Mbytes. The Lisp system used for the measurements had a sequential garbage collector, but no garbage collection times are included. In the table, "Interpreted" means interpreted execution. "Slow Call" is the compiled mode execution with debugging setting. "Fast Call" is the fastest compiled mode execution.

For the details of the Lisp system, see [8].

[1] Incorporation of bignum data type is nearly complete.

4 Parallel Garbage Collection

Garbage Collection Units of SYNAPSE are constantly performing parallel garbage collection. Our garbage collection algorithm is based on one by Kung and Song [4].

4.1 Kung and Song's Algorithm and Its Problems

Kung and Song's algorithm assumes one LP (List Processor) and one GC (Garbage Collector) organization. *Roots* are fixed cells from which all active cells are reachable. For communication the LP and the GC use a deque (double ended queue), whose different ends are accessed to avoid access conflicts. The GC repeats this three-phase cycle:

Root Insertion Phase The GC inserts roots into the deque as starting point for marking.

Marking Phase Starting from roots in the deque, the GC recursively traces list cells and marks them. If a cell is found that may need to be marked, the LP marks it and inserts it into the deque.

Collecting Phase The GC collects the unmarked cells as garbage, and unmark the marked cells.

Kung and Song's algorithm has the following implementational problems.

1. Implementation of a deque is difficult. Also, a deque does not solve access conflicts in a multiprocessor system such as SYNAPSE.
2. The LP does the marking when a pointer is added and when a new cell is created. This casts a large overhead on the LP.
3. Roots are considered as fixed, while in a real Lisp system they change dynamically. If a newly created root is processed the same way as when a cell is destructively modified, a large overhead would result.

4.2 Our Solutions

Implementing Deque

Because of the implementational problems with a deque, we opted for a stack designed with special considerations for indivisible operations.

Replacing Pointers and Creating New Cells

In Kung and Song's algorithm, the LP marks the newly created cells and cells to which a pointer is added. This is in order to avoid a same cell being pushed many times when the cell is multiply referenced by creation of pointer(s) to it. But this rarely occurs. When taking the LP's overhead into account, we decided not to have the LP mark the cells, even though this may cause the GC's inefficiency.

Creation of New Roots

After a pointer to a cell is copied into a register or pushed on the stack, if all the pointers to that cell are deleted except for the ones in the register or stack, the cell becomes a root. If the cell is not marked by the time all the other pointers are deleted, it can be collected even though it is active. This is in principle the same problem as when a pointer of a cell is modified. In Kung and Song's

```
[Root insertion phase]

  begin
    <<push all roots onto the stack>> ;
    MARKING := true
  end

[Marking phase]

  begin
    while <<the stack is not empty>> do
      begin
        n := pop ;
        while (n <> NIL) and
              (n.left <> f) and
              (n.color <> black) do
          begin
            n.color := black ;
            push(n.right) ;
            n := n.left
          end
      end ;
    MARKING := false
  end

[Collecting phase]

  begin
    for i := 1 to M do
      if i.color = white then
        APPEND(i)
      else if i.left <> f then
        i.color := white
  end

Procedure APPEND(n)

  begin
    n.color := off-white ;
    n.left := f ;
    n.right := NIL ;
    region _append do
      begin
        FREE.right.right := n ;
        FREE.right := n
      end
  end
```

Figure 4: Algorithm of the GC

Procedure LPa

```
begin
  if MARKING then
    push(m.left) ;
  m.left := n
end
```

Procedure LPc

```
begin
  region _lpc
  when FREE.left <> FREE.right do
    begin
      NEW := FREE.left ;
      FREE.left := FREE.left.right ;
      NEW.left := m ;
      NEW.right := n
    end
end
```

Figure 5: Algorithm of the LP

algorithm, when a new pointer to a cell is added, the LP inserts the newly pointed cell into the deque to inform the GC of this cell. If the newly created root is processed this way, every copying of registers or pushing onto the stack would require insertion into the deque, resulting in a very large overhead.

So instead of inserting the newly pointed cell, we decided to insert (push) the deleted cell. This may delay the GC by one cycle, but the LP's efficiency is greatly improved.

4.3 Garbage Collection Algorithm

We first describe the data structure necessary to present the algorithm, then the algorithm itself.

The Data Structure

Let M cells of fixed size be numbered from 1 to M. A cell has two pointer fields and a color field. The contents of the left (right) pointer field of cell n is written as "n.left" ("n.right"). The color field of the cell is denoted as "n.color". The possible colors for a cell are black, gray, off-white, and white.

The free list is maintained by two pointers named FREE.left and FREE.right. These pointers are placed at a fixed location, and point respectively the head and the tail of the free list. The free list is made up of cells $n_1, n_2, \ldots, n_k$, and has the following properties.

- **F1.** FREE.left=n_1, n_k.right=NIL
- **F2.** for $1 \leq i < k$, n_i.right=n_{i+1}
- **F3.** for $1 \leq i \leq k$, n_i.left=f
- **F4.** for $1 \leq i \leq k$, n_i.color=off-white
- **F5.** FREE.right=n_k

The initial condition is n_1=1 and n_k=M. The left pointer field of each cell in the free list contains the special value "f".

When a new cell is created from the free list, a pointer variable NEW points to it. The value of NEW is a root.

Algorithm of the GC

Figure 4 shows the algorithm of the GC in a Pascal-like notation. MARKING is a boolean variable which is true when the GC is in the marking phase and false otherwise.

Note that the phases of all the GCs must be synchronized. For instance, assume that a GC enters the marking phase when a root of an LP has not been pushed onto the stack, and the GC finds the marking stack to be empty, causing the GC to enter the collecting phase. Then the root and the cells pointed only from that root are collected even though they are active.

Also, operations to append the garbage cells to the free list and those for creation of new cells must be made indivisible. In our algorithm, we use the following notation for indivisible operations.

```
region sem_var [when <cond>] do
      <statement>
```

This is to be read as defining the portion <statement> as an indivisible operation with respect to the variable sem_var. That is, this must be a critical section. Variable _lpc is used here for procedure LPc, and variable _append for APPEND. When the optional portion when <cond> is present, <cond> is used for a condition to enter the critical section. First the value of <cond> is checked indivisibly, and if it's true, <statement> is indivisibly processed. If the value of <cond> is false, the check is repeated until it turns true.

Stack operations push and pop are indivisible.

Algorithm of the LP

To define the algorithm of the LP is to give a specification for each kind of operation that modify list structures (Figure 5). LPa is an operation that changes the contents of the left pointer of the cell m to point to cell n, and LPc is an operation that creates a new cell whose left and right pointer fields contain pointers to cell m and n. We can safely restrict LPa and LPc this way with no loss of generality.

4.4 Implementation

Inter-Processor Communication

Entry to each phase must be synchronized among all GCUs. To do this, one of GCUs is made the supervisor for all. This processor is called the SV (Supervisor). In the root insertion phase, SV interrupts LPUs, causing them to push their roots onto the stack. The synchronization of exits from phases is realized using a shared variable in control memory.

The SV also initializes the free list and the work area, and does exception processing.

Support from Hardware

Hardware supports efficient execution of indivisible operations required by our algorithm. One such support is hardware stack. Hardware stack enables indivisible push and pop operations by accessing a fixed address in memory.

Other support are bus duplication and division of CMU. Instead of just dividing the memory equally we divided CMU into four differently used blocks. They are cell block, tag block, hardware stack block, and control block (see Section 2). Because LPU mainly uses cell block whereas GCU mainly uses tag block, access conflicts are reduced.

Efficiency Considerations

In our system, LPUs push the cells which need to be marked on the hardware stack. Then for subsequent marking, the local stacks of GCUs are used. This reduces access conflicts.

In the collecting phase, the entire cell space is scanned to reclaim the garbage cells. Each GCU is assigned an equally divided portion of the cell space for this task.

In the original Kung and Song's algorithm, the GC inserts roots in the root insertion phase, requiring that roots be available to GCU. This may mean that all operations must be done on the common memory instead of machine registers, or to maintain a copy of the registers in the shared memory. We examined a garbage collection system which adopts the former method, and found it inefficient. So we decided to let LPU do the root insertion. This interrupts LPU's list processing, but the overall performance is much better this way.

5 Performance Evaluation

To evaluate the performance of the parallel garbage collection system (henceforth "parallel system"), we made benchmark measurements and compared the results with a sequential garbage collection system ("sequential system").

Benchmark Conditions

We took several programs from "Lisp Contest"[2] [6] and made extensive comparisons (reaching 100 total hours) of the following systems.

- As the parallel system, using one LPU, two GCUs, and CMU of 8 Mbytes for cell block and 2 Mbytes for each of hardware stack block, tag block, and control block
- As the sequential system, using one LPU and CMU of the same configuration as above

[2] "Lisp Contest" provides a set of standard benchmark problems, which are widely used in Japan to evaluate Lisp systems.

The benchmark programs we used were for evaluating the performance of Lisp systems and do not consume many cells. Therefore to increase cell consumption and execution time, the programs were run interpreted, rather than compiled. Some measurements were made with about half of the cell space (500,000 cells) in constantly active state, to simulate application programs that use a large data base.

Summary of the Results

From the results we obtained a graph (Figure 6). GC Ratio and Improvement Ratio in the graph are defined as follows.

$$GC\ Ratio = \frac{Tseq.gc}{Tseq.total}$$

$$Improvement\ Ratio = \frac{Tseq.total - Tparallel}{Tseq.total}$$

Tseq.gc is the garbage collection time in the sequential system, *Tseq.total* is the total execution time in the sequential system, and *Tparallel* is the total execution time in the parallel system.

The sequential system is faster if no garbage collection occurs. But if garbage collection occurs even once, the parallel system shows better performance.

Improvement Ratio shows the improvement of the parallel system over the sequential counterpart. But when no garbage collection occurs, this value is negative and it can be taken as indicating the amount of overhead that the parallel system's extra processing introduces. Results of the measurements show that the overhead is at most 5%, and approximately 4% in average.

Improvement Ratio ranges from about 2.5% to 28%. The improvement of the parallel system is especially large when there is a load due to constantly active cells. In the sequential system, not only is there an increase in the time for one garbage collection, but also garbage collection is entered more

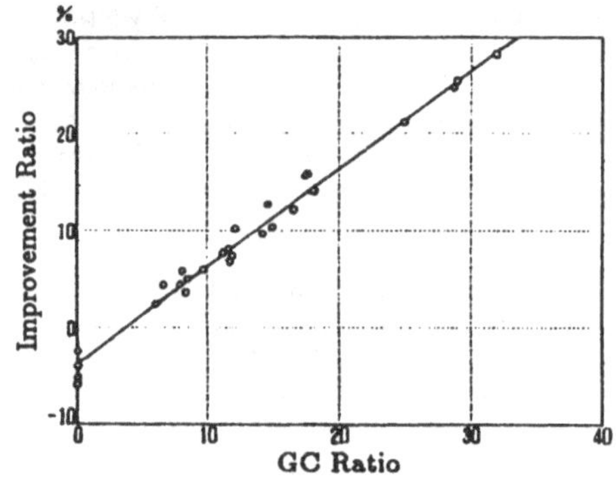

Figure 6: GC Ratio vs. Improvement Ratio

frequently because there are less free cells. This is not the case for the parallel system.

But once the cell consumption exceeds the reclamation, the parallel system's performance greatly degrades. This is mainly due to the longer period for one cycle in the parallel system.

In our measurements for the sequential system, each measurement was made after garbage collection was forced beforehand. In real use however, even for a small processing an unlucky user may be kept waiting for a long interruption caused by garbage collection. One definite advantage of the parallel system, which does not turn up in numbers or figures, is that the garbage collection is always performed, even while the Lisp system is waiting for user input. Thus such an unlucky interruption seldom occurs in the parallel system.

We summarize our comparison of the two systems in the experiment:

- The overhead for extra processing in the parallel system is approximately 4%.
- The parallel system shows improvement of 2.5% to 28% over the sequential system.
- The relationship between GC Ratio and Improvement Ratio can be expressed by a linear equation. The parallel system shows better performance over the sequential system when GC Ratio exceeds 4%.
- When cell consumption is within reach of reclamation, the parallel system shows better performance.
- Once cell consumption exceeds reclamation, the parallel system performs worse than the sequential system.

6 Conclusions and Future Work

Our goal is to construct a multi-microprocessor Lisp machine capable of providing a highly productive environment to many users. Although the final evaluation is not yet available, experiments of the parallel garbage collection system has given us promising results, as we have shown.

At present we have five LPUs and four GCUs. Four LPUs are used as personal computers for software development. The remaining LPU is connected to CMU, and is used for garbage collection experiments. From the experiments we are investigating the optimal number of LPUs and GCUs.

The current Lisp system does not include the array data type because the garbage collection algorithm could not be extended to handle compaction of the heap storage. We are examining the possibility of incorporating other garbage collection algorithms [1,2,5] to our parallel system.

We are considering the idea of developing a communication facility between LPUs, which will enable users to exchange programs or data. Parallel Lisp system is also a possibility.

Interested in the object oriented programming methodology, we are designing an object oriented operating system, as well as testing our ideas by implementing in Lisp a Smalltalk-80 virtual machine.

Prototype SYNAPSE, nearing completion, is planned to be used in an introductory Lisp programming course at Keio University.

Acknowledgements

The design of SYNAPSE Lisp V 1.0 owes much to the Spice Lisp source code placed in public domain, which we obtained through courtesy of Professor Scott E. Fahlman and other members of the Spice Lisp project at Carnegie-Mellon University. and we'd like to express our gratitude.

We'd also like to thank Kimio TSUJI whose onboard monitor, Tsujibug Ver2.23, is still alive and well.

References

[1] Baker, H. G. "List-Processing in Real Time on a Serial Computer". Comm. ACM, Vol. 21, No. 4 (April 1976) 280–294.

[2] Deutsch, L. P. and Bobrow, D. G. "An Efficient Incremental Automatic Garbage Collector". Comm. ACM, Vol. 19, No. 9 (September 1976) 522–526.

[3] Gabriel, Richard P. *Performance and Evaluation of Lisp Systems.* The MIT Press (Cambridge, Massachusetts, 1985).

[4] Kung, H. T. and Song, S. W. "An Efficient Parallel Garbage Collection System and its Correctness Proof". Tech. Note, Dept. of Computer Science, Carnegie-Mellon University (Pittsburgh, Pennsylvania, 1977).

[5] Lieberman, H. and Hewitt, C. "A Real-Time Garbage Collector Based on the Lifetimes of Objects". Comm. ACM, Vol. 26, No. 6 (June 1983) 419–429.

[6] Okuno, H. G. "The proposal of the benchmarks for The Third Lisp Contest and The First Prolog Contest". Report of WGSYM, No. 28-4, Information Processing Society of Japan (June 1985).

[7] Steele, Guy L. Jr., et al. *Common Lisp: The Language.* Digital Press (1984).

[8] Tanaka T. *Optimizations in a Lisp Compiler.* Master's thesis. Keio University (Yokohama, Japan, 1987).

A NOTE ON OPTIMAL PARALLEL TRANSFORMATIONS OF REGULAR EXPRESSIONS TO NONDETERMINISTIC FINITE AUTOMATA

Wojciech Rytter [1)]

In this note we show that the transformation of regular expressions to corresponding nondeterministic finite automata can be done in log(n) time using n/log(n) processors on a parallel random access machine without write conflicts (P-RAM). It is easy to parallelise the classical transformation of Hopcroft and Ullman [5]. The parallelisation of the more economical transformation of Sedgewick [8] is more interesting and it is obtained by applying (in two stages) a homomorphism which relates the automaton obtained through the transformation from [5] to the one obtained through the transformation from [8]. Our aim is not only the construction of the corresponding finite automaton, but also a development of a method for very efficient parallelisation of two known sequential algorithms. One can imagine that the input to our method is a known sequential algorithm and the output is its parallel version. It is sensible to provide such parallelisation for the best known sequential algorithm for a given problem. This is why we deal also with Sedgewick's transformation which is more economic (compare Fig.1 and Fig.4) than the one presented in [5], though it does not change the order of the complexity of algorithms obtained. We develop the following technique for the recursive construction. The tree of the recursion is constructed and some parameters associated with the nodes of this tree (pairs of states) are computed. This is the main step. Then, instead of simulating the recursion bottom-up or top-down, appropriate constructing actions are executed for each node of the recursion tree in parallel. The previously computed parameters (associated with the nodes) are such that the action for a given node is, at this stage, easy and independent of the action for any other node.

1. Introduction

We show that the problem of the synthesis of nondeterministic finite automata with ε-moves (nfa's, for short) is very well parallelizable. By an optimal parallel algorithm (for a given problem computable sequentially in linear time) we mean one that satisfies p*t=O(n), where p is the number of processors used, t is the parallel time and t is very small (usually logarithmic). Optimal parallel algorithms are known for few interesting computational problems: computing associative function of n variables, selection, string matching, converting an expression to its parse tree, evaluating expressions, parsing bracket languages (see [1,2,3,7,9]). We add to this list another problem: the synthesis of nfa's. Our model of parallel computation is a parallel random access machine without write conflicts (P-RAM). Such a model is known also as a CREW P-RAM. It consists of a number of synchronously working processors (RAM's) which are using a common memory . No two processors can attempt to write in the same step into the same location, however many processors can read from the same location.

1) Dept. of Computer Science, University of Warwick, Coventry CV4 7AL,U.K. and
Institute of Informatics, Warsaw University, PKiN VIII p, 00-901 Warszawa, sk.poczt.1210, Poland

The representation for nfa's chosen here is the same as the one used by Sedgewick, who called such nfa's pattern matching machines (see [8], chapter 20). However we start with the classical construction of nfa's from [5], this and the one given by Sedgewick are similar. The latter one is more economic (creates less states), but the Hopcroft and Ullman construction is easier to start with.
The nfa consists of a number of states, which are consecutive integers from 1 to m. The automaton can be represented by a diagram, with edges labelled by symbols or empty string,see Fig.1, or by arrays, see Fig.2. There are two special designated states: initial and final state. There is no edge outgoing from the final state. The automaton is represented by three tables called symbol, next1 and next2. If there is only one outgoing edge from the state s and if this edge is labelled c then symbol[s]=c, otherwise symbol[s] contains the empty string. The state next1[s] is the first state accessible from s by an edge, and next2[s] is the second state. If there is only one outgoing edge then next2 is undefined. Given a regular expression our algorithms construct the array representation of the automaton.

2. Parallelising Hocroft and Ullman transformation

The construction of the nfa is recursive. Automata are constructed for subexpressions and these automata are composed according to the operator: +, * or • (concatenation). The rules of the composition are presented in Fig.2. If one applies these rules to the expression a^*•b•$(a+c)^*$ then the automaton presented in Fig.1 is obtained (up to a renumeration of states). We shall construct the nfa using the parse tree of the expression. With every node of this tree there is associated the pair [p1,p2] of initial and terminal state of a nfa correspoding to the subexpression rooted at this node. The input to our algorithms is a regular expression given in a vector (containing consecutive symbols of the expression) of the length n (the same representation as in [1]). Such a representation allows a consecutive numbering of the leaves of the tree of the expression easily in log(n) time using n/log(n) processors. We demonstrate the construction on the expression a*•b•(a+c)*.

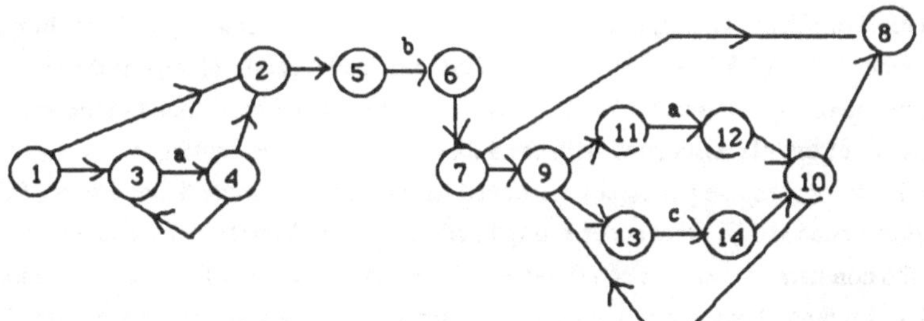

Fig.1

Algorithm1 {parallel version of Hopcroft and Ullman transformation}
Step 1
We construct the parse tree for a given regular expression. This can be done in log(n) time with

n/log(n) processors using the conversion of Bar-on and Vishkin [1]. The nodes of the tree are numbered in preorder in log(n) time with n/log(n) processors. The algorithm of Gibbons and Rytter [3] can be used.The nodes are numbered from 1 to r, where r=O(n).

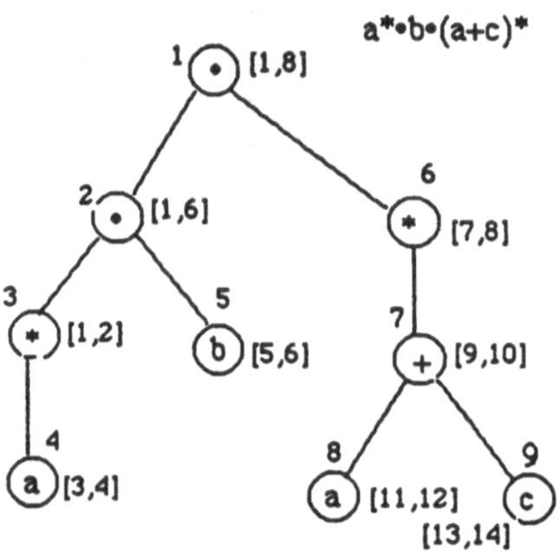

state	symbol	next1	next2
1		3	2
2		5	
3	a	4	
4		2	
5	b	6	
6		7	
7		9	8
8			
9		11	13
10		8	
11	a	12	
12		10	
13	c	14	
14		10	

Fig.2. The parse tree for the expression $W = a^{*} \bullet b \bullet (a+c)^{*}$

Step 2

The next step is the creation of the set of states and a distribution of these states among nodes of the tree. Each leaf and each node with the operator * or + needs two new states (according to the rules of combining smaller automata into larger ones). Hence the total number m of states equals twice the number of such nodes.This number can be easily computed in log n time with n/log(n) processors in the same way as computing an associative function of n variables [6]. Hence the set of states is {1,2,..,m}. We can rank the nodes requiring two new states. This corresponds to to the ranking of marked entries of a vector and can be done by an optimal parallel algorithm reducing this problem to the prefix computation problem. Then the node with the rank k receives states [2k-1,2k]. In our example these are nodes 3,4,5,6,7,8,9. The node 3 is the first node and receives [1,2], 4 is the second and receives [3,4] and so on. The states [p,q] associated with a given node correspond to the initial, respectively, final state of the nfa associated with the subexpressions corresponding to the subtree rooted at that node. Now we compute pairs [p,q] associated with nodes containing the operator •. Call such nodes nonmarked nodes and all other nodes marked nodes. Let left(v) be the left son and right(v) be the right son of the nonmarked node v .Let leftmarked(v)=left^k(v), where k is the minimal number such that left^k(v) is marked. Define analogously rightmarked(v). Then we associate with the nonmarked node v the states [p,q], where p is the initial state associated with leftmarked(v) and q is the final state associated with rightmarked(v).

In our example leftmarked(1)=3, rightmarked(1)=6. The states associated with the node 1 are [1,8].

If the functions leftmarked and rightmarked are computed then the computation of the pairs of states associated with nonmarked nodes can be easily done in O(1) time with n processors or in log(n) time with n/log(n) processors (grouping actions into portions of size log n).

We show how to compute the function leftmarked(v) for all nonmarked nodes v in parallel in log(n) time with n/log(n) processors. We can take the vector of the nodes in preorder. For each nonmarked element v of this vector leftmarked(v) is the first marked element to the right of v. Observe that such an element always exists, because leaves are marked.In our example the corresponding vector is: [1, 2, 3, 4, 5, 6, 7, 8, 9], the only nonmarked nodes are 1,2. Let us take the vector of zeros and ones whose entries correspond to the nodes. A given entry contains one iff the corresponding node is nonmarked. In our example this vector is [1, 1, 0, 0, 0, 0, 0, 0, 0].

It is enough to compute for each position v containing one the number d of consecutive ones from this position to the right.Then leftmarked(v)=v+d. Define the following operation on integers:

k©j= if k,j>0 then k+j else if k≤0 then k else -(k+|j|)

If we have a vector of zeros and ones then the number of consecutive ones starting from a given position to the right is equal to the absolute value of the product (using ©) of all numbers (which are, in our case, zeros and ones) to the right of that position (including this position). This as a standard prefix computation of computing $x_i © x_{i+1} .... © x_r$ for i=1,..,r . The operation © is associative. Such computation can be made by an optimal parallel algorithm, see for example [6].

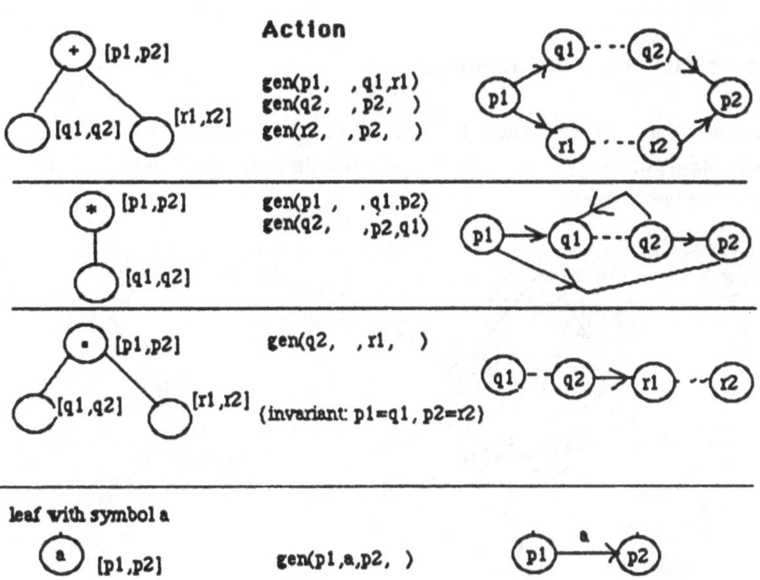

Fig.3

Analogously the function rightmarked is computed. Hence the assignment of pairs [p,q] to the nodes of the parse tree of the expression can be done in log(n) time with n/log(n) processors.

Step 3

We declare the following procedure:

procedure gen(s,sym,s1,s2); {sym is a letter or the empty string, s2 could be not defined (a blank)}

begin

if sym is a letter **then** symbol[s]:=sym; next1[s]:=s1; **if** s2 is defined **then** next2[s]:=s2 **end**;
Assume that initially the table symbol contains only empty strings. Next we execute:
for each node v **do in parallel**
if [p1,p2] is the pair of states associated with v then perform the local action corresponding to the operator associated with v, see the column titled action in Fig.3.

In Fig.3 the missing parameter (in the calls of gen)) corresponds to the emty space (in the column symbol) or to the undefined state (in the column next2).
(One action for a given node can be done in O(1) sequential time. Hence step 3 can be performed in O(1) time using n processors or in log n time using only n/log(n) processors.)
end of Algorithm1.

The following fact follows directly from the construction of the algorithm and the comments included.
Fact1
Algorithm1 simulates Hopcroft and Ullman transformation in parallel time log(n) using n/log(n) processors.

3. Parallelising Sedgewick's transformation

The rules of the compositions for the finite automaton synthesis from [8] are presented in the last column in Fig.5. If one applies them to our example expression then one obtains the nfa presented in Fig.4 (up to a renumeration of states).

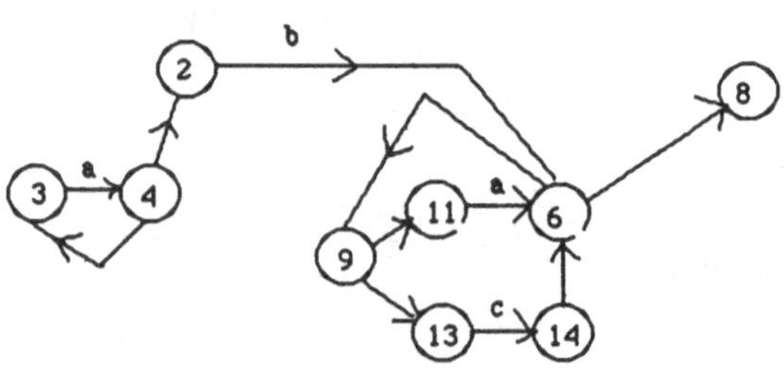

Fig.4.

Algorithm2 {parallel version of Sedgewick transformation}

Step 1 The same as step1 in Algorithm1.
Step 2 The same as step 2 in Algorithm1.
At this moment we have for our example the same tree as in Fig.2 ,with the same pairs of states for each node. In the next step we start to change these pairs.
Step 3
Initialize the array contract. For each state s initially set contract[s]=s. Then for each node v containing the operator + or * (in parallel) change one entry of the array contract usi local information about

the sons of v . Make this according to the assignments enclosed in rectangles in the column titled "dependency" in Fig.5. Next compute the table contract*[s]=contract^k[s], where k is the minimum integer such that contract^k[s]=contract^{k+1}[s]. (The array contract is treated here as a function which is iterated.) Then execute the following:

for each node v **do in parallel** {states contraction corresponding to + and * }
 let [p1,p2] be the pair associated with v;
 replace this pair by [contract*[p1],contract*[p2]].

For our example (see Fig.2) we obtain contract[7]=10, contract[10]=12,and contract[1]=4. Then we obtain contract*[7]=12, contract*[10]=12, and contract*[1]=4. For all other entries s there is contract*[s]=s. The tree with the actual pairs of states is the first tree presented in Fig.6.

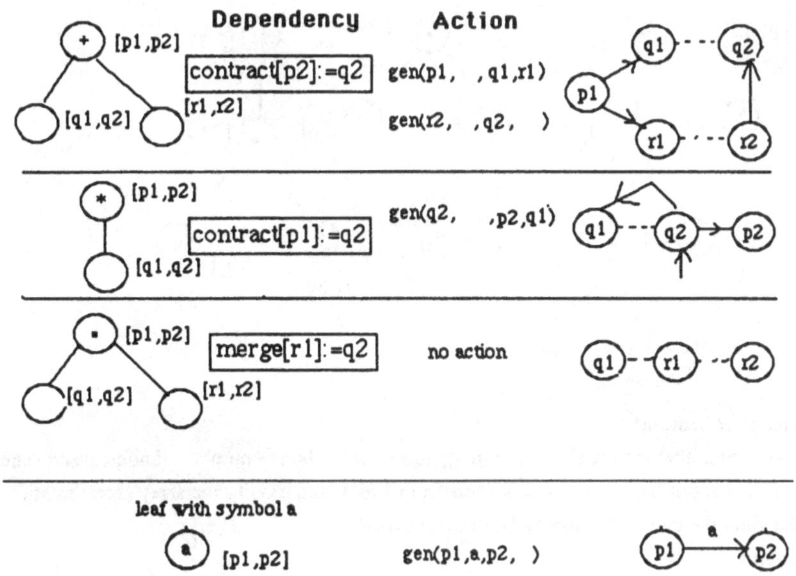

Fig.5

Step 4

Initialize the array merge, initially for each state s set merge[s]=s. Then execute:

for each node v containing the operator • **do in parallel**
 let (q1,q2), (r1,r2) be pairs associated with left and right sons of v;
 merge[r1]:=q2;

for each node v **do in parallel** {merging states with respect to • }
 let [p1,p2] be the pair associated with v;
 replace this pair by [merge[p1],merge[p2]].

In our example we set merge[5]=2 and merge[12]=6. Then the states 5 and 12 are replaced everywhere by 2 and 6, respectively. We obtain the tree named final tree in Fig.6.

Step 5

for each node v do in parallel

perform the local action specified in column "action" in Fig.5 according to the type of v; Use local informations about states of a given node and its sons in the final tree updated in steps 3 and 4.

For our example at this moment we have the array representation corresponding to the nfa from Fig.4.

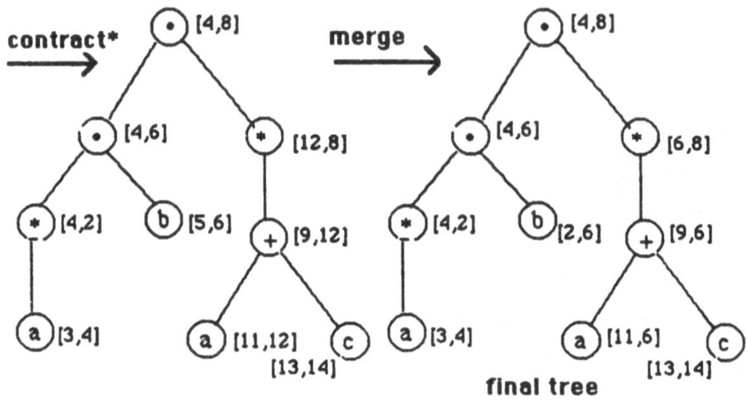

Fig.6

Step 6 {garbage collection}

Mark each state s such that contract*[s]≠s or merge[s]≠s. Let m be the number of nonmarked states. Number nonmarked states by consecutive integers from 1 to m and modify the array representation is such a way that only the entries for nonmarked states remain.

end of Algorithm2.

Fact 2

Algorithm2 can be implemented to work in log(n) time using n/log(n) processors.

Proof.

The parallel instructions "for each ... do in parallel" in steps 3, 4 and 5 can be obviously done in O(1) time with n processors or in log(n) time with n/log(n) processors (grouping actions).

It is enough to show how the computation of contract* can be done in log(n) time with n/log(n) processors. It can be easily computed in log(n) time with n processors using the doubling technique. Now observe that if s is in a pair associated with a node v then contract[s] is in a pair associated with v or its son. Hence contract* can be computed using the structure of our tree.The method from [3] or [7] of compressing the tree by a factor of log(n) and computing the function for the compressed tree can be used. This method works in log(n) time with n/log(n) processors.We refer the reader to [3, 4]. The main idea is a partition of leaves into segments of length log(n) and making some preprocessing. Such methods work well for trees whose leaves can be consecutively numbered by an optimal parallel

algorithm, this is the case when leaves correspond to operands in the expression given as a vector. A parallel prefix computation can be used,see [6]. The renumeration of states in the last step can be done easily in log(n) time with n/log(n) processors. It can be also reduced to a parallel prefix computation. This completes the proof.

Remark

In general, if one knows which pairs of elements are to be mapped into one (let us join such elements by an edge) then computing a homomorphism is analogous to the connected components problem. Let us look at pairs of states associated with the nodes in Fig.2. The operator • at node 1 implies that (when applying the more economical Sedgewick's construction) states 6 and 7 should be identified. We join them by an edge. Analogously 2 and 5 should be joined by an edge. The composition rule in Fig.5 for the operator * implies that states 1, 4 should be joined by an edge. Proceeding in this way we obtain the following graph whose nodes are states and whose edges indicate which states are to be identified:

6-7-10-12 1-4 2-5 3 8 9 11 13 14 .

This graph has 9 components and they correspond to the states of the automaton in Fig.4. It has a very special property. Generally, the subgraph consisting of edges implied by the operators * and + is a set of edge-disjoint paths (top-down in our parse tree). The subgraph consisting of all other edges (which are implied by •) is a set of disjoint edges (cross edges in our tree).

It is not even known whether the connected components problem (in the general case) can be computed in log(n) time on a parallel random access machine without write conflicts. In our case log n time and n/log(n) processors were enough because of a special structure of the corresponding graph and the homomorphism involved and because of the method of computing this homomorphism in two stages (steps 3 and 4). This part of the algorithm can be viewed as an optimal parallel algorithm for the connected components problem restricted to a simple subclass of undirected graphs.

Acknowledgment

The author thanks A.M.Gibbons for linguistic corrections.

References

[1] I.Bar-On,and U.Vishkin.. Optimal parallel generation of a computation tree form. ACM Trans.on Progr.Lang.and Systems 7,2 (1985) 348-357

[2] R.Cole. An optimal selection algorithm. Ultracomputer Note #97, Courant Institute of Math.Sciences, march (1986)

[3] A.Gibbons, W.Rytter. An optimal parallel algorithm for dynamic expression evaluation and its applications.Accepted for Found.of Software Techn.and Theor. Comp. Science,to appear in Lect.Notes in Comp. Science, Springer-Verlag, december (1986),

[4] S.Fortune, J.Wyllie. Parallelism in random access machines, Proceedings of 10th ACM Symp. on tHeoretical Computer SCience (1978) 114-118

[5] J.Hopcroft,J.Ullman. Introduction to automata theory, languages and computations. Chapter 2. Addison-Wesley (1979)

[6] G.Kindervater and J.Lenstra. An introduction to parallelism in combinatorial optimization. Report OS-R8501,Centre for Mathematics and Computer Science, Amsterdam (1985)

[7] W.Rytter. Optimal parallel parsing of bracket languages. Research Report RR84, Dept. of Computer Science, University of Warwick (1986)

[8] R.Sedgewick. Algorithms. Chapter 20. Addison-Wesley (1983)

[9] U.Vishkin. Optimal parallel pattern matching in strings. in Automata, languages, computation (ed.W.Brauer), Lect.Notes in Comp. Science 194 (1985) 497-508

OPTIMAL PARALLEL PARSING OF BRACKET LANGUAGES

Wojciech Rytter [1) and Raffaele Giancarlo [2)

(All correspondence to the first author)

Abstract: We prove that the parsing problem for bracket context-free languages can be solved in log(n) time using n/log(n) processors on a parallel random access machine without write conflicts (P-RAM).On the way we develop a new technique for tree compression based on the bracket structure of the tree. It is especially useful when a function is to be computed for <u>all</u> nodes of the tree, because the decompression is easy, while the technique from [2] is best suited for computing the value associated only with the root.

An optimal parallel algorithm (for a given problem computable sequentially in linear time) is one that satisfies p*t=O(n), where p is the number of processors used, t is the parallel time and t is very small (i.e., log(n), $\log^2 n$). Optimal parallel algorithms are known for few nontrivial computational problems: computing associative function of n variables, selection, string matching, converting an expression to its parse tree, dynamic evaluation of expressions. We add to this list another problem: parsing bracket languages. In some sense it can be treated as a generalization of optimal conversion of expressions into parse trees (if we assume that expressions are fully paranthesized).

Bracket languages are one of the few interesting subclasses of context-free languages known to be recognizable sequentially in logarithmic space, it is natural to expect that a problem easy with respect to the space complexity could be also solvable by an efficient parallel algorithm.Another subclass of context-free languages recognizable in logarithmic space is the class of input driven languages [10]. For such languages it was also shown that an optimal parallel algorithm for the recognition problem is possible, see [2].

For bracket languages we give a much stronger result, since we deal with the parsing problem which seems to be more difficult than the recognition problem. As far as we know the only nontrivial context-free languages for which an optimal parallel parsing algorithm is (implicitly) known are Dyck languages (well formed sequences of constant types of brackets). In fact the algorithm given in [5] is not an optimal parallel algorithm, since p=n and t=log(n) in [5]. However the number of processors can be reduced to n/log(n) using the result of [1] in a straightforward way.

Our model of parallel computation is a parallel random access machine without write conflicts (P-RAM). It consists of a number of synchronously working processors (RAM's) which are using a common memory . No two processors can attempt to write in the same step into the same location, however many processors can read from the same location.

1) Dept.of Computer Science, University of Warwick, Coventry CV4 7AL,England, and Institute of Informatics, Warsaw University, Poland

2) Dept .of Informatics, University of Salerno,Italy, and Dept. of Computer Science, Columbia University, New York, USA.

The best algorithms for parallel general context-free recognition on a P-RAM work in $\log^2(n)$ time using $O(n^6)$ processors, see [11] (such complexity can even be achieved on much weaker models of parallel computations, cube connected computers and perfect shuffle computers, see [9]).
Recently it was proved in [2] that bracket languages can be recognized using an optimal parallel algorithm (log n time and n/log(n) processors). We show that the parsing problem for these languages can be also solved using an optimal parallel algorithm.
A context-free grammar is given by a 4-tuple G=(N,T,P,S), where N is the set of nonterminals, T is the set of terminal symbols, P is the set of productions and S is a starting nonterminal symbol. G is a bracket grammar iff each production is of the form A->(u), where u does not contain brackets "(", ")". A language is a bracket language iff it is generated by a bracket grammar. A typical example of a bracket language is the set of paranthesized arithmetic expressions with constants a,b. It is generated by the grammar:

E->(E) | (E*E) | (E+E) | (E-E) | (E/E) | (a) | (b)

The text generated by a bracket grammar contains explicit information about the "shape" of the parsing tree (given by the bracket structure of the text). However such information does not give directly the full information about the parsing tree, the labels (nonterminals) associated with the nodes are missing. The aim of this paper is to prove that the computation of these labels can be done by an optimal parallel algorithm. The number of possible correct labellings can be exponential, though for each text the shape of its parse tree is uniquely determined.
We are concerned with finding any correct labelling (a parse tree if there is any).

For ease of exposition assume that G is in a Chomsky-like Normal Form, each production being of the type A->(BC), or A->(a), where B,C are nonterminals and a is a terminal.Our method can be extended to arbitrary bracket grammar. Instead of binary trees one has to consider trees with degrees bounded by a constant.
We write A->*w iff the string w can be derived from A. Let S be the starting symbol of the grammar. Let w be a given input string of length n. The parsing problem is: construct a parsing tree PT (if $S\rightarrow^{*}w$). The size of the problem is n.
(We assume that the grammar is given and has a constant size independent of n.)
The tree PT is represented by arrays whose entries correspond to the nodes of the tree. With each node x there is associated information about its sons, father and label. The label of the root is S.

Example

Consider the grammar:

S -> (BA) | (BC) | (AS)
A-> (BA) | (AA) | (BB) | (a)
B-> (CC) | (CS) | (b)
C-> (AB) | (CA) | (BC) | (a)

and the input text

w = ((b)(((a)(a))((b)(a)))).

The bracket structure of w is given by the tree in Fig.1. Each node corresponds to a pair of matching brackets. The sons of a given pair are pairs enclosed within it. This determines the shape of the parse tree, which is shown in Fig1 (if we disregard the values associated with nodes). The nonterminals corresponding to internal nodes of such a tree are at present unknown. Their computation by an optimal parallel algorithm is the aim of our paper.

It was shown in [1] that such a tree (without values associated with the nodes) can be constructed by an optimal parallel algorithm. At this stage (computing the "shape" of the tree) all symbols except brackets can be ignored. Hence we can assume that the shape of the parsing tree (without nonterminal symbols) is computed.

Define the operation * on sets of nonterminals as follows:

S1*S2= {A : A->(BC) is a production and B∈S1, C∈S2 }.

For our example grammar we have {A,B,}*{B,C} = {A,S,C}.

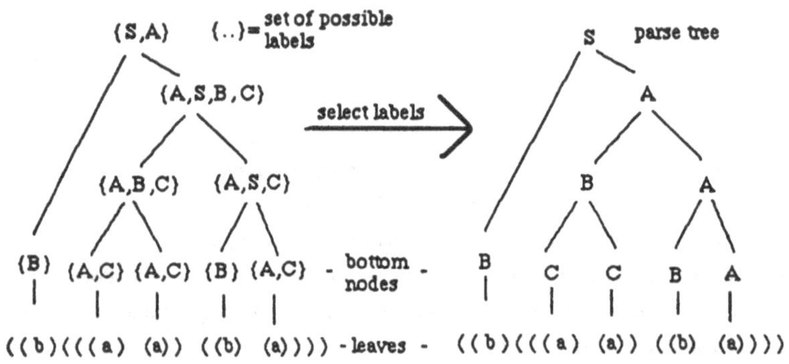

Fig.1

We say that a node in our tree is a **bottom node** if it corresponds to a derivation X->(x), where X is a nonterminal and x is terminal symbol. (The bottom nodes are nodes of height one in our tree, if we remove leaves (corresponding to terminal symbols) in Fig.1 then the leaves of the tree obtained will be bottom nodes.) Each node v covers a substring of w consisting of all symbols corresponding to leaves of the tree rooted at v. Denote this substring by sub(v), for a given tree and input text w.

For each internal node v define val(v)= $\{X : X\text{->}^{*}\text{sub}(v)\}$. It is easy to compute val(v) for each bottom node, it takes O(1) time per one node since the size of the grammar is constant.For a bottom node v sub(v)="(x)" for some terminal symbol x, and we have to find all nonterminals X such that X->(x) is a production. Hence val(v) can be computed for all bottom nodes in O(1) time using n processors or in log(n) time using n/log(n) processors.

If v is an internal node which is not a bottom node then it has two sons. Denote them by v1 and v2. It follows from the definition that val(v)= val(v1)*val(v2). Hence the problem of computing val(v) for all v turns out to be the problem of computing values of all nodes in a tree of an algebraic expression (assuming that the values of bottom nodes are already computed). The underlying algebra is not very regular. For example the operation * can be nonassociative. However the carrier of the algebra is finite. It was proved in [2] that the computation of val can be done by an optimal parallel algorithm.

Hence we can assume now that val(v) is computed for each node v. Now we have to choose one nonterminal from each set val(v). We cannot make this choice locally, since many conflicts (with respect to the grammar) would occur.

We associate with each node v a partial function D_v, called the dependancy function.The arguments and values of this function are nonterminals. The interpretation of $D_v(A)=B$ is: if label(father(v))=A then label(v)=B.Next we execute the following algorithm.

<u>for each</u> internal non-bottom node v <u>do in parallel</u>

let v1, v2 be the left and right son of v, respectively ;

for each X∈ val(v) choose Y ∈ val(v1) and Z ∈ val(v2) such that X->(YZ) is a production;

$D_{v1}(X)$:=Y; $D_{v2}(X)$:=Z; {invariant: suitable Y,Z can always be found}

<u>Example</u>

Let val(v)={A,S,B,C}, val(v1)={A,B,C}, val(v2)={A,S,C}.

Then for A we can choose B∈ val(v1), A∈ val(v2), since A->(BA) is a production.

We set $D_{v1}(A)$=B,$D_{v2}(A)$=A.For S∈ val(v) we can choose also B, A and set $D_{v1}(S)$=B, $D_{v2}(S)$=A. Analogously we can set $D_{v1}(B)$=C, $D_{v2}(B)$=C and $D_{v1}(C)$=C, $D_{v2}(C)$=A. The functions associated with nodes (written vertically) are presented in Fig.2 for our example tree. The functions D_v for all nodes v can be easily computed in O(1) time with n processors or in O(log n) time with n/log(n) processors. Observe that we resolve the (possible) ambiguity of the grammar when computing the functions D_v. We have many possibilities to choose corresponding nonterminals and we fix one of them.The choices are from sets whose sizes are bounded by a constant. There are always some suitable nonterminals because of the definition of the operation *.

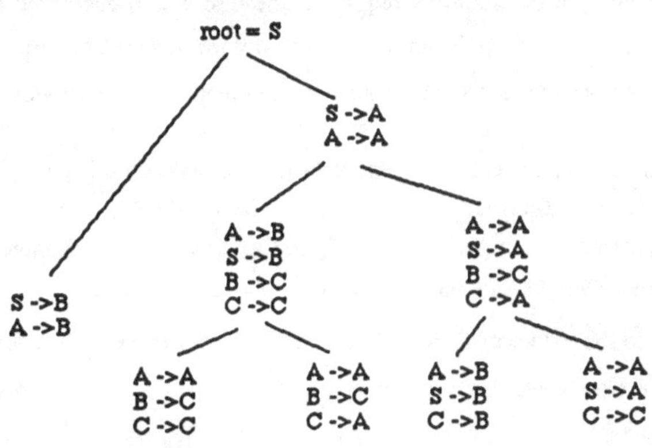

Fig.2. A ->B means here: if the father has the label A then this node should have the label B. We know that the root should have label S. What are labels implied for other nodes?

If we require that the root has the label S then the functions D_v determine uniquely the label for each node in a top-down way. The value in the root determines the values in the sons of the root through their functions D, this determines values for their sons etc.

Define the function composition $f \bullet g\ (x) = g(f(x))$.

For each internal nonroot node v let $F_v = f_1 \bullet f_2 \bullet \ldots \bullet f_k$, where $f_1,..,f_k$ are functions D associated with the nodes on the path (top-down) from the root to v (excluding the root and including v).

For each node v in parallel we set label(v)=F_v(S). This gives the full parse tree.

The parse tree determined by the functions in Fig.2 is shown in Fig.1. The selection of labels can be done in O(1) time with n processors, or in log(n) time with n/log(n) processors if the values of F_v are already computed for each v. Hence the parse tree can be constructed by an optimal parallel algorithm if the functions F_v can be computed by an optimal parallel algorithm

Theorem

Every bracket language can be parsed in log(n) time using n/log(n) processors on a P-RAM.

Proof.

It is enough to show that the functions F_v for all internal nonroot nodes v can be computed in log(n) time using n/log(n) processors. One possiblity is to extend the method used in [2] . However we develop a different method, which is more suitable in this case.We first show how to compute the functions F_v in log(n) time with n processors using the doubling technique. Initially for each nonroot node v F_v=D_v and assume that father(root)=root and F_{root}=identity. Then execute the following.

<u>repeat</u> log(n) <u>times</u>
<u>for each</u> internal nonroot node v <u>do in parallel</u>
<u>begin</u> $F_v := F_{father(v)} \bullet F_v$; father(v):=father(father(v)) <u>end</u>.

The above algorithm works in log(n) time using n processors. In order to reduce the number of processors by a factor of log n some preprocessing is required. The tree T is transformed to the reduced tree RT with n/log n nodes and functions F_v are computed only for nodes of this tree using the above algorithm. Then the tree RT is expanded and the functions are computed for all nodes.

We say that a path from v1 to v2 (in a given tree T) is reducible if each node on this path, except maybe v1and v2, has a son which is a leaf. (Formally, a single edge is also a reducible path)

The reducible path p can be compressed into single edge, see Fig.3. Call this operation compress(p).

The compression does not affect the value of F_v for any node v except those eliminated.

If the value of F_{v1} is computed then the values of F_v for all eliminated nodes can easily be computed in log(n) time using one processor. One has to decompress the compressed path and compute values F_v going along this path top-down.

Our aim is to find n/log(n) edge-disjoint reducible paths whose removal will reduce the tree by a factor of log(n).We use the approach of Bar-on and Vishkin. We refer the reader to [1], page 351 and assume a familiarity with the method and (especially) the claim related to subintervals induced by brackets chosen in step (3) of the Bar-on,Vishkin's algorithm.

At this moment we have the parse tree T without labels (with the functions D_v computed).

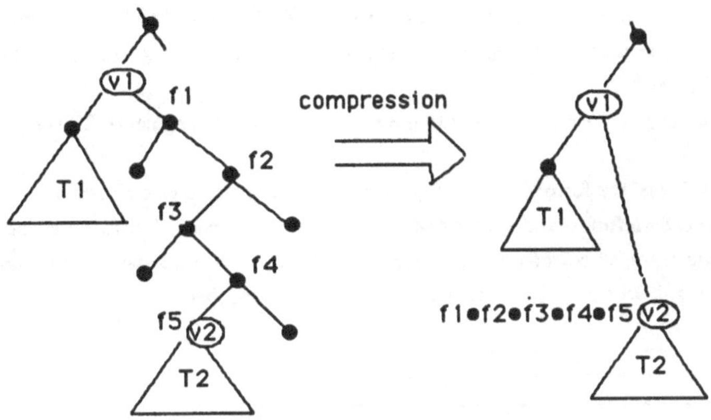

Fig.3

Such a tree and the bracket structure of the input text are two different representation of the same object. The bracket structure will help to find a good decomposition into reducible paths.We illustrate the method on the following example. Let

w = ((((a)((a)(((a)(((a)(((a) (a))(a)))((a)(a))))((a)(((a) (a))(a))))))((((a)((a)((a) (a))))(a))(a)))(a))(a)).

In the general case, partition the text into n/log(n) segments of the length (approximately) log n. For ease of presentation example let us disregard for a moment the true value of log(n) and assume that the partition is as follows:

((((a)((a)(((a)(((a)(((a) | (a))(a)))((a)(a))))((a)(((a) | (a))(a))))))((((a)((a)((a) | (a))))(a))(a)))(a))(a))

Assign a processor to each segment. Each segment contains some matching pairs of brackets and some brackets whose matches are outside the segment. The processor (assigned to a given segment) finds which brackets have their matches inside the segment. Let us define the maximal matching pair in a given segment to be a pair of matching brackets, both within this segment, which is not enclosed by any pair with the same property.The subsegment whose endpoints are such brackets (including them) is called the maximal subsegment.Consider the second segment (a))(a)))((a)(a))))((a)(((a). This segment (with maximal subsegments enclosed in [..]) is:

[(a)]) [(a)])) [((a)(a))]))([(a)] (([(a)] .

The maximal matching pair corresponds to a subtree all of whose leaves are within the given segment. The maximal subsegments correspond to the leaves of this tree. If we know the value of F_V for the root of each such tree in a given segment then one processor can easily compute the values of F_V for all other nodes in this segment.

Our first step is the replacemnt of all such trees by new single leaves. In terms of symbols we replace each maximal subsegment by a special symbol •. Hence the second segment will be transformed into •)•))•))(•((• . For the whole string we obtain the following sequence

w'= (((•(•((•((•(((• | •)•))•))(•((• | •)•)))))(((•(•(• | •))•)•))•)•))

This sequence corresponds to the tree with some subtrees replaced by leaves. Denote this tree by T.

The symbols • correspond to leaves of the tree and each pair of matching brackets corresponds to an internal node of T. The tree T for our example string is illustarted in Fig.5 and the bracket structure in Fig.4. The numbers of rectangles (corresponding to matching brackets) placed in Fig.4 correspond to the numbers of nodes of the tree T.

Let w" be the string w' with symbols • erased and with the same partition into segments. The crucial property of w" is:

each segment of w" is of the form)))...)((((..(, possibly with only one type of brackets.

We mark in each segment each leftmost and each righmost left and right bracket. There are at most four brackets marked in one segment. Next for each marked bracket (in parallel) we mark its matching bracket. This is shown in Fig.4, where marked brackets are indicated by arrows.

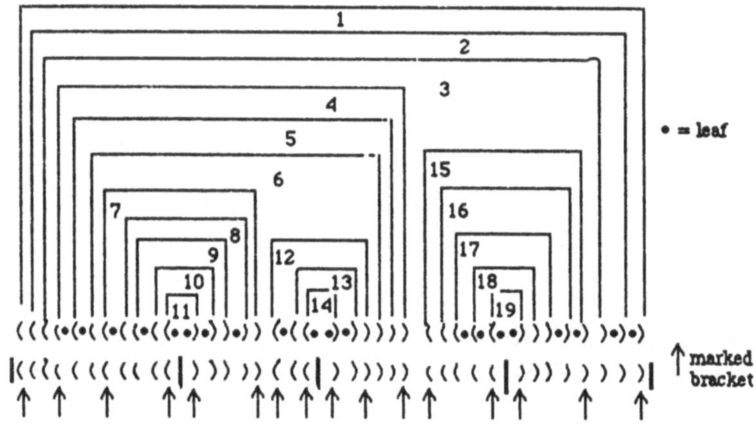

Fig.4

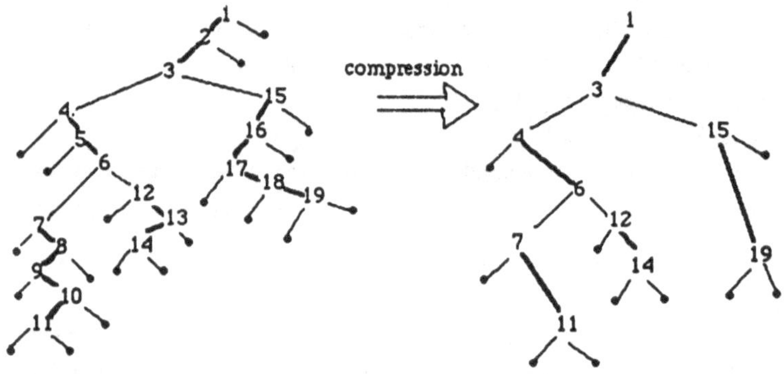

Fig.5

We define the following transformation for the tree T.

Transformation (tree compression)

(1) For each pair of marked matching brackets we mark the corresponding node of T.

(2) Additionally for each node of the tree (in parallel) we mark it if both of its sons were marked in step (1).

(3) For each marked nonroot node v denote by path(v) the path from v (bottom-up) to the next marked node. Compress each such path p =path(v) into a single edge using the operation compress(p).

In our example in step (1) we mark the nodes 1,4,15,7,12,19,14 and 11. Then in step (2) we mark additionally the nodes 3 and 6.

Claim

For each marked node v path(v) is a reducible path and its length is O(log n). If we compress paths path(v) for all marked nodes v then the resulting tree RT will have O(n/log(n)) nodes.

Proof (of the claim)

Let us look at the bracket structure. We consider first the paths from marked nodes down.

Let v' be a marked node and $(_{v'}\ )_{v'}$ its corresponding pair of brackets. These brackets are marked. Assume that one of the descendants of v' is marked and the son of v' is not marked.

Let us go, in the bracket sequence w", to the left of $)_{v'}$ until we find a marked bracket (it is some bracket $)_{v2}$ corresponding to a node v2), and to the right of $(_{v'}$ until we find a marked bracket (it is some bracket $(_{v1}$ corresponding to some node v1).

We have the situation

$$(_{v'}(_1(_2(_3((\,..(_{v1}\,..\,)_{v2}...)))_3)_2)_1)_{v'}\ .$$

<u>Case 1</u>. v1=v2=v (for example when v'=7 in our tree)

The nodes v' and v are marked. The brackets corresponding to v' enclose the brackets corresponding to v. We have the following situation if we disregard the symbol • :

$$(_{v'}(_1(_2(_3((\,..(_{v}\,..\,)_{v}...)))_3)_2)_1)_{v'}.$$

All brackets between $(_{v'}$ and $(_v$ are left brackets and all brackets between $)_v$ and $)_v$ are right brackets. Moreover the bracket $(_1$ matches the bracket $)_1$, $(_2$ matches $)_2$, and so on. It can be proved using the same argument as in [1], page 351. We refer the reader to a claim proved there.

Now look at two consecutively enclosed pairs of brackets, for example $(_1..)_1$ and $(_2..)_2$. The node x corresponding to the first pair is the father of the node y corresponding to the second pair. Look at the other son z of the node x. We claim that this other son is a leaf. If we look at these pairs of brackets in the string w' then there are only two possible situations. $(_1\bullet(_2...)_2)_1$ or $(_1(_2...)_2\bullet)$. The son z should correspond to . If it were not a leaf then it could be reduced to one leaf during the preprocessing of one segment, because all its leaves are in the same segment (they are between brackets lying in the same segment). Hence the path from v to v' is reducible.

<u>Case 2</u>. v1≠v2 (for example when v'=4 in our tree)

We have the following situation

$$(_{v'}(_1(_2(_3((\dots(_k (_{v1} \dots)_{v1}(_{v2} \dots)_{v2})_k \dots)))_3)_2)_1)_{v'}.$$

Now the node v" corresponding to $(_k)_k$ has both sons marked (because of marking corresponding brackets), hence it is a marked node (after our additional marking).It follows that the path from v' to v" is reducible using the same argument as in the previous case.

Take any nonroot marked node v and its path path(v) which ends at v' (a proper ancestor of v). We have proved that if we go down from v' then at some moment we encounter a marked node x and the path from v' to x is reducible. However x must be equal to v, because there are no marked nodes between v and v' and v is not a leaf. Hence path(v) is reducible.

It is easy to see that there are only O(n/log(n)) marked brackets (constant number per segment), hence there are also only O(n/log(n)) marked nodes.There can be in fact more marked nodes than pairs of matching marked brackets (because of additionally added marked nodes). However it is of the same order.Hence the size of compressed tree is O(n/log(n)). This completes the proof of the claim.

We have described at the beginning of the proof (of the theorem) an algorithm to compute all functions F in log(m) time with m processors for a tree with m nodes. We compress our tree and compute the functions F for the compressed tree RT. The size of RT is n/log(n). If we take m=n/log(n) and the algorithm mentioned above, then we can compute the functions for RT in log(n) time using n/log(n) processors.Now we can assign a processor to path(v),for each marked nonroot node, and we can easily decompress each such a path and compute functions F for reconstructed nodes in log n time per one path using one processor.There are O(log n) paths. This completes the proof.

References

[1] I.Bar-On,and U.Vishkin., Optimal parallel generation of a computation tree form. ACM Trans.on Progr.Lang.and Systems 7:2 (1985),348-357

[2] A.Gibbons,W.Rytter. An optimal parallel algorithm for dynamic expression evaluation and its applications. accepted for Found.of Software Techn.and Theoretical Comp.Science,december (1986), to appear in Lect.Notes in Comp.Science,Springer-Verlag.

[3] Fortune,S.and Wyllie,J. Parallelism in random access machines, Proceedings of the 10th ACM Symp. Theory of Comp.(1978) 114-118 .

[4] G.Kindervater,J.Lenstra. An introduction to parallelism in combinatorial optimization. Report OS-R8501, Centre for Math.and Comp.Science,Amsterdam (1984)

[5 R.Mattheyses,and C.M.Fiduccia, Parsing Dyck languages on parallel machines. 20th Allerton Conference on Comm.Control and Computing (1982)

[6] K.Mehlhorn. Bracket languages are recognizable in logarithmic space. Inf.Proc.Letters 5:6 (1976) 169-170

[7] W. Ruzzo. On the complexity of general context free language parsing and recognition. Automata, languages and programming. Lect.Notes in Computer Science (1979),pp.489-499

[8] W.Rytter. On the complexity of parallel parsing of general context-free languages. Accepted for Theoretical Computer Science

[9] W.Rytter. On the recognition of context free languages. Computation Theory, Lect.Notes in Comp.Science 208,Springer Verlag (1985),pp.318-325

[10] W.Rytter. An application of Mehlhorn algorithm for bracket languages to log n space recognition of input driven languages. Inf.Processing Letters,23:2 (1986) 81-84

[11] W.Rytter. The complexity of two-way pushdown automata and recursive programs. in Combinatorial algorithms on words (ed.A.Apostolico,Z.Galil),Springer-Verlag (1985) 341-356

[12] W.Rytter. Parallel time log n recognition of unambiguous cfl's. Fund.of Computation Theory, Lect.Notes in Computer Science 199 (1985) 380-389,full version to appear in Inf. and Control

ON RELIABLE NETWORKS FROM UNRELIABLE GATES

Dietmar Uhlig [1)]

ABSTRACT: The study of networks with small error probability was inaugurated by J.v. Neumann in [1] in 1952. Assume there is a complete set of (unreliable) gates with error probability ε smaller than 1/2. One of the central results in this field (argued heuristically by von Neumann and proved rigorously by R.L. Dobrushin and S.I. Ortyukov [5] in 1977) is the following: Let γ be any (extremely small) positive constant. Further let A be a network realizing Boolean function f provided no gate has failed. (The error probability of A may be very great.) Let C(A) be the complexity of A (i.e. the sum of "costs" of its elements). Then the function f can be realized by a (reliable) network $\tilde{A}$ with error probability not greater than $\varepsilon + \gamma$ and complexity O(C(A)logC(A)). N. Pippenger [2] showed in 1985 that for almost all Boolean functions f there are networks $\tilde{A}$ with complexity O(C(A)) instead of O(C(A)logC(A)). The proof is very easy and ingenious. Note that O(C(A)) means the following: There is a constant c_1 such that $C(\tilde{A}) \leq c_1 C(A)$. Constant c_1 was not determined by Pippenger, but it seems to be very great. We show that there is a constant $c_2 = c_2(\varepsilon)$ such that $C(\tilde{A}) \leq c_2 C(A)$, where $c_2(\varepsilon) \to 1$ if $\varepsilon \to 0$. Thus, for almost all Boolean functions networks constructed by our method have very small error probabilities (near that of the elements) and almost minimal complexity.

1. Definitions and Dobrushin, Ortyukov and Pippenger's main results

We consider (combinatorial) networks. Precise definitions are given in [3,4]. A set $\mathfrak{G}$ of gates (elements) is called complete if every Boolean function canbe computed (realized) by a network consisting of these gates. For example, the set consisting of 2-input AND, 2-input OR and the NOT function is complete. A cost or weight (a positive number), $C(\mathfrak{g})$, is associated with each of the gates $\mathfrak{g} \in \mathfrak{G}$. The cost C(A) of a network A is the sum of costs of its gates.

Let f be an arbitrary Boolean function. We set C(f)=minC(A), where A ranges over all networks realizing the function f assuming no gate failed. Let us further assume that each of the gates of the set $\mathfrak{G}$ has an error probability ε ($\varepsilon < 0.5$), i.e. the probability of the event "the gate $\mathfrak{g}$ realizes the function according to it" is $1-\varepsilon$ and the probability of the event "the gate $\mathfrak{g}$ does not realize the function according to it" is equal to ε. Let $\tilde{a} = (a_1, \ldots, a_n)$ be any input vector of a network A. We define the error probability $p_{\tilde{a}}(A)$ according to input vector $\tilde{a}$ and

1) Ingenieurhochschule Mittweida, Platz der DSF 17, Mittweida, 9250, DDR

to network A as the probability that network A for input vector $\tilde{a}$ does not compute the value which it computed in case no gate failed. The error probability p(A) of a network A is defined as $\max p_{\tilde{a}}(A)$, where $\tilde{a}$ ranges over all input vectors of network A. We set $C_\delta(f)=\min C(A)$, where A ranges over all networks realizing function f in case no gate failed and having error probability not greater than δ. Number C(f) is called complexity of f. Number $C_\delta(f)$ is called complexity of f limited by error probability δ. Furthermore, we define $C(n) = \max C(f)$, $C_\delta(n) = \max C_\delta(f)$, where f ranges over all n-argument Boolean functions.

We will use the following notations:
$a(n) \sim b(n)$ denotes $a(n) = b(n)(1+\vartheta_n)$, where $\vartheta_n \to 0$ if $n \to \infty$,
$a(n) = o(b(n))$ denotes $a(n) = \vartheta_n b(n)$, where $\vartheta_n \to 0$ if $n \to \infty$,
$a(n) \precsim b(n)$ denotes that there is a constant c_3 such that $a(n) \leq c_3 b(n)$,
$a(n) \lesssim b(n)$ denotes $a(n) \leq b(n)(1+\vartheta_n)$, where $\vartheta_n \to 0$ if $n \to \infty$,
$\log a$ denotes $\log_2 a$.

If φ is an arbitrary element of the given complete set, then we consider number $\varrho(\varphi)$ defined as costs of elements divided by the number of its inputs diminished by one. Let ϱ be the minimum of all those numbers. We call the element for which we get this minimum the "cheapest" element of set $\mathcal{G}$. An important result describing the complexity of Boolean functions was proved by O.B. Lupanov [3] in 1958. He showed that

$$C(n) \sim \varrho 2^n/n \qquad (1)$$

and that for every positive number η the number of Boolean functions f having a complexity $C(f) \leq (1-\eta)\varrho 2^n/n$ is $o(2^{2^n})$, i.e. almost all Boolean functions of n variables have nearly the same complexity as the function with the highest complexity.

For the reader's convenience let us assume that set $\mathcal{G}$ contains a gate realizing the 3-argument majority function $xy \vee xz \vee yz$ (having also error probability ε). First assume ε=const. R.L. Dobrushin and S.I. Ortyukov have shown in [5] if $\varepsilon < 0.07$ and $\delta > q(\varepsilon)$ where $q(\varepsilon)$ is the minimum of the positive roots of expression $\varepsilon + (1-\varepsilon)(3q^2-2q^3)=q$ then there is a constant $c_4=c_4(\varepsilon)$ such that for each network A there is a network $\tilde{A}$ (realizing the same function as A in case no gate has failed) with error probability $p(\tilde{A}) \leq \delta$ and complexity

$$C(\tilde{A}) \lesssim c_4 C(A) \ln C(A) \text{ if } C(A) \to \infty. \qquad (2)$$

We will use this result in our proof together with Lupanov's method.

Dobrushin and Ortyukov have also shown [6] that there are an infinite number of Boolean functions f and a number c_5 such that $C(f) \leq c_5 C(f) \cdot \ln C(f)$.

Note further that Pippenger's result [2] is obtained from (2) if $\ln C(A)$ will be omitted and another (very great) constant c_6 is taken instead of c_5. S.I. Ortyukov [7] also considered error probabilities ε_n with $\varepsilon_n \to 0$ if $n \to \infty$. Let $\varepsilon = \varepsilon_n$, where $\varepsilon_n \in (0,1/2)$ and

$$\overline{\lim}\, n^{-1} \log \varepsilon_n \leq -1. \tag{3}$$

Then for each constant $c_7 > 0$ if $\delta_n \geq (1+c_7)\,\varepsilon_n$ then

$$C_{\delta_n}(n) \sim C(n) \sim \varrho 2^n/n.$$

But (3) is a very strong and artificial restriction.

2. New results, sketch of proof

We are able to prove two theorems, where the second is a carollary of the first.

T h e o r e m 1 . For each arbitrarily small positive number c there exists a number ε where $\varepsilon \in (0,1/2)$ with the property that if each element of the given complete set $\mathfrak{G}$ has an error probability not greater than ε and if $\delta \geq (1+\gamma)\varepsilon$ where γ is an arbitrarily small positive number, then

$$C_\delta(n) \lesssim (1+c)\,\varrho\, 2^n/n \sim (1+c)C(n). \tag{4}$$

T h e o r e m 2 . There is a sequence $\varepsilon'_1, \varepsilon'_2, \ldots$ with the properties

1. $\varepsilon'_{n+1} < \varepsilon'_n$ and $\varepsilon'_n \in (0,1/2)$ $(n=1,2,..)$
2. $\varepsilon'_n \to 0$ if $n \to \infty$

such that for each sequence $\varepsilon_1, \varepsilon_2, \ldots$ with the properties

3. $\varepsilon_n \geq \varepsilon'_n$ and $\varepsilon_n \in (0,1/2)$ $(n=1, 2, \ldots)$
4. $\varepsilon_n \to 0$ if $n \to \infty$

and for each arbitrarily small positive number γ if each network realizing a Boolean function of n variables consists only of elements with an error probability not greater than ε_n and if $\delta_n \geq (1+\gamma)\,\varepsilon_n$ then

$$C_{\delta_n}(n) \sim C(n) \sim \varrho 2^n/n. \tag{5}$$

N o t e . Suppose the complete set $\mathfrak{G}$ does not contain an element realizing function $xy \vee xz \vee yz$. Then Theorem 1 and 2 would remain valid if we take δ (respectively δ_n) as follows: $\delta \geq (1+\gamma)m\varepsilon$ ($\delta_n \geq (1+\gamma)\cdot m\,\varepsilon_n$), where m is the minimal number of elements which are sufficient to realize this function.

We present a method of realisation of Boolean functions by which we obtain networks with complexities which are asymptotically limited by $(1+c)\varrho\, 2^n/n$ but with error probabilities being a multiple of ε (see Lemma 4). To prove Lemma 4 we need Lemmata 1,2,3. The main idea of our construction is the following. Let us consider Lupanov's method of realization of Boolean functions by networks with complexities satisfying (1). These networks consist of subnetworks with a complexity $o(2^n/n)$ and of a lot of subnetworks each of them in turn consisting of many "cheapest" elements and only of them. They are connected in such a way that each subnetwork has one output and a maximum of inputs. For example, if the "cheapest" element is the two-input AND, then each of these subnetworks realizes a conjunction, the number of its variables being by one greater than the number of elements of the subnetwork. We call the subnetworks with "cheapest" elements the "main" subnetworks. They have a very great error probability. The common complexity of all of them is $\lesssim \varrho 2^n/n$. We replace them by networks having (1+c)-fold complexity but having a very small error probability referring to those input vectors which are possible (assuming the input signals are correct). Furthermore, the "main" subnetworks are constructed in such a way that for each of the possible input vectors the failures of only a small number of gates or input signals may cause a false output signal. We apply Dobrushin/Ortyukov's method to the networks with common complexity $o(2^n/n)$ and obtain networks with a small error probability and a greater complexity but also with an upper bound $o(2^n/n)$. Further we vary Lupanov's method in such a way that each output signal depends only on a small number of output signals of the subnetworks. For this reason we need, among others, constructions as given by Lemma 1.

Let us shortly review Lupanov's representation of Boolean functions [3]. For that we need several notations. Let y be an arbitrary Boolean variable or Boolean function. Denote $K_0(y)=\bar{y}$, $K_1(y)=y$. If $\tilde{\sigma} = (\sigma_1,\dots,\sigma_u)$ is an arbitrary Boolean vector then by $K_{\tilde{\sigma}}(y_1,\dots,y_u)$ we denote the conjunction $K_{\sigma_1}(y_1)\dots K_{\sigma_u}(y_u)$ and by $|\tilde{\sigma}|$ denote $\sigma_u 2^{u-1} + \sigma_{u-1}2^{u-2}+\dots+\sigma_1$. Further, by $\theta_i(y_1,\dots,y_k)$ we denote the Boolean function defined for a natural number s by

$$\theta_i(\alpha_1,\dots,\alpha_k) = \begin{cases} 1, & (i-1)s \le |(\alpha_1,\dots,\alpha_k)| < is, \\ 0, & \text{otherwise} \end{cases} \tag{6}$$

Let $k<n$, let

$$p = \left]2^k/s\right[\tag{7}$$

and let $f(x_1,\dots,x_n)$ be an arbitrary Boolean function. Denote

$$f_i(x_1,\dots,x_n) = \theta_i(x_{n-k+1},\dots,x_n)\, f(x_1,\dots,x_n), \tag{8}$$

$i=1,\dots,p$. Let

$$f_{i\tilde{\sigma}}(x_1,\dots,x_n) = f_i(\sigma_1,\dots,\sigma_u,x_{u+1},\dots,x_n), \tag{9}$$

$$f(x_1,\dots,x_n)= \bigvee_{i=1}^{p} f_i(x_1,\dots,x_n)= \bigvee_{i=1}^{p} \bigvee_{\tilde{\sigma}} K_{\tilde{\sigma}}(x_1,\dots,x_u) f_{i\tilde{\sigma}}(x_{u+1},\dots,x_n). \tag{10}$$

For the reader's convenience let us assume that the "cheapest" element of the given complete set $\mathcal{G}$ is a two-input gate. Denôte the Boolean function realized by it by λ. Let

$$\Phi_N(v_1,\dots,v_N) = \lambda(v_1,\lambda(v_2,\lambda(v_3,\dots,\lambda(v_{N-1},v_N)\dots))) \tag{11}$$

where

$$N = 2^{n-k-u}. \tag{12}$$

In [3] is shown that there are Boolean functions $\Psi_{\xi}(x_{u+1},\dots,x_{n-k},y)$,

$1 \le \xi \le N$, satisfying expression

$$\left.\begin{aligned} & f_{i\tilde{\sigma}}(x_{u+1},\dots,x_n) = \\ & = \Phi_N(\psi_1(x_{u+1},\dots,x_{n-k}, f_{i\tilde{\sigma}}(0,\dots,0,0,x_{n-k+1},\dots,x_n)), \\ & \qquad \psi_2(x_{u+1},\dots,x_{n-k}, f_{i\tilde{\sigma}}(0,\dots,0,1,x_{n-k+1},\dots,x_n)),\dots, \\ & \qquad \psi_N(x_{u+1},\dots,x_{n-k}, f_{i\tilde{\sigma}}(1,\dots,1,1,x_{n-k+1},\dots,x_n))). \end{aligned}\right\} \quad (13)$$

Let $\tilde{\delta} = (\delta_{u+1},\dots,\delta_{n-k})$. We set

$$\psi_{\xi,i,\tilde{\sigma},\tilde{\delta}} = \psi_\xi(x_{u+1},\dots,x_{n-k}, f_{i\tilde{\sigma}}(\delta_{u+1},\dots,\delta_{n-k},x_{n-k+1},\dots,x_n)). \quad (14)$$

Note that the functions $\psi_1,\dots,\psi_N$ do not depend on f_i. Resulting from (6),(8),(9),(10) for each i, $1 \le i \le p$ the number of functions $f_{i\tilde{\sigma}}(\delta_{u+1}, \dots,\delta_{n-k},x_{n-k+1},\dots,x_n)$ which are different to each other is at most $p2^s$. Therefore

$$|\{\psi_{\xi,i,\tilde{\sigma},\tilde{\delta}}\}| = p2^sN. \quad (15)$$

(Here and in what follows $|Q|$ means the number of elements of set Q.)

Now we consider a more complicated representation of Boolean functions than those given by (10) and some of its properties (see Lemmata 1,2,3). Let $z_{i,j}$ be Boolean variables, $i=1,\dots,p$; $j=0,\dots,2^u-1$. We define a Boolean function

$F = F(x_1,\dots,x_u,x_{n-k+1},\dots,x_n,z_{1,0},\dots,z_{i,j},\dots,z_{p,2^u-1})$ by

$$\left.\begin{aligned} & F(\sigma_1,\dots,\sigma_u,\sigma_{n-k+1},\dots,\sigma_n,z_{1,0},\dots,z_{p,2^u-1}) = \\ & \quad = \begin{cases} z_{i,j} & \text{if } |(\sigma_1,\dots,\sigma_u)| = j \text{ and } \Theta_i(\sigma_{n-k+1},\dots,\sigma_n) = 1 \\ 0 & \text{otherwise} \end{cases} \end{aligned}\right\} \quad (16)$$

L e m m a 1 . An arbitrary network realizing function F has the following property. If it computes correctly and if all signals on the inputs for $x_1,\dots,x_u,x_{n-k+1},\dots,x_n$ are correct, then the output signal can only be false if all of the following 3 conditions are satisfied:
1. $|(\sigma_1,\dots,\sigma_u)| = j$, 2. $\Theta_i(\sigma_{n-k+1},\dots,\sigma_n) = 1$,
3. The signal on the input for variable $z_{i,j}$ is false.

Let g be an arbitrary Boolean function. Then by Rg we denote the network realizing g (assuming no gate failed) and having (minimal) complexity $C(Rg)=C(g)$. It is easy to show that $C(RF) \le (u+k)p2^u$. Thus, by

$$s = [n - 30\log n], \quad (17)$$

$$k = [5\log n], \quad (18)$$

$$u = [n - 10\log n] \quad (19)$$

and by (7) follows $C(RF) \le n2^{u+k}$. By (2) we obtain

$$C_{2\varepsilon}(F) \le n^2 2^{u+k} = o(2^n/n). \quad (20)$$

Instead of function Φ_N used in Lupanov's representation (see (11), (13)) we take a Boolean function $G_N=G_N(v_1,\dots,v_N)$ defined as follows. Let $H_4(v_1,v_2,v_3,v_4)=v_1v_2 \vee v_3v_4$. Let $H_N(v_1,\dots,v_N)$ be defined. Then we define H_{4N}, by

$$H_{4N}(v_1,\dots,v_{4N}) = H_N(v_1,\dots,v_N)\, H_N(v_{N+1},\dots,v_{2N}) \vee \quad (21)$$

$$\vee H_N(v_{2N+1},\dots,v_{3N})\ H_N(v_{3N+1},\dots,v_{4N}).$$

Let be $N_1=4^{a'}$, $N_2=2^{a''}$, where a' and a'' are positive integers. Let

$$N = N_1N_2. \tag{22}$$

Then, with function Φ_N defined by (11) we set

$$G_N(v_1,\dots,v_N) = H_{N_1}(\Phi_{N_2}(v_1,\dots,v_{N_2}),\dots,\Phi_{N_2}(v_{N-N_2+1},\dots,v_N)). \tag{23}$$

Function H_N has linear complexity according to the number of variables. Therefore, by (2)

$$C_{2\epsilon}(H_{N_1}) \lesssim N_1\log N_1. \tag{24}$$

Due to our assumption that the "cheapest" element of $\mathcal{G}$ is a two-input gate we have $C(\Phi_M) = \varrho(M-1)$. It follows

$$C_{\epsilon N_2}(\Phi_{N_2}) = \varrho(N_2-1). \quad (N_2=\text{cost.}) \tag{25}$$

Let $\bar{R}G_N$ be a network realizing G_N according to the representation (23) and consisting of subnetworks with complexities which are limited by (24) and (25) and with error probabilities 2ϵ and ϵN_2, respectively. Then for a constant c_{10} we obtain

$$C(\bar{R}G_N) \le \varrho N_1(N_2-1) + c_{10}N_1\log N_1. \tag{26}$$

With functions F, G_N and analogous to $\psi_1,\dots,\psi_N$ chosen functions $\varphi_1,\dots,\varphi_N$ we represent Boolean function $f(x_1,\dots,x_n)$ as follows.

$$\left.\begin{aligned}
&f(x_1,\dots,x_n) = F(x_1,\dots,x_u,x_{n-k+1},\dots,x_n,z_{1,0},\dots,z_{i,j},\dots,z_{p,2^u-1})\\
&\text{where } z_{i,|\tilde{\sigma}|} = f_{i\tilde{\sigma}}(x_{u+1},\dots,x_n) =\\
&= G_N(\varphi_1(x_{u+1},\dots,x_{n-k},f_{i\tilde{\sigma}}(0,\dots,0,0,x_{n-k+1},\dots,x_n)),\\
&\qquad \varphi_2(x_{u+1},\dots,x_{n-k},f_{i\tilde{\sigma}}(0,\dots,0,1,x_{n-k+1},\dots,x_n)),\dots,\\
&\qquad \varphi_N(x_{u+1},\dots,x_{n-k},f_{i\tilde{\sigma}}(1,\dots,1,1,x_{n-k+1},\dots,x_n))).
\end{aligned}\right\} \tag{27}$$

Analogous to $\psi_{\xi,i,\tilde{\sigma},\tilde{\delta}}$ (see (14)) we consider functions $\varphi_{\xi,i,\tilde{\sigma},\tilde{\delta}}$. Then

$$|\{\varphi_{\xi,i,\tilde{\sigma},\tilde{\delta}}\}| = p2^sN. \tag{28}$$

L e m m a 2 . For each positive number c there are numbers $N_2>0$ and $c_{11}>0$ with the following properties.

1. $c_{10}N_1\log N_1 \,/\, \varrho N_1(N_2-1) \le c/2$ (see (26)).

2. Functions $\varphi_1,\dots,\varphi_N$ can be chosen in such a way that for each Boolean vector $(a_1,\dots,a_n)$ and for each $f_{i\tilde{\sigma}}(x_{u+1},\dots,x_n)$ if the input signals of the ξth input, $1\le\xi\le N$, of $\bar{R}G_N$ do no depend on the signals of the other inputs of $\bar{R}G_N$ and if the probability of the event "the signal of the ξth input is the signal $\varphi_\xi(a_{u+1},\dots,a_{n-k},f_{i\tilde{\sigma}}(\delta_{u+1},\dots,\delta_{n-k},a_{n-k+1},\dots,a_n))$, where $|(\delta_{u+1},\dots,\delta_{n-k})| = \xi$)" is at least $1-4\epsilon$, then the probability of the event "the output signal of $\bar{R}G_N$ is not the signal $f_{i\tilde{\sigma}}(a_{u+1},\dots,a_n)$" is not greater than $c_{11}\epsilon$, where ϵ is the error probability of the gates.

The proof of Lemma 2 is very complicated and space-consuming. Therefore we shall omit it.

Lemma 3. There exists a number c_{12} with the following property: Each of the functions $\varphi_{\xi,i,\tilde{6},\tilde{\delta}}$ can be realized with

$$C_{4\varepsilon}(\varphi_{\xi,i,\tilde{6},\tilde{\delta}}) \lesssim c_{12}(2^{n-u} + 2^k). \qquad (29)$$

Proof of Lemma 3. Obviously, by (1) and (2)
$C_{2\varepsilon}(\varphi_{\xi}(x_{u+1},\dots,x_n)) \lesssim (n-u)2^{n-u}/(n-u)$,
$C_{2\varepsilon}(f_{i\tilde{6}}(\delta_{u+1},\dots,\delta_{n-k},x_{n-k+1},\dots,x_n)) \lesssim k2^k/k$, from which follows (29)

Lemma 4. For each arbitrary small number c, $c>0$, there is a constant c_{13} satisfying expression

$$C_{c_{13}\varepsilon}(n) \lesssim (1+c)\varrho 2^n/n$$

(c_{13} does not depend on ε).

Sketch of proof of Lemma 4. We realize an arbitrary Boolean function $f(x_1,\dots,x_n)$ according to (27) by using a network for function F with an error probability 2ε (see (20)), by using at most $p2^sN$ networks for functions $\varphi_{\xi,i,\tilde{6},\tilde{\delta}}$ with error probabilities not greater than 4ε (see (28),(29)) and by using $p2^u$ networks $\overline{R}G_N$ for the function G_N with error probabilities at most $c_{11}\varepsilon$ (more precisely see Lemma 2) which are connected in a certain manner. By this and by Lemma 1 we obtain that for an arbitrary input vector $\tilde{a}$ the error probability according to $\tilde{a}$ and to the constructed network is at most $(c_{11}+2)\varepsilon = c_{13}\varepsilon$. By this and by (7),(12),(17)-(20),(22),(26), (28) and Lemma 3 we obtain the statement of the lemma.

The proof of Theorem 1 is obtained by a method firstly considering by G. I. Kirienko [8] for so-called self-correcting networks (by a spezial coding) applied to the networks with properties given by Lemma 4.

References

[1] Neumann von, J.: Probabilistic Logic of Reliable Organism from Unreliable Components. In: C. E. Shannon and J. Mc Carthy (Eds.), Automata studies, Princeton University Press (1956) 43 - 98.

[2] Pippenger, N.: On Networks of Noisy Gates. 26. Symposium on Foundation on Computer science, 21. - 23.10.1985, Portland, 30 - 38.

[3] Lupanov, O.B.: On a Method of Synthesis of Networks. Izv. Vysš. Učebn. Zaved. Radiofizika 1 (1958) 1, 120 - 140. (Russian)

[4] Savage, J.E.: The Complexity of Computing. Wiley-Interscience, New York, 1976.

[5] Dobrushin, R.L. and S.I. Ortyukov: Upper Bound for Redundancy of Self-Correcting Arrangements of Unreliable Functional Elements. Prob of Info Transm. 13 (1977), 203 - 218.

[6] Dobrushin, R.L. and S.I. Ortyukov: On the Lower Bound for Redundancy of Self-Correcting Networks of Unreliable Functional Elements. Prob. Peredači Informacii 13 (1977) 1, 82 - 89 (Russ.)

[7] Ortyukov, S.I.: On the Synthesis of Asymptotically Non-redundant Self-Correcting Networks of Unreliable Functional Elements. Prob. Peredači Informacii 13 (1977) 4, 3 - 8. (Russ.)

[8] Kirienko, G.I.: Synthesis of Combinatorial Networks which are Self-Correcting Referring to a Growing Number of Errors. Diskrenij analiz, Sb. Trudov IM SI AN SSSR 16 (1970) 38 - 43. (Russian)

AREA-TIME TRADEOFFS FOR SELECTION

Imrich VRŤO[1/]

ABSTRACT

We prove nearly optimal lower and upper bounds on the AT^2 complexity of the problem of selecting the ℓ-th smallest from a set of integers. Our VLSI model satisfies the property that I/O ports lie on the border of the circuit.

1. INTRODUCTION

Increased use of VLSI for the fabrication of digital circuits has led to increased interest in complexity results on the inherent VLSI difficulty of various problems. The most attention has been paid to the problem of ordering. The problems of the area and the area-time lower and upper bounds for VLSI sorters have been completely solved in [1-4, 6,8-10]. The question of the area complexity of selection the ℓ-smallest of n k-bit integers has been answered in [5]. The AT^2 complexity of the ℓ-selectors was first studied in [11] by Thompson and Yasuura. They proposed seven VLSI circuits differing in the area, time and a special choice of the parameters k, ℓ, n. For short integers ($k = O(\log n)$), some of the circuits were optimal regarding the lower bound $AT^2 = \Omega(kn(\log kn))$. But for long integers ($k \gg \log n$), the AT^2 performance of the best ℓ-selector was at least $\Omega(k)$ worse than the lower bound. The above result were based on the most used - synchronous VLSI model characterized by the unit delay of wires.

In this paper, we investigate the ℓ-selection problem in a stronger but more realistic VLSI model. This model is an extension of the synchronous one by the assumption that I/O ports lie on the border of the circuit. We shall call it the boundary model. We shall derive a stronger lower bound and describe some upper bounds which meet our lower bound to within a polylogarithmic function of k or n. In some special cases these algorithms turn optimal.

Note that the problem of finding the minimum element of a set(ℓ=1) in the boundary model with linear delays of wires was studied in [13].

1/ Institute of Technical Cybernetics, Slovak Academy of Sciences, Dúbravská 9, 842 37 Bratislava, Czechoslovakia

2. LOWER BOUND

Before proving the lower bound, we introduce some useful notions and lemmas. Consider a boolean function $y = f(x_1,x_2,\dots,x_n)$.

LEMMA 1 [14]: If y is functionally dependent on all input variables i.e. for any i, $i = 1,2,\dots,n$ there exist two boolean vectors x, x' that differ only in the i-th component such that

$$f(x) \neq f(x'),$$

then computing of f by the boundary VLSI circuits satisfies the bound

$$AT^2 = \Omega(n\log^2 n).$$

Let X denote the set of the input variables of f. Let $\pi=(X_L,X_R)$ be a partition of X into X_L, X_R satisfying $X_L \cup X_R = X$, $X_L \cap X_R = \emptyset$ and $|X_L| = \lceil n/2 \rceil$, $|X_R| = \lfloor n/2 \rfloor$. If α, β are assignments of values to the variables from X, we use α_L for α restricted to X_L and β_R for β restricted to X_R. Also we use $\alpha_L\beta_R$ for the input assignment that agrees with α on X_L and with β on X_R.

A fooling set for the function f and the partition π is a set $\mathcal{A}$ of input assignments with the property that for any distinct α and β in $\mathcal{A}$, one of the following cases must hold:

1. $f(\alpha_L\beta_R) \neq f(\alpha)$
2. $f(\alpha_L\beta_R) \neq f(\beta)$

Define $I(f,\pi)$ to be the logarithm, base 2, of the size of the largest fooling set for f and π. Define

$$I(f) = \min_{\pi} \{I(f,\pi)\},$$

where the minimum is taken over all possible partitions π defined above. $I(f)$ is called the information content of f [12].

LEMMA 2 [7,12]: Computing of f by the boundary VLSI circuit satisfies the bound

$$AT^2 = \Omega(nI(f)).$$

Now we can state the following theorem on the lower bound for the ℓ-selection.

THEOREM: The area and time of any boundary VLSI circuit selecting the ℓ-smallest of n k-bit integers satisfies the bound

$$AT^2 = \begin{cases} \Omega(kn(k + \log^2 n)), & \text{for } k \leq n \\ \Omega(kn(\log^2 k + n)), & \text{for } k \geq n \end{cases}$$

PROOF: Consider n integers $x_1,x_2,\dots,x_n$, each being represented on k bits: $x_i = x_{i,k-1}x_{i,k-2}\dots x_{i,0}$. We shall prove a lower bound for the problem of finding the least significant bit (LSB) of $\min\{x_1,x_2,\dots,x_n\}$. Denote this problem by a boolean function f of kn variables $x_{i,j}$, $i=1,2,\dots,n$, $j=0,1,\dots,k-1$. Clearly, the lower bound for computing f is also the lower bound for the original problem.

First, we apply Lemma 1 and show that $y = LSB(\min\{x_1,x_2,\dots,x_n\})$

functionally depends on each input variable $x_{i,j}$.

1. Let $j \neq 0$.

Set $x_{i,o} = 0$

$x_{m,o} = 1$, for $m \neq i$

other variables to zeros.

Now if $x_{i,j} = 0$, then $y = 0$

and if $x_{i,j} = 1$, then $y = 1$.

2. Let $j = 0$. Set all variables to ones.

If $x_{i,o} = 1$, then $y = 1$,

if $x_{i,o} = 0$, then $y = 0$.

Hence using Lemma 1, we obtain

$$AT^2 = \Omega(kn \log^2 (kn)) = \begin{cases} \Omega(kn\log^2 n), & \text{for } k \leq n \\ \Omega(kn\log^2 k), & \text{for } k \geq n \end{cases} \qquad (1)$$

Further, we shall prove that $I(f) = \Omega(\min\{k,n\})$. According to Lemma 2, it yields

$$AT^2 = \Omega(kn\min\{k,n\}) = \begin{cases} \Omega(k^2 n), & \text{for } k \leq n \\ \Omega(kn^2), & \text{for } k \geq n \end{cases} \qquad (2)$$

Combining (1) and (2) we obtain the required result.

Put $m = \lfloor \min\{k,n\}/6 \rfloor$. Choose a partition $\pi = (X_L, X_R)$. In [13], the combinatorial lemma is proved which asserts that for any partition π, at least one of two following cases must happend:

1. There exist such i,j and $p_1 > p_2 > \dots > p_m = 0$ that

$$x_{i,p_1}, x_{i,p_2}, \dots, x_{i,p_m} \in X_L,$$

$$x_{j,p_1}, x_{j,p_2}, \dots, x_{j,p_m} \in X_R$$

2. There exist such i,j and $p_1 > p_2 > \dots > p_m$ that

$$x_{p_1,i}, x_{p_2,i}, \dots, x_{p_m,i} \in X_L$$

$$x_{p_1,j}, x_{p_2,j}, \dots, x_{p_m,j} \in X_R,$$

whereby $i = 0$ or $j = 0$.

Assume that the case 1. is fulfiled. We shall construct a fooling set of the size 2^{m-1}. For $t = 1,3,5,7,\dots,2^m - 1$, define assignments $\alpha(t)$ to the input variables in such a way that

$x_{i,p_1} x_{i,p_2} \dots x_{i,p_m}$ is a binary representation of t,

$x_{j,p_1} x_{j,p_2} \dots x_{j,p_m}$ is a binary representation of $t - 1$,

the other variables are set to ones.

We assert that $\alpha(t)$, $t = 1,3,5,\dots,2^m - 1$ is the fooling set.

Choose $t_1 < t_2$. Then

$$1 = f(\alpha(t_1)_L \beta(t_2)_R) \neq f(\alpha(t_1)) = 0,$$

because

$$f(\alpha(t_1)_L \beta(t_2)_R) = LSB(\min\{x_i, x_j\}),$$

where $x_i < x_j$ and x_i is odd and

$$f(\alpha(t_1)_L) = LSB(\min\{x'_i, x'_j\}),$$

where $x_i > x_j$ and x'_j is even.

Now assume that the case 2, is fulfiled. Let $j = 0$. If $i = 0$, the proof is similar. For $t = 0,1,2,\ldots,2^m - 2$, define assignements $\alpha(t)$ to the input variables as follows:

$x_{p_1,i}x_{p_2,i}\ldots x_{p_m,i}$ is a binary representation of t,

$x_{p_1,j}x_{p_2,j}\ldots x_{p_m,j}$ is a binary representation of $2^m - t - 1$

the other variables are set to ones.

We assert that $\{\alpha(t), t = 0,1,2,\ldots,2^m - 2\}$ creates the fooling set. Choose $t_1 < t_2$. Then

$$0 = f(\alpha(t_1)_L \beta(t_2)_R) \neq f(\alpha(t_1)) = 1.$$

This situation is illustrated in Fig. 1, for m = 3. The rows (columns) of the table are indexed by all values of $X_L(X_R)$

	$x_{p_1,0}x_{p_2,0}x_{p_3,0}$ / $x_{p_1,i}x_{p_2,i}x_{p_3,i}$	$\alpha(6)_R$ 001	$\alpha(5)_R$ 010	$\alpha(4)_R$ 011	$\alpha(3)_R$ 100	$\alpha(2)_R$ 101	$\alpha(1)_R$ 110	$\alpha(0)_R$ 111
$\alpha(0)_L$	000	0	0	0	0	0	0	1
$\alpha(1)_L$	001	0	0	0	0	0	1	1
$\alpha(2)_L$	010	0	0	0	0	1	0	1
$\alpha(3)_L$	011	0	0	0	1	1	1	1
$\alpha(4)_L$	100	0	0	1	0	0	0	1
$\alpha(5)_L$	101	0	1	1	0	0	1	1
$\alpha(6)_L$	110	1	0	1	0	1	0	1

Fig. 1.

defined above. The corresponding entries contains the values of f. For the sake of simplicity, we described only the assignments to the variables $x_{p_1,i}, x_{p_2,i}, \dots, x_{p_m,i}$ and $x_{p_1,o}, x_{p_2,o}, \dots, x_{p_m,o}$. It is easy to show that there are zeros above the secondary diagonal and the values of f on the secondary diagonal are equal to 1. Our fooling set is created by those assignments that correspond to the entries on the secondary diagonal.

Thus for any partition π, we have constructed the fooling set of the size at least 2^{m-1}. Therefore it holds

$$I(f,\pi) = \Omega(m)$$

and consequently

$$I(f) = \quad (m) = \Omega(\min\{k,n\}) .$$

3. UPPER BOUNDS

Our upper bounds are only some adaptations of known algorithms to the boundary model. If $k \leq n$, the best upper bounds are achieved by implementation of the algorithm from [11] with I/O ports on the border. This algorithm occupied O(n) area using "H-type" layout of the VLSI tree counter - the largest consument of the circuit area. The layout of this circuit with I/O ports on the border occupies $O(n\log^2 n)$ area and computation time remains $O(k\log n)$. This leads to the area-time upper bound in the boundary model

$$AT^2 = O(k^2 n\log^4 n).$$

In the same paper [11], the original algorithm was slightly improved to the following performances:

$$A = O(n\log\log n),\ T = O(k\log n/\log\log n).$$

Again, the boundary layout of this circuit leads to the best upper bound in the boundary model:

$$A = O(n\log^2 n \log\log n),\ T = O(k\log n/\log\log n).$$

$$AT^2 = O(k^2 n\log^4 n/\log\log n).$$

If $k \geq n$ the best upper bound is achieved by the sorting algorithm for long keys proposed in [2]. Its area-time complexity is

$$AT^2 = O(kn^2\log^2 k \log n).$$

We can see that our upper bounds meet the lower bound within $O(\log^4 n/\log\log n)$ or $O(\log^2 k \log n)$. In some special cases, the lower bound is optimal. For $\ell = 1$ and $k = O(\log n)$, the circuit from [11] for finding the minimum element can be adapted to the boundary model. The original circuit was based on a binary "H"-tree of serial comparators. The layout of this circuit with I/O ports on the border leads to the circuit of the complexity

$$A = O(kn\log n/(k + \log n)) = O(kn)$$
$$T = O(k + \log n) = O(\log n)$$
$$AT^2 = O(kn\log^2 n).$$

For n = 2, the sorting algorithm from [2] mentioned above is optimal satisfying

$$AT^2 = O(k\log^2 k).$$

Our nearly optimal bounds provide space for further improvments. It is a question whether the lower or the upper bound can be improved. But it seems that the information content method for lower bounds is limited because we are able to show that $I(f) = O(\min\{k\log \ell, n\})$.

We recall the open problem of the gap between the upper and lower bound for the ℓ-selection in the synchronous model.

4. REFERENCES

[1] Bilardi,G.,Preparata,F.P.: Area-time lower bound technique with application to sorting. Algorithmica,1, 1986,1, 65-91.

[2] Bilardi,G.,Preparata,F.P.: The influence of key length on the area-time complexity of sorting. In: Proc. 12-th ICALP, 1985.

[3] Cole,R.,Siegel,A.R.: On information flow and sorting. In: Proc. 26-th FOCS, Portland 1985, 208-221.

[4] Ďuriš,P.,Sýkora,O.,Thompson,C.D.,Vrťo,I.: Tight chip area bounds for sorting. Computers and Artificial Intelligence, 4, 1985, 6, 535-544.

[5] Ďuriš,P.,Sýkora,O., Thompson,C.D.,Vrťo,I.: A minimum area for ℓ-selection. To appear in Algorithmica 1987.

[6] Leighton,F.T.: Tight bounds on the complexity of parallel sorting. In: Proc. 16-th STOC, Washington 1984, 71-80.

[7] Lipton,R.J.,Sedgewick,R.: Lower bounds for VLSI. In: Proc. 13-th STOC, Milwaukee 1981, 300-306.

[8] Siegel,A.R.: Tight area bounds and provably good AT^2 bounds for sorting circuits. Tech. Rep.,Comp.Sci.Dept., New York University, New York 1984.

[9] Siegel,A.R.: Aspects of information flow in VLSI circuits. In:Proc. 18-th STOC, 1986, 448-459.

[10] Thompson,C.D.: Area-time complexity for VLSI. In: Proc. 11-th STOC, 1979, 81-88.

[11] Thompson,C.D.,Yasuura,H.: On the area-time optimal design of ℓ-selectors. In: Proc. Asilomar Conf. on Circuits, Systems and Computers, 1985.

[12] Ullman,J.D.: Computational Aspects of VLSI. Rockville, Computer Science Press 1984.

[13] Vrťo,I.: Optimal VLSI algorithm for finding the maximum element of a set. In: Proc. PARCELLA'84, Berlin, Academie Verlag 1985,232-238.

[14] Vrťo,I.: The area-time complexity of the VLSI counter. Submitted to IPL.

Optimization of special permutation networks using simple algebraic relations

F. Wächter[1)]

1. Parallel memory with permutation network

The development of special processors for digital signal processing with an architecture adapted to the favoured algorithms also demands special memories. To get fast signal processing these memories have to be organized in parallel together with a special permutation network. Fig.1 shows the structure of such a memory whose conception was developed in the ZKI /1/. It consists of N memory moduls M_i, N address processors A_i to compute the addresses of the accesses to the memory moduls and a permutation network PNW which adapts the turn of the dates fetched from the memory moduls to the format of access (window), wherein N is a prime number.

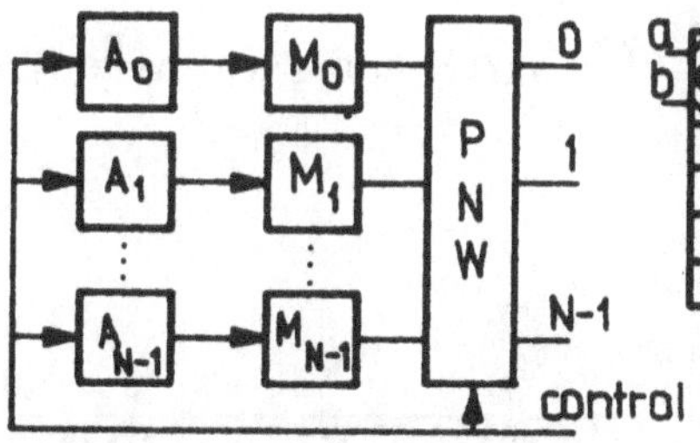

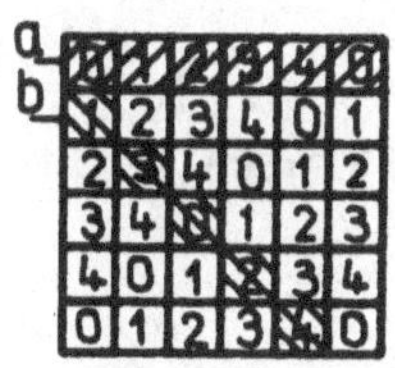

Fig.1 structure of a parallel memory

Fig.2 linear windows of access, N=5

With this memory the access with connected and unconnected linear windows is possible. Fig.2 shows two of such windows for N=5.
Linear windows are used to solve problems of image processing /1/, of matrix operations /2/ and of parallel access to nodes of a tree /3/. The permutation needed for the access with linear windows can be described with

$$P(S,F) = \begin{pmatrix} S & S+F & S+2F & \dots & S+(N-1)F \\ 0 & 1 & 2 & & N-1 \end{pmatrix} \qquad (1)$$

wherein S is the number of the memory modul in which first element of the window is stored, F is the distance of the elements of the window. The operations in (1) have to be done modulo N. This permutation con-

1) AdW der DDR, Zentralinstitut für Kybernetik u. Informationsprozesse, IT Dresden, Zeunerstr. 38, Dresden 8027

trolled by S and F changes the turn of the dates fetched from the memory moduls so, that the dates of the i-th element of the window appear at the i-th output line of the PNW. The parameters of the windows in fig.2 are a) S=0, F=1 and b) S=1, F=2.

2. Structure of the PNW

A PNW to realize the permutation P can be structured as a combination of two rotators for N respectively N-1 inputs /4,5/. The first rotator realizes the permutation V: $x \rightarrow x-S \bmod N$. With a special interconnection between the rotators and the second rotator a permutation M: $x \rightarrow x \cdot F^{-1} \bmod N$ will be performed. This is possible because the integers 1...N-1 with N prime form a cyclic group under the operation of multiplication modulo N. The outputs $r^x \bmod N$ of the first rotator must be connected with the inputs x of the second rotator and the outputs x of the second rotator are the outputs r^x of the whole PNW, wherein r is a primitive root of N.

If the rotators are structured in levels of switches with shift amounts of 2^i, $i=0,\dots,\lceil \mathrm{ld} N \rceil$, the control signals of the switches are the c_i, c_j of the decomposition

$$(-S) \bmod N = \sum_{i=0}^{n-1} c_i 2^i, \quad (F^{-1}) \bmod N = \prod_{j=0}^{m-1} r^{2^j c_j} \bmod N, \; c_i, c_j \in \{0,1\}, n = \lceil \mathrm{ld}\, N \rceil, m = \lceil \mathrm{ld}(N-1) \rceil \quad (2)$$

Fig. 3 shows such a PNW with N=7, r=3.

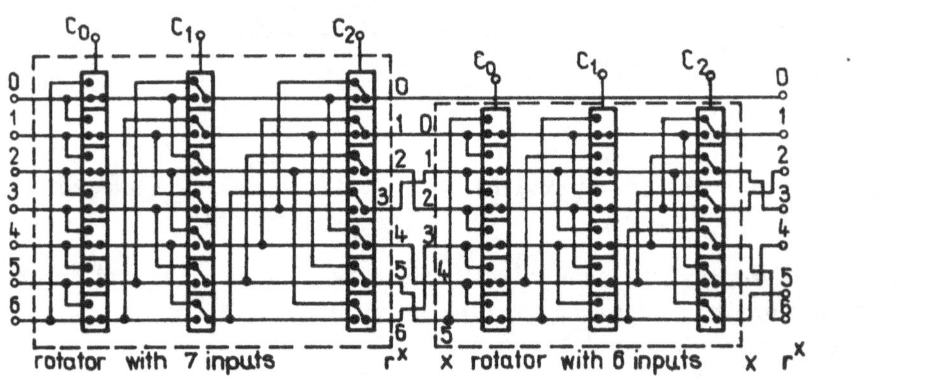

Fig.3 decomposed PNW for n=7, r=3 with control for S=1, F=2

For great values of N there is a high wiring amount by realizing the PNW. Two ways to optimize the wiring of rotators will be discussed here: at first a more general description of the shift amount and at second the decomposition of the permutations in the levels.

3. Optimization of rotators by selecting special bases

3.1. General description of the shift amount

The shift amount t of a rotator with q inputs can be expressed in a more general form /6/

$$t = \sum_{i=0}^{n-1} c_i a_i \bmod q \text{ with } n = \lceil \mathrm{ld}\, q \rceil,\ c_i \in \{0,1\},\ 0 < a_i < q \qquad (3)$$

The set (a) of the parameters $a_0, a_1, \ldots, a_{n-1}$ will be called a base. The base elements will be chosen so, that with (3) all values from 0 to N-1 can be generated. In general there are many different bases (a) for a given N. For instance in the case of N=17 there are 4176 different bases without changing the turn of the elements in the bases. The calculation of the bases must be done by a computer /6/. Only in the special case of $q = 2^i$ a general expression exists to calculate the base elements. In this case the base elements are given by $a_i = (2^i + k \cdot 2^{i+1}) \bmod 2^i$ with k integer.

By computing the bases it can be obtained, that there are bases with pairs of elements $a_i = \pm a_j \bmod q$. This is possible if $q/2^{-\lceil \mathrm{ld} q \rceil} \leq 3/4$. If $q/2^{-\lceil \mathrm{ld} q \rceil} \leq 9/16$ also two such pairs of elements are possible. For instance, bases (1,1,3,3,8) and (1,6,6,15,15) exists for q = 17. Using bases with pairs of elements, the wiring amount can be decreased. This will be shown at the example of the rotator with the base (1,1,3,3,8) for q=17 in fig. 4. The placement of the levels must be done so, that levels with pairs of elements are neighbouring. In fig. 4 the first two levels have the elements 1,1 and the last two levels the elements 3,3. If the placement of the switching cells is in the turn of $x \cdot a_i \bmod q$, in these four levels a wiring amount of only one track is possible. The whole wiring amounts is 21 tracks.

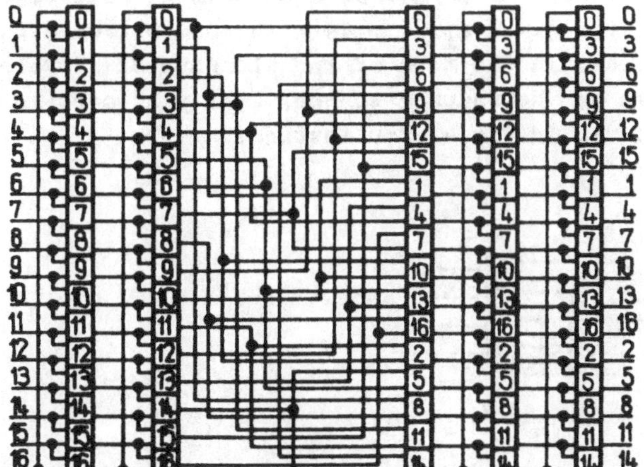

Fig. 4 rotator q=17, (a_i)=(1,1,3,3,8)

By using a base with $a_i = 2^i$ 33 tracks are needed /6/.

3.2. Cycles of the rotation

In the rotator of fig. 4 the number of tracks is reduced, but there are long wires which increase the time delay of the network. To reduce the wiring length the permutations in the levels must be decomposed. Comparing the properties of the additive residue group modulo q R and the description of the permutation $V_i : x \rightarrow (x+a_i) \bmod q$ as a product of disjoint cycles it can be shown, that at a determined turn of the elements of the subgroup generated by a_i and its cosets in R are equal the cycles of V_i. If m_i is the order of a_i in R, the rotation V_i has N/m_i cycles with m_i elements.

$$V_i(a_i) = \prod_{l=1}^{N/m_i} (0+b_l\ (a_i+b_l) \bmod q,\ (2a_i+b_l) \bmod q, \ldots \ldots ((m_i-1)\ a_i+b_l) \bmod q) \tag{4}$$

The values of the b_l must be chosen so, that disjoint cycles will be generated. For instance at q=8, $A_i=4$, $V_i(4)$ is given by $V_i(4)$ = (0 4) (1 5) (2 6) (3 7), wherein the first cycle is the subgroup generated by 4.

3.3. Optimization considering the orders of the base elements

Considering the cycles of V_i given by (4) the wiring amount of the rotator can be reduced. There are two heuristic rules for optimization, which demands special placement of levels and switches.

a) The wiring amount of one level can be reduced, if all switches of one cycle are placed neighbouring and the turn of the inputs of the level is like the turn of the switches. In this case no more than m_i tracks are needed to wire the level and wiring length are not greater than m_i times the length of a switching cell. Fig.5 shows a part of a level for q=12, $a_i=3$, $m_i=4$ with this placement. If the switches are placed in the turn of the elements of a cycle, the number of tracks can be reduced to one. This placement is shown in the first two level in fig.4, for instance.

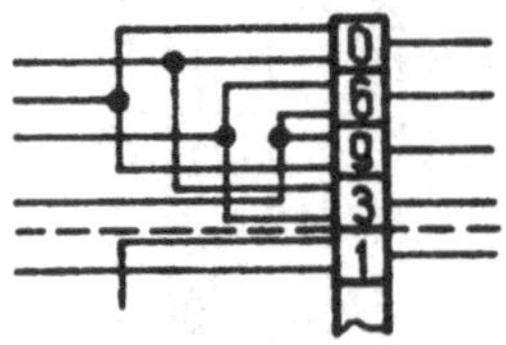

Fig.5 placement considering cycles, q=12, $a_i=3$

b) If there are base elements a_i, a_j with $m_i=k\cdot m_j$ the wiring amount can be reduced by neighbouring placement of the levels with these elements. In the case k=1 the cycles of $V(a_i)$ and $V(a_j)$ have the same elements and by placement of the switches corresponding the cycles no more than $2\cdot m_i$ tracks are needed to wire both levels. Fig.6 shows this placement for the example q=12, $a_i=3$, $a_j=9$, $m_i=m_j=4$. In the case k > 1 the elements of one cycle of $V(a_i)$ are the elements of k cycles of $V(a_j)$, because the subgroup generated by a_j in R is a subgroup of the subgroup generated by a_i. The wiring amount can be reduced by neighbouring placement of the levels with a_i, a_j, if the switches of k cycles of $V(a_j)$ whose elements are the elements of one cycle of $V(a_i)$ are placed neighbouring. Hence no more than m_i+m_j tracks are needed to wire both levels. Fig.7 shows this placement for the example q=8, $a_i=2$, $a_j=4$, $m_j=2$.

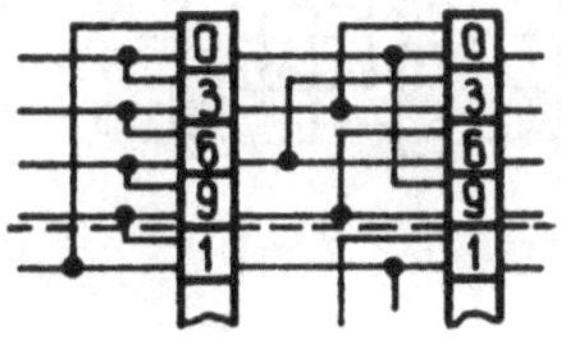

Fig.6 placement at q=12, $a_i=3$, $a_j=9$, $m_i=m_j=4$

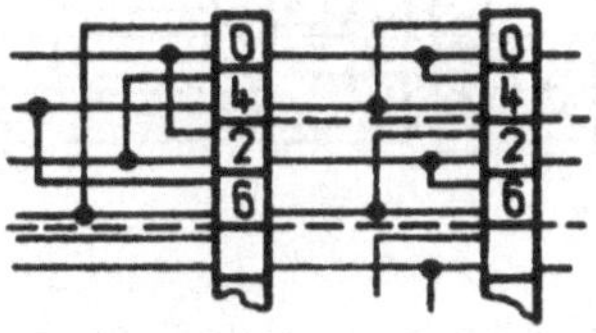

Fig.7 placement at q=8, $a_i=2$, $a_j=4$, $m_i=4$, $m_j=2$

3.4. Criteria of selecting bases

Considering the described rules of placement, the wiring amount of a rotator with a base (a) can be estimated without a detailed realization of the wiring. A good wiring is possible if the base has following properties:

1) base elements with small orders
2) base elements with orders $m_i=k\cdot m_j$
3) base elements with $a_i= \pm a_j \mod q$.

3.5. Example

The effects which can be obtained by a placement considering these rules will be shown in fig.8. There is a rotator for q=21. The base is (a) = (7,14,3,6,9) with orders (m) = (3,3,7,7,7). The whole wiring needs 26 tracks and the wiring lengths are short in 4 of the 5 levels. Using the more common base (a) = (1,2,4,8,16) 41 tracks are needed and the maximum wiring length in all levels is greater than 14 times the length of a switching cell /6/. Further it can be obtained, that the regularity of the structure increases by considering the cycles of permutation.

In fig.8 the blocks I,II repeated 7 times or 3 times.

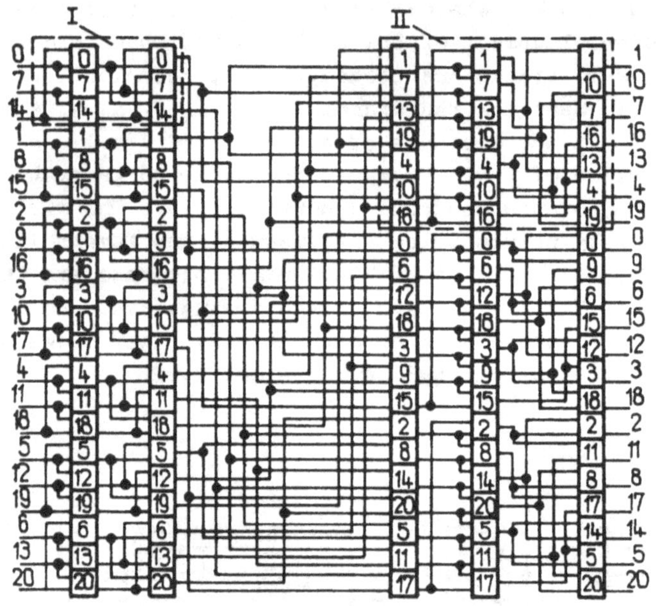

Fig.8 rotator with optimized placement, q=21,
(a) = (7,14,3,6,9)

4. Optimization of a PNW for N=17

A PNW for N=17 was optimized using the said results and other methods of optimization which not depend of the mathematical description of the permutation /6/. This methods are: combining of two levels to one level of more complicated switches and using both switches with several inputs and one output and switches with one input and several outputs. Fig.9 shows the structure of the PNW.

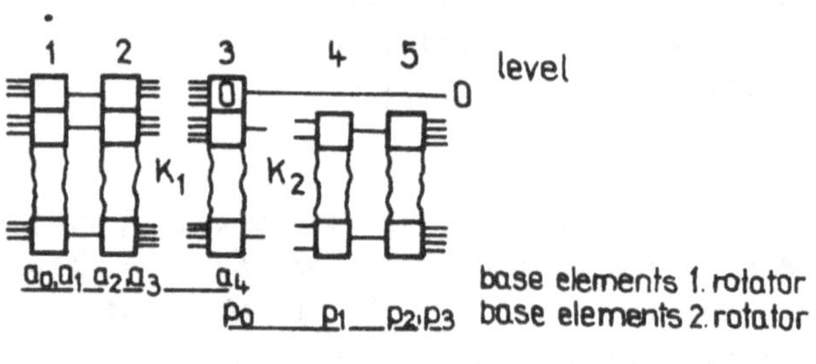

Fig.9 structure of an optimized PNW for N=17

The wiring of first and last level will be done in wiring channels with 17 tracks, between the PNW is embedded. In the levels 1,2 are base elements $a_0=a_1$, $a_2=a_3$ combined and there are switches with 3 instead of

4 inputs or outputs, which would be needed by combining levels of single switches with $a_i \neq \pm a_j$ mod N. Level 3 combines the two rotators. The interconnection of the rotators following powers of a primitive root of N is considered in the wiring of channel K_1. Base element p_1 of level 4 has an order of $m_1=2$ and a wiring amount of two tracks is possible in channel K_2. The wiring amount between the levels of the PNW will be minimized observing following conditions:

- equal placement of switches in levels 1,2
- placement of switches in level 3 corresponding to the cycles of V(16)
- equal placement of cycles of V(16) in levels 3,4
- equal placement of switches in levels 4,5.

Corresponding this conditions only channel K_1 has to be optimized. This was done for (a_i) = (15,15,11,11,14), (p_i) = (5,8,6,12) with a result of 13 tracks in K_1. Hence the wiring between the levels of the PNW needs only 15 tracks.

5. Summary

To realize fast parallel memories permutation networks PNW are needed. For a parallel memory developed by the ZKI the PNW can be decomposed in two rotators with a special connection structure. The rotators are decomposed in levels of switches. Each level can realize shift amounts of a_i or 0. The whole rotation consists of rotations with shift amount $c_i a_i$ in the level with c_i=0 or 1. The wiring amount of the level depends of the set of the a_i (base). Considering the cycles of the rotation in the levels criteria were found to select bases for a small wiring amount. Good bases for rotations of q inputs have elements with small orders in the additive residue group modulo q and with orders $m_i=k \cdot m_j$ for base elements a_i, a_j. Using such bases the number of tracks and the wiring lengths in the levels can be reduced and the regularity of the structure increases. A PNW for N=17 was optimized corresponding the said results.

Ref.

/1/ Rebel,Gössel: Ein parallel Speicher,AdW d.DDR, ZKI, Berlin 1982
/2/ Kung, Leiserson: Systolic apparatus for matrix computations US-PS 4,493,048
/3/ Rebel, Gössel: Adressenberechnungsschaltung, Patentschr. 1985
/4/ Pöschel et al: Ein dekomponiertes Permutationsnetzwerk für einen parallelen Bildspeicher. Proc.INFO84, Bd.5, 840-844, Dresden 1984
/5/ Barnes: Parallel access alignment network with barrel switch implementation for d-ordered vector elements US-PS 4,223,391, 1980
/6/ Wächter: Zur Strukturierung spezieller Permutationsnetzwerke ZKI-Informationen 2/85, AdW der DDR

Computing a Rectilinear Steiner Minimal Tree in $n^{O(\sqrt{n})}$ Time

*Clark D. Thomborson (a.k.a. Thompson)**
Linda L. Deneen
Gary M. Shute

Computer Science Department
University of Minnesota
Duluth, Minnesota 55812
U.S.A.

Abstract

We propose an algorithm for computing a rectilinear Steiner minimal tree on n points in $2^{O(\sqrt{n}\log n)}$ time and $O(n^2)$ space. This is an asymptotic improvement on the $2^{O(n)}$ time required by current algorithms. If the points are distributed uniformly at random on the unit square, the Steiner tree calculated by our algorithm is minimal with high probability. The "constant factors" of our algorithm are such that it should be feasible to obtain exact solutions for n-point problems whenever $n \leq 25$. Previously, only problems of size $n \leq 20$ were feasible.

1 Introduction

The earliest formulation of Steiner's Problem is attributed to Fermat in the early 17th century, but a generalization is the problem we know today: given as input a set V_{in} of vertices in the Euclidean plane, find a set S of points, called *Steiner points*, and a set E of edges on $V_{in} \cup S$ such that E forms a tree on $V_{in} \cup S$ and the sum of the lengths of the edges in E is minimal.

Kuhn's excellent survey paper [14] traces the development of work on this Euclidean Steiner Tree Problem. It has important applications, such as the design of telephone networks, and has captured the attention of computer scientists interested in its computational aspects. In 1977 Graham, Garey, and Johnson showed that the Euclidean Steiner Tree Problem is NP-Complete [7], dashing hopes of optimal algorithms for large sets V_{in}, but legitimizing interest in heuristics [4,10,13,19,20,24] and easier variants of the problem [1,22].

A variant of the Euclidean Steiner problem has important applications to circuit design. The Euclidean problem can be translated to the rectilinear (L_1) metric by simply changing the distance function. The resulting *Rectilinear Steiner Problem,* surveyed by Hwang in [11], asks for a minimal Steiner tree with edges parallel to the x- and y-axes. Such a tree is called a *Rectilinear Steiner Minimal Tree* (RSMT).

Any VLSI design system must cope with RSMT problems (usually in suboptimal ways) in order to connect the terminals of subcircuits. The rectilinear restriction arises because of technological difficulties in creating non-rectilinear wiring paths on the surface of a semiconductor substrate. RSMT problems also arise at another level of circuit design, when one deposits metal on a printed circuit board in order to connect one chip's pins to another's. In both applications, it is important to have a minimal or near-minimal length wiring path to reduce stray capacitance, and thus to increase circuit speed. A constraint of secondary importance is to minimize the number of bends in the RSMT. This makes it easier to perform the "detailed routing" that assigns slightly different positions to parallel edges in unconnected RSMTs.

*Supported by the National Science Foundation, through its Design, Tools and Test Program under grant number MIP 84-06408.

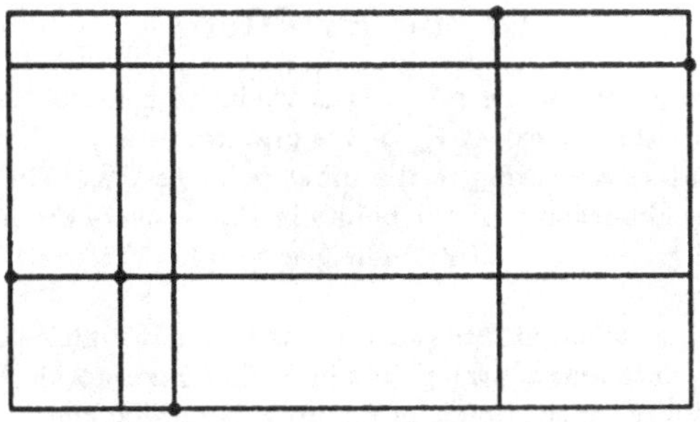

Figure 1: A grid graph on five points.

Most RSMT algorithms find Steiner trees that are subgraphs of a "grid graph" formed by drawing horizontal and vertical line segments through the vertices, where the segments are limited to the rectangle enclosing the vertices [9]. See Figure 1. Despite this restricted search space, the RSMT problem is NP-complete [8].

The published literature contains two exact algorithms for finding a RSMT on a set of points. Both algorithms are exponential and can only be used if the set is small. Yang and Wing describe a branch-and-bound algorithm running in $2^{O(n^2)}$ time and $O(n^2)$ space [23]. Apparently, Yang and Wing's algorithm is feasible for vertex set sizes up to $n = 20$. Dreyfus and Wagner use dynamic programming to solve the more general problem of computing a minimal Steiner tree for a graph [6]. Their algorithm is easily adapted to solve the Rectilinear Steiner Problem in $O(n^2 3^n)$ time, where n is the number of vertices. Unfortunately, the Dreyfus and Wagner algorithm requires $O(n^2 3^n)$ space, making it infeasible for $n \geq 18$.

In this algorithm we begin by dividing the vertex set of size n in half by a vertical cut line. Any RSMT on the vertex set has $k \geq 1$ edges that cross the cut line. (Our preliminary analysis shows that if $n \geq 20$ points are uniformly distributed at random on the unit square, then with probability $p > 0.9$ there is a RSMT for which $k \leq 2\lceil\sqrt{n}\rceil$.) For each possible value of k, then, we choose k edges of the associated grid graph where the RSMT is assumed to cross the cut line. Next we find all pairs of forests that can join together at the k edges to form a Steiner tree. The forest pairs define "terminals" on the edge of two Steiner tree subproblems. By solving all subproblems, and choosing the pair with minimal total length, we find a minimum Steiner tree with high probability.

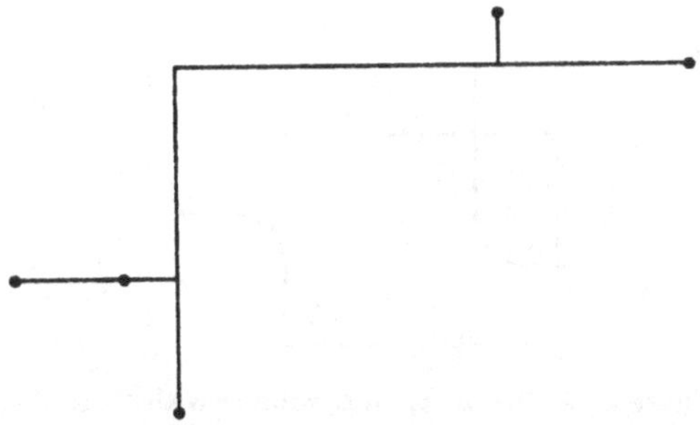

Figure 2: A minimum Steiner tree on the graph of Figure 1.

We have developed a new algorithm using a technique called *nonserial dynamic programming* [5]. When calculations on each half are done recursively with cut lines alternating between vertical and horizontal, straightforward analysis shows that our algorithm runs in $2^{O(\sqrt{n}\log n)}$ time. This is a clear improvement on the $2^{O(n)}$ performance of the best previous algorithm, at least for large n. We believe it is also a significant improvement for feasibly-small n, say $n \leq 25$.

2 Formal Description of the Problem

Given a set V_{in} of $|V_{in}| = n$ points in the plane, it is trivial to construct a grid graph like the one shown in Figure 1. Formally, the vertex set V_{gg} of the grid graph G_{gg} is $X \times Y$, where X and Y are the sets of x- and y-coordinates appearing in the input point set V_{in}. The edge set E_{gg} of the grid graph is defined by the 4-neighborhoods of the points in V_{gg}. If there are no degeneracies, there are $2n(n-1)$ edges in the grid graph on n points. The grid graph of Figure 1 has one y-degeneracy, so it has only $(2n-1)(n-1)$ edges.

To find a rectilinear Steiner minimal tree (RSMT) for V_{in}, it is sufficient to find a minimal-length connected subgraph of G_{gg} containing all the points in V_{in} [9]. Figure 2 shows one of the two RSMTs that can be obtained in this way for the points of Figure 1. Note that the RSMT would not be unique even if the y-degeneracy were removed. Another trivial observation is that there are in general many RSMTs that are not subgraphs of a grid graph (because extra jogs can be inserted anywhere in an "L" shaped wire). In some applications [17], it is important to produce several RSMTs or near-minimal rectilinear Steiner trees for a given set of points. Such algorithms are beyond the scope of this paper.

A trivial algorithm for finding a RSMT is to search the space of subgraphs of V_{gg}, picking a shortest one that satisfies the connectedness and point inclusion properties. A naive implementation of this algorithm would take $2^{O(n^2)}$ time. (Yang and Wing's algorithm, mentioned in the introduction, is a branch-and-bound improvement on the trivial algorithm. Unfortunately, they neither prove nor conjecture an asymptotic decrease in time [23].)

3 Description of the New Algorithm

As outlined in the introduction, the new algorithm searches the space of subgraphs of V_{gg} in a recursive fashion, solving RSMT subproblems on nearly-square subgrids. A typical subproblem is shown in Figure 3. The desired solution to a subproblem is actually a forest of RSMTs, one Steiner tree for each star graph in the subproblem. (Figure 3 has three star graphs. The one on the top right has degree one, the one on the bottom right has degree two, and the one on the left has degree four.) We seek a forest of RSMTs of minimal total length, connecting the terminals on the boundary of the subproblem in the same way as the star graphs. Additionally, we require the solution forest to contain every vertex in the input set V_{in} that lies within the boundary of the subproblem.

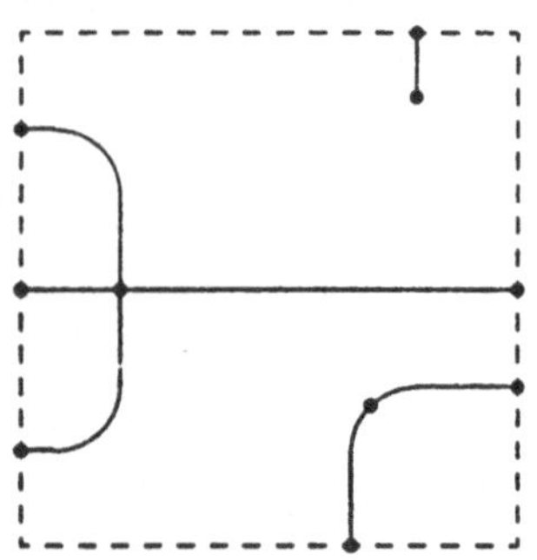

Figure 3: A 7-terminal subproblem with three stars.

A typical recursive subdivision of Figure 3 is shown in Figure 4. Here, we show how Figure 3 can be solved by two subproblems joined by three cut-edges. The left-hand subproblem has three stars and six terminals; the right-hand subproblem has three stars and seven terminals. The gap shown between the subproblems is one "column" of the grid graph. It contains no vertices.

To obtain an optimal solution to a (sub)problem, we must examine all possible subdivisions. A convenient way to generate all subdivisions is outlined below. Before doing this, we note that, without loss of generality, no two star graphs intersect. If they did, their solution RSMTs would also intersect, forming a cycle; and a shorter composite RSMT could be formed by omitting one of the edges in that cycle. Thus the star graphs divide the region inside a RSMT problem into a set of planar faces.

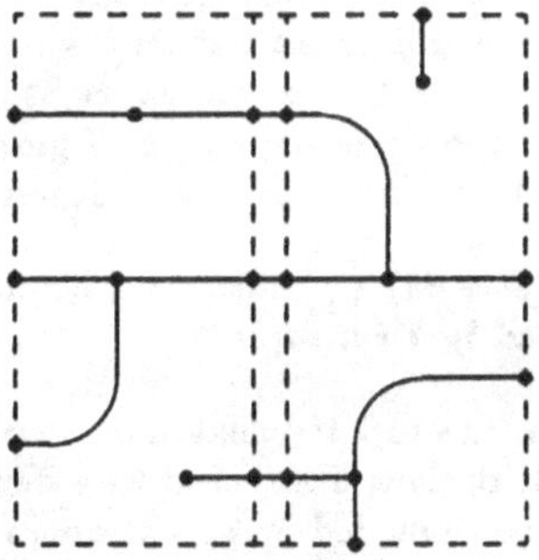

Figure 4: A vertical subdivision of Figure 3 into a 6-terminal problem and a 7-terminal problem.

Graphically, a recursive subdivision of a RSMT problem is a pair of dashed lines running from mid-bottom to mid-top of the problem region. See Figure 4. We start the subdivision process by enumerating the star graphs on the boundary of the planar face containing the mid-bottom "start" point of our subdividing line. After choosing (exhaustively) one of these star graphs, we have several options of how to generate a cut-edge.

The simplest case is that of a degree-1 star. Figure 5 shows how we must always split such a star into a degree-1 star and a degree-2 star, where the degree-1 star may be either on the left (Figure 5b) or the right (Figure 5c) of the cut-edge. After choosing one of these options, the cut-edge can be assigned a y-coordinate to locate it precisely in the grid graph. If there are n_r rows in this problem's region of the grid graph, then, there are $2n_r$ ways of creating a cut-edge by splitting a degree-1 star.

Similar reasoning gives an exhaustive analysis for generating cut-edges from a degree-2 star. Figure 6 shows the three possibilities. We may form two degree-2 stars, one on each side of the cut-edge, as in Figure 6b. Alternatively, we may form one degree-1 star and one degree-3 star, as in Figures 6c and 6d.

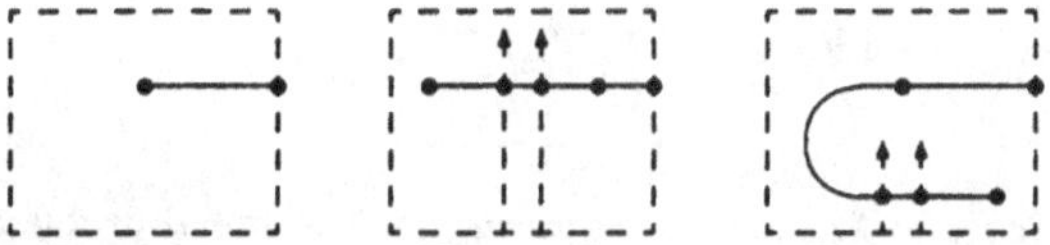

Figure 5a. Figure 5b. Figure 5c.

Figure 5: Two options for splitting the degree-1 star of Figure 5a.

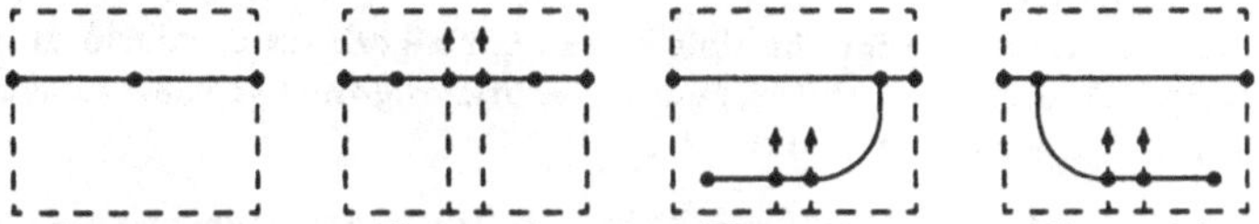

Figure 6a. Figure 6b. Figure 6c. Figure 6d.

Figure 6: Three options for splitting the degree-2 star of Figure 6a.

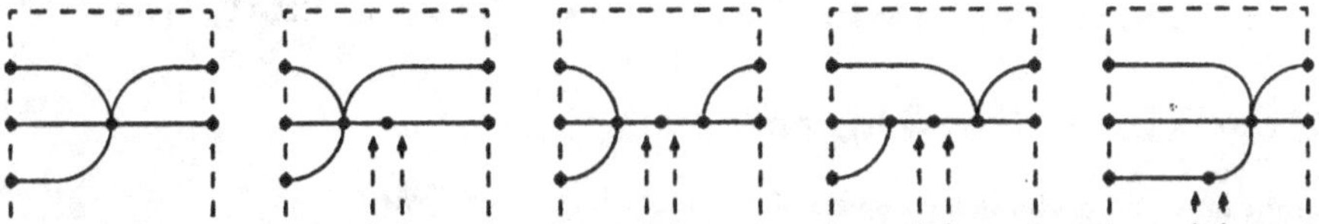

Figure 7a. Figure 7b. Figure 7c. Figure 7d. Figure 7e.

Figure 7: Four ways of getting a degree-2 star from the degree-5 star of Figure 7a.

Higher-degree stars are a little more complicated. It seems best to start by enumerating all $d-1$ planar partitions of a degree-d star into a degree-c star on the left (where $0 \le c \le d-2$), a degree-2 star in the middle, and a degree-$(d-c-2)$ star on the right. See, for example, Figure 7. The middle degree-2 star can then be split in three ways, as in Figure 6. In all, then, there are $3(d-1)$ topologically distinct ways of generating a cut-edge from a degree-d star, for all $d \ge 2$.

Lemma 1 *There are fewer than $k(3t+5k)^k\binom{n_r}{k}$ distinct ways to subdivide a n_r-row problem with t terminals into two subproblems joined by k cut-edges.*

Proof sketch. Each terminal gives rise to 2 topological options if it is attached to a degree-1 star, and d terminals give rise to $3(d-1)$ options if attached to a degree-d star. The number of options per terminal per cutedge is thus upper-bounded by 3. The operations of Figures 5b, 5c, and 6b add a degree-2 star to the problem, increasing the number of options for subsequent cuts by at most 3. (Note that fewer options are available, in general, because not all stars are be on the boundary of the planar face containing the current endpoints of the dashed lines.) The operations of Figure 6c and 6d add a degree-1 star and increase the degree of an adjoining star by one. This increases the number of options for subsequent cuts by at most 5.

The factor of $\binom{n_r}{k}$ arises because we must assign each cut-edge to one of the n_r rows in the current region of the grid graph. The leading factor of k is a (crude) allowance for the possibility of subdividing the problem with fewer than k cut-edges. □

It remains to set up the basis and starting-point for the recursion. The most convenient basis for the recursion is formed by a zero-height, zero-width subproblem. Such a subproblem is solved by an RSMT with no edges.

The RSMT problem we wish to solve at the outset has zero terminals and thus no stars. Figure 8 shows how to generate the first cut-edge in this situation. Successive cut-edges can then be generated in the usual fashion, by splitting stars.

One last difficulty: due to degeneracies, one may encounter a subproblem of zero width but non-zero height. Such subproblems should be rotated by 90 degrees before being subdivided. This

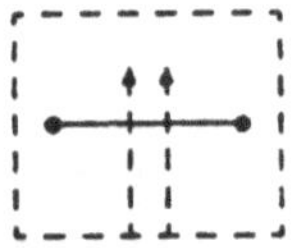

Figure 8: First cut-edge through a 0-terminal problem.

"rotation before subdivision" operation can be put to more general use to obtain the best solution time: one should always rotate a problem if there are more rows than columns in its region of the grid graph.

We can now write a recurrence for the time to run our algorithm on a grid graph with n_r rows and n_c columns ($n_r \le n_c$), with at most $f(n_r)$ cut-edges bridging the two sub-problems. We write the recurrence in terms of the perimeter $m = 2n_r + 2n_c$:

$$T(m) \le \begin{cases} 2f(m)(3m+5f(m))^{f(m)}\binom{m}{f(m)}T(\lfloor m/2 \rfloor), & \text{if } m > 1; \\ 1, & \text{otherwise.} \end{cases}$$

In the next section, we argue that $f(n) = 2\lceil\sqrt{n}\rceil$ will yield a tree that is a RSMT with high probability. Solving the recurrence above, we find that the time to solve an n-point RSMT, $T(4n)$, is $n^{O(\sqrt{n})}$.

4 How Many Cut-Edges?

We present here the preliminary results of our probabilistic analysis.

Lemma 2 *[9] Let V_{in} be a set of points in the plane, and let T be any RSMT on V_{in}. Without changing the length of T, T can be transformed to a RSMT T' with the property that each edge of T' has at least one endpoint in V_{in}.*

We say a RSMT T is in normal form if it obeys the end-point property of T' in Lemma 2.

Lemma 3 *Let S be a 1×1 square, and let V_{in} be any set of n points in S. Let C be a vertical line through X, and let R be the $2w+1$ rectangle consisting of all points of S within distance w of C. Let V_R be the points of V_{in} lying in R. Finally, let T be a normal-form RSMT on V_{in}, and let E be the set of edges of T which cross C. Then*

$$|E| \leq |V_R| + 2\left\lceil \frac{1}{w} \right\rceil + 2.$$

Proof sketch. The key observation here is that the edges which cross C must either have length greater than w or have an endpoint in V_R. Long edges crossing C must be at least w units apart, otherwise we can develop a contradiction to T being an RSMT. □

By elementary probability theory, if n points are chosen uniformly at random in the unit square, the probability of seeing at most j points in a predetermined $1 \times 1/(2\sqrt{n})$ rectangle is

$$\sum_{0 \leq i \leq j} \binom{n}{i} \left(\frac{1}{\sqrt{n}}\right)^i \left(1 - \frac{1}{\sqrt{n}}\right)^{n-i}.$$

This sum is lower-bounded by $1 - \epsilon$ if we set

$$j = \sqrt{n}/2 + (e-1)\sqrt{\sqrt{n/4}\ln\frac{1}{\epsilon}},$$

for any $0 < \epsilon < 1$ [16,18]. (Here, $e = 2.718...$, the natural base for logarithms.)

For our algorithm to find a RSMT, we must have a high-probability upper bound on the number of points near our $n^2 - 1$ recursive cuts (one of length 1, six of length 1/2, twenty-four of length 1/4, etc.). We find that our algorithm will succeed with probability p if we use up to $f(n_r)$ cut-edges when subdividing a problem on n_r grid-graph rows, where

$$f(n) = \sqrt{n} + (e-1)\sqrt{\sqrt{n}\ln\frac{n^2-1}{1-p}}.$$

A simpler formula that gives a probability of success greater than 0.9 for all $n \geq 20$ is

$$f(n) = 2\left\lceil \sqrt{n} \right\rceil.$$

We note, in passing, that we can use Lemma 3 to bound the number of cut-edges to allow at each stage of the recursion. We would then obtain an exact algorithm for the RSMT that runs in $O(n^{\sqrt{n}})$ time with high probability.

5 Experimental Results

We have not yet completed coding the general case of our algorithm. We do, however, have experimental results for the simple case of $f(n) = 1$, in which at most one cut-edge separates subproblems. This algorithm runs in $n^{O(\log n)}$ time, and is feasible for $n \leq 50$ on a Sun-3/50 workstation. See Figure 9 for the result of a 20-hour computation, in which 841 million subproblems were solved. Possibly this algorithm will be of value as a heuristic, although the competition is fierce: an $O(n \log n)$ time minimum spanning tree algorithm, suitably modified, is an excellent heuristic [4,13].

6 Future Work

We have described an exact algorithm for computing a rectilinear minimal Steiner tree (RMST) on n points that runs with high probability in time $n^{O(\sqrt{n})}$, as well as an algorithm that runs in $n^{O(\sqrt{n})}$ deterministic time that with high probability produces a RMST.

The results reported here are preliminary in nature. We intend to improve our algorithm in several ways.

- We can reduce the size of the grid graph over which the algorithm must search for solutions [24,12].

- We can tabulate the results of frequently-occurring intermediate computations (e.g., those with one terminal) so that these results need not be recomputed.
- We can short-circuit the algorithm when it reaches small cases that can be solved more quickly, using algorithms for point sets satisfying special constraints [1,3].
- We can terminate the algorithm before examining all cut sets, by proving that a previously obtained solution is in fact optimal. Such termination criteria are well established for the Euclidean TSP [15], but no one has applied this idea to the RSMT (but see [2,21]).
- Most importantly, we don't have to cut every point set at the same x-coordinate. By positioning the cut line appropriately, or possibly by applying the planar separator theorem, we can reduce either the expected or maximum number of cut edges.

Using the techniques listed above, we expect to develop faster approximate and exact algorithms for calculating an RSMT.

References

[1] A. V. Aho, M. R. Garey, and F. K. Hwang. Rectilinear Steiner trees: efficient special-case algorithms. *Networks*, 7:37–58, 1977.

[2] Y. P. Aneja. An integer linear programming approach to the Steiner problem in graphs. *Networks*, 10:167–178, 1980.

[3] Marshall W. Bern. A more general special case of the Steiner tree problem. 1986. Manuscript submitted to STOC–19.

[4] Marshall W. Bern. Two probabilistic results on rectilinear Steiner trees. In *Proceedings of the 18th Annual ACM Symposium on the Theory of Computing*, pages 433–441, May 1986.

[5] U. Bertele and F. Briosche. *Nonserial Dynamic Programming.* Academic Press, New York, 1972.

[6] S. E. Dreyfus and R. A. Wagner. The Steiner problem in graphs. *Networks*, 1:195–207, 1972.

[7] M. R. Garey, R. L. Graham, and D. S. Johnson. The complexity of computing Steiner minimal trees. *SIAM Journal of Applied Mathematics*, 32(4):835–859, 1977.

[8] M. R. Garey and D. S. Johnson. The rectilinear Steiner tree problem is NP-complete. *SIAM Journal of Applied Mathematics*, 32(4):826–834, June 1977.

[9] M. Hanan. On Steiner's problem with rectilinear distance. *SIAM Journal of Applied Mathematics*, 14(2):255–265, March 1966.

[10] F. K. Hwang. An $O(n \log n)$ algorithm for suboptimal rectilinear Steiner trees. *IEEE Transactions on Circuits and Systems*, CAS–26(1):75–77, January 1979.

[11] F. K. Hwang. The rectilinear Steiner problem. *Design Automation and Fault Tolerant Computing*, 2:303–310, 1978.

[12] Alfred Iwainsky, Enrico Canuto, Oleg Taraszow, and Agostino Villa. Network decomposition for the optimization of connection structures. *Networks*, 16:205–235, 1986.

[13] Janos Komlos and M. T. Shing. Probabilistic partitioning algorithms for the rectilinear Steiner tree problem. *Networks*, 15:413–423, 1985.

[14] Harold W. Kuhn. "Steiner's" problem revisited. In G. B. Dantzig and B. C. Eaves, editors, *Studies in Mathematics, Vol. 10: Studies in Optimization*, pages 52–70, Mathematical Association of America, 1974.

[15] E. L. Lawler, J. K. Lenstra, A. H. G. Rinnooy Kan, and D. B. Shmoys, editors. *The Traveling Salesman Problem: A Guided Tour of Optimization.* John Wiley and Sons Ltd., 1985.

[16] Prabhakar Raghavan. *Randomized Rounding and Discrete Ham-Sandwich Theorems: Provably Good Algorithms for Routing and Packing Problems.* PhD thesis, U. C. Berkeley, Computer Science Division, August 1986.

[17] Prabhakar Raghavan and Clark D. Thompson. Provably good routing in graphs: regular arrays. In *Proceedings of the 17th Annual ACM Symposium on the Theory of Computing*, pages 79–87, ACM, May 1985.

[18] Prabhakar Raghavan and Clark D. Thompson. Randomized rounding: a technique for provably good algorithms and algorithmic proofs. *Combinatorica*, to appear, 1987.

[19] Michal Servit. Heuristic algorithms for rectilinear Steiner trees. *Digital Processes*, 7:21–32, 1981.

[20] J. MacGregor Smith, D. T. Lee, and Judith S. Liebman. An $O(n \log n)$ heuristic algorithm for the rectilinear Steiner minimal tree problem. *Engineering Optimization*, 4:179–192, 1980.

[21] David I. Steinberg. The fixed charge problem. *Naval Research Logistics Quarterly*, 17:217–225, 1970.

[22] V. A. Trubin. Subclass of the Steiner problems on a plane with rectilinear metric. *Cybernetics (U.S.A.)*, 21(3):320–325, 1985. translated from *Kibernetika 21:3*, 37–40, May-June 1985.

[23] Y. Y. Yang and Omar Wing. Optimal and suboptimal solution algorithms for the wiring problem. In *IEEE International Symposium on Circuit Theory*, pages 154–158, 1972.

[24] Y. Y. Yang and Omar Wing. Suboptimal algorithm for a wire routing problem. *IEEE Transactions on Circuit Theory*, 508–510, September 1972.

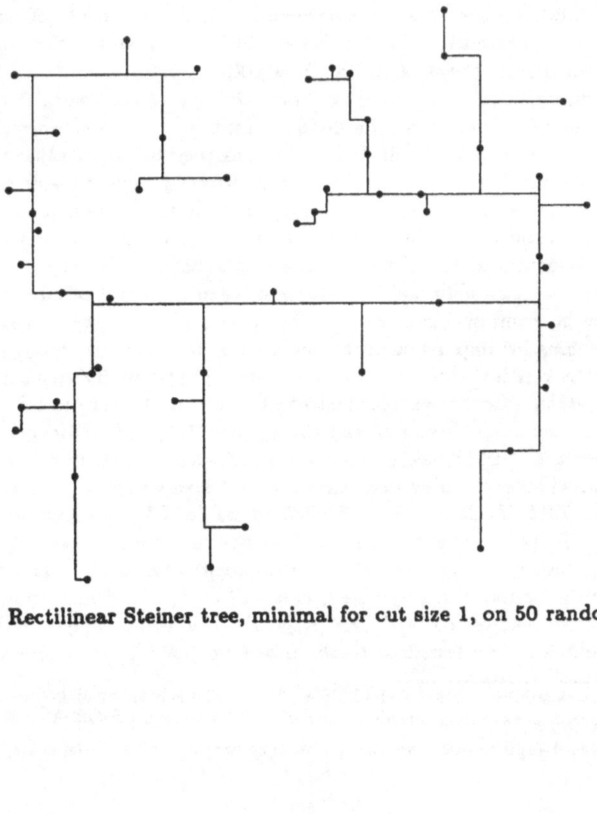

Figure 9: Rectilinear Steiner tree, minimal for cut size 1, on 50 random points.

What can be Parallelized in Computational Geometry?

Chee-Keng Yap[1]
Courant Institute of Mathematical Sciences
New York University
251, Mercer Street
New York, NY 10012

ABSTRACT

This paper has two goals. First, we point out that most problems in computational geometry in fact have fast parallel algorithms (that is, in NC^*) by reduction to the cell decomposition result of Kozen and Yap. We illustrate this using a new notion of generalized Voronoi diagrams that subsumes all known instances. While the existence of NC^* algorithms for computational geometry is theoretically significant, it leaves much to be desired for specific problems. Therefore, the second part of the paper surveys some recent results in a fast growing list of parallel algorithms for computational geometry.

1 Introduction

Computational geometry treats basic problems that are building blocks in larger systems of many applications. Because many of these applications require fast (often real-time) algorithms, it follows that efficient parallel solutions are important or even required. The study of parallel algorithms in computational geometry has recently begun in earnest [2][6], although the first major work goes back to the largely unpublished PhD thesis of Anita Chow [12].[2]

One goal of this paper is to point out that the existence of fast parallel algorithms for most problems in computational geometry can be deduced from the cell decomposition result of Kozen and Yap [26]. In [26] it is shown that cell decompositions together with adjacency information can be computed in NC for fixed dimensions. So, in principle, we have an affirmative answer to the question posed in our title. This consequence is not generally known and some authors continue to pose questions whether certain geometric problem is in NC (e.g. [20]). In any case, we feel it is an important theoretical conclusion. On the other hand, it is not satisfactory for particular problems of interest because the solutions obtained by reductions to any general cell decomposition algorithm can be expected to be far from optimal. So the second part of our paper surveys recent progress in finding efficient algorithms for important problems in computational geometry.

Since parallel architecture is a very diverse subject, we begin by clarifying our model of parallelism. We are mainly interested in synchronous parallelism embodied in the various PRAM models, and also in the closely related circuit model in complexity theory. See [17],[33],[35] for surveys on these models. One first refinement of the PRAM model is according to whether we allow concurrent or exclusive reads (CR or ER), and whether we allow concurrent or exclusive writes (CW or EW). Typically, three classes are considered: EREW, CREW and CRCW. In case of CW, we must also specify how write conflicts are resolved. To be specific, we will say that the smallest numbered processor succeeds in writing. In the present paper, we parameterize the complexity of a parallel algorithm by its processor bound $P(n)$ and its time bound $T(n)$, writing this as $(P(n), T(n))$. When using the O-notation, we will say $O(P(n), T(n))$ instead of $(O(P(n)), O(T(n)))$. For simplicity, we ignore the space bound and in any case the space bound is often close to the processor bound. (Paraphrasing [2], it is hard to

[1]Supported by NSF Grants #DCR-84-01898 and #DCR-84-01633. This is based on an invited talk at the *International Workshop on Parallel Algorithms and Architectures*, Humboldt University, Berlin, DDR, May 25-30, 1987.

[2]Indeed, this remarkable thesis is several years ahead of its time since it treated all the major problems that are topics of current research.

imagine a world where space is a more valuable resource than processors.)

Although there is interest in other models such as mesh connected or cubed connected computers (and for practical reasons since such machines are easier to build), we feel that the PRAM models are more interesting algorithmically. For instance, many problems have a complexity of $\theta(n, n^{1/2})$ in the mesh connected model [27]. Since $\Omega(n^{1/2})$ is a lower bound on any problem requiring general movement of data on such computers, this indicates that the main limitation in such algorithms is data movement. More pertinently, it seems that PRAM complexity addresses the inherent limits of parallelizing solutions to a problem rather than the limitations imposed by the connectivity of the model. (Of course the influence of connectivity is an extremely interesting study in its own right.)

The next issue is the class of algorithms that ought to be the target of our algorithmic design. Namely, when shall we say that a parallel algorithm is a 'good' solution? Just as the class P is 'good' in deterministic sequential computations, it is generally agreed that the class of problems solvable by PRAMs within processor-time bounds $O(n^{O(1)}, \log^{O(1)} n)$ is a robust class which can play this role; we will denote this class by NC^+ (perhaps modified by CRCW, CREW or EREW). We write $NC_k^+(f(n))$ for the subclass with bounds $O(f(n), \log^k n)$; if one of the parameters are omitted, we have NC_k^+ or $NC^+(f(n))$. This superscript '+' is intended to distinguish the class from another class NC studied in complexity theory and defined as those problems solvable by Boolean circuits of polynomial size and poly-logarithmic depth. In [2], we identify a superclass of NC, consisting of those problems solvable by circuits with similar parameters as NC circuits except that each node computes a basic arithmetic operation or solves a bounded degree polynomial equations, with infinite precision in unit time; we denote it by NC^*. Here we follow [11] in adding solving bounded degree polynomial equations to our primitive operations. We intend NC^+ to have these capabilites as well. Clearly, $NC \subseteq NC^* \subseteq NC^+$. As is customary, we almost exclusively describe NC^+ algorithms even when we are really interested in the NC^* or NC version; when appropriate, we then ask for the reader's indulgence to accept that we could have translated the algorithm into NC^* or even NC. Another remark is that we are only interested in *uniform* versions of these classes -- the precise notion of uniform is not important here.

2 Geometric Complexes

In computational geometry we seem to have a natural language in which to embed most problems of interest. I refer to Tarski's language L_T of elementary geometry and algebra. Essentially, L_T is the first order language with variables ranging over the real numbers $\mathcal{R}$, constants of 0 and 1, the equality and inequality relation, and the functions of $+, -$ and $\times$. We could attempt to formalize the concept of a geometric problem in the style of [42],[41]: a computational problem is a formula $\phi(\bar{x}; \bar{y})$ in some logical language L where $\bar{x}$ are the input variables and $\bar{y}$ are the output variables. Unfortunately, most problems in computational geometry do not fit this formulation nicely. In any case, most problems require the weak second order version of L_T, since we need to introduce variables for finite sets or tuples (e.g. polygons). Here we prefer a more combinatorial approach.

First we ask what are the geometric objects typically computed. Basically, each geometric object is a subset of $\mathcal{R}^d$ for some $d \geq 1$, with some additional structure. We proceed as follows: for any set $F \subseteq \mathcal{Q}[\bar{x}] = \mathcal{Q}[x_1, \ldots, x_d]$ of polynomials with rational coefficients, let $V(F)$ and $U(F)$ be the sets

$$V(F) = \{\bar{a} \in \mathcal{R}^d : \forall f \in F, f(\bar{a}) = 0\}, \qquad U(F) = \{\bar{a} \in \mathcal{R}^d : \forall f \in F, f(\bar{a}) > 0\}.$$

A ***fundamental set*** is a maximal connected subset of $V(F)$ or $U(F)$ for some finite set F. An ***elementary set*** is a maximal connected subset of a finite intersection $S_1 \cap S_2 \cap \cdots \cap S_n$ where S_i are fundamental sets. Each elementary set is homeomorphic to an open i-ball or a i-sphere (boundary of a $(i+1)$-ball); i is the dimension of the object. For any collection K of subsets of $\mathcal{R}^d$, let the ***support*** $|K|$ of K refer to the union of the subsets in K. A ***geometric complex*** is a finite collection K of pairwise disjoint elementary sets such that if $s \in K$ then $cl(s) \subseteq |K|$ where $cl(s)$ is the closure of s. For any two sets s, s', we say s is ***incident on*** s' if $cl(s) \subseteq s'$, writing this as

$$s \prec s'.$$

We say s and s' are ***adjacent*** if $cl(s) \cap cl(s')$ is non-empty. Note that s and s' are adjacent in a geometric complex K iff there is some elementary set t in K such that $t \prec s$ and $t \prec s'$. In general, incidence is too restrictive for geometric complexes, and we prefer adjacency relations.

Thus supports of geometric complexes are closed. Note that a simple polygon is a geometric complex, but a non-simple polygon should be broken up at points of self-intersection in order to get a geometric complex. To connect our study of geometric complexes with cell decompositions we introduce some definitions (see [26]).

For any set $\Sigma \subseteq \mathcal{Q}[\bar{x}]$ of polynomials, a *sign-assignment* σ to Σ is a function $\sigma : \Sigma \to \{-1, 0, +1\}$. The *sign-class* X_σ is

$$X_\sigma = \{\bar{a} \in \mathcal{R}^d \ : \ \forall f \in \Sigma, \sigma(f) = sign(f(\bar{a}))\}$$

where $sign(a) = -1, 0$ or $+1$ according to whether a is negative, zero or positive. We say σ is *consistent* if X_σ is non-empty. A subset $S \subseteq \mathcal{R}^d$ is said to be Σ-*invariant* if S is contained in some sign-class X_σ. The sign-assignment of a point $\bar{a}$ is σ if $\bar{a} \in X_\sigma$.

A geometric complex K is *based* on Σ if each elementary set in K is a union of Σ-invariant sets.

3 Generalized Voronoi diagrams

Many problems of computational geometry amount to *the construction of geometric complexes, together with the adjacency relations.* It is difficult to make this a completely formal statement, but our strategy here is to illustrate it with a large class of well-studied problems related to Voronoi diagrams. The usefulness of such objects are fully documented in the literature.

We follow [19] who suggests that the large variety of Voronoi diagrams calls for some unifying view. We reconsider their work using a more general and different terminology. First we introduce the following class

$$\mathcal{Q}\langle u_0, \ldots, u_n\rangle$$

of *generalized polynomial expressions* over variables $\bar{u} = (u_0, \ldots, u_n)$:

1. $\alpha, u_0, \ldots, u_n \in \mathcal{Q}\langle u_0, \ldots, u_n\rangle$ for each $\alpha \in \mathcal{Q}$. Each of these expressions have *depth* 0, *size* 1.
2. If $f, g \in \mathcal{Q}\langle u_0, \ldots, u_n\rangle$ then also $f + g, f - g, fg \in \mathcal{Q}\langle u_0, \ldots, u_n\rangle$, and they each have depth $1 + \max\{depth(f), depth(g)\}$ and have size $1 + size(f) + size(g)$,
3. If $f_1, \ldots, f_m \in \mathcal{Q}\langle u_0, \ldots, u_n\rangle$ $(m \geq 1)$ and $1 \leq k \leq m$, then also $\max_k\{f_1, \ldots, f_m\}$, $\min_k\{f_1, \ldots, f_m\} \in \mathcal{Q}\langle u_0, \ldots, u_n\rangle$; the depth is $1 + \max\{depth(f_i) \ : \ i = 1, \ldots, m\}$ and size is $1 + \sum_{i=1}^m size(f_i)$.

Here, $\max_k$ represents the kth largest element (so $k = 1$ gives the largest element), and similarly for $\min_k$. Each expression $\beta \in \mathcal{Q}\langle u_0, \ldots, u_n\rangle$ represents a function of $u_0, \ldots, u_n$, and we normally do not distinguish between the function and the expression. Note that even if u_i does not explicitly appear in β the function is still nominally a function of u_i. It is easy to see that these functions are continuous. (We will call polynomials in the usual sense 'regular' for emphasis.)

Let $\Sigma = (f_1, \ldots, f_n) \subseteq \mathcal{Q}\langle u_0, \ldots, u_{d-1}\rangle$ be a fixed sequence of n generalized polynomials in d variables, and let $\beta \in \mathcal{Q}\langle u_0, \ldots, u_n\rangle$. For any sign-assignment σ of Σ, define the (generalized) sign-class $X_{\sigma,\beta}$ (or simply X_σ if β is understood) as follows:

$$X_\sigma = \{\bar{a} \in \mathcal{R}^d \ : \ \forall f \in \Sigma, \sigma(f) = sign(\beta(f(\bar{a}), \Sigma(\bar{a})))\}$$

where $\Sigma(\bar{a}) = (f_1(\bar{a}), \ldots, f_n(\bar{a}))$. Thus the earlier definition of sign-class corresponds to β projecting onto its first variable. The collection $K_\beta(\Sigma)$ of non-empty sign-classes is called the β-*diagram* of Σ, and the elements of the diagram are called *cells*.

We estimate of the complexity of β-diagrams:

Lemma 1 *Let $r > 0$ be fixed as n varies. Let $\Sigma \subseteq \mathcal{Q}\langle u_0, \ldots, u_{d-1}\rangle$ $(d < r)$ be a sequence of n generalized polynomials where each generalized polynomial has depth and size at most r, and let $\beta \in \mathcal{Q}\langle u_0, \ldots, u_n\rangle$ have depth at most r and at most size n^r.*

1. *The β-diagram $K(\Sigma)$ of Σ is a geometric complex.*
2. *The β-diagram is based on $O(n^{r+1})$ polynomials, each of bounded degree.*
3. *The number of cells in the diagram is polynomial in n.*

Proof. For any generalized polynomial $\beta \in \mathcal{Q}\langle u_0, \ldots, u_n\rangle$, define $\bar{\beta}$ to be the following set of (regular) polynomials: if $depth(\beta) = 0$ then $\bar{\beta} = \{\beta\}$. If $\beta = \beta_1 - \beta_2$ then $\bar{\beta} = \{\alpha_1 - \alpha_2 : \alpha_i \in \bar{\beta}_i\}$. Similarly when $\beta = \beta_1 + \beta_2$ or $\beta = \beta_1\beta_2$. If $\beta = \max_k\{\beta_1, \ldots, \beta_m\}$ then $\bar{\beta}$ is the union over all the $\bar{\beta}_i, (i = 1, \ldots, m)$, and over all $\bar{\beta}_i - \bar{\beta}_j, (i, j = 1, \ldots, m)$.

If β satisfies the conditions of the lemma, then the degrees of polynomials in $\bar{\beta}$ is bounded (but single exponential in r). To bound the cardinality of $\bar{\beta}$: one sees inductively that this is $n^{O(1)^r}$. In the same way, for each $f \in \Sigma$, the set $\bar{f}$ has bounded degrees and bounded cardinality.

Let $\Sigma = (\alpha_1, \ldots, \alpha_n)$. Then let $\bar{\beta}(\Sigma)$ denote the set of all polynomials obtained by substituting u_0 with any element from $\bigcup_{i=1}^n \bar{f}_i$, and substituting the variables $u_1, \ldots, u_n$ with some sequence $(f_0, \ldots, f_n)$ where $f_i \in \bar{\alpha}_i$ $(i = 1, \ldots, n)$. It is not hard to see that K is based on the set $\bar{\beta}(\Sigma)$. Since $\bar{f}, (f \in \Sigma)$, has bounded cardinality (depending singly exponentially on r), we see that K is based on a set of $O(n^{r+1})$ polynomials. This proves the first two parts of the lemma. The third part depends on the observation that the cells of the diagram are union of $\bar{\beta}(\Sigma)$-invariant components. The conclusion then follows from the fact that the number of sign-invariant components of a set of $n^{O(1)}$ polynomials, each of bounded degree, has $n^{O(1)}$ sign-invariant components. This bound can be deduced by the cell-decomposition technique of Collins'. (Although crude it is accessible and more direct than the oft-quoted Milnor-Thom bound. Indeed, the Milnor-Thom result bounds the number of components in an algebraic variety, and so does not directly bound the number of sign-invariant components which is what we need.) **Q.E.D.**

Examples.

1. Computing of *hyperplane arrangements* fit this framework. The function $\beta(u_0, \ldots, u_n)$ simply projects onto its first coordinate u_0. But note that convex hulls do not fit our scheme.

2. Let us see how the *standard Voronoi diagram* for a set of points fits into this framework: for any set of points $P \subseteq \mathcal{R}^d$, let

$$\Sigma(P) = \{D(\bar{x}, \bar{a}) : \bar{a} \in P\}$$

where $D(\cdot, \cdot)$ denotes the square of the Euclidean distance and $\bar{x} = (x_1, \ldots, x_d)$. Let $\beta(u_0, \ldots, u_n) = u_0 - \min_1\{u_1, \ldots, u_n\}$. Then we see that the usual Voronoi cell associated with a point $\bar{a} \in P$ is given by the sign-class X_σ where $\sigma(D(\bar{x}, \bar{a})) = 0$ but $= +1$ elsewhere.

3. The *farthest-point Voronoi diagram* of P is obtained if $\Sigma(P)$ is as above, β uses the maximum function instead, and with consistent sign-assignments σ that are zero at one polynomial but non-positive otherwise.

4. The *degree-k Voronoi diagrams* ([19],[15]) are obtained as in the Voronoi diagram above but where $\beta(u_0, u_1, \ldots, u_n)$ is $u_0 - \min_k\{u_1, \ldots, u_n\}$. The *order-k Voronoi diagrams* are obtained when the regions are unions of degree-i regions (for $i = 1, \ldots, k$). Here we have $\beta(u_0, \ldots, u_n) = u_0 - \min_1\{u_0, \min_k\{u_1, \ldots, u_n\}\}$.

5. Voronoi diagrams in the L_p-metric fits this formulation. This is obvious for $1 < p < \infty$ but it holds even for $p = 1$ or $p = \infty$. This is because the absolute value function is a generalized polynomial: $|c| = \max_1\{c, -c\}$. Note that in this example, the use of generalized polynomials in the set Σ is essential.

6. The following interesting diagram arises in motion planning [29] in the space $\mathbf{S} = \mathcal{R}^2 \times \mathcal{S}^1$ where $\mathcal{S}^1$ is the circle (1-sphere). Here a point in $\mathbf{S}$ is given by $Z = (x, y, \theta)$ where θ is an angle. Note that we can embed $\mathbf{S}$ in $\mathcal{R}^4$ using $(x, y, \theta) \mapsto (x, y, \sin\theta, \cos\theta)$. Thus, we could assume that we are actually given $\sin\theta, \cos\theta$. As input, we have a set S of line segments (walls) and their endpoints (corners). The motion planning is for a directed line-segment (the 'rod') which we denote by PQ, with endpoints given by P and Q. For any $Z = (x, y, \theta) \in \mathbf{S}$ and $s \in S$, we define $D(s; Z)$ to be the square of the distance from the (nearest point on the) rod to s when the rod is placed in position Z. A sign-assignment is a function $\sigma : S \to \{-1, 0, +1\}$ and the sign-class X_σ is given by

$$X_\sigma = \{Z \in \mathbf{S} : \forall s \in S, \sigma(s) = sign(D(s; Z) - \min\{D(s'; Z) : s' \in S\})\}$$

We see that the 'Voronoi cell' belonging to each $s \in S$ is given by the non-empty sign-classes X_σ with $\sigma(s) = 0$ and $\sigma(s') = +1$ for $s' \neq s$. In addition to Voronoi edges and vertices, there are also Voronoi surfaces. We must show that $D(s; Z)$ is actually a generalized polynomial. We may write $D(s; Z) = d^2 + (\max_1\{0, t_P - t_s, t_s - t_Q\})^2$ where d^2 is the distance from s to the line L through the line segment PQ and t_P, t_Q, t_s is the parameter of the projections of points P, Q, s onto the line L; we choose the parameter to denote the distance of the point from P, with Q having a positive distance. (This form is suggested by Tom Dubé.) One verifies that the formula is correct.

This last example raises an interesting issue: in most of computational geometry, the input is assume to be exact, and finitely specified using rational numbers. In this example, we need 'exact finite representation' of angles. Here the convention is less well-established. We note three possible representations: directly in radians, or by its ratio with π (i.e. α represents $\alpha\pi$), or by its trigonometric value (say, as $\sin\alpha$) but since there is some ambiguity, we also need another bit (say, to denote the sign of $\cos\alpha$). Each representation has its advantages but they do not capture the same class of exactly representable angles. We could adopt all three but we would have to interrelate them.

4 Reduction to Cell Decomposition

First we review the cell decomposition problem. Given a set of (regular) polynomials $\Sigma \subseteq \mathcal{Q}[x_1, \ldots, x_d]$ the goal is to construct a geometric complex K that partitions $\mathcal{R}^d$ so that each $c \in K$ is Σ-invariant. The partition K is called a ***cell decomposition*** if each $c \in K$ is homeomorphic to $\mathcal{R}^i$ for some $i \leq d$. Collins' algorithm [16],[4] computes such a decomposition in polynomial time (assuming the dimension d is fixed). Unfortunately, this algorithm is inadequate for our purposes on two counts: it is not in NC^+ and it yields no information on incidence relationship among the cells. ([34] has a partial solution for finding incidence relationships efficiently.) In [26] we resolve both shortcomings partly by incorporating techniques from [8] (see also [38]) into Collins' algorithm. David Prill [31] independently gave a method for computing incidences based on entirely different principles. The output of the algorithm in [26] on input Σ is a cell decomposition K represented by a labelled graph in the following way:

$$G = (V, E, \Delta, \delta, \tau, N)$$

1. V are vertices (we may assume $V = \{1, 2, \ldots, |V|\}$), one for each cell of the decomposition K; let $R_v \subseteq \mathcal{R}^d$ denote the cell represented by $v \in V$.

2. E is the edge set such that uEv iff R_u is incident on R_v.

3. Δ is a set of polynomials that contains the input set Σ. $\Delta - \Sigma$ is the set of 'auxiliary' polynomials.

4. τ represents the sign assignment of the cells. More precisely, for each $v \in V$, $\tau(v)$ is a sign-assignment for Δ such that when $\tau(v)$ is restricted to Σ (since $\Sigma \subseteq \Delta$), then R_v is contained in the sign-class of the restricted $\tau(v)$. Of course several R_v may belong to the same sign-class and it is the sign-assignment to the auxiliary polynomials that distinguish among these cells.

5. N is an NC-circuit that "defines" the cells. For any sign-assignment σ to the polynomials in Δ, $N(\sigma)$ computes the cell index $v \in V$ corresponding to σ (or outputs "inconsistent").

The circuit N is used as follows: suppose that we want to know which cell a point $\bar{a} \in \mathcal{Q}^d$ lies in. We first evaluate $sign(p(\bar{a}))$ for each $p \in \Delta$; this can be done in NC since all the evaluations can be done in parallel. Then the output (which corresponds to a sign assignment) is then fed into the circuit N to tell us the $v \in V$ such that $\bar{a} \in R_v$.

We now investigate the requirements for the construction of a geometric complex to be NC-reducible to the cell decomposition algorithm of [26]. To do this, we must understand the connection between different instances of a problem: Let $\Gamma = \Gamma(u_0, \ldots, u_{d-1}; v_1, \ldots, v_n)$ be a sequence of generalized polynomials on $d + n$ variables where we think of the v_i's as parameters. A pair (Γ, β) is called a ***n-scheme***. For any substitution of real values a_i for the parameters v_i, we obtain an ***instance*** $(\Gamma(u_0, \ldots, u_{d-1}; a_1, \ldots, a_n), \beta)$ of the n-scheme. A ***generalized Voronoi diagram problem*** corresponds to an infinite sequence $\{(\Gamma_n, \beta_n) : n = 1, 2, \ldots\}$ where each (Γ_n, β_n) is a n-scheme. An ***input*** to the problem is a sequence $a_1, \ldots, a_n$ of rational numbers and the corresponding output is the β-diagram of $\Gamma_n(u_0, \ldots, u_{d-1}; a_1, \ldots, a_n)$.

If Σ, β are generalized polynomials satisfying the conditions of the above lemma, we say (Σ, β) is of ***type*** (r, n). If each instance of a scheme is of type (r, n) then we say that the scheme is of ***type*** (r, n). If the n-scheme of a generalized Voronoi diagram problem is of type (r, n) for some fixed r, we say the *rank* of the problem is r.

In order for a problem $\{(\Gamma_n, \beta_n) : n = 1, 2, ...\}$ to be in NC^*, here are some sufficient conditions:

1. *For each n, the scheme (Γ_n, β_n) can be generated in NC^*.* This simply means that the problem is *uniform*.

2. *The problem must be of rank r for some finite r, and the scheme (Γ_n, β_n) must be of type (r, n).* Bounded rank and instances with bounded depth seems natural – this holds in all our examples in the previous section. Unbounded rank or unbounded depth problems seldom occur naturally (exceptions: theorem proving, root isolation and solving systems of polynomial equations). Our requirements so far ensure that lemma 1 is applicable and so size of the required β_n-diagram is polynomial in n. Let (Σ_n, β_n) be an instance of (Γ_n, β_n) and suppose that the β_n-diagram of Σ_n is based on a set Φ_n of regular polynomials (recall that in the proof of lemma 1, $\Phi_n = \bar{\beta}_n(\Sigma_n)$). We can invoke the algorithm of Kozen-Yap to compute the Φ_n-invariant cell-decomposition.

3. *The ability to reconstruct the sign-classes of Σ_n.* We need to compute those sign-assignments σ of Σ_n for which X_{σ,β_n} is non-empty. Of course we do not wish to check the exponentially many possibilities. Suppose that $\tau : \Sigma_n \to \{-1, 0, +1\}$ is the sign-assignment that we wish to construct corresponding to the sign-assignment $\sigma : \Phi_n \to \{-1, 0, +1\}$. We recall that in constructing the set $\bar{\beta}$ (for any generalized polynomial β), if $\beta = \max_k\{\beta_1, \ldots, \beta_m\}$ then we add the pairs $f_i - f_j$ for all $f_i \in \bar{\beta}_i$ ($f_j \in \bar{\beta}_j, i \neq j$). This amounts to the pairwise comparison of all arguments of the the function $\max_k$, and allows us to decide (given σ) which is the kth largest argument. Thus we may deduce the corresponding sign $s(f)$ of $\beta_n(f, \Sigma_n)$ (recall the definition of X_σ) for each $f \in \Sigma_n$; we simply let $\tau(f)$ equal $s(f)$. It is not difficult to give NC-circuits to compute all such consistent sign-assignments τ. Of course, several consistent σ's may yield the same τ: the sign-class X_{τ,β_n} is simply the union over all these Φ_n-invariant classes. The adjacency relation among the cells can easily be deduced from the incidence relation of the Φ_n-invariant decomposition.

Corollary 2 *All the six examples in the previous section are in NC^*.*

Of course, the bounds obtained by such general constructions are crude. The point we wish to make is that there is a systematic procedure to draw such conclusions. Here we focused on a generalization of Voronoi diagrams that includes all known examples of Voronoi diagrams.

Remark: *When is NC^* really NC?* We have stated our bounds as NC^* in the corollary even though the Kozen-Yap algorithm is NC. To understand this, we must recall that there are two outstanding numerical problems that are not known to be in NC: the problems of root isolation and of integer GCD. Because of this, the Kozen-Yap algorithm does not compute 'sample points' for each cell in the decomposition, unlike in the Collins' procedure. For many geometric applications, the symbolic representation of a decomposition as a labelled graph above is sufficient. However, for something like Voronoi diagrams, it seems that we would really like to obtain more numerical information about, say, the Voronoi vertices. This is precisely the sample point information. The coordinates of Voronoi vertices would be algebraic numbers represented, as usual, by isolating intervals with defining polynomials. This calls for root isolation, but for fixed degree polynomials. Recall that we have defined NC^* so that it can isolate roots of fixed degree polynomials in constant time. This is not an artificial choice to accommodate the present discussion; in [11], we have already suggested that isolating roots of fixed degree polynomials should be added because the solving simple trigonometric functions is important in many applications and they can be reduced to root isolation. Another example arguing for their inclusion is that we always solve shortest path problems assuming the ability to take square roots in unit time.

5 Survey of parallel algorithms

Some preliminary remarks are in order. Many of these problems will require sorting as a basic step. Since the breakthrough in [3], it is known that sorting of n numbers is in $NC_1^*(n)$ (the method is known as AKS sorting). The implicit constants render the AKS method impractical and it is often goal to avoid AKS sorting. But if we are willing to work with PRAMs, the best algorithm is now due to Cole [14] who gives a CREW $NC_1^+(n)$ algorithm with very small constants ($2.5n$ comparisons); he also gives a EREW $NC_1^+(n)$ solution with larger constants. Cole's work improves an earlier solution of Preparata [30] (which requires some details supplied by Borodin and Hopcroft [9]). Another remark is that we must now pay attention to the particular subclasses of NC^+ an algorithm falls into. For instance, $NC^+(n^3)$ would not be practical by present day technology while $NC^+(n)$ seems feasible. Most of the results are for low dimensions and tend to be in $NC^+(n)$.

5.1 Convex hulls

We begin with one of the first problems studied in this context, the convex hull of a set of points. The obvious method of divide and conquer, when parallelized gives an $O(n, \log^2 n)$ solution. This was achieved by Chow [12] and Nath et al [28]. Independently, [2], [6] and [36] improved this to $O(n, \log n)$. The idea in the first two papers is to divide the n points into $\sqrt{n}$ subsets and recursively solve them. The technique here of $\sqrt{n}$ divide-and-conquer is an important paradigm in parallel algorithms. As it turns out, this paradigm is not crucial for convex hulls: Wagener in his thesis ([36],[37]) described an $O(n, \log n)$ divide-and-conquer solution where the division is the usual halving.[3]

In Chow's thesis, she also showed that convex hulls in 3-dimensions is in $NC_3^+(n)$, by a reduction to an optimal sorting algorithm (viz. AKS sorting). In [2], we give an $NC_3^+(n)$ method that avoids sorting but is based on a data-structure (of independent interest) for answering queries on tangent planes from a line to a convex polyhedra.

5.2 Voronoi diagrams

The standard Voronoi diagram for a point set in the plane is reducible to 3-D convex hull by well-known transformations. So the problem is in $NC_3^+(n)$. In [2][4], the bound is improved to $NC_2^+(n)$. There are many generalizations of Voronoi diagrams but perhaps the most important case (with applications in motion planning, etc) is to compute the Voronoi diagram for an *essentially disjoint*[5] set of line segments. There are two known optimal sequential solutions here: Yap [39] has a divide-and-conquer method and Fortune [22] has a plane sweep method. In [23] we have been able to parallelize the technique of Yap to obtain an $O(n, \log^2 n)$ solution.

Closely related to Voronoi diagrams is the Delaunay triangulation of a point set. The same complexity bounds for Voronoi diagrams immediately apply. Saxena, Bhatt and Prasad [32] gave an interesting a spectrum of processor-time tradeoffs achievable for Delaunay triangulation:

$$O(\log n, n), \quad O(n^2, \log n \log\log n), \quad O(n^3, \log\log n), \quad O(n^4, 1)$$

The first three results are for CREW PRAM, but the last one requires a CRCW PRAM. Actually, the write conflicts only occur with processors writing the same value to a common memory location, the so-called 'common' CRCW model.

If we are interested in triangulating (the interior of the convex hull of) a set of points, not necessarily the Delaunay triangulation, then ElGindy [21] shows that in d-dimensions, the bounds $O(f(d) \log^n, \frac{n}{\log n})$ are achievable on a CREW PRAM. Here $f(d) = d^4 / \log\left(\frac{4^d}{4^d-1}\right)$. Another direction is to triangulate a set of line segments, as considered next.

5.3 Triangulating a set of disjoint line segments

We are given a set of n (closed) line segments in the plane. First we want to detect if they are essentially disjoint. If they are essentially disjoint, we want to connect their endpoints with additional line segments so that the interior of their convex hull is triangulated.

The first parallel algorithm was given by Aggarwal, Chazelle, Guibas, Ó'Dúnlaing and Yap [2] giving an NC^+ solution with bounds $O(n \log n, \log n)$. This implies, of course, an $O(n, \log^2 n)$ solution. Atallah and Goodrich [7] improved this to $O(n, \log n \log\log n)$. Recently, together with Cole [5], they obtained a further improvement to $O(n, \log n)$.

[3] Recently, Atallah and Goodrich independently discovered similar solutions.

[4] i.e. the journal version, not the preliminary conference version.

[5] This means that for every pair s, s' of segments, if $s \cap s'$ is non-empty then $s \cap s'$ consists of a single point that is a common endpoint of s and s'

The parallel triangulation algorithms all depend on computing the so-called ***trapezoidal map***, i.e. for each vertex v, we compute the edges $A(v)$ and $B(v)$ of the simple polygon that are vertically visible from v, with $A(v)$ above v and $B(v)$ below v. The complexity bounds cited in the last paragraph all come from computing this map. In the course of computing this map, we also detect whether the set is essentially disjoint.

Suppose that we have also computed the convex hull of the set of line segments. Using the trapezoidal map, the interior of the convex hull can be partitioned into the so-called ***one-sided monotone polygons***. The triangulation of these monotone polygons in [2],[7] is relatively involved. Recently we discovered an elegant new method, by two (parallel) calls to the trapezoidal map [40].

As is well-known, the triangulation of a simple polygon immediately leads to a host of other problems that can be solved efficiently. We refer to [2] for two instances (balanced recursive partition of a polygon, optimal placement of guards in an art gallery). See also [13] for the related problem of reporting intersection of rectangles.

5.4 Point location

The (planar) point location problem begins with a triangulation T_0 of the interior of a triangle Δ_0, and we are required to construct a data-structure so that for any query point p inside Δ_0, we must respond with the triangle of T_0 containing p. There are now several sequential methods known for constructing such a data-structure in linear time and answering queries in $O(\log n)$ time. For parallel solutions, Anita Chow's thesis constructs a suitable data-structure in bounds $O(n, \log^2 n)$. Unfortunately, the data-structure answers queries in suboptimal time $O(\log^2 n)$.

A very elegant optimal data-structure here is due to Kirkpatrick [25]: the structure consists of a hierarchy of $O(\log n)$ triangulations $T_0, T_1, T_2, \ldots$ ending in the single triangle Δ_0. The construction of T_{+1} given T_i boils down to: how to find a large (i.e. some constant fraction of the size of T_i) subset of independent vertices of T_i with bounded (say ≤ 6) degree. One should be careful here: the similar looking "MIS problem", finding any maximal independent subset of an arbitrary graph, is notoriously difficult to parallelize (the best algorithm uses $O(n^3)$ processors). Fortunately, Kirkpatrick and Dadoun [18] was able to find an $O(n, \log n)$ solution to this question. This implies an $O(n, \log^2 n)$ solution for constructing the hierarchy of triangulations. Again, point location leads to other efficient solutions. See [18] for some applications.

5.5 Miscellaneous

There are other results which we briefly note: Goodrich [24] shows that the all nearest-neighbor problem for a convex polygon can be solved with optimal speedup, i.e. $O(p, n/p + \log n)$ for any p. In [2], we consider the problem of computing the smallest triangle enclosing a convex polygon. A solution using an interesting 'back-and-forth' technique solves this in $O(n, \log n)$. ElGindy [20] gave an $O(n, \log^2 n)$ solution to the problem of computing the shortest path between two points inside a monotone polygon. Goodrich and Atallah [6] computes a closest pair of points among n planar points in complexity of $O(n, \log n \log\log n)$.

6 Several Questions

We suggest some directions for future work.

1. ***Parallel techniques.*** It is inevitable that new techniques are discovered as we apply ourselves to parallel algorithms. Some of them are analogues of sequential ones: the square-root divide and conquer method ([6], [2]), parallel plane sweep ([2],[7]). Others do not seem to have sequential analogues: the back-and-forth technique ([2]). We ask: is dynamic programming parallelizable in NC^+? Note that dynamic programming has a belated appearance in computational geometry (see ([10], [11],[1]) mainly because geometric optimization problems have not been studied much.

2. ***Convex hulls.*** Although there are no explicit convex algorithms for higher dimensions, it is not hard to see that convex hulls in any dimension is NC-reducible to cell decomposition. The interesting question is to determine the precise $k = k(d)$ such the d-dimensional problem is in NC_k^+. Note that

$k(1) = 1, k(2) = 1, k(3) \leq 3$.

3. *Complexity theoretic questions.* We notice that although convex hulls in 2 and 3 dimensions and planar Voronoi diagrams are all solved in $O(n \log n)$ sequentially, their parallel complexity using n processors is $O(\log n)$, $O(\log^3 n)$ and $O(\log^2 n)$, respectively. We ask a basic question: is it true that for any $k \geq 1$, there are problems with sequential time complexity of $O(n \log n)$ which is not in $NC_k^+(n)$ but in $NC_{k+1}^+(n)$? We think this is true, but it would be nice to even generate conjectured examples for each k.

4. *NC, NC^* and NC^+.* We need more systematic organization of the precise relationships between these classes. This touches on an issue that is little studied even in the sequential setting: how does converting from the infinite precision model to the bit model affect the complexity? The answers seems to be known (i.e. varies from folk knowledge to faith) but someone needs to work the appropriate theorems for easy application.

5. *Generalized problems.* We formulated the generalized Voronoi diagram problem to serve as a vehicle for demonstrating reduction to cell-decomposition. However, the definitional structure may have independent interest. For example, convex hulls do not fit our formulation directly. What is the power of the logical language needed to capture all or most problems in computational geometry? What are the logical properties of such classes of problems? This would contribute towards the program of "a theory of computational problems" ([42],[41]). It seems that in computational geometry we have a good chance of succeeding: we could begin with some generalization of Tarski's language.

References

[1] A. Aggarwal, J. S. Chang, and C. K. Yap. Minimum area circumscribing polygons. *The Visual Computer*, 1:112–117, 1985.

[2] A. Aggarwal, B. Chazelle, L. Guibas, C. Ó'Dúnlaing, and C. Yap. Parallel computational geometry. In *IEEE Foundations of Computer Science*, pages 468–477, 1985. To appear, special issue **Algorithmica**.

[3] M. Ajtai, J. Komlós, and E. Szemerédi. Sorting in $c \log n$ parallel steps. *Combinatorica*, 3:1–19, 1983.

[4] Dennis S. Arnon. *A Cellular Decomposition Algorithm for Semi-Algebraic Sets*. Tech. Rep. No. 353, Dept. of Comp. Sci., Univ. of Wisconsin, 1979. PhD thesis.

[5] M. J. Atallah, R. Cole, and M. T. Goodrich. Private communication.

[6] Mikhail J. Atallah and Michael T. Goodrich. Efficient parallel solutions to geometric problems. In *Proc. 1985 Int. Conf. on Parallel Processing*, pages 411–417, 1985. To appear, J. of Parallel and Distributed Computing.

[7] Mikhail J. Atallah and Michael T. Goodrich. Efficient plane sweeping in parallel. In *2nd ACM Symp. on Computational Geometry*, pages 216–225, 1986.

[8] M. Ben-Or, D. Kozen, and J. Reif. The complexity of elementary algebra and geometry. In *ACM Symposium on Theory of Computing*, pages 457–464, 1984.

[9] Alan Borodin and John Hopcroft. Routing, merging and sorting on parallel models of computation. In *14th STOC*, pages 338–344, 1982.

[10] J. E. Boyce, D. P. Dobkin, R. L. Drysdale, and L. J. Guibas. Finding extremal polygons. *SIAM J. Computing*, 14:134–147, 1985.

[11] J. S. Chang and C. K. Yap. A polynomial solution for the potato-peeling problem. *Discrete and Comput. Geo.*, 1:155–182, 1986.

[12] Anita Chow. *Parallel algorithms for geometric problems*. PhD thesis, Department of Computer Sci., University of Illinois, Urbana-Champaign, 1980.

[13] Anita L. Chow. A practical parallel algorithm for reporting intersection of rectangles. In *IEEE Symp. Parallel Processing*, pages 304–305, 1981.

[14] Richard Cole. *Parallel Merge Sort*. Technical Report 278, Courant Institute, NYU, 1987. Earlier version in 27th FOCS, submitted for publication.

[15] Richard Cole and Chee Yap. Geometric retrieval problems. *Information and Control*, 63:39–57, 1984.

[16] George E. Collins. Quantifier elimination for real closed fields by cylindrical algebraic decomposition. In *2nd GI Conf. on Automata Theory and Formal Languages, Lecture Notes in Computer Science*, pages 134–183, Springer-Verlag, 1975.

[17] Stephen A. Cook. *Towards a Complexity Theory of Synchronous Parallel Computation*. Technical Report 141/80, Dept. of Computer Science, University of Toronto, 1980.

[18] N. Dadoun and D. Kirkpatrick. Parallel processing for efficient subdivision search. In *3nd ACM Symp. Comput. Geo.*, 1987. to appear.

[19] H. Edelsbrunner and R. Seidel. Voronoi diagrams and arrangements. In *ACM Symposium on Computational Geometry*, pages 251–262, 1985.

[20] Hossam ElGindy. A parallel algorithm for the shortest path problem in monotone polygons. may 1986. Dept of Comp. and Inf. Sci., Univ. of Penn.

[21] Hossam ElGindy. A parallel algorithm for triangulating simplicial point sets in space with optimal speed-up. April 1986. Manuscript.

[22] Steven Fortune. A sweepline algorithm for Voronoi diagrams. In *2nd ACM Symp. Comput. Geo.*, pages 313–322, 1986.

[23] M. Goodrich, C. Ó'Dúnlaing, and C. Yap. *Fast Parallel Algorithms for Voronoi Diagrams.* Technical Report CSD-TR-538, Dept. of Comp. Sci., Purdue Univ., 1985.

[24] Michael T. Goodrich. *An Optimal parallel algorithm for the all nearest-neighbor problem for a convex polygon.* Technical Report CSD-TR-533, Dept. of Comp. Sci., Purdue Univ., 1985.

[25] David G. Kirkpatrick. Optimal search in planar subdivision. *SIAM J. Computing*, 12:28–35, 1983.

[26] Dexter Kozen and Chee Yap. Algebraic cell decomposition in NC. In *IEEE Foundations of Computer Science*, pages 515–521, 1985.

[27] Russ Miller and Quentin F. Stout. *Mesh Computer Algorithms for Computational Geometry.* Technical Report 86-18, Dept. of Computer Science, SUNY at Buffalo, 1986.

[28] D. Nath, S. N. Maheshwari, and P. C. P. Bhatt. Parallel algorithms for the convex hull in two dimensions. In *Conf. on Analysis Problem Classes and Programming for Parallel Computing*, pages 358–372, 1981.

[29] C. Ó'Dúnlaing, M. Sharir, and C. Yap. Generalized Voronoi diagrams for moving a ladder: I. Topological analysis. *Comm. Pure and Applied Math.*, 1984.

[30] Franco Preparata. New parallel-sorting schemes. *IEEE Trans. on Computers*, C-27:669–673, 1978.

[31] David Prill. On approximations and incidence in cylindrical algebraic decompositions. *SIAM J. Computing*, 15:972–993, 1986.

[32] S. Saxena, P. C. P. Bhatt, and V. C. Prasad. Fast parallel algorithms for Delaunay triangulation. 1986. Extended abstract.

[33] Jacob T. Schwartz. Ultracomputers. *ACM Trans. on Programming Languages and Systems*, 2:484–521, 1980.

[34] Jacob T. Schwartz and Micha Sharir. On the piano movers' problem: II. General techniques for computing topological properties of real algebraic manifolds. *Advances in Math.*, 4:298–351, 1983.

[35] Uzi Vishkin. *Synchronous Parallel Computation - a Survey.* Technical Report 71, Courant Institute, NYU, 1983.

[36] Hubert Wagener. Optimally parallel algorithms for convex hull determination. *Algorithmica*, 1987. (submitted).

[37] Hubert Wagener. *Parallel computational geometry using polygonal order.* PhD thesis, Technical University of Berlin, 1985. West Germany.

[38] Chee K. Yap. *Parallel subresultant Sturm sequences.* Technical Report, Robotics Lab. Report, Courant Institute, NYU, 1987. To appear.

[39] Chee-Keng Yap. *An $O(n \log n)$ algorithm for the Voronoi diagram of a set of simple curve segments.* Technical Report 43, Robotics Lab, Courant Institute, NYU, 1985. Submitted for publication.

[40] Chee-Keng Yap. ***Parallel triangulation of a simple polygon in three calls to the trapezoidal map.*** Technical Report, Robotics Lab, Courant Institute, NYU, March 1987.

[41] Chee-Keng Yap. Space-time tradeoffs and first order problems in a model of programs. In ***12th ACM Symp. Theory of Computing***, 1980.

[42] Chee-Keng Yap. ***Three studies on Computational Problems***. PhD thesis, Yale University, 1980.

A Co-Operative Programming Environment for a Back-End Type Sequential Inference Machine CHI

Akihiko Konagaya Ryousei Nakazaki Mamoru Umemura*

Abstract

The outline of a language and a software system developed on a co-operative high performance sequential inference machine (*CHI*) are described. *CHI* is a back-end type sequential inference machine which aims for high-speed execution of large scale logic programming programs. It consists of a high performance processor and large main memories, dedicated for logic programming languages, and a host machine for input/output services. The novelty of the work is in its use of *co-operative processes* and the extension of a *logic programming language* to make an interactive programming environment on a back-end type machine. Separation of language processing processes and input/output server processes makes it possible to utilize host machine software systems, such as a file system, a window system and a network system, in order to realize a comfortable, high performance, reliable programming environment on the back-end machine. In addition, an inter-machine communication protocol based on "virtual objects" considerably reduces the difficulty of developing bus-transparent input/output operations between the host machine and *CHI*. This approach is quite general and applicable to any loosely coupled distributed system.

1 Introduction

Logic programming languages, as typified by Prolog[10,17], have come to be known as knowledge programming languages due to their advantageous knowledge programming facilities, such as pattern matching (unification), automatic backtracking and database searching. Such languages are also well known as kernel languages in the *Fifth Generation Computer Systems Project* in Japan[6]. The main current difficulty concerning logic programming languages is the lack of a high performance language processor. This problem comes from the fact that logic programming languages require uncommon programming functions, such as dynamic type checking and dynamic resource management, as well as large address spaces to hold backtracking information.

To overcome this problem, we developed a *co-operative high performance sequential inference machine (CHI)*[11] between fiscal 1983 and 1986 within the Fifth Generation Computer Systems Project in Japan, sponsored by MITI. *CHI* is a back-end type sequential inference machine designed to be attached to a general purpose computer system or a work station such as a personal sequential inference machine (PSI)[18]. Currently, we use the VAX system 750 or PSI as a host machine for our inference machine. Furthermore, we have developed *New-CHI* as the successor of the inference machine *CHI*. *New-CHI* has an architecture similar to *CHI*, but uses compact hardware based on LSI technology. The host machine for *New-CHI* is an engineering work station developed by NEC.

In this paper, we focus on how to realize an interactive logic programming environment on *CHI*. The technology we used is a *co-operative programming environment* which consists of several processes working together. This environment consists of language processing processes and input/output server processes connected by inter-machine communication protocols called "virtual objects". The separation of the language processing processes and the input/output server processes makes it possible to utilize complicated input/output software systems, such as a file system, a window system and a network system which have already been provided on the host machine. This implies that we can concentrate our efforts more on developing an interpreter, a compiler and a resource management system specifically for a logic programming language.

The biggest difficulty in developing the co-operative programming environment is to realize sophisticated input/output operations, known as *bus-transparent input/output operations*, which enable the *CHI* processes to use the host machine devices as if the devices were directly equipped with the *CHI*

*C&C Systems Research Laboratories, NEC Corporation 4-1-1 Miyazaki Miyamae-ku, Kawasaki 213, Japan

processor. To accomplish this, we propose *virtual objects*, as the highest level inter-machine communication protocol between *CHI* and its host machine. The *virtual objects* represent host devices, such as files and windows, and each access operation causes corresponding remote procedure calling to the host machine. This abstraction makes it possible for *CHI* processes to use host devices, as a kind of data objects provided in *CHI*, and greatly reduces the difficulty of developing an interactive programming environment.

In the next section, we introduce the design overview of the sequential inference machine *CHI*. In section 3, the new logic programming language *SUPLOG*, which we designed to develop the co-operative programming environment, is described. After that, we present the outline of the co-operative programming environment and a new inter-machine communication protocol *virtual objects*, and some experimental results of their implementation.

2 Sequential Inference Machine CHI

CHI is a micro-programmable tagged architecture machine based on the Warren Abstract Machine (WAM)[16]. Logic programming language requires special execution mechanisms and large address spaces to realize unification and automatic backtracking facilities. To meet these requirements, *CHI* provides a micro-programmed special purpose processor which executes an instruction set designed for logic programming languages, and large main memories (64 M words) with a tag field.

Several authors insist on the benefit of "reduced instruction set" from the view point of VLSI chip design. This approach would also be applicable to logic programming-oriented processor design. However, we chose the micro-programmed processor approach for the following reasons:

- We needed to enrich the *CHI* instruction set according to system development, because we had no concrete logic programming instruction set powerful enough to develop whole software systems on *CHI*.
- A rich and fairly big instruction set can reduce the "semantics gap" between hardware and language. As a result, it can save considerable compile time, which is one of the most important issues in designing an interactive programming environment.

The biggest problem in computer architecture is the trade-off between hardware and software. To achieve maximum performance at reasonable cost, we adopt the WAM instruction set, on which sophisticated optimization techniques are applicable[16]. We provide about 80 instructions[1] for unification, predicate calling, automatic backtracking and clause indexing. In addition, we provide about 100 micro-programmed built-in predicates, which support backtracking control, checking types, data object handling, process management, memory management and inter-machine communication[2].

The WAM compiler can compile logic programs into a sequence of fairly simple stack operations. However, these operations still require special functions such as dynamic type checking, dynamic mode checking and dynamic address checking, which cause considerable overheads when executing on conventional general purpose computers. To overcome this, the *CHI* processor includes such special features as a tag/value comparator, a multi-port read/write register file and an automatic address checker. The *CHI* processor also includes conventional performance improvement hardware such as a cash memory (8 K words) and a simultaneous function block execution controller which enables three-stage pipelining.

Another performance improvement results from the more sophisticated memory system. *CHI* provides word addressable tagged memory (64 M words, 36 bits/word)[3], which can be divided into 8 segments per each process. The tagged memory is effective for both performance improvement and debugging of logic programming languages. It enables one to check data types without additional memory reference by means of representing a (data) pointer and its data type in a word. In fact, *CHI* achieves any dynamic tag checking within 1 machine cycle (100 nano second) using the tag-value comparator. The tagged memory is also useful as a debugging aid. *CHI* uses instruction tag fields for illegal instruction checks and traps. *CHI* causes software traps when it encounters non-instruction words or spied instruction words marked by the programmer. This mechanism greatly helps program debugging on *CHI*, especially in the early stage, by protecting execution of non-code area and by enabling compiled

[1] We have improved WAM instruction set so that we can compile clauses incrementally in *New-CHI*.
[2] We realized most of these built-in predicates by the lower level register-to-register operations in *New-CHI*.
[3] 100 M words, 40 bits/word in *New-CHI*.

code trace traps. The tag field is 2 bits for numbers and 5 bits for other data objects which are represented by their addresses (29 bits). One bit is used for indicating short tag or long tag, and 1 bit is reserved for garbage collection.

The *CHI* memory system also provides segment-based multiple address spaces up to 8 segments per process. Four of them are process-owned segments, and the rest are shared. The multiple address spaces make it possible to extend stacks and heaps without relocating data objects. We use the process-owned segments for stacks (a trail stack, a local stack and a global stack) for storing dynamic data such as variable bindings, control information and backtrack information. We use the shared segments for heaps for storing static data such as programs and symbol tables. In the current implementation, all *CHI* processes share all the programs and symbol tables in the heaps. However, we will separate system programs/symbol tables and user programs/symbol tables in the next version, to realize the more sophisticated memory management system. The user programs/symbol tables will be stored in the reserved process-owned segment.

Providing such processor and memory systems, *CHI* achieves very high performance for various types of logic programs. For example, it achieves 280 KLIPS (Kilo Logical Inferences Per Second) for a list concatenation program called "append". In addition, the large memory capacity (64 M words) makes it possible to run fairly large practical programs without the support of a virtual memory management system which would considerably reduce execution performance on the back-end type machine.

3 Logic Programming Language SUPLOG

We designed a new logic programming language *SUPLOG* to develop software systems on *CHI*. The language provides various programming facilities which are effective not only for knowledge programming but also for system programming.

Since *CHI* was designed as a logic programming language-oriented machine, the best way to develop the whole software system is by means of a logic programming language. However, the language facilities of conventional logic programming languages are not sufficient to develop system programs such as a process scheduler, a memory manager and input/output operation handlers. To solve this problem, *SUPLOG* provides various extended facilities, such as destructive data types, inter-process communication primitives, non-local exit control, multiple name spaces and unification handlers, some of which may be considered to be *unsuitable* in the classical logic programming languages. In the following, we show their design principle and usages in *SUPLOG*.

3.1 Objects in logic programming

SUPLOG provides "destructive data types" to represent objects which hold history-dependent information. It is true that *side-effects are harmful* in logic programming because we need precise control flow when backtracking occurs. However, it is also true that most practical programs, e.g., operating systems, require some kind of history-dependent information. One elegant solution to this contradiction is to introduce "objects" in the sense of object-oriented programming[4]. The object-oriented programming style makes it possible to hide low-level side-effect primitives from the outer world, and to treat history-dependent information more logically.

Several authors have already proposed such objects in logic programming[14,5]. However, today's computer technology is not fast enough to allow realizing the history-dependent information in 'objects' by means of *object copying* or *assert/retract operations* which insert/remove a clause to/from a clause database. *SUPLOG* solves this problem simply by providing traditional destructive data types, whose side-effects are retained after backtracking. The most important point is that *SUPLOG* treats such objects as constants in order to keep consistency in unification and backtracking. That is, *SUPLOG* treats an object as an individual with a unique name represented by its address. This means that we do not need to note the states of objects in unification, because any side-effect operation does not change the address of objects. This simple definition makes it possible to avoid confusion when we use side-effects in unification and backtracking.

3.2 Parallelism in logic programming

Parallelism is one of the most important programming paradigms in developing large complex software systems such as operating systems. Although several authors have already proposed elegant parallel logic programming languages[13,2,12,15], *SUPLOG* adopts a rather conventional approach to creating a multiple process environment on *CHI*: indirect inter-process communication via 'mailboxes'. We have designed the language this way, because it is asynchronous behavior not nondeterministic behavior that we want to realize on *CHI*. That is, we want to create a multiple process environment that enables inter-machine communication between *CHI* and the host machine, and process scheduling on the level of programming tools such as interpreters and compilers. Parallel execution of logical connectives, such as *And-goals* and *Or-goals*, is an important issue in logic programming research, but it is not the current target issue in the *CHI* project.

The mailbox model is practical and sufficient in programming environment development if it supports dynamic process creation, labeled mailboxes, both blocked and unblocked message communication operations, and interruption-handling mechanisms from hardware and software. However, it is too primitive to develop application systems such as co-operative problem solving and co-operative knowledge databases. To overcome this problem, we are now developing a more sophisticated parallel programming paradigm called "remote unification". The remote unification is a bi-directional message passing protocol represented on the mailbox model. We will be able to integrate various parallel programming paradigms in the single concept *remote unification*[7].

3.3 Other extension facilities

Other extension facilities provided in *SUPLOG* are multiple name spaces, unification handlers and non-local exit control, some of which are already familiar from recent logic programming languages[1,3]. The multiple name spaces are useful for realization of module structures in developing large complex systems from a system programming point of view. It is also useful for expressing "multiple worlds" from a knowledge programming point of view. The key features of the *SUPLOG* multiple name spaces are:

- Exports/imports predicate symbols identified by their names and the number of arguments, among multiple name spaces.
- Provides a "name type" which represents constant symbols in multiple name spaces.

The unification handler is a mechanism which invokes a handler when some condition is satisfied in unification, for example, variable instantiation. This enables realization of various extended unification algorithms[8], and constraint programming on logic programming[9]. The non-local exit control is used mainly for exception handling. In addition, the combination of the unification handlers and the non-local exit control enables realization of a sophisticated control mechanism which could be called "intelligent backtracking".

4 Co-Operative Programming Environment

There are many approaches to constructing a programming environment. There are design choices such as the number of target languages (single language vs. multiple languages), processor types (a general purpose processor vs. a special purpose processor), system configurations (a stand-alone machine vs. a back-end type machine), etc. However, it is beyond the scope of this paper to delineate these choices in more detail. Therefore, we restrict our discussion to how to construct an interactive programming environment on a back-end type sequential inference machine.

In designing such an environment on the back-end type machine, we must make certain choices, e.g., which machine should hold a clause database and a symbol table, whether the back-end machine should support a multiple process environment, and what kind of protocols should be used for the communication between them. We designed the *CHI* system as if *CHI* were a stand-alone machine. That is, we developed the *CHI* system that has its own clause database, symbol tables, multiple process environment and interpreters. Then, we connected *CHI* with the host machine so that *CHI* could handle the input/output devices on the host machine via virtual objects. The following are our design principles for the choices we made.

4.1 Program Management

CHI manages not only compiled predicates, but also interpretive predicates. That is, *CHI* provides a clause database which serves for interpreters. *CHI* has a special processor which executes compiled predicate codes. Therefore, it is natural decision that *CHI* manages compiled predicates. However, there is a design choice whether the back-end machine should manage interpretive predicates, in other words, should have an interpreter. One may prefer to use a host machine for program debugging, and a back-end machine for program execution. In this case, *CHI* would be an accelerator which executes highly optimized programs provided by the host machine. This approach is attractive only for its simplicity. We did not choose it for the following reasons:

- A clause database is an important facility in logic programming languages. Most knowledge application programmers prefer to use interpretive predicates for knowledge representation as well as debugging.
- To facilitate *incremental programming*, we allow the mixed use of interpretive predicates and compiled predicates, which greatly enhances debuggability in an interactive programming environment.

4.2 Symbol Management

CHI has its own symbol tables to manage all information concerning symbols. It is also possible to place the symbol tables on the host machine. In this case, a symbol will be represented by a number which indicates the offset of a symbol table in the host machine. However, this implementation causes considerable overhead when the programmer wants to get print names of the symbols for composition of new symbols or for debugging.

The other design choice concerning the symbol tables is whether the user processes should share the same symbol tables or not. This issue is closely related to the issue of program sharing, because logic programming languages call procedures via predicate symbols. In *CHI*, we adopted shared symbol tables in order to save making a redundant copy of system programs each time a new process is created. However, this implementation causes intolerable conflict when the *CHI* processes update the same clause database in parallel. To solve this problem, *New-CHI* provides both shared symbol tables and process-owned symbol tables. This makes it possible to construct process-owned name spaces and process-owned clause databases.

4.3 Multiple Process Environment

CHI provides a multiple process environment in order to realize asynchronous remote input/output operations and parallel execution of programming tools, such as interpreters and compilers. The multiple process environment might not be necessary if we restricted our target programming environment such that it consisted of only a single interpreter that handles input/output operations by polling. However, such restriction produces nothing but redundant idle time of the *CHI* hardware. The multiple process environment not only makes good use of the *CHI* hardware, but also provides a flexible test bed for simulating various parallel logic programming languages and systems.

4.4 Inter-Machine Communication

We introduced *virtual objects* as the highest level inter-machine communication protocol between *CHI* and the host machine. The *CHI* hardware provides a DMA controller that can transfer data up to 256 K bytes per second. Direct usage of the DMA controller of course achieves fast inter-machine communication. However, it is painful to program remote input/output operations using such a low-level operation. Therefore, we developed a three-level inter-machine communication protocol.

Figure 1 shows the conceptual models describing the inter-machine communication protocols between a client process on *CHI* and a server process on the host machine. The lowest-level protocol is a remote inter-process communication between the client process and the server process. The processes send/receive messages to/from each other via the DMA controller. Note that message passing is uni-directional in this level.

The middle-level protocol is a remote procedure calling mechanism from the client process to the server process. At this level, the client process can invoke file operations, such as open, close, read and write, by calling the corresponding procedures defined in the server process. Remote procedure calling is a good way to realize the remote input/output operations. However, such procedure-oriented abstraction still has the drawback that the programmer must be aware of the existence of inter-machine communication, and carefully write more optimized data-transfer algorithms, such as buffer blocking, according to the kinds of devices. To solve this, we provide *virtual objects* which cause the corresponding procedure calling, when they are accessed. Since virtual objects are data objects in *SUPLOG*, we can deal with virtual objects like any other object on *CHI*. Therefore, we need no longer be aware of the existence of the remote input/output operations. These operations are completely encapsulated in the virtual objects. In this sense, we consider the virtual objects as the realization of object-oriented abstraction of the remote input/output operations.

5 Implementation

We developed our software system using only *SUPLOG* from a basic resource management system to an interpreter. Such an approach greatly increases the flexibility and expandability of a programming environment, because we can utilize any function of the *CHI* hardware in *SUPLOG*. The total program size is about 50 K lines in *SUPLOG*, and its object size now occupies about 1 M words.

The system consists of a three-level hierarchy; a system kernel layer, a basic resource management system layer and a programming tool layer. The system kernel layer provides various system calls for memory allocations, primitive data structure access operations, multiple name space operations and others, most of which should run in noninterrupt mode. They are used for the primitive predicates in developing the basic resource management system. The basic resource management system layer consists of a process management system, a memory management system, an input/output management system and an exception handling system. They are used for the realization of a multiple process environment and remote input/output operations. The programming tool layer consists of a shell, an interpreter and a compiler. The shell is a command interpreter for controlling user processes. The interpreter realizes an interactive *SUPLOG* programming environment including a program loader and a tracer/debugger. The compiler compiles a *SUPLOG* source file into the bulk of compiled predicates which can be incrementally loaded by the program loader. In the current implementation, all user processes are initialized as a *SUPLOG* interpreter.

Figure 2 shows the inter-process interaction in the current co-operative programming environment. We use two system processes: a DMA handler process and an input/output manager process for the realization of asynchronous remote input/output operations. The DMA handler process acts as a device handler for the DMA operation. It is directly invoked by the *CHI* hardware, and serves buffer allocation and data transfer for the user processes. The input/output manager process arbitrates all input/output requirements from the user processes. This makes it possible to handle the asynchronous remote input/output operations. In this implementation, the user processes can release the *CHI* processor to other processes until remote input/output operations are completed, or can execute their contexts in parallel with the remote input/output operations.

The multiple process environment, as realized on *CHI*, is a good vehicle for constructing a co-operative programming environment. However, it requires some additional implementational improvements from a practical point of view. The first problem is the context switching overhead when an interruption occurs. Process-oriented system design is simple and beautiful, but it is difficult to handle all interruptions as processes; for example, a timer interrupt for time slicing. We will solve this problem by providing interrupt handlers which execute in the context of the interrupted process. Unfortunately, we cannot define such interrupt handlers in *SUPLOG* because interruptions may occur even in the unification process.

The other problem results from resource management among user processes. We forsake inter-process garbage collection because it may interrupt program execution for a long time in order to reclaim the large memory address spaces. We will solve this problem by placing process-owned resources in a process-owned segment, and by managing the number of sharing processes for the shared resources. Such implementation may cause some overhead for inter-process communication between user processes. However, we will be able to reclaim all the resources when the user processes are released. We must make more of an effort to deal with resource management problems in a multiple process environment since it is the one of the most important issues in distributed processing system research.

6 Evaluation

It is very difficult to evaluate the worth of a programming environment because it depends not only on processor performance, but also on the feasibility of programming and debugging. However, program

Compiled Program	Preprocessing	Clause Compilation	Procedure Compilation
Sample A	3.4	147.8	20.5
Sample B	2.8	213.9	18.0
Sample C	4.2	109.8	20.1
Sample D	2.9	425.4	19.0

Table 1: Performance Comparison between *CHI* and a C-Prolog interpreter on a VAX system 750 using a *SUPLOG* Compiler. (unit = execution time on C-Prolog/elapsed time on *CHI*)

execution performance is one of the measures used to evaluate a programming environment if the target programs are fairly large.

Table 1 shows the performance comparison of compile times between *CHI* and a VAX system 750. We used a C-Prolog interpreter as a competitor. Although the C-Prolog interpreter does not have a compiler, it is well known as a fast interpreter due to its fast parser and clause database operations being wholly written in the language C. The measured program is a *SUPLOG* compiler (12000 lines) written in Prolog so that it runs on both *CHI* and the C-Prolog interpreter. The *SUPLOG* compiler consists of three parts: a preprocess part, a clause compilation part and a procedure compilation part. The results shows that *CHI* achieves good performance compared with the C-Prolog interpreter on the VAX system 750. The most important point is that the *CHI* version *SUPLOG* compiler runs three times faster than the C-Prolog version *SUPLOG* compiler in the preprocess part which includes remote input operations to read compiled programs. This shows that the *CHI* processor is fast enough to compensate for the overhead caused by the separation of the language processing process and the input/output process. Furthermore, note that the C-Prolog parser is wholly written in the programming language C, while the *CHI* parser is written in *SUPLOG*. This implies that we can execute logic programming languages faster than imperative languages if appropriate hardware is provided.

Other differences are nearly obvious because the *CHI* processor executes the unification processes about 150 - 250 times faster than the C-Prolog interpreter on the VAX system 750, and *SUPLOG* programs are highly optimized by a compiler. The difference in the procedure compile part will be greater, if *CHI* tunes up the assert/retract operations, which are currently about 10 times slower than those in the C-Prolog interpreter.

7 Conclusion

In this paper, we show the effectiveness of co-operative processes with the design of an interactive programming environment on a back-end type sequential inference machine. The key ideas are the separation of input/output server processes and language processing processes, and introduction of an object-oriented inter-machine communication protocol "virtual objects".

The separation makes it possible to develop a high performance reliable programming environment with relatively small effort by utilizing host machine input/output systems, such as a file system, a window system and a network system. The performance results show that the overhead caused by such separation can be compensated for, if the back-end processor is much faster than the host machine.

The ***virtual objects*** make it possible to deal with the host machine devices as data types. Such object-oriented abstraction of remote input/output operations can encapsulate complicated protocols into virtual objects and free us from the need to consider the existence of inter-machine communication.

These results convince us that we can develop a more powerful computer system by means of loosely coupled systems, each of which has a language-oriented processor and main memories dedicated for its owned language processes.

Acknowledgements: We thank to Professor Arvind and the MIT Laboratory for Computer Science for making it possible for Akihiko Konagaya (one of the authors) to spend a one-year study leave there, and for having a chance to prepare this paper. We also thank to Dr. Shun'ichi Uchida (ICOT) who gave us the chance to develop this system. Thanks are also due to Dr. Yasuo Kato, Dr. Katsuya Hakozaki and Dr. Masahiro Yamamoto (NEC) for their continuous encouragement, to Shin'ichi Habata, Minoru Yokota, Hideo Shimazu, Atsushi Atarashi (NEC) for their willingness to discuss their machine implementation research efforts, to Noriko Kijima (NEC) and the members of *CHI* software development group for their assistance, and to Natalie Tarbet and Greg Papadopoulos (MIT) for their valuable comments in regard to this paper.

References

[1] J. Bendl, P. Koves, and P. Szeredi. The MPROLOG system. In *Logic Programming Workshop*, pages 14–16, Debrecen, Hungary, 1980.

[2] K. Clark and S. Gregory. *PARLOG: Parallel Programming in Logic.* Research Report DOC 84/4, Imperial College, 1984.

[3] A. Colmerauer. *Prolog II: Reference Manual and Theoretical Model.* Groupe Intelligence Artificielle, Universite Aix-Marseille II, 1982.

[4] A. Goldberg and D. Robson. *Smalltalk-80: language and its implementation.* Addison-Wesley, 1983.

[5] K. Kahn, E.D. Tribble, M.S. Miller, and D.G. Bobrow. Objects in concurrent logic programming languages. In *OOPSLA'86*, pages 242–257, 1986.

[6] K. Kawanobe. Current status and future plans of the fifth generation computer system project. In *Int'l. Conf. on Fifth Generation Computer Systems 1984*, 1984.

[7] A. Konagaya. Parallelism in logic programming. in Preparation.

[8] A. Konagaya. Typed unification and object oriented interpretation of a clause. *Computer Software*, 4(1), 34–43, 1987. in Japanese.

[9] A. Konagaya and M. Umemura. Knowledge information processing language: SHAPEUP. *New Generation Computing*, 2(2), 1984.

[10] R. Kowalski. *Logic for Problem Solving.* North Holland Publishing Co., 1979.

[11] R. Nakazaki, A. Konagaya, S. Habata, H. Shimazu, M. Umemura, M. Yamamoto, M. Yokota, and T. Chikayama. Design of a high-speed prolog machine HPM. In *Int'l. Symp. on Computer Architecture*, 1985.

[12] L.M. Pereira and Nasr R. Delta-prolog: a distributed logic programming language. In *Int'l. Conf. on Fifth Generation Computer Systems 1984*, pages 283–291, 1984.

[13] E. Shapiro. *A Subset of Concurrent Prolog and Its Interpreter.* Technical Report TR-003, ICOT, 1983.

[14] E. Shapiro and A. Takeuchi. Object oriented programming in concurrent prolog. *New Generation Computing*, 1(1), 1983.

[15] K. Ueda. *Guarded Horn Clause.* PhD thesis, University of Tokyo, 1985.

[16] D.H. Warren. *An Abstract Prolog Instruction Set.* Technical Report 309, SRI Artificial Intelligence Center, 1983.

[17] D.H. Warren. *Implementing PROLOG—Compiling Predicate Logic Programs.* Research Report 39, Dept. of Artificial Intelligence, Univ. of Edinburgh, 1977.

[18] M. Yokota, A. Yamamoto, K. Taki, H. Nishikawa and S.Uchida. The Design and Implementation of a personal sequential inference machine: PSI. *New Generation Computing*, 2(1), 1984.

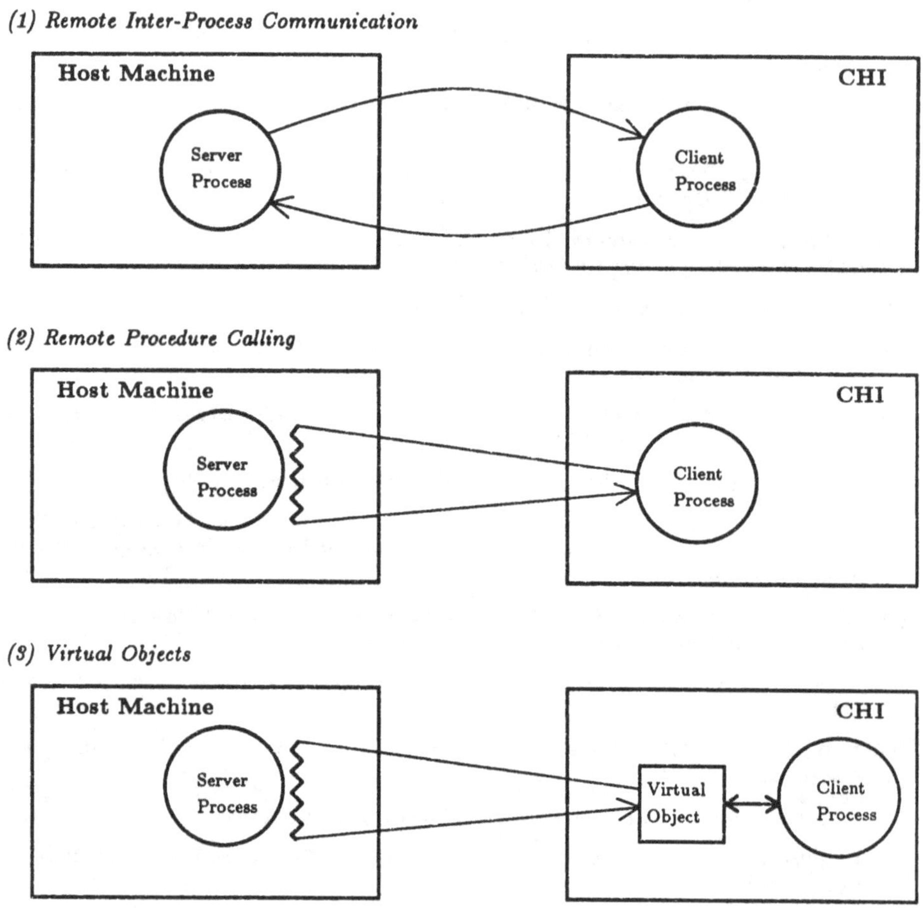

Fig. 1 Inter-Machine Communication Protocols

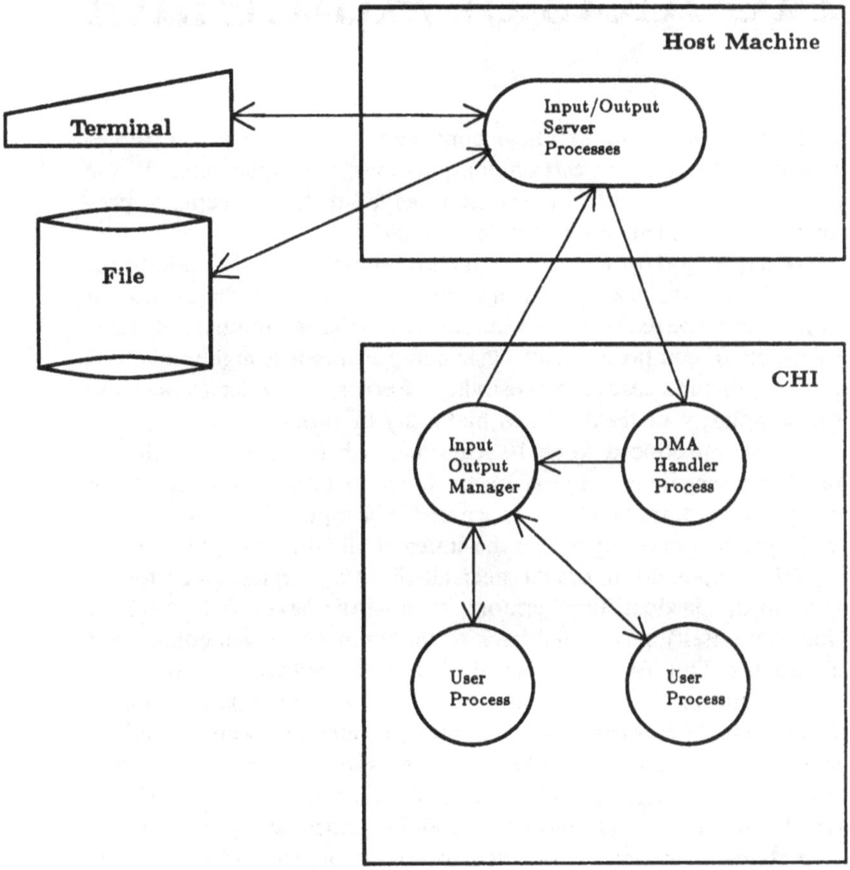

Fig.2 Inter-Process Interaction in a Co-Operative Programming Environment

Ferenc Gécseg

Products of Automata

Both theoretical and practical considerations motivate the representation of objects as certain compositions of simpler ones. In the theory of automata this observation has led to the concepts of products and complete systems of automata.

In the general form of the products of automata all the component automata are fed back to one another. With this very broad notion of products, the realization of automata with large numbers of states by means of compositions of basic components is a highly involved process; this increases the possibility of errors. In order to decrease the complexity of feedbacks, a hierarchy of products called α_i-products was introduced some 10 years ago, where i runs over the set of all non-negative integers. In an α_i-product the index set of the component automata is linearly ordered. The input of each automaton in the product may depend on the states of all automata preceding it, i.e., all component automata steer all those automata which follow them in the product. Furthermore, at most the next $i - 1$ automata (including itself) may be fed back to the input of a given component automaton. Thus for α_i-products the lengths of feedbacks are at most i.

The aim of this monograph is to give a systematic account of α_i-products. It consists of five chapters, a reference section, and an index. The first chapter contains the necessary concepts and results from universal algebra, automata, and sequential machines. Chapters 2 and 3 deal with homomorphic and isomorphic representations, respectively. Chapter 4 is devoted to homomorphic and isomorphic simulations with respect to a generalization of α_i-products. The final chapter is concerned with infinite products and representations of automaton mappings in finite lengths.

(Mathematische Lehrbücher und Monographien, II. Abteilung, Band 70)

Leinen DDR 64,– M; Ausland 64,– DM
ISBN 3-05-500326-8
Bestell-Nr. 763 710 5
Bestellwort: Gécseg, Automata 9043 engl.

Akademie-Verlag Berlin 1986

Band 1

Inverse and Improperly Posed Problems in Differential Equations

Proceedings of the Conference on Mathematical and Numerical Methods, held in Halle/Saale (GDR) from May 29 to June 2, 1979

Edited by Gottfried Anger
296 Seiten, 1979 (vergriffen)

Band 2

Fundamentals of Computation Theory FCT '79

Proceedings of the Conference on Algebraic, Arithmetic and Categorial Methods in Computation Theory, held in Berlin/Wendisch-Rietz (GDR) September 17–21, 1979

Edited by Lothar Budach
576 Seiten, 1979

Band 3

Decidability and Generalized Quantifiers

By Andreas Baudisch, Detlef Seese, Hans-Peter Tuschik, and Martin Weese
XII, 235 Seiten, 1980

Band 4

Zur Elastizitäts- und Thermoelastizitätstheorie

Potentialtheoretische Methoden in Anwendung auf verschiedene Modelle

Von Lothar Jentsch und Johannes Maul
157 Seiten, 1980

Band 5

Systems Analysis and Simulation 1980

Proceedings of the International Symposium held at Berlin (GDR) September 1–5, 1980

Edited by Achim Sydow
496 Seiten, 1980 (vergriffen)

Band 6

Nichtlineare diskrete Optimierung

von Eberhard Girlich und Michail M. Kowaljow
218 Seiten, 1981

Band 7

Completeness Problems in the Structural Theory of Automata

By Jürgen Dassow
148 Seiten, 1981

Band 8

Darstellung von Lösungen linearer elliptischer Differentialgleichungen

Von Günther Wildenhain
92 Seiten, 1981

Band 9

Introduction to the Spectral Theory of Operators in Spaces with an Indefinite Metric

By I. S. Iohvidov, M. G. Krein, and H. Langer
120 Seiten, 1982 (vergriffen)

Band 10

Nonlinear Time-discrete Systems

A General Approach by Nonlinear Superposition

By Michael Gössel
115 Seiten, 1982 (vergriffen)

Band 11

Preprimal Algebras

By Klaus Denecke
162 Seiten, 1982

Band 12

Ergodic Theory and Related Topics

Proceedings of the Conference held in Vitte/Hiddensee (GDR) October 19–23, 1981

Edited by Horst Michel
232 Seiten, 1982

Band 13

Singularly Perturbed Differential Equations

By H. Goering, A. Felgenhauer, G. Lube, H.-G. Roos, and L. Tobiska
176 Seiten, 1983

Band 14

Leben wir in einer Volterra-Welt?

Ein ökologischer Zugang zur angewandten Systemanalyse

Von Manfred Peschel und Werner Mende
233 Seiten, 1983

Band 15

Markov Decision Problems with Countable State Spaces

Optimality Criteria – Algorithms – Clustering

By Hans Michael Dietz and Volker Nollau
174 Seiten, 1983

Band 16

Stochastische Verfahren zur Suche nach dem Minimum einer Funktion

Von Ryszard Zieliński und Peter Neumann
133 Seiten, 1983

Band 17

Invertibility and Asymptotics of Toeplitz Matrices

By Albrecht Böttcher and Bernd Silbermann
200 Seiten, 1983

Band 18

Structural Induction on Partial Algebras

Introduction to Theory and Application of Partial Algebras – Part II

By Horst Reichel
205 pages, 1984

Band 19

Algebraic Methods for Toeplitz-like Matrices and Operators

By Georg Heinig and Karla Rost
212 pages, 1984

Band 20

Frege Conference 1984

Proceedings of the International Conference held at Schwerin (GDR), September 10–14, 1984

Edited by Gerd Wechsung

408 pages, 1984

Band 21

Numerical Analysis of Selected Semilinear Differential Equations

Edited by Christian Großmann, Thomas Riedrich, and Hartmut Schönheinz

203 pages, 1984

Band 22

Singular Ordinary Differential Operators and Pseudodifferential Equations

By Johannes Elschner

200 pages, 1985

Band 23

Lotka-Volterra-Approach to Cooperation and Competition in Dynamic Systems

Proceedings of the 5th Meeting of UNESCO's Working Group on Systems Theory held on the Wartburg, Eisenach (GDR) at March 5–9, 1984

Edited by Werner Ebeling and Manfred Peschel

271 pages, 1985

Band 24

Convergence Structures 1984

Proceedings of the Conference on Convergence held in Bechyně (Czechoslovakia), September 24–28, 1984

Edited by Josef Novák, Werner Gähler, Horst Herrlich, and Jan Mikusiński

254 pages, 1985

Band 25

Parcella '84

Proceedings of the II. International Workshop on Parallel Processing by Cellular Automata and Arrays held in Berlin (GDR), September 25–27, 1984

Edited by Wolfgang Händler, Tamás Legendi, and Gottfried Wolf

239 pages, 1985

Band 26

Multiobjective and Stochastic Optimization Based on Parametric Optimization

By Jürgen Guddat, Francisco Guerra Vasquez, Klaus Tammer, and Klaus Wendler

175 pages, 1985

Band 27/28

Systems Analysis and Simulation 1985
I: Theory and Foundations
II: Applications

Proceedings of the International Symposium held in Berlin (GDR), August 26–31, 1985

Edited by Achim Sydow, Manfred Thoma, and Robert Vichnevetsky

per volume 495 pages, 1985

Band 29

Parcella '86

Proceedings of the III. International Workshop on Parallel Processing by Cellular Automata and Arrays held in Berlin (GDR), September 9–11, 1986

Edited by Tamás Legendi, Dennis Parkinson. Roland Vollmar, and Gottfried Wolf

272 pages, 1986

Band 30

Fuzzy Sets Applications, Methodological Approaches, and Results

Proceedings of the International Workshop on Fuzzy Sets Applications cosponsored by IIASA and convened in cooperation with IAEA held on the Wartburg, Eisenach (GDR), at March 3–8, 1985

Edited by Steffen Bocklisch, Sergei Orlovski, Manfred Peschel, and Yasushi Nishiwaki

233 pages, 1986

Band 31

Mathematical Methods of Specification and Synthesis of Software Systems '85

Proceedings of the International Spring School, held in Wendisch-Rietz (GDR), April 22–26, 1985

Edited by Wolfgang Bibel and Klaus P. Jantke

245 pages, 1986

Band 32

A Model Theoretic Oriented Approach to Partial Algebras

Introduction to Theory and Application of Partial Algebras – Part I

By Peter Burmeister

319 pages, 1986

Band 33

Finite-difference Methods on Irregular Networks

A Generalized Approach to Elliptic Problems of Second Order

By Bernd Heinrich

206 pages, 1986

Band 34

Modern Algorithms for Large Sparse Eigenvalue Problems

By Arnd Meyer

125 pages, 1987

Band 35

Parametric Optimization and Related Topics

Edited by Jürgen Guddat, Hubertus Th. Jongen, Bernd Kummer, and František Nožička

407 pages, 1987

Band 36

Discretization in Differential Equations and Enclosures

Edited by Ernst Adams, Rainer Ansorge, Christian Großmann, and Hans-Görg Roos

250 pages, 1987

Band 37

Factorization of Measurable Matrix Functions

By Georgi Semenovich Litvinchuk and
Ilya Matveyevich Spitkovskiĭ

372 pages, 1987

Band 38

Parallel Algorithms and Architectures

Proceedings of the International Workshop
on Parallel Algorithms and Architectures
held in Suhl (GDR), May 25–30, 1987

Edited by Andreas Albrecht, Hermann Jung,
and Kurt Mehlhorn

205 pages, 1987

Band 39

Parametric Integer Optimization

By Bernd Bank and Reinhard Mandel

138 pages, 1987

Band 40

Computer Analysis of Images and Patterns 1987

Proceedings of the II. International Conference
CAIP '87 on Automatic Image Processing,
held in Wismar (GDR), September 2–4, 1987

Edited by Leonid P. Jaroslavskiĭ,
Azriel Rosenfeld, and Wolfgang Wilhelmi

282 pages, 1987

This volume contains the papers of the International Workshop "Parallel Algorithms and Architectures" held in Suhl (GDR) from May 25 till 30, 1987. The program of the workshop consists of invited lectures given by acknowledged scientists as well as short communications. It covers both theoretical and practical aspects of parallel computing.

The main topics are

- models of parallel computations
- parallel algorithms for individual problems, e. g. from graph theory, logic programming, combinatiorics and computational geometry
- hardware algorithms and parallel computers.

Dieser Tagungsband enthält die Beiträge der internationalen Arbeitstagung „Parallel Algorithms and Architectures", die vom 25. bis 30. Mai 1987 in Suhl (DDR) stattfand.

Das Tagungsprogramm umfaßt Hauptvorträge anerkannter Wissenschaftler und Kurzvorträge, die sowohl auf theoretische als auch auf praktische Aspekte paralleler Berechnungen gerichtet sind.

Die Schwerpunkte der Tagung sind

- parallele Berechnungsmodelle
- parallele Algorithmen für spezielle Probleme, z. B. aus der Graphentheorie, der logischen Programmierung, der Kombinatorik und der algorithmischen Geometrie
- Hardware-Algorithmen und Parallelrechner.

ISBN 3-05-500397-7
ISSN 0138–3019

FSC
www.fsc.org
MIX
Papier | Fördert gute Waldnutzung
FSC® C083411

Zeitfracht Medien GmbH
Ferdinand-Jühlke-Straße 7
99095 Erfurt, Deutschland
produktsicherheit@kolibri360.de